Special Economic Zones in India

Financial Inclusion: Challenges and Opportunities

Special Economic Zones in India

Financial Inclusion: Challenges and Opportunities

Editor

P. K. Manoj

SERIALS PUBLICATIONS

NEW DELHI (INDIA)

First Published – 2009

ISBN: 978-81-8387-275-1

Published by

SERIALS PUBLICATIONS
4830/24, Prahlad Street, Ansari Road
Darya Ganj, New Delhi-110002 (India)
Phone : 23245225 Fax : 91-11-23272135
E-mail: serials@satyam.net.in

CONTENTS

PREFACE

Indian economy in general and the financial system in particular have been witnessing quite a large number of radical changes ever since the initiation of the economic deregulation measures in the early nineties. There have been many favourable developments in the banking sector resulting in a growingly resilient banking sector, as is evidenced by the constantly improving financial stability of the banks, steadily declining NPA levels, high levels of capital adequacy ratio and the like. Generally favourable macro economic environment since the early 2000s have added momentum to the above growth. In spite of all these, there are growing apprehensions regarding the long term sustainability of the current growth rate,, primarily in view of the fast declining inclusiveness of the Indian financial system. In the above context, there is a strong argument in favour of social banking and financial inclusion, particularly in favour of time-tested development models like micro finance. On the other extreme there is a view point that the current reform measures need to be continued as such with the ultimate aim of attaining international competitiveness. The proponents of the latter argue in favour of Special Economic Zones and such other governmental measures for enhanced competitiveness of domestic industries in the international market. In the midst of pretty diverse development paradigms as above, formulating appropriate business strategy for banks is indeed a formidable task. Department of Applied Economics, Cochin University of Science and Technology which has got an enviable track record in pure and applied research in such diverse and emerging fields as technology, business, finance and economics has felt it expedient to bring together industrialists, academicians, scientists and technologists into a common nation-wide forum to deliberate on the development dilemma as discussed above. Accordingly, it has been decided to organize a National level Seminar on the relevant theme viz. "Banking in the Era of Diverse Development Paradigms: from Financial Inclusion to Special Economic Zones". As in the past, this time also there has been an overwhelming response from all corners to the Seminar.

The book contains a total of 25 technical papers touching upon a very wide range of issues confronting Indian banks in the contemporary centrality. These range from financial inclusion to SEZs, from corporate governance to bancassurance and from Securitization Act to data mining. It is very much expected that this book containing research papers on such a wide range of sub-themes would be immensely valuable to social scientists, technologists, industrialists, and academicians.

The editor is thankful to Dr. Gangan Prathap, the Honourable Vice-Chancellor of CUSAT and all other top officials of the University for their support and co-operation. The editor is grateful to the faculty, library staff and non-teaching staff of the Department of Applied Economics and its sister department, School of Management Studies. Special thanks are due to the staff and management of SNGIST, North Parur for their technical-cum-research support as well as the provision for use of a wide array of electronic journals in relevant fields. Likewise, the support and co-operation from Cochin Special Economic Zone (CSEZ) worth special mention. The editor is greatly thankful to the authors of all the papers who have contributed their papers and have also modified the same within the stipulated time as per the review comments.

Editor

P. K. MANOJ

1

INTERNET BANKING AND CUSTOMER ACCEPTANCE: THE INDIAN SCENARIO

SUDEEP S. & K. C. SANKARANARYANAN

Introduction

Tremendous growth of internet during the mid-nineties prompted banks to utilize Internet as a medium for offering banking services. In Internet Banking banks allow their customers to perform banking transactions through their web site in a secure way. ICICI Bank was the first bank in India which offered this delivery channel, by kicking off its online banking services in 1996. Other private sector banks like Citibank, IndusInd Bank and HDFC Bank and Timesbank (now part of HDFC Bank) started offering internet banking services in 1999. SBI launched its internet banking services in July 2001. Other public sector banks like State Bank of India, Bank of Baroda, Allahabad Bank, Syndicate Bank and Bank of India, also rolled their services during the same time. Banks in India currently offer 'Fully Transactional Websites' to their customers. The customers could conduct variety of transactions through internet banking facility which includes: account summary, details of historical banking transactions, funds transfer, new service announcements, loan applications, bill payment, cheque book request, cheque status enquiry, stop cheque request, credit card payments/statement, facilities to contact account manager etc. In a survey conducted by IAMAI and IMRB (IMRB & IMAI, 2006), estimates the number of internet users as of September 2006 to around 37 million and the number or 'active' users is pegged around 25 million. The survey also estimates around 2.4 million E-Commerce users, which included internet banking users. An estimated 4.6 million Indian internet users are availing internet banking services as of 2007 (Kothari, 2007).

Need for the Study

Introduction of new technologies allowed banking institutions to offer new channels of service outlets like ATM facility, Internet Banking, Telephone Banking and Mobile Banking. Indian consumers too have access to many new channels to interact with their bank. Banks race against each other in bringing the latest technology for the benefit of their customers and themselves.But not many studies have been conduced to evaluate if "Internet Banking" channel is utilized properly by the customers in India. Reasons for customer apathy towards Internet banking channel, if that exist, have also not been analyzed in an Indian context earlier.

Objective of the Study

This study plans to "plug" gap of research in the acceptance of Internet banking among Indian customers. The primary objectives of this study are to:

- Identify factors influencing the adoption and usage of Internet banking in India
- Examine whether Theory of Planned Behaviour (TPB) or Technology Acceptance Model can be applied in Internet banking adoption and usage.
- Develop a model to explain behavioral intention to use internet banking.

Research Model

Based on the literature review and findings of the qualitative study conducted on a focus group, the researcher developed a research model indicating the acceptance of internet banking among customers. The model contained seven factors that the researcher posits to have an effect on internet banking acceptance (Figure 1). The research model developed is primarily based on the Theory of Planned Behaviour (TPB) (Ajzen, 1985) and the Technology Acceptance Model (TAM) (Davis *et al.*, 1989). The constructs for *consumer security concerns, customer security awareness* and *trust and privacy* was added to the model to make it more relevant for internet banking acceptance. Research constructs and hypotheses posited are given in Table 1. Questionnaire for the survey was designed to gather the respondent's personal information and views about the factors included in the research model. The survey questionnaire contained four sections. Section I contained questions for capturing respondent's demographic details. Section II, questions to collect respondent's computer and internet usage, Section III, questions to collect users banking

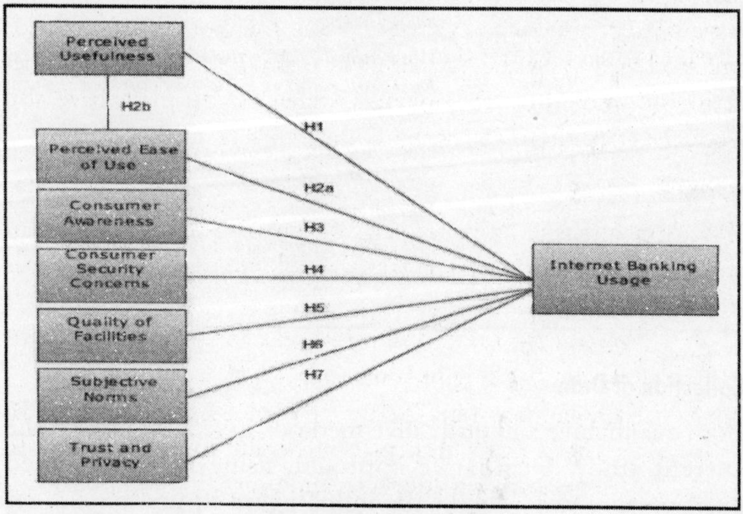

Figure 1: **Research Model**

patronage and usage of e-banking channels and finally Section IV, questions to measure the respondent's views on the research model. In total, fifty four items were added in the survey questionnaire for measuring the seven constructs used in the research model. Pre-testing of the survey questionnaire was carried out. Respondents in the pre-test mentioned that questions were straight forward and they did not face any problems in responding.

Table 1
Research Constructs and Hypotheses

Research Construct	*Hypotheses*
Perceived Usefulness (PU)	H1: *Perceived Usefulness (PU) has a positive effect on the customer acceptance of online banking*
Perceived Ease of Use (PEOU)	H2a: *Perceived Ease of Use (PEOU) has a positive effect on the customer acceptance of online banking*
	H2b: *Perceived Ease of Use (PEOU) has a positive effect on the perceived usefulness of online banking*
Consumer Awareness (CA)	H3:*Perceived consumer awareness (CA) has a positive effect on the customer acceptance of online banking*
Consumer Security Concerns (SC)	H4: *Perceived consumer security concerns (SC) has a negative effect on the customer acceptance of online banking*
Quality of Facilities (QF)	H5: *Perceived quality of facilities for accessing bank site has a positive effect on the customer acceptance of online banking.*
Subjective Norms (SN)	H6: *The beliefs associated with subjective norms are significantly related to an individual's intention to adopt Internet banking.*
Trust and Privacy (TP)	H7: *Perceived trust and privacy on the bank has a positive effect on the customer acceptance of online banking*

Collection of Data

Both quantitative and qualitative methods have been used in the current study. Qualitative approach using an open-ended questionnaire was used in the initial phase to understand the outlook of customers to online banking. The research model developed for this study was tested using quantitative method by conducting a survey. In this study two different data collection method were employed viz. web based (online) survey and paper based survey. Web based survey was chosen as Internet is the most suitable medium for communicating the target group of the survey i.e. internet banking customers. The researcher resorted to a choice-based or convenient sampling approach for selecting the respondents for this survey. Respondents to this survey were chosen from the alumni list of Cochin University, membership list of professional associations like ICAI, IEI, ISACA etc and employees of service industry companies. For the research study 500 invitation e-mails were sent and 169 responses were received. To increase response rate three reminders were sent to the respondents. The survey was made online during May 2006 and data were collected for a period of 3 months. The response rate of 33.8% falls in the typical response rate of web surveys. Paper based survey was also conducted to gather data for the study. 300 survey questionnaires were distributed among the participants, 250 questionnaires were filled and returned, and 97 fully filled questionnaires were taken for the final analysis. Thus the effective response rate of paper based survey is 32.3%. After discarding incomplete and vague responses 266 responses were taken for final analysis.

Data Analysis

Data collected from the survey were analyzed and interpreted using various statistical techniques usually employed in positivistic study. Statistical analysis was carried out using SPSS (Statistical Package for Social Sciences) version 14.0. Descriptive analysis techniques like average, percentage, frequencies etc were performed on the data for getting an overall structure of the sample. The reliability and construct validity of the research instrument were assessed before final analysis of the data. The Cronbach alpha coefficient for each research variable was computed to test for reliability. To analyze for convergent and discriminant validity of the constructs, factor analysis was used. Hypotheses were tested using linear regression analysis and multi linear regression analysis was used to test model's prediction capabilities.

Major Findings

The main objective of the study was to identify the factors that were influencing internet banking adoption among customers in India. The survey produced empirical confirmation of seven factors which did influence internet banking acceptance. The factors produced by survey were: *perceived usefulness, perceived ease of use, consumer awareness, consumer security concerns, quality of facilities, subjective norms* and *trust and privacy.* The survey instrument's reliability and construct validity test results were found satisfactory.

Second objective of the study was to check if theoretical base of internet banking acceptance could be developed, in particular, two theories in social psychology area were tested for their applicability in this study. One of the model tested was Technology Acceptance Mode (TAM) (Davis, 1989), which is a widely used model for predicting technology adoption. In this study two constructs in TAM namely *perceived usefulness* and *perceived ease of use* is tested in the context of internet banking acceptance. The results gave empirical evidence that the acceptance of internet banking was significantly influenced by the two constructs of the TAM. Results showed that the factors *perceived usefulness* and *perceived ease of use* had positive influence on internet banking acceptance.

Third objective of the study was to develop a model that could explain behavioral intention of internet banking adoption. The researcher developed a model for predicting internet banking adoption and framed eight hypotheses vis-a-vis with that model. All the hypotheses framed for the study were found to be empirically accepted (Table 2). Overall research model is statistically significant ($F = 10.264$ and $p < 0.001$) and all the independent variables together explain for 21.8% ($R^2 = 0.218$) variance on the dependent variable (*Internet Banking Use*). But out of the independent variables β coefficient of only *Perceived Usefulness*

(β = 0.290, t = 2.915, p=0.004) and *Consumer Security Concerns* (β = -0.197, t = -3.290, p < .001) are statistically significant. The significant levels of other five independent variables are higher than the accepted level of p < .005. The β coefficient of five variables *Perceived Usefulness, Perceived Ease of Use, Consumer Awareness, Quality of Facilities* and *Subjective Norms* are positive showing that they help acceptance of dependent variable Internet *Baking Use.* On the other hand, β coefficient of two variables *Consumer Security Concerns* and *Trust and Privacy* are negative indicating that these factors hinder acceptance of dependent variable *Internet Banking Use.*

Table 2
Hypotheses Testing (Regression Analysis)

Hypothesis	*Dependent Variable*	*Independent Variable*	*β*	*t-value*	*p-value*
H1	Internet Banking Use	Perceived Usefulness	.422	7.560	.000
H2a	Internet Banking Use	Perceived Ease of Use	.371	6.497	.000
H2b	Perceived Usefulness	Perceived Ease of Use	.698	15.821	.000
H3	Internet Banking Use	Consumer Awareness	.246	4.124	.000
H4	Internet Banking Use	Consumer Security Concerns	-.186	-3.083	.002
H5	Internet Banking Use	Quality of Facilities	.286	4.855	.000
H6	Internet Banking Use	Subjective Norms	.231	3.861	.000
H7	Internet Banking Use	Trust & Privacy	.303	5.172	.000

Concluding Observations

Indian economy is witnessing stellar growth over the last few years. There have been rapid developments in infrastructural and business front during the growth period. Internet adoption among Indians has been increasing over the last one decade. Indian banks have also risen to the occasion by offering new channels of delivery to their customers. Internet banking is one such new channel which has become available to Indian customers. Customer acceptance for internet banking has been good so far. In this study the researcher tried to conduct a qualitative and quantitative investigation of internet banking customer acceptance among Indians. The researcher tried to identify important factors that affect customer's behavioral intention for internet banking. The researcher also proposes a research model which was extended from Technology Acceptance Model for predicting internet banking acceptance. The findings of the study would be useful for Indian banks in planning and upgrading their internet banking service. Banks could increase internet banking adoption by making their customer awareness about the usefulness of the service. It is seen that from the study that the variable *perceived usefulness* has a positive influence on internet banking use, therefore internet banking acceptance would increase when customers find it more usefulness. Banks should plan their marketing campaigns taking into consideration this factor. Proper marketing communications which would increase consumer awareness would result in better acceptance of internet banking. The variable *perceived ease of use* had a positive influence on internet banking use. That means customers would increase internet banking usage when they find it easier to use. Banks should therefore try to develop their internet banking site and interface easier to use. Banks could also consider providing practical training sessions for customers at their branches on usage of internet banking interface. The findings of the study would be useful for Indian banks in planning and upgrading their internet banking service.

References

Ajzen, I. (1985). From Intentions to Actions: A Theory of Planned Behaviour. in Action Control (Kuhland, J. and Beckman, J. (Eds), From Cognition to Behaviour, pp. 11-39). Heidelberg: Springer.

Davis, F., Bagozzi, R. & Warshaw, R. (1989). User Acceptance of Computer Technology: A Comparison of Two Theoretical Models. *Management Science*, 35(8), pp. 982-1003.

Davis, F. D. (1989). Perceived Usefulness, Perceived Ease of Use, and User Acceptance of Information Technology. MIS Quarterly, 13(3), pp. 318-339.

IMRB, & IMAI (2006), *Internet in India-2006 (Summary Report of I-Cube 2006)*, New Delhi, IMRB International *(eTechnology Group@IMRB)*.

Kothari, D. (2007), Count on IT: Banks are now just a click or SMS away. *The Week*, Vol. 25, No. 48, October 28, 2007, pp. 63-76.

2

A STUDY AND IMPLEMENTATION OF CLASSIFICATION ALGORITHMS IN DATA MINING FOR A CRM BASED BANKING APPLICATION

SUMITRA BINU

Introduction

A traditional CRM system typically focuses on reengineering the transactions and workflows to make them customer centric. However to gain competitive advantage it is equally important to analyze the business data for identifying trends in customer behavior that would help in customer acquisition, retention, and building customer loyalty. Data mining with traditional CRM will help achieve these twin benefits.

Banks have many and huge databases containing transactional and other details of its customers. These data stores carry valuable business information, which can be used to expand the business opportunities. The traditional query languages fail to support such an extensive analysis and decision making because human analysis breaks down with volume and dimensionality. Traditional statistical methods do not have the capacity and scale to analyze these data. Hence modern data mining methodologies and tools are increasingly being used for decision-making process not only in banking and financial institutions, but also across the industries.

This work attempts to compare the performance of two types of data mining algorithms. The two types of classification algorithms adopted for this work include statistical-based algorithms and distance-based algorithms. The algorithms are compared on the basis of their efficiency in classifying the bank customers according to their risk level.

Several previous studies have compared classifiers. Most of the studies have limited their comparison to at most two algorithms. The most elaborate and inclusive study that was ever done was the STATLOG Project carried out in Europe (Michie, Spiegellhalter, and Taylor, 1994). After a study of the various classification algorithms, they came to the assumption that the fragmentation among the different disciplines that have worked on classification problems has hindered communication and progress. A procedure that worked best on one type of dataset may not be exhibiting the same type of performance level on another dataset. The three individual procedures most often among the best for each of the datasets were one type of neural net (DIPOL 92) and two types of statistical procedures (ALLOC 80 and logistic discriminant analysis). Decision trees performed well if the data set was multimodal. Other variations of decision trees were also considered. Among the decision tree group of methods, almost all performed about the same. Among the neural nets one type was frequently one of the best overall (DIPOL 92) and another type was rarely among the best (Kohonen's LVQ).

Thus it is seen that majority of the studies conducted on the comparison of classification algorithms were focusing on Decision tree – based algorithms and Neural Network-based algorithms. The present work involves the comparison of Statistical-based algorithms and Distance-based algorithms. Statistical based algorithm adopted for this work is Naïve-Bayes classification technique and the Decision tree based algorithm is K-nearest Neighbor technique. The algorithms are applied on data sets with varying number of records and a comparative analysis is done based on their classification accuracy and time.

Problem Statement

The bank wants to identify the existing customers who are may be offered car loans or house loans. This process is carried out under the assumption that either the customers are not having any loan or they have only one of the two loans. They may be given loans at a reduced interest rate as a measure of retaining the existing customers. After identifying the customers who may be offered loans, it is necessary to evaluate them on the basis of their "risk" level. For this the customers are evaluated with the help of a number of parameters like age, income, debt, gender, marital status and the like. For a given customer these parameter values may be presented in the form of an input vector.

Selection of Algorithms

The algorithms employed are selected on the basis of type of data, size of data as well as requirement of the results. The K-Nearest Neighbour algorithm is applied to predict the risk of, a potential loan customer as, good or bad. Again to compare the efficiency of two classification algorithms, Naïve Bayes algorithm is also applied to classify a prospective borrower into two classes like "good risk" and "poor risk". K-Nearest Neighbor is a supervised learning algorithm where the result of a new instance query is classified based on majority of K-Nearest neighbour category. The purpose of the algorithm is to classify a new object based on attributes and training sample. The classification is using majority vote among the classification of the K-objects.

Naïve-Bayes is a classification technique that is both predictive and descriptive. It analyses the relationship between each independent variable and the dependent variable to derive a conditional probability for each relationship.

Methodology Adopted

Classification Algorithms

The classification algorithms are categorized into five types, based on the methodology or procedure adopted by the algorithm to carry out the classification process. The different categories of classification algorithms are Statistical-Based, Distance Based, Decision-Tree Based, Neural Network Based and Rule based algorithms. Statistical-Based algorithms comprises of Regression and Naïve-Bayes classification. Regression problems deal with the estimation of an output value based on input values. Naïve-Bayes classification algorithm has its origin from Bayes theorem. This algorithm assumes that all attributes contribute equally to the classification problem and that all attributes are independent of each other. The algorithm is very easy to understand and implement. Compared to other classification techniques, Naïve-Bayes requires only one scan of the training data. Naïve-Bayes approach can handle missing values easily by simply omitting that probability when calculating the likelihoods of membership in each class. The technique yields good results when there is a simple relationship between data.

K-Nearest Neighbor is a distance-based algorithm, which tries to find the nearest neighbors of new instance, by calculating the distance between the new instance and the instances in the training set. After calculating the distance, the neighbors are arranged in the ascending order of distance. After that, depending on the value of K, the nearest neighbors are selected.

Decision tree algorithms represent supervised learning, and hence require pre classified target variables. A training data set, which provides the algorithm with values of the target variables, must be provided. Decision trees learn by example and examples should be provided in the training set for all possible subsets of records. The objective of decision tree approach is to iteratively partition the given data set into subsets where all elements in each final subset belong to the same class. With this technique, a tree is constructed to model the classification process. Once the tree is built, it is applied to each tuple in the database and results in a classification for that tuple.

Using neural networks, as with decision trees, a model representing how to classify any given database tuple is constructed. The activation functions typically are sigmoidal. When a tuple must be classified, certain attribute values from that tuple are input into the directed graph at the corresponding source nodes. There often is one sink node for each class. The output value that is generated indicates the probability that he corresponding input tuple belongs to that class. The tuple will then be assigned the class with the highest probability of membership. The learning process modifies the labeling of the arcs to better classify the tuples. Given a starting structure and value for all the labels in the graph, as each tuple in the training set is sent through the network, the projected classification made by the graph can be compared with the actual classification. Based on the accuracy of the prediction, various labeling in the graph can change this leaning process continuous with all the training data or until the classification adequacy is accurate.

Techniques of Java used for the present work

The following section explores the features of Java packages and classes, Interfaces, Threads, applets and JFC exclusively used for the programming purpose.

*Package: Java.lang.**

The java.lang package is indispensable when programming in Java. It is automatically imported into every source file at compile time. The package contains the Object class, which is the mother of all classes, and the wrapper classes used to manipulate primitive values as objects. All classes directly or indirectly extend the Object class. Wrapper Classes are introduced to manipulate primitive data types.

Interfaces

A collection-sometimes called a container-is simply an object that groups multiple elements into a single unit.Action listener interface is the listener interface for receiving action events. The class that is interested in processing an action event implements this interface, and the object created with that class is registered with a component, using the components add Action Listener method. When the actionevent occurs, that objects action Performed method is invoked.

Threads

On an operating system a running program is known as a process. A single process can have separate runnable tasks called threads. A thread is also referred to as a lightweight process. Javax.swing.J Internal Frame is a lightweight object that provides many of the features of a native frame, including dragging, closing, becoming an icon, resizing, title display, and support for a menu bar. Generally, we add JInternalFrames to a JDesktoppane. The user interface delegates the look-and-feel-specific actions to the DesktopManager object maintained by the JDesktoppane. The JInternalFrame Contentpane is where you add child components. As a convenience add and its variants, remove and SetLayout have been overridden to forward to the contentpane as necessary. SWINGS.

Sun Microsystems is leveraging the technology of Netscape Communications, IBM, and Lighthouse design to create asset of Graphical User Interface (GUI) classes that integrate with JDK 1.1.5. These classes are standard with the Java ® 2 platform and provide a more polished look and feel than the standard AWT component set. The collection of APIs coming out of this effort, called the Java Foundation Classes (JFC), allows developers to build full-featured enterprise–ready applications.

JFC is composed of five APIs: AWT, Java 2D, Accessibility, Drag and Drop, Swing. The AWT components refer to the AWT as it exists in JDK versions 1.1.2 and later. Java 2D is a graphics API based on technology licensed from IBM/Taligent. It is currently available with Java® 2 Platform (and not usable with JDK 1.1). The Accessibility API provides assistive technologies, like screen magnifiers which could be used with various pieces of JFC. Drag and Drop support is part of the next JavaBean generation, "Glasgow," and is also available with the Java ® 2 platform.

Swing includes a component set that is targeted at forms-based applications. Loosely based on Netscape's acclaimed Internet Foundation Classes (IFC), the Swing components have had the most immediate impact on Java development. They provide a set of well-groomed widgets and a framework to specify how GUIs are visually resented, independent of platform.

Swing can expand and simplify the development of cross-platform applications. The Swing collection consists of seventeen packages, each of which has its own distinct purpose.

Classification Process

Steps in Classification Process

The classification process may result in the categorization of data into predefined classes. Hence before the classification task is carried out, the classes to which the entities are to be assigned must be predefined. Thus, there is a need of preprocessing before we assume a classification task in a data set. The basic steps involved in the classification process may be summarized as follows:

- Feature Selection. The ultimate aim is to select the relevant attributes for classification process. Thus, preprocessing of data may be necessary prior to their utilization in classification task.
- Classification algorithm: This step refers to the choice of an algorithm that, results in the accurate classification of a data set. The classification algorithm is chosen on the basis of several features such as type of data (categorical or numerical), size of data, type of result required etc. After the preprocessing steps, the following

methodology is adopted by most supervised learning methods for building and evaluating a model .The algorithm is provided with a training set of data, which includes the pre classified values of the target variable in addition to the predictor variables. For example, if we are interested in classifying that a patient without a disease is normal, otherwise abnormal. The classification will be predicted on the basis of variables such as age, gender, smoking habits, blood pressure etc. and these variables are the predictor variables. The target field is Class (normal or abnormal) to which the patient belongs. In other words, the records in the training set need to be pre classified. A provisional data-mining model is then constructed using the training samples provided in the training data set.

- The next step is to examine how the provisional data-mining model performs on a test set of data. In the test set, a holdout data set, the values of the target variable are hidden temporarily from the provisional model, which then performs classification according to the patterns and structure it learned from the training set. The efficacies of the classifications are then evaluated by comparing them against the true values of the target variable. The provisional data-mining model is then adjusted to minimize the error rate on the test set.
- The adjusted data-mining model is then applied to a validation data set, another holdout data set, where the values of the target variable are again hidden temporarily from the model. The adjusted model is itself then adjusted, to minimize the error rate on the validation set. Estimates of model performance for future unseen data can then be computed by observing various evaluative measures applied to the validation set.
- Validation of results: The correctness of classification algorithm results is verified using appropriate criteria and

techniques. There are several measures like accuracy, precision, recall, confusion matrix etc that can be used to evaluate the classifier.

- Interpretation of results: The results given as output by the classification process may have to be examined by the experts in the application area by integrating the results with other experimental evidence and analysis in order to draw the right conclusion.

Application of Classification in CRM

Banks would like to provide value added services to the customers, as this may ultimately lead to better customer relationship management. It is assumed that the strategy adopted by the bank for better customer relationship management is to offer loans to existing customers of the bank, at a reduced interest rate. For this the deserving and eligible customers have to be identified. Eligibility means, the customers should be capable of paying off their loans. A deserving customer is one, who is committed towards paying off his loans. Thus the bank should be able to identify "Good Risk" and"Bad Risk" customers before deciding to offer them loans.

Assumptions

Loans are offered only to those customers who have no loans or have a maximum of one loan. Bank offers only two types of loan, viz. Vehicle loan and House loan. Income eligibility for hue loan is that take home pay should be at least 30% of monthly income. Income eligibility for car loan is that take home pay should be at least 40% of monthly income.

Computations Performed as part of preprocessing

The risk of customers is predicted by the dependent variables, Debt, Income and Marital status. Hence before trying to predict the risk, the customers had to be categorized into different groups, based on their income level and debt level. Customers are categorized into three groups based on their income. The salary scale for classification and the corresponding categories are as follows:

Table 1
Salary Category

Monthly salary scale	*Income group*
Above 50,000	High
35,000<Monthlyincome<50,000	Upper Middle
20,000<Monthly income<35,000	Middle

Debt Category

In the case of customers who have not taken any loan from the bank, debt is calculated as,

Debt = Monthly Income – Take Home Pay,

Where take home pay is calculated as,

Take Home Pay = Monthly Income – (Savings + Income Tax + PF)

In the case of customers of who have taken a loan from the bank, debt is calculated as,

Debt = Take home pay – Monthly income – Equated Monthly Income (EMI)

For calculating EMI, the following criterion is used by the bank:

Table 2
Calculating EMI

Monthly salary slab (Rs.)	*% of Monthly salary Considered*
8.000 – 10,000	45
10,000 – 20,000	50
20,000 – 35,000	55
Above 35,000	60

EMI = $p * r * (1+r)^n / ((1+r)^n - 1)$

Where P = Principal Amount

R = Rate of Interest = (Annual rate of Interest/12)/100

n = tenure * 12

Teaching Data

After analyzing the behavior of previous customers who had taken loans from the bank, the bank has formulated certain combinations for Debt, Income and marital status, which can be used in predicting the risk category of customers. The combinations are as follows:

Table 3

Debt	*Income*	*Marital status*	*Risk*
High	High	Yes	Good
High	Middle	No	Poor
High	High	No	Poor
High	Low	Yes	Poor
High	Low	No	Poor
High	Middle	Yes	Poor
High	Upper Middle	Yes	Good
High	Upper Middle	No	Poor
Low	High	Yes	Good
Low	Low	No	Poor
Low	Middle	Yes	Good
Low	Middle	No	Poor
Low	High	No	Poor
Low	Upper Middle	Yes	Good

After calculating the debt, the customers are categorized into two groups as follows:

Table 4
For House Loans

Debt Amount	*Category*
>70% of Monthly Income	Very High
50% of Monthly Income < Debt < 70% of Monthly Income	High
<50% of Monthly Income	Low

Table 5
For Vehicle Loans

Debt Amount	*Category*
>60% of Monthly Income	Very High
40% of Monthly Income < Debt < 60% of Monthly Income	High
<40% of Monthly Income	Low

Algorithms are applied and their accuracies are measured, after taking the assumptions into consideration.

Algorithms Implemented

K-Nearest Neighbor Technique

The K-nearest neighbor (k-NN) algorithm is a method of classifying objects based on closest training examples in the feature space. K-NN is a type of instance based learning where the function is only approximated locally and all computation is deferred until classification.

The nearest method represents one of the simplest and most intuitive techniques [CH67] in the field of statistical discrimination. It is a nonparametric method, where a new observation is placed into the class of the observation from the learning set that is closest to the new observation, with respect to the covariates used. The determination of this similarity is based on the distance measures.

Formally this simple fact can be described as follows: Let,

$$L = \{ (yi, xi), I = 1,2,\ldots,nL\}$$

be a training or learning set of observed data, where yi $\in$ (1… c} denotes class membership and the vector xi = (xi1,…,xip) represents the predictor values. The determination of the nearest neighbors is based on an arbitrary distance function d (x, y). Then for a new observation (y, x) the nearest neighbor (y(1), x(1)) within the learning set is determined by

And Y = y(1), the class of the nearest neighbor, is selected as prediction for y. The notation x(j) and y(j) here describes the jth nearest neighbor of x and its class membership, respectively.

For example, such typical distance functions are the Euclidean distance

$$D\,(xi, xj) = \sqrt{\left(\sum_{s=1}^{p}(x_{is} - x_{js})^2\right)}$$

Or the absolute distance

$$D (xi, xj) = \sum_{s=1}^{p} |x_{is} - x_{js}|$$

In general, both measures can be seen as special cases of the so called MinKowski distance

$$D (xi, xj) = (\sum_{s=1}^{p} |xis - xjs|^{q})^{1/q}$$

The Euclidean distance results for the selection q = 2, the absolute distance for the parameter value q = 1.

The method has been explained by the random occurrence of the learning set, by studies conducted in this area. The class label $y_{(1)}$ of the nearest neighbor x(1) of a new case x is a random variable. So the classification probability of x into class $y_{(1)}$ is $P(y_{(1)} | x_{(1)})$. For large learning sets x and $x_{(1)}$ coincide very closely with each other, so $P(y_{(1)} | x_{(1)}) \approx P(y | x)$ results approximately. Therefore the new observation x is predicted as belonging to the true class y with the probability approximately P (y|x)

It is an extension of this idea that has become popular in the form of K-Nearest Neighbor algorithm. Here not only the closest observation within the learning set is referred for classification, but also the k most similar cases. The parameter k has to be selected by the user. Then the decision is in favor of the class label, most of these neighbors belong to.

Let Kr denote the number of observations from the group of the nearest neighbors that belong to class r:

$$\sum_{r=1}^{c} K_r = K$$

Then a new observation is predicted into the class l with

Kl = max r (kr)

This prevents one singular observation from the learning set deciding about the predicted class. The degree of locality of this technique is determined by the parameter K: For K = 1 one gets the simple nearest neighbor method as maximal local technique, for $k \rightarrow n_L$ a global majority vote of the whole learning set results. This implies a constant prediction for all new observations that have to be classified: always the most frequent class within the learning set is predicted.

Experiment Performed with K-NN

K-Nearest Neighbor is a predictive technique suitable for classification models. Unlike other predictive algorithms, the training data is not scanned or processed to create the model. When a new case or instance is presented to the model, the algorithm looks at all data to find a subset of cases that are most similar to it and uses them to predict the outcome.

The K-Nearest Neighbor algorithm classifies a new instance into one of the predefined classes.

The algorithm accepts as input, the training data, number of nearest neighbors to be considered and the input tuple or the new instance to be classified. The training phase of the algorithm consists only of storing the feature vectors and class labels of the training samples. K-NN does not make a learning pass through the data.

Determine the parameter K, which indicates the number of neighbors to be considered: Each use of the K-NN algorithm requires that we specify a positive integer value for K. This determines how many existing cases are looked at when predicting a new case. The best value for K will require some experimentation with the data at hand, comparing results for different K values against a test dataset. Usually K is chosen to be an odd number. Larger values of K reduce the effect of noise on the classification, but make boundaries between classes less distinct.

Calculate the distance between the query-instance and all the training samples: The term nearest implies, that K-NN is based on a concept of distance, and this requires a metric to determine distances. All metrics must result in a specific number for comparison purposes. Whatever metric is used is both arbitrary and extremely important. It is arbitrary because there is no preset definition of what constitutes a "good" metric. It is important because the choice of metric greatly affects predictions.

Sort the distance and determine the nearest neighbors based on the k-th minimum distance: Arrange the distance between the query instance and the records in the training set in the order of distance. Then depending upon the value of k, choose the nearest neighbors. For example if k is 3, choose the first three records hat are nearest in distance to the query instance.

Gather the category of the nearest neighbors. i.e. determine the class labels of all the 3 nearest neighbors, in the case of k = 3.

Use simple majority of the category of nearest neighbors as the prediction value of the query instance: For example, if three neighbors are chosen, and if two of them have their class label as "Good risk" and one has its class label as "Poor risk", the majority of the category is "Good Risk". Hence "Good Risk" will be chosen as the class label of the new instance.

Naïve Bayes Method

Naïve Bayes classification method assumes that contribution by all predictor variables or attributes towards the classification problem are equal and that the attributes are independent of each other. Naïve Bayes classification is a simple classification scheme that is based on the Bayes rule of conditional probability. This method analyzes the contribution of each "independent" attribute and then determines a conditional probability. A classification is made by combining the impact that the different attributes have on the prediction to be made.

The approach is called "naïve" because it assumes the independence between the various attribute values. Given a data value xi the probability that a related tuple, ti, is in class c_j is described by P $(C_j | X_i)$. Training data can be used to determine P (x_i), P $(x_i | C_i)$ and P (C_i). From these values, Bayes theorem allows us to, estimate the posterior probability P $(C_j | X_i)$ and the P $(C_j | t_i)$. Naive Bayes do not handle continuous data, so any dependent or independent continuous variables must be binned or bracketed.

Experiment Performed with Naïve-Bayes

Naïve Bayes Algorithm Classifies a New Instance into Predefined Classes by Calculating the Conditional Probabilities.

Given a training set, the Naive Bayes algorithm adopts the following procedure to carry out the classification process:

- The probability of each outcome or dependent variable $P(C_j)$ is computed by counting how many times each class occurs in the training set. This is called the apriori probability. For example, if the "Good risk" outcome occurs three out of 5 cases, then the prior probability of "Good Risk" is 3/5.
- The algorithm determines how frequently each independent variable value occurs in combination with each dependent variable or class category. These frequencies are then used to compute the conditional probabilities. Thus if xi is an independent variable the $P(x_i | C_j)$ denotes the probability of occurrence of xi in conjunction with a class Cj. This is the *likelihood probability*.
- The likelihood probabilities are combined with apriori probabilities to determine the posteriori probabilities. These probabilities are used to predict the class membership of a target tuple. Combining the effects of the different attribute values that form the tuple does this.

Implementation

Data Sets Used

The two algorithms, K-Nearest Neighbor and Naïve Bayes, which are the subject of the study, attempts to find out the risk value of the customers, who may be offered loans. As a part of evaluating their performance, the algorithms are applied on data sets of varying size. The execution time and the accuracy of classification are the two constraints applied on the data sets. Based upon the constraints, both the algorithms are examined and the final conclusion is derived.

The sample data sets used are one with 69 records, another with 529 records and a third one with 1029 records. The comparison study is carried out on the database of the bank, with several tables such as Deposit, Loan, Loan-Transaction, Deposit-Transaction, Savings Bank, Product-Type, Job-Type, Customer-Type and Loan-Scheme-Master. In addition to these data sets, several data sets from the UCI repository have been used for the purpose of comparing the algorithms. These data sets include Contact lens data set, Soya bean data set and the segment data set.

Preparing the Data for the Application of Algorithms

The first step in preparing the data was to identify the customers who may be offered loans. The bank offers loans only to those customers who have either no loans or have at most one loan. The details of those customers who don't have any loan are extracted from the customer-master-table and the customers who have at most one loan are extracted from the loan-master table.

While extracting the details of customers from the customer-master-table, their debt amount is calculated as the difference between income and take-home-pay. Finding the sum of take-home-pay and EMI and then subtracting it from income, we calculate the debt of the customers, extracted from the loan table. After calculating the debt amount, the customers are categorized into three different Debt scales, viz. Very high, high and low. If the debt-amt of a customer is greater than 70 per cent of monthly income, then the customer is categorized as a "very high" debt customer. These customers are not offered loans at all. If the debt-amt is less than 70 per cent and greater than 40 per cent of monthly income, then the customer is categorized as a "high" debt customer. . If the debt-amt is less than 40 per cent of monthly income, then the customer is categorized as a "low" debt customer.

These customers may be offered vehicle loans or house loans after examining their "risk" level.

The customers are categorized into four income groups on the basis of their monthly-income scale. The income field corresponding to each customer record is checked for its value. If cust-income is above 50,000, then the customer falls in the "high" income group. If the customer's income lies between 35,000 and 50,000, he falls in the "upper middle" income group. If the income lies between 20,000 and 35,000, he falls in the "middle" income group. If income is less than 20,000, he falls in the "low" income group. Thus the customers who may be offered loans along with their income-category and debt-category have been identified. But before offering loans, the bank wants to identify the "risk" of the customers. Based on the behavioral pattern of previous "loan customers", the bank has derived certain rules regarding the identification of "risk" level of customers. A sample record values may be cust-id = 220, debt = high, income = high, marital status = no the risk = poor. I.e. if the customer has a high debt, high income and he is not married, then he is a poor risk customer. In other words, he may not be a good customer for loan. The teaching-set table contains the cust-id, income-category, debt-category, marital status and the risk level of the previous customers. The training-set is populated with the fields that contribute to the prediction of risk of the customers. Thus the cust-id, income-category, debt-category and marital status of the potential customers, are moved to the training-set table.

Application of K-Nearest Neighbor

The application of the K-NN algorithm is carried out in three phases. In the first phase, called the teaching-phase, each record of the training-set is compared with the all the records in the teaching-set to determine whether there is a match with any of the combinations in the teaching-set. If there is a match, the corresponding "risk" will be assigned as the "risk" of the customer in the training-set. For comparison purpose, only the independent attributes viz. debt-category, income-category and marital status are used. The process is continued until all the customers have been classified according to their "risk".

Next is the validation phase, where the real application of the K-NN algorithm comes in. This phase is carried out to determine, the accuracy of performance of the algorithm. During this phase, only the records in the training-set are considered. All the fields except the "risk" will be extracted and placed into the validation-set table. The risk field of this table will be initially empty. Then the "Euclidean distance" of each record of this table from all the other records is calculated in the same table is calculated. For calculating the distance, we need numerical variables. Hence the categorical values of debt, income and marital status are assigned numerical values. High debt is assigned a value of 1 and low debt a value of 0. High income is assigned the value 3, upper middle a value of 2, middle a value of 1 and low a value of 0. Similarly, married is assigned the value 1 and unmarried the value 0.

The calculated distances are stored into an array. Then the distances are sorted in the ascending order by comparing each distance with its immediate successor. If the value of the successor is less, then that distance will be moved to the front. Similarly all the distances are sorted. The value of K, the number of neighbors is chosen to be 5. From the sorted list, the first 5 distances and the corresponding cust-id's are determined. Then the "risk" of these 5 customers is determined from the training set. The "risk" that is repeated the maximum number of times will be the risk of the concerned record of he validation-set table. This process is continued until all the records of the validation-set have been assigned a "risk" category. Then the "predicted risk" of all the customers in the validation-set table is compared with the "actual risk" in the training-set table, to determine the accuracy of classification.

The next-phase is the test phase. During this phase, the details of a new set of customers initially unknown to the algorithm will be stored in the test-set table. Each record in this table is compared with all the records in the training-set table. I.e. their "Euclidean distance" from all the records in the training-set table will be calculated. Then the cust-id of the first 5 neighbors will be determined based upon the distance and their corresponding "risk" category will be determined from the training-set table. The simple majority will be assigned as the "risk" of the tested customer in the test-set table. The process is repeated until all the customers in the test-set are classified on the basis of "risk".

Table 6
Sample Method for Classification using K-Nearest Neighbor

A sample data set

Name	*Debt*	*Income*	*Married*	*Risk*
Teaching Data Set				
Krishnan	High	High	Yes	Good
Maria	Low	High	Yes	Good
John	Low	High	No	Poor
Mary	High	Low	Yes	Poor
Latha	Low	Low	Yes	Poor
Coded Data Set				
Krishnan	1	3	1	Good
Maria	0	3	1	Good
John	0	3	0	Poor
Mary	1	0	1	Poor
Latha	0	0	1	Poor

The given data set is the training data set, which will be scanned by the classifying program every time a test data is entered for classification. This data set contains information about people to whom the institution previously loaned money. The lender determined if each applicant was a good or poor credit risk. Because risk is what we wish to predict, it is the dependent variable, also called the target variable. The other columns used to build the model are known as independent columns. Here, the independent columns include debt level (High or Low), income level (High, Upper middle, Middle, Low) and Marital Status

(Yes or No). The name column will be ignored because it is highly unlikely that a person's name affects his credit risk. Suppose K = 3 or 3-NN. The distance measure used is the Euclidean distance, which is the square root of the sum of the squares of the distances between corresponding variables of the compared records.

Test data

The test data variables are given in the form of an input vector as (Harish, High, High, Yes). The classification program has to predict whether the potential customer is a good risk or a bad risk on the basis of the behavioral pattern of previous loan customers. Hence the program finds the distance between Harish and the customers of the training set.

Applying the Algorithm

Determine the parameter K = number of nearest neighbors:

Let us assume that K = 3

Calculate the distance between the new instance of tissue and all the training samples:

Coordinate of query instance is (1, 1, 1). Here the distance measure that we are making use of is the Euclidean distance measure, where in we take the square root of the square of the distance between the observations.

Table 7
Euclidean Distance between Query Instance and Training Sample

X1 = debt	*X2 = income*	*X3 = marital status*	*Euclidean distance to (1,3,1)*
1	3	1	$\sqrt{(1-1)^2 + (3-3)^2 + (1-1)^2} = 0$
0	3	1	$\sqrt{(0-1)^2 + (3--3)^2 + (1-1)^2} = 1$
0	3	0	$\sqrt{(0-1)^2 + (3-3)^2 + (0-1)^2} = 1.414$
1	0	1	$\sqrt{(1-1)^2 + (0-1)^2 + (1-1)^2} = 1$
0	0	1	$\sqrt{(0-1)^2 + (0-1)^2 + (1-1)^2} = 1.414$

Sort the distance and determine the nearest neighbor based on the K- th minimum distance: Arranging the distance between Harish and all his neighbors and selecting the neighbors whose distance corresponds to the first three in the order obtain the 3-nearest neighbors of Harish. Thus the 3-nearest neighbors of Harish are Krishnan, Mary and Maria.

Table 8
Neighbors Ranked According to Their Distance

X1 = debt	*X2 = income*	*X3=marital status*	*Euclidean distance to query instance(1,1,1)*	*Rank minimum dist*
1	3	1	0	1
0	3	1	1	2
0	3	0	1.414	4
1	0	1	1	3
0	0	1	1.414	5

Gather the Category of the Nearest Neighbors

In the above table, the data in the second row is not included in the list of neighbors, because the rank of this data is more than 3.

Table 9
Neighbors Categorized on the Basis of Their Quality

X1 = debt	*X2 = income*	*X3 = marital status*	*Euclidean distance*	*Rank minimum dist*	*Is it included in 3-NN*	*Y = Category of NN*
1	3	1	0	1	Yes	Good
0	3	1	1	2	Yes	Good
0	3	0	1.414	4	No	Good
1	0	1	1	3	Yes	Poor
0	0	1	1.414	5	No	Poor

Use simple majority of the category of the nearest neighbors as the prediction value of the query instance: In the above table we can see that we have 2 neighbors with their category as *"Good"* and 1 neighbor, whose category is *"Bad"*. Since 2 >1, we conclude that the majority category is *"Good"*. Hence the risk category of Harish is Good.

Classification Accuracy and Processing Time of K-Nearest Neighbor

The validation phase of K-NN is carried out to determine the accuracy of performance of the algorithm. In the validation phase, all the records in the validation set are classified according to their "risk". To determine whether this classification is correct or not, the "predicted risk" of each customer in the validation-set table will be compared with the "actual risk" of the same customer in the training-set table. If the two risks match, then the corresponding record s a correctly classified instance. Otherwise it is a wrongly classified instance. Similarly all the records are verified and the total number of correctly classified instances and wrongly classified instances are determined. This result is represented in the form of a confusion matrix, which clearly shows the accuracy in classification.

The processing time of K-NN is determined by observing the time taken by the algorithm to perform the classification on varying number of records. This information is represented in the form of a histogram, with the number of records represented in the X-axis and time-taken to process the records in the Y-axis.

Application of Naïve-Bayes

The Naïve-Bayes classification algorithms involves the performance of cross-tabulation of data, calculating the "total-by-risk", calculating "likelihood" probabilities of "good risk" score and "poor risk" score, calculating the prior probabilities of "good risk" and "poor risk", calculating the "posterior probabilities of "good risk" score and "poor risk " score, comparing the "good risk score" and "poor risk score" and predicting the risk of the customers.

Sample Method for Classification using Naïve-Bayes

Consider the credit risk classification problem goal of which is to predict whether an applicant will be a "Good Risk" or a "Poor Risk" type. The sample data set contains only categorical values. Hence there is no need to do binning (grouping) of data.

From the following sample training data set, we cross-tabulate counts of each risk outcome (Good or Poor) and each value in the independent variable column. For example, there are two customers whose income is "High" and risk is "Good" and one customer whose income is "high" and "risk" is poor.

Table 10
Training Data

Name	*Debt*	*Income*	*Married*	*Risk*
Krishnan	High	High	Yes	Good
Maria	Low	High	Yes	Good
John	Low	High	No	Poor
Mary	High	Low	Yes	Poor
Latha	Low	Low	Yes	Poor

Now we calculate the *"Total by risk"* for the two categories. *Total by Risk for Good Risk* is to look at out of the total number of customers considered, how many customers belong to the Good Risk category. In our sample out of the 5 customers considered, 2 customers belong to the "Good Risk" category.

Hence Total by Risk for Good Risk = 2.

Total by Risk for Poor Risk: is to look at out of the total number of customers considered, how many customers belong to the Poor Risk category. In the training data, out of a total of 5 customers, 3 belong to the poor risk category.

Hence Total by Risk for Poor Risk = 3.

These figures are summarized in the following table:

Table 11
Total by Risk

Independent Variable	*Value*	*Counts Good Risk*	*Counts Poor Risk*
Debt	High	1	1
Debt	Low	1	2
Income	High	2	1
Income	Low	0	2
Married	Yes	2	2
Married	No	0	1
Total by Risk		2	3

Likelihood Probability

The likelihood of occurrence of an event given that another may have contributed to the occurrence of the event, is known as likelihood probability. The likelihood that one of the independent variable has a particular value, given a known risk level, can be obtained by using the count of corresponding risk level and dividing by the "Total by Risk" number (on the bottom row of Table 11). Eg. the likelihood that a "Good Risk" has high income is obtained as,

$$\text{Likelihood (High Income/Good Risk)} = \frac{\textit{Counts of Good Risk for High Income}}{\text{Total by Risk for Good Risk}}$$

i.e. P (High Income/Good Risk) = 2/2 = 1

This is because both the instances of Good Risk have high Income. In the same way, the conditional probability that a poor risk has a low income is 0.67, because 2 out of 3 poor risks have low income (row 4 of Table 8). The Likelihood Probabilities are summarized in Table 12.

Table 12
Likelihood Probabilities

		Counts	*Counts*	*Likelihood*	
Independent Variable	*Value*	*Good Risk*	*Poor Risk*	*Given good Risk*	*Given Poor Risk*
Debt	High	1	1	1/2 =0.5	1/3=0.33
Debt	Low	1	2	½=0.5	2/3=0.67
Income	High	2	1	2/2=1	1/3=0.33
Income	Low	0	2	0/2=0	2/3=0.67
Married	Yes	2	2	2/2=1	2/3=0.67
Married	No	0	1	0/2=0	1/3=0.33
Total by Risk		2	3		

Prior Probability

Prior probability is the probability of occurrence of an event that is calculated prior to conducting the experiment. The last row of Table 12 is also used to compute the Prior Probabilities for Good and Poor Risk. In our data the *Prior Probability* for Good Risk is calculated as the ratio of the number of cases of Good Risk to the total number of customers.

P (Good Risk) = 2/5 = 0.4

Similarly the prior probability for Poor is calculated as the ratio of the number of cases of Poor risk to the total number of customers. Out of the 5 customers, 3 customers are of the Poor Risk category.

P (Poor Risk) = 3/5 = 0.6

Posterior Probability

Posterior probability is obtained by multiplying the prior probability for risk level by all the likelihood figures from Table 12 for the independent variables (Bayes' theorem). The highest scoring value becomes the predicted value. In Table 10 the first row for Krishnan in the training set has High debt, High Income and Marital Status as "yes". In Table 11 the likelihoods associated with these values and Good risk are 0.5, 1.0 and 1.0 respectively (rows 1, 3 and 5 of Table 11). The product of these three numbers and the prior probability for Good i.e. 0.40 is 0.5*1.0*1.0*0.4 = 0.2. Similarly we can obtain poor risk values. The related figures are shown in the following table.

Table 13
Good Risk & Poor Risk scores

Name	*Debt*	*Income*	*Married*	*Risk Actual*	*Good Risk Score*	*Poor Risk Score*
Krishnan	High	High	Yes	Good	0.4*0.5*1*1	0.6*0.33*0.33*0.67
Maria	Low	High	Yes	Good	0.4*0.5*1*1	0.6*0.67*0.33*0.67
John	Low	High	No	Poor	0.4*0.67*1*0	0.6*0.67*0.33*0.33
Mary	High	Low	Yes	Poor	0.4*0.5*0*1	0.6*0.33*0.67*0.67
Latha	Low	Low	Yes	Poor	0.4*0.5*0*1	0.6*0.67*0.67*0.67

Now we compare the Good Risk score and the Poor Risk score for each customer, and whichever value is higher for a Risk category will be the predicted risk category of the customer.

For example, the Good Risk score of Krishnan is 0.2 and the Poor risk score is 0.044. Since 0.2 is greater then 0.44, Krishnan is predicted to be a Good risk customer. The category of all the data in the training set is summarized as follows:

Table 14
Risk Predicted

Name	*Debt*	*Income*	*Married*	*Risk Actual*	*Good Risk Score*	*Poor Risk Score*	*Risk Predicted*
Krishnan	High	High	Yes	Good	0.2	0.044	Good
Maria	Low	High	Yes	Good	0.2	0.09	Good
John	Low	High	No	Poor	0	0.04	Poor
Mary	High	Low	Yes	Poor	0	0.09	Poor
Latha	Low	Low	Yes	Poor	0	0.18	Poor

The Table 14 presents the actual risk, the scores for Good Risk and Poor Risk, and the predicted Risk for all cases in the sample data. With all the outcomes predicted correctly, it is confirmed that the algorithm has 100 percent accuracy on the training set.

Now we shall validate the model by using it to predict the outcomes for a separate test data.

Classification Accuracy and Processing Time of Naïve-Bayes

The validation phase of naïve-Bayes is carried out to determine the accuracy in the performance of the algorithm. In the validation phase, all the records in the training-set, except for the "risk" field is moves to the validation-set. The algorithm is applied to the records in the validation-set, after eliminating the "risk" field. The algorithm predicts the "risk" of all the records in the validation-set. To determine whether this classification is correct or not, the "predicted risk" of each customer in the validation-set table will be compared with the "actual risk" of the same customer in the training-set table. If the two risks match, then the corresponding record is a correctly classified instance. Otherwise it is a wrongly classified instance. Similarly all the records are verified and the total number of correctly classified instances and wrongly classified instances are determined. This result is represented in the form of a confusion matrix, which clearly shows the accuracy in classification. The processing time of Naïve-bayes is determined by observing the time taken by the algorithm to perform the classification on varying number of records. This information is represented in the form of a histogram, with the number of records represented in the X-axis and time-taken to process the records in the Y-axis.

Evaluation of the Performance of K-Nearest Neighbor and Naïve-Bayes

The performance of the algorithms is compared on the basis of classification accuracy and the time taken for the entire classification process. The classification accuracy is obtained from the confusion matrix of both the algorithms as well as the percentage of correctly classified instances and the percentage of wrongly classified instances. The algorithms are applied on different datasets with the intention of assessing the performance level with the change in number of attributes and number of instances.

Results

Analysis of Classification Accuracy for Varying Number of Instances

The results of the application of algorithms on data sets with varying number of instances were obtained in the form confusion matrices. The results show that the classification accuracy of Naïve-Bayes is affected by the variation in the number of instances. But K-NN performs equally well when applied to all the three data sets with varying instances. In other words, accuracy in classification of K-NN is independent of number of instances.

Analysis of Classification Accuracy for Varying Number of Attributes

Both the algorithms were applied on three data sets from the UCI machine learning repository. The contact lens data set has 5 attributes and 24 instances, Soya-Bean data set has 36 attributes and 683 instances and the Segment data set has 20 attributes and 810 instances. The performances of the two algorithms were comparable when applied to the contact lens data set. When the algorithms were applied on Soya-Bean data set with a comparatively large number of attributes, the classification accuracy of Naïve-Bayes was better than that of K-NN. Again the algorithms were applied on the segment data set with a very large number of instances. In this case, the classification accuracy of K-NN was better compared to that of Naive-Bayes. The result shows that K-NN is a better.

Observation on the performance of the two algorithms on the basis of a comparison of the results of application of the algorithms on the Contact-lens, Soya-beans and Segment data set, can be put forward as follows:

Taking the case of Contact-lens data set, the number of attributes and number of instances are less. From the results of application of the algorithms we can see that both the algorithms perform in exactly the same manner. Thus the algorithms are equally efficient, in the case of data sets with a small number of attributes and instances.

Now when we consider the Soya-Beans data set, the numbers of attributes as well as the number of instances are very high compared to the Contact-lens data set. When the results of correctly classified instances are compared, we find that Naive-Bayes is exhibiting a better performance compared to K-NN.

As part of determining whether it is an increase in the number of attributes or an increase in the number of instances that contributed to the variation in performance, the algorithms were again applied on, Segment data set. The number of attributes in the case of segment data set was less compared to the Soya-beans data set, but the numbers of instances were more. When comparing the results of the application of both the algorithms on this data set, it was found that K-NN was showing a better performance compared to Naïve-Bayes.

Thus on the basis of the experiment conducted on these three data sets, it can be concluded that, Naïve-Bayes is a better performer, when the number of attributes is more and K-Nearest Neighbor performs well in comparison to Naïve-Bayes , when the number of instances is more.

Concluding Observations

The comparative study of Classification Algorithms, K-Nearest Neighbor and Naïve-Bayes has paved the way to explore the similarities and differences between the two categories of classification techniques viz. Distance-Based and Statistical-Based. This thesis has been formulated with an experimental approach and the algorithms are implemented in Core Java to provide a detailed view of the classification process.

The conclusion after discussion on classification algorithms is given by a comparative presentation and stressing the pros and cons of each category. Another important issue that is discussed in this paper is the features selection or relevance analysis, which involves the process of selecting the attributes relevant to the classification process. The deviations in the performance of the algorithms with variation in the number of instances and attributes have also been the subject of study.

The paper also examines the approaches for estimating the classifier accuracy. This is related to the inherent features of the data sets under concern. Using training data alone to derive a classifier and then to estimate the accuracy of the classifier can result in misleading overoptimistic estimates due to overspecialization of the learning algorithm to the data.

The Performance of the two algorithms varies depending upon the features of the data sets under consideration. The time taken by the K-Nearest Neighbor algorithm to perform the classification does not vary much with variation in the number of instances or the number of attributes. But the K-Nearest Neighbor algorithm is suitable only for small data sets. When the number of instances exceeds 5000 records, the algorithm exhibits a very poor performance. The classification accuracy of the K-Nearest Neighbor algorithm is nearly 100 percent in the case of small data sets with varying number of instances. But when the number of attributes increases, the classification accuracy decreases with K-Nearest Neighbor. The performance time of Naïve-Bayes technique varies with the variation in the number of instances. The number of instances also affects the classification accuracy. But the change in the number of attributes does not affect the performance of naive-Bayes.

A comparison of the two algorithms reveals that, K-Nearest neighbor is best suitable for small data sets. The time taken by K-Nearest Neighbor is less compared to the time taken by Naïve-Bayes, for the same set of records. When the number of instance is more, the classification accuracy of K-Nearest Neighbor is more compared to that of Naïve-Bayes. But when the number of attributes is more, the classification accuracy of Naïve-Bayes is better compared to the classification accuracy of K-Nearest Neighbor.

References

[AC03], Wai-Ho Au and Keith C. C. Chan (2003), *"Mining Fuzzy Association Rules in a Bank-Account Database,"* *IEEE Transactions on Fuzzy Systems,* "Vol. 11, No. 2, pp. 238-248.

[AIS93] R. Agrawal, T. Imielinski, and A. Swami, *"Mining Association Rules between Sets of Items in Large Databases,"* in Proc. ACM SIGMOD Int. Conf.

[Alp04] Ethem Alpaydin (2004), *"Introduction to Machine Learning,"* pp. 153, MIT Press.

[AMEM03] C. d'Amato, D. Malerba, F. Esposito, M. Monopoli (2003), *"Extending the K-Nearest Neighbour classification algorithm to symbolic objects,"* Convegno Scientifico Intermedio SIS, 9-11 Giugno 2003, Università degli Studi di Napoli "Federico II".

[AS94] R. Agrawal and R. Srikant (1994), *"Fast Algorithms for Mining Association Rules,"* in Proc. 20th Int. Conf. Very Large Databases, Santiago, Chile, pp. 487-499.

[AZ04] Pieter Adriaans and Dolf Zantinge (2004), "*Data Mining*", Pearson Education, pp. 56-57.

[BCP93] Brown, D., Corruble, V. and Pittard, L. (1993), *"A Comparison of Decision Tree Classifiers With Back Propagation Neural Networks for Multimodal Classification Problems"*, Pattern Recognition Vol. 26, pp. 953-961.

[Brad97] Bradley, A. (1997), *"The use of the Area under the ROC curve in the Evaluation of Machine Learning Algorithms"*, Pattern recognition 30, pp. 1145-1159.

[Bre96] Breriman (1996), *"Bagging Predicators,"* Machine Learning, pp 123-140.

[BW90] Harper W. Boyd, and Orville C. Walker (1990),*"Marketing Management - A Strategic Approach,"* Irwin.

[CH05] Yongqiang Chen and Leifang Hu (2005), *"Study on Data Mining Application in CRM System Based on Insurance Trade,"*, in Proc ACM Int. Conf. Electronic Commerce, Xi'an, China, Vol. 113 , pp. 839-841.

[CH67] Cover and Hart (1967), *"Nearest Neighbor Pattern Classification"*, IEEE Transactions on Information Theory 13; pp. 21-27.

[CM98] V. Cherkassky and F. Mulier (1998), *"Learning From Data: Concepts, Theory and Methods,"* New York: Wiley.

[DHB95] Dietterich, T., Hild, H., and Bakiri. G. (1995), *"A Comparison of ID3 and Backpropagation for English Text-To-Speech Mapping,"* Machine Learning, Vol. 18, 51-80.

[Dun04] Margaret H. Dunham (2004), *"Data Mining-Introductory and Advanced Topics"*, Pearson Education, pp. 76-100.

[EPH98] A. Episcopos, A. Pericli, and J. Hu (1998), *"Commercial Mortgage Default: A Comparison of Log it with Radial Basis Function Networks,"* J. Real Estate Finance and Econ., Vol. 17, pp. 163-178.

[Ger99] R. Gertsen (1999), *"Assessing Loan Risks: A Data Mining Case Study,"* IT Professional, Vol. 1, pp. 16-21.

[GW02] Gora, g., Wojna, A. (2002), RIONA: *"A Classifier Combining Rule Induction and K-NN Method with Automated Selection of Optimal Neighbourhood"*, Proceedings of the Thirteenth European Conference on Machine Learning, ECML 2002, Lecture Notes in Artificial Intelligence, 2430, pp. 11-123, Springer-Verlag.

[Har75] John A. Hartigan (1975), *"Clustering Algorithms"*, New York: John Wiley & Sons.

[HHGY00] Hongxing He, Simon Hawkins, Warwick Graco and Xin Yao (2000), *"Application of Genetic algorithm and K- Nearest Neighbour Method in Real World Medical Fraud Detection Problem"* , *Journal of Advanced Computational Intelligence and Intelligent Informatics,* Vol. 4, No. 2, pp. 130-137.

[HK05] Jiawei Han, Micheline Kamber (2005), *"Data Mining Concepts and Techniques,"* Elsevier, pp. 323-324, pp. 382-389.

[HL85] F.E Harrell, and K.L. Lee (1985), *"A Comparison of the Discrimination of Discriminant Analysis and Logistics regression under Multivariate Normality,"* P.K Se (ed.) Biostatistics: statistics in Biomedical, Public Health, and Environmental Sciences, North-Holland, Amsterdam.

[HMS01] David Hand, Heikki Mannila, Padhraic Smyth (2001), *"Principles of Data Mining"*, Prentice-Hall India, pp. 260-262.

[Hol93] Holte (1993), *"Very Simple Classification Rules Perform Well on Most Commonly used Datasets"*, Seminar paper.

[JC00] Jensen, D. D. and Cohen. P.R (2000), *"Multiple Comparisons in Induction Algorithms"*, Machine Learning 38, pp. 309-338.

[JZ97] G.H. John and Y. Zhao (1997), *"Mortgage Data Mining,"* in Proc. IEEE/ IAFE, New York, pp. 232-236, March.

[Kas80] G.V. Kas (1980), *"An Exploratory Technique for Investigating large Quantities of Categorical Data"*, Applied Statistics, 29, pp. 119-127.

[KC01] Ling Jing Kao and Chih Chou Chiu (2001), *"Mining the Customer Credit by Using the Neural Network Model with Classification and Regression Tree Approach,"* IFSA World Congress and 20th NAFIPS International Conference, Vancouver, Canada, Vol 2., pp. 923-928, July.

[KLRRL98] Ruby L. Kennedy, Yuchun Lee, Benjamin Van Roy, Christopher D. Reed, and Richard P. Lippman (1998), *"Solving Data Mining Problems through Pattern Recognition,"* Englewood Cliffs, N.J.: Prentice Hall.

[KN96] E. Knorr and R. Ng. (1996), *"Finding Aggregate Proximity Relationships and Commonalities in Spatial Data Mining"*, IEEE Trans. Knowledge and Data Engineering, 8, pp. 884-897.

[Lan02] Markus Lang (2002), *"Implementation of Naïve Bayesian Classifiers in Java,"*, Presented at the Seminar for *"Intelligent Systems and Intelligent Agents,"*, Kaserslautern Uty of Applied sciences, March.

[Lar05] Daniel. T. Larose (2005), *"Discovering Knowledge In Data-An Introduction to Data Mining,"* John Wiley & Sons, Inc., pp. 34.

[LSDCZD04] Dongqing Liu, Ting Shi, Joseph A. DiDonato. John D Carpten, Jian Ping Zhu, Zhong-Hui Duan (2004), *"Application of Genetic Algorithm/ K-Nearest Neighbor Method to the Classification of Renal Cell Carcinoma,"*, CSB, IEEE Computational Systems Bioinformatics Conference, pp. 558-559.

[LY06] Xiangyan Li and Nong Ye (2006), *"A Supervised Clustering and Classification Algorithm for Mining Data with Mixed Variables,"* IEEE Transactions on

Systems, Man, and Cybernetics-Part A: Systems and Humans. Vol. 36, No. 2, pp. 396-406, March.

[MCS93] C.J. Matheus, P.K. Chan, and G. Piatetsky-Shapiro (1993), *"Systems for Knowledge Discovery in Databases,"* IEEE Trans. Knowledge data Eng., Vol. 5, pp. 903-913.

[Mil02] Miller, A. (2002), *"Subset Selection in Regression"*, Chapman & hall/CRC.

[Mit97] T. Mitchell (1997), *"Machine Learning,"* Boston, MA: WCB/McGraw-Hill.

[MR] Metz, C. ROCKIT 0.9B User's Guide Department of Radiology, University of Chicago, Available at www- radiology.uchicago.edu/krl/toppage11.htm

[MWKSE06] Ing Mierswa, Michael Wurst, Ralf Klinkenberg, Martin Scholz and Timm Euler, "YALE: Rapid Prototyping for Complex Data Mining Tasks", in Proc. ACM SIGKDD Int. Conf. Knowledge discovery, Philadelphia, PA, USA, 2006, pp. 935-940.

[PCY95] J.S. Park, M.S. Chen, and P.S.Yu, *"An Effective hash based Algorithm for Mining Association Rules,"* in Proc. ACM SIGMOD Int. Conf. Management Data, San Jose, CA, 1995, pp. 175-186.

[Pep00] J. Peppard (2000), *"Customer Relationship Management (CRM) in Financial Services,"* Eur. Manage.J., Vol. 18, No. 3, pp. 312-327.

[PFK98] Provost, F. Fawcett, T. and Kohavi, R. (1998), *" The Case Against Accuracy Estimation for Comparing Induction Algorithms"*, Proceedings of the Fifteenth International Conference on Machine learning, Madison, WI.

[Qui86] J. Quilan (1986), *"Induction of Decision Trees"*, Machine Learning, 11(1), pp. 81-106.

[Rip94] Ripley, B. D. (1994), "Neural Networks and Related Methods for Classification", *Journal of The Royal Statistical Society,"* pp. 409-456.

[RCW00] A.K. Reichert, C.C.Cho, and, G.M Wagner (2000), "An examination of the Conceptual Issues Involved in developing Credit Scoring Models," *Journal of Business and Economic statistics,* Vol. 1, pp. 101-114.

[SC98] Alberto Saccardi, and Guido Cuzzocrea (1998), *"Database Marketing Applications in the Italian Banking Sector,"* SEUGI 16 Proceedings, Heidelberg, Germany.

[SG87] William F. Schell and Joseph P. Guiltinan (1987), Marketing Contemporary Concepts and Practices, Allyn and Bacon.

[SL04] Surendra K. Singhi and Huan Liu, *"Feature Subset Selection Bias for Classification Learning,"* ICML'04, ACM, pp. 849-856.

[SMT91] Shavlik, J.W., Mooney, R.J and Towell, G.G. (1991), "Symbolic and Neural Learning Algorithms, An Experimental Comparison", Machine Learning Vol. 6, pp. 111-143.

[Sri92] R.P. Srivastava (1992), *"Automating Judgmental Decisions Using Neural Networks"* A Model for Processing Business Loan Applications," presented at the ACM Annual Conf. Communications, Kansas City, MO.

[Swe73] Swets, J. (1973), *"The Relative Operating Characteristic in Psychology"*, Science 182, pp. 990-1000.

[SZD06] Aihua Li Yong Shi, Meihong Zhu, Jingran Dai (2006), *"A Data Mining Approach to Classify Credit cardholders' Behavior"*, ICDM Workshops, pp. 828-832 .

[Vra01] Ivan Vrancic. *"Pattern Recognition Approach to Customer Analysis,"* - Proceedings of 2nd Int'l Symposium on Image and Signal Processing and Analysis, Pula, Croatia, 2001. pp. 325-329.

[WB06] C.M Van der Walt and E. Bernard (2006), *"Data Characteristics that Determine Classifier Performance,"* in Proceedings of the Sixteenth Annual Symposium of the Pattern Recognition Association of South Africa, pp. 160-65.

[WF05] Ian H Witten and Eibe Frank (2005), *"Data Mining-Practical Machine Learning Tools and Techniques,"* Morgan Kauffman, pp. 296-297.

[Zad04] Zadrozny, B., *"Learning and Evaluating Classifiers under Sample Selection Bias"*, ICML '04, ACM.

[ZZ04] Dongsong Zhang and Lina Zhou (2004), *"Discovering golden Nuggets: Data Mining in Financial Application"*, IEEE Transactions on Systems, Man, and Cybernetics-Part C: Applications and Reviews. VOL 34, NO. 4, pp. 513-522, November.

3

MULTI-RATER ASSESSMENT AND TOTAL QUALITY MANAGEMENT: THE PRESENT NEED FOR BANKING SECTOR IN INDIA

R. Balasubramaniyan

I

Introduction

India has a long history of both public and private banking. Modern banking in India began in the 18th century, with the founding of the English Agency House in Calcutta and Bombay. In the first half of the 19th century, three Presidency banks were founded. After the 1860 introduction of limited liability, private banks began to appear, and foreign banks entered the market. The beginning of the 20th century saw the introduction of joint stock banks. In 1935, the presidency banks were merged together to form the Imperial Bank of India, which was subsequently renamed the State Bank of India. Also that year, India's central bank, the Reserve Bank of India [RBI], began operation. Following independence, the RBI was given broad regulatory authority over commercial banks in India. In 1959, the State Bank of India acquired the state owned banks of eight former princely states. Thus, by July 1969, approximately 31 per cent of scheduled bank branches throughout India were government controlled, as part of the State Bank of India.

The post-war development strategy was in many ways a socialist one, and the Indian government felt that banks in private hands did not lend enough to those who needed it most. In July 1969, the government nationalized all banks whose nationwide deposits were greater than Rs. 500 million, resulting in the nationalization 54 per cent more of the branches in India, and bringing the total number of branches under government control to 84 per cent.

After nationalization, the breadth and scope of the Indian banking sector expanded at a rate perhaps unmatched by any other country. Indian banking has been remarkably successful at achieving mass participation. Between the time of the 1969 nationalizations and the present, over 58,000 bank branches were opened in India; these new branches, as of March 2003, had mobilized over 9 trillion Rupees in deposits, which represent the overwhelming majority of deposits in Indian banks. This rapid expansion is attributable to a policy, which required banks to open four branches in unbanked locations for every branch opened in banked locations.

In India, the last decade saw the transformation of banking into a totally new experience. Technology has enabled banks to overcome the barriers of time and space in extending their service to customer. New channels like Internet Banking, ATM's, EFT [Electronic Fund Transfer], Debit cards, Mobile banking, Tele Banking etc. provide access to customers on a 24x7 basis across the world. The value proposition to customers through these channels has been tremendous.

A banks reputation for its credibility and trustworthiness provides consumers with the best possible solution for their financial needs. The Customer Relationship Management [CRM] has a massive influence in banking services. It has resulted in much hyped gains in the banking sector. The forces of deregulation, globalization and advancing technology have greatly increased the competitive pressures in the banking industry. The Indian banking industry is going through a turbulent time. Since the financial reforms started, banks have been given a greater degree of freedom in determining their rate structure for deposits and advances, as well as their product range. The freedom of choice which bank customers did not have earlier because of standardized products and regimented interest rates has now been given to customers. Banks are functioning increasingly under competitive pressures emanating from within the banking system, from non-banking institutions as well as from the domestic and international capital markets.

The rest of the paper is organized as follows. Section II captures the objectives and methodology. Section III examines the spread, Burden and profit analysis of public sector Banks. Section IV presents the need for Multi-Rater Assessment and Total quality management for banking sector in India and section V provides the summary and conclusion.

II

Objectives of the Study

1. To examine the trends in spread and burden of public sector banks.
2. To analyse the pattern of profits in public sector banks.
3. To find out the factors influencing Multi-Rater Assessment (MRA) and Total Quality Management (TQM) in public sector banks.
4. To suggest policy measures for improving MRA and TQM in public sector banks.

Methodology

The study is predominantly based on secondary data. The banking data at the national level is primarily considered to gauge the spread pattern, burden issues and profit making units in public sector banks in India. The study attempts, to unravel the mysteries behind certain 'failures' of public sector banks by considering factors such as spread, burden and profits and their interrelationships. To make the Study more meaningful and appropriate, Multi-Rater Assessment and Total quality management device have been used to increase the operational viability of the public sector banks in India. Finally, the study covers a period between 2003-2006. Largely, the data is derived from banking information of RBI.

III

Spread, Burden and Profit Analysis of Public Sector Banks

Conceptualization

Profit is an absolute difference between Total Revenue [TR] and Total Cost [TC] during a specific period normally denoted by an accounting year. If TR is more than TC, it results in profit and vice versa results in loss. The important components of profit planning are SPREAD i.e. the difference between interest earned on advances and interest paid on deposits and the BURDEN i.e. the difference between non-interest income and non-interest expenditure. Thus Spread and Burden are critical factors in generating profit.

Table 1
Analysis of Spread

[Rs. In crore]
[By the end of March 31st]

Year1	*Interest earned 2*	*Interest expended 3*	*Spread [2-3]*
2003	1,07,193	69,853	37,340
2004	1,09,496	65,766	43,730
2005	1,20,364	68,764	51,600
2006	1;37,615	80,272	57,343

Source: Complied from Statistical Tables relating to Banks in India. RBI.

Spread is a function of cost of resources and yield on funds deployed. Interest earned includes interest/discount on advances and bills, income on investments, interest on balances with RBI and other inter bank funds and others. Table 1 gives the details of analysis of Spread in public sector banks. It reveals that there is an increasing trend in the Spread of the public sector banks. The growth in interest earned is more in the year 2006 when compared to previous years. It is because of investments are more during the years.

Table 2
Analysis of Burden

(Rs. In crore)
(By the end of March 31st)

Years [1]	*Operating expenses [2]*	*Provisions and contingencies [3]*	*Non-Interest expenditure 4 [2+3]*	*Non-Interest income [5]*	*Burden 6 [4-5]*
2003	28,895	17,420	46,315	21,271	25,044
2004	32,361	22,929	55,290	28,107	27,183
2005	37,055	23,319	60,374	24,196	36,178
2006	41,532	22,603	64,135	23,332	40,803

Source: Compiled from Statistical Tables relating to Banks in India, RBI.

The analysis of Burden of the PSBs is explained in Table 2. Burden is a function of non-interest expenditure and non-interest income. Non interest expenditure includes operating expenses and provisions and contingencies, whereas non-interest income is the other income of the banks except interest earned. The above Table clearly indicates that the Burden component of PSBs is increasing rapidly. Payments to and provisions for employees is the major expenditure under operating expenses. Banking is a man power oriented industry and a large workforce is employed to run and maintain the banks. Managements of banks have little control over salaries as the employees unions have their say in deciding the salary structure as they are highly organized and have better bargaining power.

Table 3
Spread–Burden–Profit Analysis

(Rs. In crore)
(By the end of March 31st)

Year [1]	*Spread* [2]	*Burden* [3]	*Net Profit* 4 [2-3]
2003	37,340	25,044	12,296
2004	43,730	27,183	16,547
2005	51,600	36,178	15,422
2006	57,343	40,803	16,540

Source: Complied from Statistical Tables relating to Banks in India. RBI.

The profit of the banks is recorded more when ever the Spread increases more and simultaneously the Burden decreases or otherwise the percentage of increase in Spread is more than the percentage of increase in Burden. Table 3 reveals the details of Spread-Burden Profit analysis of public sector banks. It is clear from the table that the profit of the public sector banks are not showing an increasing trend. It is decreasing in the year 2005 and further the growth in profit is very low due to increase in operating expenses and provisions.

Table 4
Banking Performance Indicators, FY 2007

Indicators	*Standard Charted Bank*	*SBI*	*All Banks Average*
Cost of funds %	4.17	4.79	4.85
Return on Assets %	3.06	0.84	1.05
Return on Advances %	5.40	3.50	4.08
Business per employee [Rs. Lakh]	924.20	357.00	522.29
Profit per employee [Rs. Lakh]	19.62	2.37	3.49

Source: A Profile of banks: 2007, RBI, Mumbai.

Table 4 shows the banking performance indicators [FY 2007] in India. The indicators reveals that the standard charted Bank's efficiency is significant in cost of funds [4.17%] return on assets [3.06%], return on advances [5.40%] and profit per employee [19.22 lakh] as compared to SBI and All-Banks' average put together. The table further pinpoints that the performances of a private bank is for greater in every aspect when compared to public sector banks.

Table 5
Sources of Borrowings:
Amount of every Rs. 1000 Borrowed by Farmers in Selected States

(In. Rs.)

State	*Money Lenders*
Andhra Pradesh	534
Tamil Nadu	397
Rajastan	365
Punjab	363

Source: Business India, September, 2007, P. 16.

Table 5 reveals that the amount of every Rs. 1000 borrowed by farmers in selected states confirms the general perceptions of the role of money lenders as the saviours of the rural people. Farmers is Andhra Pradesh have borrowed money [Rs. 534], Tamil Nadu [Rs. 397], Rajastan [Rs. 365], and Punjab [Rs. 363] of every Rs. 1000 from the money lenders.

Table 6
Sources of Borrowing: Amount of every
Rs. 1000 Borrowed by Farmers from the Banks in Selected States

(In Rs.)

State	*Banks*
Andhra Pradesh	200
Rajastan	270
Tamil Nadu	281
Punjab	284

Source : Business India, September, 2007, P. 16.

Table 6 captures the amount of borrowings per Rs. 1000 by Farmers from Banks in rural areas. It significantly confirms the general public opinion that the public sector banks disbursement of loans are highly insignificant. Andhra Pradesh farmers got only [Rs. 200] followed by

Rajastan [Rs. 270], Tamil Nadu [Rs. 281] and Punjab [Rs. 284] respectively for every Rs. 1000 as loan from the public sector banks. It clearly reveals that the Indian farmers are still depending on local moneylenders for finance.

IV

Multi-Rater Assessment and Top Quality Management in Banking Sector in India

Multi-Rater Assessment

The 360-degree feedback or Multi-rater assessment has become a worldwide phenomenon. It was extensively used in the Indian Institute of Management, Ahmedabad in India even though the term 360- degree feedback was coined in USA in early nineties. This tools has become a popular change management tool and leadership competence-building tool. This is evident from the increase in the number of Indian companies adopting it. The 360-degree feedback process is an important development to enrich human resources, organizational development and training and development, It provides a wider and more realistic forum for frank evaluation by direct reports, peers and others, resulting in new motivation and direction for the people. Though people may express initial apprehension of being assessed by superiors subordinates, colleagues and others in actual practice many prefer to be assessed by a group who see their performance from a variety of perspectives, rather than from the limited perspective of their immediate superiors. They find 360-degree feedback as more accurate and fair. [Srinivasan, 2007]. Most organizations appear to be using this process for:

- Leadership development [implementing their leadership models or reinforcing the same]
- Individual growth and development
- Competency building

- Performance Appraisals, rewards and recognition, collecting data on employees, succession planning and career development.

Top Quality Management–The Need

In late 80's Japan initiated an array of quality improvement techniques which moved beyond, "checking for and measuring faults". The emphasis shifted. Even in manufacturing, to the prevention of quality breakdowns rather than the detection of faults that had occurred.

Chopin [1994] has given the following principles of TQM in service industry.

1. Highest priority given to quality throughout the organization.
2. Quality is defined in terms of customer satisfaction.
3. Customer is defined as those who have both internal and external relationships with the organization [employees, shareholders, etc].
4. Customer satisfaction and building of long–term relations are at the satisfaction of the organization.
5. Organization aims will be clearly stated and accessible to all.
6. Principles, beliefs, valves and quality are communicated throughout the organization.
7. Total quality management creates an ethos that pervades all aspects o the organization's activities.
8. Core values of honesty, integrity, trust and openness are essential ingredients of TQM.
9. The total quality organization is intended to be mutually beneficial to all concerned and operation in a climate of mutual respect for all stakeholders.
10. The health and safety of all organization members and customers are given priority.

11. Performance measurement, assessment and auditing of the organization activities is a common feature of TQM.

V

Summary and Conclusion

Profit is the motive for any business organization. The most important function of profit is establishment of viability of operations and continued stability of the organization. In the post nationalization era, the profitability in public sector banks ceases to be an important parameter for measuring their performance and instead their developmental and social role got precedence over profits and profitability. Fixation of targets for priority sector lending, lead bank scheme, trust on small scale industry and agricultural lending opening large number of branches in rural, unbanked areas etc., were some of the indicators which hinted at the role, banks were expected to play and the PSBs did exceedingly well in these areas. However, what has been compromised in the process is the operational efficiency, generally reflected through profits and profitability.

Since the banking sector reforms [1991] there had been a shift of emphasis from development or social banking to commercially viable banking. Profitability became the buzzword and the prime mover of the financial strength and performance of banks. The Indian public sector banks. The Indian public sector banks are facing stiff competition from the private sector banks in attracting customers. There has already been a great rise in the cost of staff and the demand for further hike in the wages is on the anvil. There has also been pressure on the PSBs to up date their work technology through computerization which is expensive for them. The public sector banks declared a loss of Rs. 3,369 crore in 1992-93 as against a profit of Rs. 803 crore in 1991-92 and a loss of Rs. 3,349 crore in 1993-94 as a result of the introduction of prudential norms. In the year 1994-95, the PSBs turned the corner, with a net profit of Rs. 1,116 crore. The net profit of the PSBs have shown an increasing trend since then and for the year ended March 31st 2006 they recorded a net profit of Rs. 16,540 crore. [Reddy *et. al*, 2007].

Deposit mobilization by commercial banks assumes great importance in the Indian context. Deposit is the largest form of household savings [around 40 per cent of total household savings in 2005]. a major component of money supply and also the key liability of commercial banks. After nationalisation, commercial banks, particularly Public Sector Banks [PSBs], were encouraged to mobilize deposits, as it was the main source of funds. This was then attempted by expanding the network of bank branches to rural areas in order to tap the hitherto untapped resources. But after financial sector liberalization, efficient functioning of the banks occupied centre stage and this was emphasized in every sphere of the activity. As deposit mobilization continues to be an important activity of the commercial banks, particularly of the PSBs, there is a need to examine how efficient these banks are in deposit mobilization.

Large banks being more efficient than the smaller ones, indicates the presence of economies of scale in Indian banking sector. This suggests that merger of smaller banks would lead to greater efficiency. Competition [measured by Interest Margin] also seems to have a positive impact on the deposit efficiency of commercial banks. Deregulation has significant positive impact on the deposit efficiency measure. Thus, the post-liberalisation reform measures followed by the Reserve Bank of India appear to have positive impact on the banking sector. However, It is an accepted fact that rural India is grossly Under-banked despite the massive rural branch expansion programmes launched by the banks during the last 38 years of public sector bankings. Out of the six lakh villages, banks are operating in 28,237 villages only, with 30,560 rural branches and officers [Industrial Economist, 2008].

References

Bell, Frederick W. and Neil B. Murphy (1986), "Costs in Commercial Banking: A Quantitative Analysis of Bank Behaviour and Its Relation to Bank Regulation", *Research Report* No.41, October. Boston: Federal Reserve Bank of Boston.

Benston, George J. (1964), "Economies of Scale and Marginal Cost in Banking Operations" *National Banking Review, II*, September, pp. 507-549.

Bhattacharya, P.C. and M.N. Sivasubramanian (2003), Financial Development and Economic Growth in India: 1970-71 to 1998-1999", *Applied Financial Economics*, Vol. 13(12), pp. 905-09.

Levine, R. and S. Zervos (1998), "Stock Markets, Banks and Economic Growth", *American Economic Revies*, Vol. 88(3), pp. 537-558.

Mahesh, H.P. (2006), "Liberalisation and Efficiency of Indian Commercial Banks: A Stochastic Frontier Analysis", Working Paper 177. Bangalore, India: Institute for Social and Economic Change.

————*et. al*, (2006), "Banking on Deposit Mobilization", *The Indian Economic Journal*, Vol. 54(3), pp. 119-132.

Narasimham, M. (1991), Report of the Committee on the Financial System. Mumbai: Reserve Bank of India.

————(1998), Report of the Committee on banking Sector Reforms. Mumbai: Reserve Bank of India.

Reddy S.V. *et. al*, (2007), " Profitability and Productivity in Indian Public Sector Banks", Banking Finance, November, pp. 13-15.

4

IMPACT OF MICROFINANCE ON THE COMMUNITY DEVELOPMENT OF RURAL SOCIETY: A CASE STUDY

JUSTINE JOSEPH

Introduction

The achievement of economic development was the major concern of economic thinkers and policy makers in various countries while organizing and implementing different programmes and activities. The economic development of any country is materialized when various socio economic problems like poverty, unemployment, illiteracy, poor quality of life, gender inequality etc. are solved to an agreeable level. Thus, economic development brings about a rise in the standard of living and improvement in the welfare of the people in an economy. In India also eradicating poverty, generating gainful employment opportunities, improving social well being and removal of regional disparities are the major goals of development efforts since independence.

India has various rural development and employment generating programmes like Integrated Rural Development

Programme (IRDP), National Rural Employment Programme (NREP), Rural Landless Employment Guarantee Programme (RLEGP), Prime Minister's Rozgar Yojana (PMRY), Swarnjayanti Gram Swarozgar Yojana (SGSY), Dry land Development Schemes, Wet land Development Schemes, Social forestry schemes under afforestation scheme etc. were since early 1980s. These programmes were formulated and implemented with the objectives of providing employment, creating productive and durable assets and improving overall quality of life especially in the rural areas. However, the above programmes organized and implemented by the Central as well as State governments have not been successful to the desired level. The problems of hunger, malnutrition, unemployment, ill health, illiteracy, gender inequality etc. continue to be major problem in rural areas.

The failure of various income and employment generating programmes has been due to the lack of involvement of the people for whom such programmes were meant. Participation of beneficiaries at various stages of the implementation of these programmes was not ensured since the State took the initiative and responsibility in their implementation. There is the need for macro level institutional arrangements to involve the people in the formulation , implementation and monitoring of these schemes. In other words, the role of the civil society has become very important in formulating and implementing such programmes.

The developmental effort of the civil society are steered by various People's Organizations, Non-Profit Voluntary Organizations and Non-Governmental Organizations (NGOs). "NGOs refer to nongovernmental organizations that attempt to address the concerns of the unprivileged and the underserved in the Third World through the development activities such as agricultural assistance, primary health care, provision of basic services and education" (Suzuki, 1998). NGO is an organization or group of people working independently of any external control with specific objectives and aims to fulfill tasks that oriented to bring about desirable change in a given community or area or situation. NGOs could be understood as a team of people with similar interest, freely joining hands to bring about improvement or changes in the society through organized and collective efforts. Many development experts consider NGOs and voluntary organizations more successful in reaching out to the poor and they can play a key role in motivating the people and ensuring the distribution of resources with a view to ensure its proper utilization. It is mainly through group process and participation in decision making that empowerment of people and thus community development take place. "Community development has been described as a process of change from the traditional way of living of rural communities to a progressive way of living; as a method by which people can be assisted to develop themselves on their own capacity and resources; as a programme for accomplishing certain activities for the welfare of the rural people; and as a movement for progress with a certain ideological context. The essential element of community development is participation by the people themselves in efforts to improve their level of living and the provision of technology and other services so as to encourage initiative, self help and mutual help. The movement combines a faith in democracy and social justice on the one hand and in science and technology on the other" (Desai,1988). The poor and downtrodden sections in the society realize their potentialities and capabilities through participation.

Voluntary organizations and non governmental organization organize and implement the development programmes and projects primarily through Self Help Groups (SHGs). SHGs are small, economically homogeneous and affinity groups of rural or urban poor voluntarily formed to save and contribute to a common fund to be lent to its members as per group decision and for working together for social and economic uplift. "An SHG is an informal association of 10-15 people who voluntarily come together for the business of saving and credit and to enhance member's financial security as primary focus and on the other, the common interests of members such as the area of development, awareness, motivation, leadership, training and associating in other social intermediation programmes for the benefit of the entire community" (Gangaiah, 2006). Usually, a SHG is a homogeneous group of poor, women users etc. This group is a voluntary one, formed on areas of common interest so that they can think, organize and operate for their development. Economic welfare of all members is their aim. The SHG strategy involves forming small ,cohesive and participative groups of the poor; encouraging them to pool their thrift regularly and using the pooled thrift to make small rest bearing loans to members. Subsequently, bank credit also becomes available to group to augment its resources for lending to its members. SHGs provide the benefits of economies of scale, cost effective alternative for different financial services, collective learning, democratic and participatory culture, a firm base and platform for dialogue and cooperation. Moreover, the benefits of SHGs are based on cooperation rather than competition. This follows the real principle of contribute according to your ability and extract according to your need.

SHGs are now emerging as major agents of development and empowerment of weaker sections in the third world. Thus, the SHG strategy aims at provision of benefits of growth process to the neglected class, especially women by socio-economic background in terms of labour, income, credit, and investment etc. It also aims at bringing the excluded and neglected women into mainstream of economic development through saving-investment-employment and income generation strategy for attaining development. Thus, SHGs play a crucial role in improving the savings and edit and also in reducing poverty and social inequalities.

SHGs are considered as the most effective mechanism for providing the vast range of financial and non-financial services including skill up gradation and entrepreneurship development to the poor for alleviating poverty and raising the rural come. They undertake micro finance services to the rural poor as a means of eradicating poverty. "Micro finance refers to the entire range of the financial and non-financial services including the skill upgradation and the entrepreneurship development rendered to the poor for enabling them to overcome the poverty" (Gireeshkumar, 2005). Micro finance is at present highlighted and accepted as a new development paradigm for alleviating poverty through the social and economic empowerment of the poor especially the women.

In India the formal beginning of the micro finance was made in the year 1992 and since then the micro finance sector has grown at an accelerated pace. The UN declared 2005 as the year of micro credit in order to increase the awareness of micro finance as a means to achieve economic and human development. It is the result of the understanding that micro finance or the provision of financial services to low income households has come to be accepted as the most effective intervention to alleviate poverty in developing countries.

Micro finance initiation was actually the result of an idea generated by the Nobel Prize winner Dr. Muhammed Yunus of Bangladesh during the period 1974–76 who initiated organizing the poor into SHGs and making them realize the very basic theory of survival. It has now become more or less revolutionary movement throughout the world and most of the developing countries have adopted it as a comprehensive and participatory method of achieving the economic progress of the country. Micro finance has been adopted even in the advanced countries of the world with the objective of women empowerment and poverty eradication.

As in the case of many developing countries, the poor in India too have not been covered by services of the formal banking system for long. It was more so in the case of rural poor. The spread of the rural credit system in India since 1947 was not equate to help the rural poor so as to get themselves out of the tentacles of the local money lenders. The poorest of the poor were not given access to finance from financial institutions like banks and they were the non bankable clients in the vocabulary of banks. For banks, they were expensive clients due to the nature of small loans and related expenditure on issuance and repayments. Soon the poor women got organized by themselves or at the initiatives of others and credit was made available to them.Voluntary organizations and NGOs entered the area of micro financing and promoted SHGs which would save small amounts for their own needs. Banks were advised to consider lending to SHGs as part of their mainstream credit operations and to identify branches having potential for linkage with the SHGs. Banks were also directed that SHGs registered or unregistered which engaged in promoting the saving habits among their members would be eligible to open savings bank accounts with banks irrespective of their availing of credit facilities from banks. Further, in India we have to focus on extending financial services in both rural and urban areas for ensuring financial inclusion of all segments of the population. The provision of micro finance through SHGs helps the neglected sections to get financial assistance for attaining development.

The community development can be achieved only with the poverty alleviation through creation of gainful employment opportunities and sustainable income generating activities. The experience of different poverty eradication, employment generation and welfare programmes have shown that the key to their success lies in mobilizing sufficient credit for them. The small enterprises especially in the rural areas can be promoted only with sufficient credit support which may be brought forth in the form of micro finance organized by SHGs. A comprehensive framework to revive the cooperative credit system, revitalize the Regional Rural Banks and reorient commercial banking system etc needs to get a high priority.

Trends In Development Theory

Earlier development represented modernization or catching up with advanced countries, but it is not at all an obvious ambition at present. Modernity no longer seems so attractive in view of ecological problems, consequences of technological changes etc. Westernization no longer seems to be attractive at a time of revaluation of local culture and cultural diversity. At present everything that development used to represent appears to be in question, in crisis.

Development may be defined as the organized intervention in collective affairs according to a standard of improvement. What constitutes improvement and what is appropriate intervention may vary according to culture, class, historical context and relations of power. These issues are negotiated in this development theory. The strength and weakness of development thinking is its policy oriented character. During the 19th century development referred to remedies for the shortcomings and maladies of progress. It involves questions such as population, job laws, social questions and urban squalor. Accordingly, progress and development contrasted and development differed from and complemented progress. Later, in the colonial period the term development referred mainly to colonial resource management, to make the colonies cost effective and later to build up economic resources with a view to national independence. In the modern development thinking and economics the core meaning of development was economic growth. In the course of time mechanization and industrialization became part of this. Later when development thinking broadened to encompass modernization, economic growth was combined with political modernization, that is, nation building and social modernization such as fostering entrepreneurship and achievement orientation. With the onset of alternative development thinking, new understanding of development came to the fore focused on social and community development. The core definition of development in the Human Development Reports of UNDP is enlargement of people's choices.

Two radically different perspectives on development came to the fore during 1980s and 1990s. Neo liberalism in return to neo classical economics, eliminates the foundations of development economics: the notion that developing economies represent a special case. According to neo liberal view there is no special case. What matters is to get the prices right and let market forces do their work. Development in the sense of government intervention is anathema for it means market distortion. The central objective of economic growth is to be achieved through structural reforms, deregulation, liberalization, privatization etc. In effect a conventional meaning of development, that is , economic growth, is retained but agency of development switches from State to market. Thus neo liberalism is an anti-development perspective, not in terms of goals but in terms of means. Here the state is accused of authoritarian engineering where the economic growth is repudiated and which are deemed a failure or disaster for the majority of population.

In all the previous development thinking the conventional unit of development was nation. The key development statistics and measures used by international institutions are still country statistics. However, while the nation remains the central domain of development, gradually development is becoming a multi-level, multi-scalar series of efforts simultaneously taking place at levels lower than the nation, at the national level and at levels beyond nation.

Beyond the national level are community development, local economic development and micro regional development. Community development received a new emphasis with alternative development. Local development in its various forms connects with questions of rural/urban disparities, urban development, regional inequality, new regionalism and new localism with a view to endogenous development and in relation to globalization.

After, development thinking has been more or less successively state led, market led and society led, it is increasingly understood that development action needs all of these in new combination. Inter sectoral cooperation and partnerships are highly necessary for human development, social choice, public action, urban development and local economic development. The trend is towards, on the one hand, formal channels and on the other hand, informal channels (NGOs and SHGs).

Significance of the Study

Even after more than five decades of planned economic development and various attempts to provide financial assistance to the poor, they still remain in a stage of poverty. The success of poverty alleviation and employment generation programmes lies in the evolution and participation of community based organizations at the grass roots level. People's participation in the credit delivery and recovery and the linking of the formal credit institutions and borrowers through intermediaries of SHGs have been recognized as a supplementary mechanism for providing credit support to the rural poor. The primacy of community organizations and people's participation in the financial service sector has been the central theme of most of the micro finance centered poverty alleviation programmes. There is a social intermediation through SHGs so that financing is cost effective and the system of group lending avoids the intermediation of credit brokers between banks and the clients and also reduces individual borrowing transactions costs.

Formation of SHGs is an important method which enables the downtrodden in the rural areas to become self reliant and obtain financial independence and freedom so that they can play an active role in the process of development. SHGs help in inculcating the positive values of cooperation, mutual help, mutual trust etc. among the members. Since most of the SHGs comprises of women members, the functioning of SHGs helps in the attainment of community development through development and empowerment of poor women.

It is important to note that the most significant area of operation of SHGs is micro finance. Micro finance is a system of providing financial assistance to the poor to free them from the clutches of local money lenders and enable them to undertake economically productive activities for attaining community development. The poor and the needy in the rural areas always had to depend on money lenders and land lords for getting financial assistance. These local money lenders always charged exorbitant rate of interest on the amount of credit advanced by them. It is, therefore, important to know whether SHGs have significantly reduced the dependence of poor on the money lenders. The SHGs provide financial assistance based on the amount of saving made by the beneficiaries. So it is worthwhile to analyse whether the functioning of the SHGs has increased the saving habit of the members It is also useful to analyse how the poor people in rural areas utilize the loans taken by them. Further , it is important to know whether the utilization of these loans leads to further generation of income and employment or not. It is again worthwhile to see whether these loans result in raising the standard of living of the people and consequent development of the community. SHGs in the country have grown in terms of number of SHGs formed, number of beneficiaries, amount of savings by members, amount of loans availed from SHGs and from banks, loan utilization by members etc. Definitely SHGs have achieved a lot in quantitative and qualitative terms. In this study an attempt has been made to review the role played by SHGs in the community development.

Micro Finance

Micro finance is a revolutionary idea and emerging concept in the development literature especially in the paradigm of alternative development. It is regarded as a powerful instrument for addressing poverty alleviation related development programmes. It enables the poor to take advantage of existing opportunities, builds up their assets, generates self employment, develops micro enterprises, raises income, builds up self confidence and self esteem, improves their purchasing power and there by consumption, empowers them economically and socially, enhances overall economic growth, domestic savings and improves financial market and provides escape route from poverty.

Micro finance refers to small savings, credit and insurance services extended to socially and economically disadvantaged segments of the society. It is the provision of thrift, credit and other financial services and products of very small amounts to the poor in rural, semi-urban or urban areas , with a view to enabling them to raise their income level and improve living standards. In simple terms, micro finance refers to the entire range of financial and non- financial services, including skill up gradation and entrepreneurship development rendered to the poor for enabling them to overcome poverty. It is recognized and accepted as one of the new development paradigms for alleviating poverty through social and economic empowerment of the poor, with special emphasis on women. Thus micro finance could be referred to as an institutional mechanism for credit support in small quantity and usually linked with small groups along with other complementary support such as training and other related services to the people with poor resources and skills for enabling them to take p economic activities. It is a financial service of small quantity provided by financial institutions to the poor. These financial services include savings, credit, insurance, leasing, money transfer, equity transaction etc.

Role of SHGs in Micro Finance

The role of micro finance was promoted primarily through organizing the poor into SHGs by which they realize the very basic theory of survival. People's participation in credit delivery and recovery, and linking of formal credit institutions borrowers through intermediaries of SHGs have been recognized as a supplementary mechanism for providing credit support to the rural poor. Experiences of different anti poverty and other welfare programmes implemented through out the world have shown that the key to their success lies in evolution and participation of community based organizations at grass root level. The earlier development programmes in the rural areas failed in alleviating poverty through creation of sustainable income generating opportunities because they lacked the participation of people and community based organizations. SHGs are the most significant institutional arrangement at the micro level for promoting micro finance. The micro finance is recognized and accepted as one of the new development paradigm by which poverty alleviation, and social and economic empowerment of the poor are brought about. Banking with poor seems to be possible through the following approaches:

(a) Conventional weaker section lending by banks.

(b) SHG linkage programme.

(c) Lending by banks and financial institutions to micro finance institutions for lending to SHGs or individuals.

Of the above three approaches, the most successful and prevalent method is micro finance through SHGs.

Micro finance activities through SHGs in the country are largely promoted by NGOs, scheduled banks, co-operative banks and also by the governmental agencies. Among these micro finance and SHG initiatives promoted by the NGOs are very strongly felt in almost all parts of the country. NGOs have distinctive advantage in this area because they are very successful in promoting community development through micro finance and SHG movement with the full participation of the people and in accordance with the needs and requirements of the local people. Large numbers of NGOs are working in different parts of the country towards organizing the poor and weaker sections of the society into SHGs and thus bringing about the development of the poor people especially in the rural areas.

Sandhya Development Society (SDS), registered in 1981, is one of the major NGOs working in the three districts in Kerala, namely, Kottayam, Idukki and Eranakulam districts. The most important achievement of SDS was the formation of SHGs from 1996 onwards. Sandhya formed Vikas Credit and Informal Banking Service Society (VICIB) as a federation of SHGs. Today VICIB has 71 branch offices in Kottayam, Idukki and Ernakulam districts.

In each of these branch offices, there are minimum 25 SHG units. Presently, there are 2960 active VICIB SHG units with 60000 beneficiary households. All these are exclusively women SHGs. The micro finance schemes for lending among the SHG members by VICIB are shown in Table 1. Table 2 shows the mobilization of small savings by the VICIB SHGs from 2000-01 to 2004-05. Table 3 illustrates the internal lending among the SHG members by the VICIB SHGs from 2000-01 to 2004-05. Table 4 shows the amount of bank linkage loans to the SHG members from 2000-01 to 2004-05.

Table 1
Micro Finance Schemes of VICIB

Loans (in Rs.)	*Term (year)*	*No. of installments*	*Interest (in Rs.)*
1000	1	50	70
2000	1	50	135
3000	1	50	210
4000	1	50	270
5000	1	50	345
6000	1.5	75	590
7000	1.5	75	710
8000	1.5	75	800
9000	1.5	75	889
10000	1.5	75	1000

Source: SDS Published Data.

Table 2
Total Savings Mobilized by VICIB SHGs from 2000-01 to 2004-05

Year	*Savings (in Rs.)*	*Cumulative Total (in Rs.)*	*Percentage Increase*
2000-01	797429	797429	
2001-02	975318	1772747	22
2002-03	1119692	2892439	15
2003-04	3624592	6517031	223
2004-05	7649521	14166552	111

Source: SDS Published Data,.

Table 3
Internal Lending by VICIB SHGs from 2000-01 to 2004-05

Year	*Internal Lending (in Rs.)*	*Percentage Increase*
2000-01	3383624	
2001-02	4290664	27
2002-03	6369635	48
2003-04	12818752	101
2004-05	33592762	162

Source: SDS Published Data.

Table 4
Bank loans to SHG Members from 2000-01to 2004-05.

Year	*Bank Loans (in Rs.)*	*Percentage Increase*
2000-01	850303	
2001-02	813533	- 4
2002-03	1163079	43
2003-04	4486721	286
2004-05	13520412	201

Source: SDS Published Data..

Concluding Observations

It has been found that community based organisations and SHGs are very much effective in solving the socio-economic problems of poverty, unemployment, poor quality of life, lack of durable assets and thus, bringing about community development in rural areas in a sustainable basis. The SHG movement has facilitated the mobilization of small savings of the poor, especially those in rural areas, which would otherwise have never been possible. It has been found that these small savings mobilized by SHGs are diverted into activities generating employment and income to the rural poor women. In addition to their individual savings, SHGs arrange linkages with banks and formal financial institutions to the SHG members which enable them to avail supplementary financial assistance. Micro credit and micro finance through SHGs have enabled to a large extent to alleviate rural poverty and attain community development. Various

agencies like Non Governmental Organizations and Governmental Organizations are promoting SHGs in the rural areas and it is a significant step in the process of empowerment of the rural poor especially the women. The changes that have emerged in the social values and attitudes of the members of the SHGs are a clear manifestation of their socio economic empowerment interventions yielding quicker results. The creation of awareness and empowerment among the members of SHGs have substantially contributed to the community development of the local people especially women.

References

Naoki Suzuki (1998), *Inside NGOs,* Intermediate Technology Publications, p. 1.

Desai, Vasanth (1988), *Rural Development: Programme and Strategies*, Vol. II, Himachal Publishing House, Bombay.

Gangaiah, C., B . Nagaraja and C. Vasudevulu Naidu (2006), Impact of Self Help Groups on Income and Employment: A Case Study, *Kurukshetra,* March, pp. 18-23.

G.S. Gireeshkumar (2005), Micro Finance in India-A Visible Option for Vulnerable Sections, *Indian Journal of Multidisciplinary Research,* Vol. I(2), p. 255.

Dantwala, M.L., Harsh Sethi and Pravin Visaria (eds.) (2001), *Social Change Through Voluntary Action,* Sage Publications India Pvt. Ltd., New Delhi.

Dreze, Jean and Amartya Sen (1995), *Economic Development and Social Opportunity,* Oxford University Press, Delhi

Fisher, Thomas and M.S Sriram (2006), *Beyond Micro Credit, Putting Development Bank into Micro Finance,* Vistar Publications India Pvt. Ltd., New Delhi.

Karnakar, K.G. (1999), *Rural Credit and Self Help Groups: Micro Finance Needs and Concepts in India,* Sage Publications Pvt. Ltd., New Delhi.

Srivastava, Alka (2004), *Self Help Groups and Civil Society-A Preliminary Study,* Indian Social Institute, New Delhi.

Chandrakavate, M. S. (2006), The SHGs Model of Microfinance: A Silent Movement Towards Empowering Rural Women, *Southern Economist,* Vol. 45, No.7, August 1, pp. 15-18.

Das R.M. (2004), Micro-finance Through SHGs: A Boom for the Rural Poor, *Kuruksetra,* Vol. 52, No. 4, pp. 43-45.

Dr. Mohanan, S. (2000), Micro Credit and Experiment of Women-Role of NGOs, *Yojana,* Vol. 44, No. 2, February.

Dr. Yunus, Muhammad (2000), Employment and Grameen Bank, *Yojana,* Vol. 44, No. 2, February.

Dr. Yunus, Muhammad (2004), Grameen Bank, Microcredit and Millenium Development Goals, *Economic and Political Weekly,* Vol. XXXIX.

Gopta, M.L. and Namita Gupta (2006), Economic Empowerment of Women Through SHGs, *Kurukshetra,* February, pp. 23-26.

Kulsherstha, L.R. and Gupta A. (2001), Self Help Groups-Innovation in Financing the Poor, *Kurukshetra,* pp. 26-29.

Nair, K. Manoharan and Girija B. (2005), Micro Finance: The New Development Paradigm for Poverty Eradication and Women's Empowerment, *Kurukshetra,* April, pp. 18-20.

Basu, Kishanjit and Krishnan Jindal (eds) (2006), *Microfinance: Emerging Challenges,* Mcgraw-hill, New Delhi.

5

SCALING UP THE MICROFINANCE ALTERNATIVE FOR FINANCIAL INCLUSION

SAJITHA P. P. & SANGEETHA K. PRATHAP

Introduction

Institutional financial intermediation in India picked up momentum following nationalization of banks firstly in 1969 and then in 1980, thereby including the masses within the financial system. But, there has been a reversal of the above inclusive policy of the government during the ongoing era of financial deregulation which focuses on instilling competition and surveillance in banks financial system of the country is one of the strongest in the world. Its financial asset position is US $437 billion; higher than the countries in this category including Argentina (US $231 billion) and Malaysia (US $331 billion) (Basu and Srivastava, 2005). The share of financial assets to GDP in India is 93 per cent, while that of Argentina is 81 per cent and Mexico is 68 per cent. This shows the depth of the Indian financial market inspite of its low per capita income. India has been well performing in the distribution of the financial services in terms of population served per branch and area served by a branch (denoting physical presence) cognizant with bench marking of other countries in the similar category.

Economic theory endorses that investment and economic growth is directly proportionate to saving rate and exclusion of a vast majority represents a missed opportunity and a vast potential for economic growth. Financial Inclusion essentially means provision of banking facilities to those who were hitherto deprived of these services at affordable cost. Finance and poverty are highly interrelated terms; financial inclusion of the poor can ultimately result in reduction of poverty instigating inclusive growth. Formal financial services in most developing economies serve only a minority, often no more than 20-30 % of the population. The institutional set up in India is risk averse; concentrating on returns on investment, leaving out low profile clients whose credit worthiness is unknown. Diligence of the financing institutions has resulted in financial exclusion of the poor, with limited physical and financial assets to fall back upon. Though the supply side of finance in the country is sound in financial assets position, its coverage among low income clients is grim due to above mentioned apprehensions. Even those who have gained access owing to recent developments in financial services for the low income people in particular, are underserved (Rao, 2004). There is significant disparity in the distribution of commercial bank branches in the rural and urban centres and between regions. Financial illiteracy and lack of knowledge of financial products have grappled the poor that they do not venture to cross the doors of any financial institutions.

Microfinance to low profile and low income clients has arisen as the best alternative in this scenario. Formation of Self Help Groups (SHGs) among the neighbourhoods promoting thrift followed by provision of internal credit and further linking to mainstream financial institutions like commercial and cooperative banks has supplied a pathway to financial inclusion of the poor

even if they are devoid of physical assets. This concept has been promoted by NABARD, central and state poverty eradication programmes and by several NGOs in social service sector. In this context, this paper attempts to analyse the efficacy of application and scaling up of microfinance alternative for including the poor into the financial landscape. The paper is organized into three parts; a. Supply side of institutional financing in the country, b. Demand and access to finance by households c. Efficacy of micro finance alternative.

Supply Side Constraints in Indian Financial System

Spatial Distribution of Banking Services

In India, nationalisation of commercial banks in 1969 laid foundation for social banking, with the main objective of institutionalising financial intermediation in unbanked centers. This aim was considered to be achieved within two decades; and almost culminated with introduction of financial sector reforms in 1991 relaxing conditions on opening bank branches. This trend is visible from Table1. Share of rural branches of commercial banks in the country increased from 22.19 per cent in 1969 to 51.20 per cent in 1998 and declined to 41.39 per cent in 2007. The share of metropolitan and urban branches to total in 2007 has almost equaled with that of 1969 showing inclination of banks to open more branches in these centers.

Table 1

Distribution of Commercial Bank Branches Population Groupwise

Particulars	*Number of Offices*			
Year	*1969*	*1998*	*2001*	*2007*
Rural	1833 (22.19)	32878 (51.20)	32585 (47.96)	30560 (41.39)
Semi-urban	3342 (40.45)	13980 (21.77)	14843 (21.85)	16484 (22.33)
Urban	1584 (19.17)	9597 (14.94)	11193 (16.48)	13840 (18.74)
Metropolitan	1503 (18.19)	7763 (12.09)	9316 (13.71)	12952 (17.54)
Total	8262 (100)	64218 (100)	67937 (100)	73836 (100)

Figures in parenthesis shows percentage to total

Source: BSR, 2006, *www.rbi.org.in*

Population group wise distribution of pattern of deposits and credit also has shown significant variations (Table 2). Though the absolute value has increased, the share of rural deposits has come down from 13.8 per cent in 2003 to 9.9 per cent in 2007 and rural credit declined from 9.8 per cent to 7.9 per cent. Similar trend is observed in case of semi urban centers also. On contrary, significant strides in deposit growth and credit growth in metropolitan centers were recorded. The deposits share of metropolitan centers has grown from 44.7 per cent to 55.9 per cent in a span of four years while the share in credit has increased from 55.9 per cent to 66.1 per cent. Growing inclination of banking services towards urban and metropolitan centers is envisaged by the delineated trend.

Table 2
Population Groupwise Distribution of Deposits and Credit of Scheduled Commercial Banks *(Amount in Rs. Crores)*

Population Group	*2003*		*2007*	
	Deposits	*Credit*	*Deposits*	*Credit*
Rural	176269 (13.8)	74776 (9.8)	258128 (9.9)	154785 (7.9)
Semi-Urban	240523 (18.8)	84684 (11.2)	356827 (13.7)	189783 (9.7)
Urban	290022 (22.7)	125290 (16.5)	531269 (20.4)	316166 (16.2)
Metropolitan	571853 (44.7)	474461 (62.5)	1452599 (55.9)	1288833 (66.1)
All India	1278667 (100)	759211 (100)	2598823 (100)	1949567 (100)

Note: Figures in bracket indicate per cent share in All-India total.
Source: Quarterly Statistics on Deposits and Credit of Scheduled Commercial Banks, March 2006 & 2007, RBI, accessed from *www.rbi.org.in*

Regional Disparities in Banking Services

Notwithstanding efforts of planners and policy makers to curb uneven development between different regions in the country, there are significant disparities in economic growth as also in the financial system. This is evident from disparity in distribution of offices of commercial banks, deposit mobilization and credit disbursement. The southern region in India comprising states of Kerala, Tamilnadu, Andhra Pradesh and Karnataka tops the list of number of offices

(28 per cent), deposit (22.33 per cent) and credit (26.03 per cent). The north eastern region in India is the least benefited and the share of this region for selected indicators remains in single digits (Table 3). It is implied that more people residing in less banked states are subject to financial exclusion compared to fairly or soundly banked ones. According to the Committee on Financial Inclusion, 2008, the inter-district variations are much sharper than the inter-state variations. The Committee estimated that there are as much as 256 districts in the country out of total 583, spread over 17 States and one Union Territory that falls under the criteria of credit gap of 95 per cent and above and exclusion per branch of rural and semi urban population above 19,272.

Table 3

Deposits and Credit of Scheduled Commercial Banks (2006)

Region	*No. of Offices*	*No. of Deposit Accounts*	*Deposit Rs Lakh*	*No. of Credit Accounts*	*Credit Outstanding Rs. Lakh*
Northern Region	11,821	833,02,811	492,58,964	92,47,193	318,31,789
	(17)	(17.17)	(23.56)	(11)	(21.03)
North-Eastern Region	1,949	113,92,103	33,03,434	16,38,893	13,45,487
	(3)	(2.35)	(1.58)	(2)	(0.89)
Eastern Region	12,308	779,09,873	237,95,306	109,67,315	117,01,520
	(17)	(16.06)	(11.38)	(13)	(7.73)
Central Region	14,104	954,94,162	252,31,645	122,70,019	111,64,293
	(20)	(19.69)	(12.07)	(14)	(7.37)
Southern Region	19,598	1326,17,943	467,02,374	389,88,542	394,04,636
	(28)	(27.34)	(22.33)	(46)	(26.03)
All-India	70,776	4850,97,771	2091,17,424	854,35,381	1513,84,213
	(100)	(100)	(100)	(100)	(100)

Figures in parenthesis shows percentage to total.

Source: BSR, 2006, www.rbi.org.in.

From the above discussion it is evident that supply side of institutional financial intermediation is crippled by issues like regional disparity in banking development and aversion of commercial banks towards rural centers. The financial exclusion of poor is an emerging issue in this context. Though there are specialized financial institutions like RRBs and cooperatives which cater to requirements of rural scene; their coverage seems to be inadequate with limited funds and poor financial performance. This situation often leads the poor to unorganized sector, where finances are hassle free, but are costlier and riskier leading to debt trap and loss of assets.

One of the objectives of banking policy after nationalization was to expand the flow of credit to agriculture and small industries, or what were termed "priority sectors." The share of priority sectors in the total credit outstanding of scheduled commercial banks rose from 14 per cent in 1969 to 21 per cent in 1972 and then went up to 33 per cent in 1980. From 1991 to 1996, the share of priority sector credit fell, in line with the recommendations of the Narasimham Committee. At first glance, the direction in priority sector lending appears to have been reversed over the last five years. This is, however, a reversal by redefinition: "priority sector" lending now includes advances to newly-created infrastructure funds, to non-banking finance companies for on-lending to very small units, and to the food processing industry. Loans to multinationals like Pepsi, Kelloggs, Hindustan Lever and ConAgra now count as priority sector advances. More recently, loans to cold storage units, irrespective of location, have been included in the priority sector.

Poorly functioning banks that simply funnel credit to connected parties and elites slow down growth and exert a disproportionately negative influence on the poor and small businesses by depriving them of the capital they need to succeed. Unfortunately, billions of people live in countries with poorly functioning banks. Thus banks influence the ability of people, rich and poor, to improve their living standards (Barth, 2006). The demand for rural credit is analysed in this context to assess the level of indebtedness and share of institutional and non institutional agencies.

Demand and Access to Finance by Households

Indebtedness of Households in India

The indebtedness of households in India has been reviewed periodically by the Government of India. The demand side of financial services of the Indian households is analysed from the All India Debt and Investment Survey (59th Round) of National Sample Survey Organization (NSSO). It was observed that the share of indebted households in the total population has been decreasing over the years (Table 4). The share of rural indebted households came down to 20.8 % in 2002-03 from 27.7% in 1971-72. This trend was found true in case of urban households also. Lower share inspite of increase in absolute number of indebted households can be explained as a consequence of increase in population. Inspite of wide expansion and calibration of the institutional financial setup to fine tune with the objective of financial inclusion, it is established that there are a wide majority who are out of coverage. The average amount of borrowings increased 21 times for rural and 9 times for urban households. However, the borrowings of the urban counterpart was higher (average by 1.5 times) than that of the rural households.

Table 4

Indebtedness of Households in India and Average Amount of Borrowings

Year	*Households reporting borrowing (% share)*		*Average amount of borrowing per household*	
	Rural	*Urban*	*Rural*	*Urban*
1971-72	27.7	NA	174	NA
1981-82	19.7	19	446	674
1991-92	19.9	18.5	1160	1892
2002-03	20.8	15.3	3726	6162

Source: Adapted from AIDIS, NSSO 59th Round, 2002-03.

Sources of Indebtedness and their Relative Share

The financial strength of the country in terms of financial inclusion can be measured by the share of institutional agencies in the borrowings of households. Of the cash borrowings of rural households, 57.2 % is from the institutional agencies while the rest is mobilized from non institutional agencies (Table 5). While in urban areas, institutional agencies account for 75.7 % of the cash borrowings of households. Among the institutional agencies, cooperatives dominate the rural scene and commercial banks dominate the urban areas. Professional money lender still takes a lead role among non institutional agencies. It is note worthy that in rural areas, cooperatives, commercial banks and professional money lenders have equal patronage in the cash borrowings of households.

Table 5
Percentage Share of Credit Agencies in Cash Borrowings of Households (2002-03)

Credit agency	*Rural*	*Urban*
Government	2.7	6.2
Cooperative societies/bank	28	22
Commercial banks	22.7	30.6
Insurance	0.3	1.5
Provident fund	1	3
Financial corporations/institutions	0.6	8.4
Financial companies	0.8	2.5
Other institutional agencies	1	1.5
Total Institutional agencies	57.2	75.7
Landlord	0.6	0.2
Agricultural moneylender	9.6	0.6
Professional moneylender	20.6	13.3
Traders	2.9	1.3
Relatives and friends	7.4	7
Others including doctors, lawyers etc.	1.7	1.8
Total Non institutional agencies	42.8	24.2

Source: Adapted from AIDIS, NSSO 59th Round, 2002-03.

It is highly essential to look into the asset composition of the households and indebtedness position to reveal the actual position of the poor regarding access to finance. It is evident from Table 6 that households with low asset holding in rural and urban areas are mostly depending on non institutional agencies. The

non institutional source dominates the asset holding class till Rs. 1,50,000-2,00,000 (Table 6). This is inevitable because of the requirement of tangible security insisted by the institutional financing agencies. The low income and low profile clients are thus excluded from the formal financial intermediation and often run into the hands of moneylenders and traders.

Table 6
Percentage Share of Institutional and Non Institutional Agencies by Asset Holding Class

Asset holding	*Rural*		*Urban*	
class Rs. '000	*Institutional*	*Non Institutional*	*Institutional*	*Non Institutional*
<15	18	82	13.4	86.6
15-30	35	64.5	40.1	59.9
30-60	26.6	73.4	46.9	53.1
60-100	39.5	60.5	59	40.8
100-150	43.6	56.4	65.6	34.4
150-200	48.1	51.9	47.9	52.1
200-300	51.5	48.5	71.7	58.3
300-450	58.7	41.3	72.5	27.5
150-800	63.4	36.6	84.9	15.1
800 & above	73.8	26.2	89.8	10.2
All	57.2	42.8	75.7	24.2

Source: Adapted from AIDIS, NSSO 59th Round, 2002-03.

The demand analysis of financial services indicates that coverage of financial services among the low income clients is still very meager though there is supply side responses like priority sector lending which stipulates that 40 per cent of the credit disbursed by commercial banks should be given to the designated priority category including agriculture, small scale industry and other priority sectors. However the advocacy of priority sector lending leading to financial inclusion is questionable due to loopholes in the stipulations discussed elsewhere in the paper. Banks are entitled to subscribe to RIDF or bonds of NABARD instead of real lending under this head and the definition of priority sector revised from time to time does not support the real envisaged objectives. Dismal performance of RRBs that cater exclusively to the requirement of rural areas has aggravated the situation.

The Microfinance Alternative

The banking sector is facing extremely challenging scenario of competition with the neo liberal banking reforms, but it has led to the reversal of public policy of extending its reach to the poor. The incapability of the formal sector in serving the rural poor has led to the establishment of micro credit projects. The micro credit system aims at removing the weaknesses of poor recovery and non viability of loans of unbanked classes. The term microfinance arose to prominence with the declaration in Micro Credit Summit organized by World Bank at Washington D.C in 1997; defining micro credit as "extending small loans to poor people for self employment projects that generate income, allocate them to care themselves and families."

The microfinance approaches combine the safety and reliability of formal finance with the convenience and flexibility that are typically associated with informal finance (Basu and Srivastava, 2005). Microfinance is provided primarily for productive activities like income generation, self employment activities and financial services. SHGs are informal groups of people where members pool their savings and re-lend in the group on rotational basis, depending upon consumption, production and investment needs. The SHGs have common decisions formed by periodical meetings with maintenance of books of accounts. The group mobilizes thrift which is used as a revolving fund to provide credit to the members according to turn. Where the resources are too meager, the NGOs support by external resources in the first phase. The members also take up micro enterprises like soap making, hotels, catering units, bakery units, candle making etc. according to skills and training that is supported by the supporting agency. Thus, SHGs are able to provide rudimentary banking services to members at a cost

effective basis and meet urgent credit requirements in time and ensure cent per cent repayment of loans (Karmakar, 1999).

The common features of microfinance can be summarized as:

- Small loans.
- No collateral.
- Borrowers among rural poor and urban poor.
- Formation of borrower group.
- Privatization especially of the mechanism of NGO control over disbursement and determination of terms and condition attached to each loan.

These features have helped microfinance to be unique and being advocated as a measure to reach out to the unreached. Modern microfinance, as in its preset form of small-scale micro-credit facilities without any collateral security for poor households was pioneered by Professor Muhammad Yunus in Bangladesh in 1976.

Microfinance in India

Unlike many countries which have implemented Self Help Groups (SHGs) after the mid-70's, as part of the formal credit delivery system, NGOs has been provided with freedom to organize and operate SHGs in India since 1960's. This initiative was given its greater impetus in 1992 by NABARD with the launch of a pilot project to link SHGs with banks. The NABARD statistics gives the extent of coverage of the linkage and assistance by the financial intermediaries. Among the SHGs linked, 90 % are women groups. SHG bank linkage is carried out by 498 participating banks in 31 States and UTs covering 587 districts in India (NABARD, 2007). It is estimated that 40.95 million poor people are benefited from SHG bank linkage programme. The average loan per SHG (New loans) is estimated to be Rs. 44,342 and the average loan per family is Rs. 3,167. In case of repeat loans this increases to Rs. 78,693 and Rs. 5621 respectively.

Bank finance to SHGs have been experiencing scaling up in the recent years, with the expansion of SHG concept endorsed by number of developmental agencies and financing institutions. The SHG financing by the commercial banks has increased from Rs. 571 million in 1992-99 to more than Rs. 1,00,000 million in 2005-06 (Table 7). There has been rapid increase in the number of SHGs from 32,995 to about 30 lakhs indicating the responsiveness of the poor to the movement.

Table 7
SHG Bank Linkage Cumulative Progress (1992-2007)

Year	*SHGs financed*	*Bank Loan (Rs. Million)*
1992-99	32,995	571
1999-00	1,14,775	1,930
2000-01	2,63,825	4,809
2001-02	4,61,478	10,263
2002-03	7,17,360	20,487
2003-04	10,79,091	39,042
2004-05	16,18,456	68,985
2005-06	22,38,565	1,13,975
2006-07	29,24,973	1,80,410

Source: NABARD, adapted and modified.

Opportunities and Challenges in Scaling up

According to some estimates, currently over 100 million poor people in the Asia and Pacific region have access to micro-credit from institutional sources. In addition, millions of poor people have gained better access to deposit facilities and other financial services of semi-formal or formal institutions. Early successes of the programme have shattered the deep-rooted myth that poor people have neither willingness nor capability to repay loans. This has led to the launch of an irreversible process of financial democratization. Later on, another myth about the poor was dispelled; that poor people have neither capacity nor willingness to save. Also the recovery system based on social intermediation and non-financial mechanisms have proved to be effective. Another important feature in microfinance is applicability of

community governance which serves as a precondition for success in participatory programmes. Effective and responsive accounting and monitoring mechanisms implemented at group level has been important and critical ingredient for the success of programs. The remarkable achievement of modern microfinance is in the provision of impetus to commercialize the financial services to the poor and low-income households. It took more than a decade to generate this momentum which has been proved invariably that there is potential for profit at the bottom of the market pyramid.

One of the biggest challenges to scaling up of microfinance is the absence of enabling policy environment. For example, interest rate caps on small loans by banks remain a major issue in a number of countries. Microfinance initiatives could be also criticised on the grounds of high interest rates. A review of interest rates in India charged on micro credit loans observe annual rates ranging from 24% to 36% on bank linked schemes refinanced by NABARD (Ramakumar, 2004; Chavan, 2004). It has been observed that informal lenders are charging lesser than 36% per annum (Rao, 2004). Thus it is proved beyond doubt that affordable rates do not matter, but what is important the accessibility to credit (Kim, 1995).

Building adequate retail capacity to provide a broad range of services in demand among the poor is yet another issue to be confronted with. This is particularly true in a developing country like India where the unserved and underserved markets continue to be very large. The institutional retail capacity limitations in many states are putting tremendous pressure on a small group of core microfinance institutions to overstretch geographically. The rural labour enquiry report supports weakening of banks in rural areas indicated by the increase in share of money lenders in total debt from 18.6% in 1983 to 34% in 1999-2000 (GOI, 2004). Development of microfinance institutions is imperative to help the poor to mobilise resources to develop resource base to setup enterprises and leverage their entity.

Transaction costs result in a wedge for the prices charged to the clients depending on the costs of the service providers. Some poor people are unable to access formal financial services due to high costs. Reducing transaction costs will therefore have a positive impact on both supply and demand for services, creating a win-win situation for all. Extended outreach to poorer clients and those in remote locations who are unreached till date, demand reduction of transaction costs. The issue of higher transaction cost is even higher in the case of NGO provided micro credit due to addition of their operating margin. In most of the cases, it is true that NGO's cannot match the economies of scale of commercial banks. However, studies have revealed better repayment of loans and lower transaction cost in NGO controlled micro credit in selected locations (Ramachandran and Swaminathan, 2002). The cost of administration increases when NGO activities are being scaled up, that are either financed by donor funds or by raising interest rates, rendering the effective interest rate to clients higher than charged by the banking system (Mosely, 1997 and Hossain, 1993).

Most of the existing microfinance institutions are facing problems regarding skilled labour which is not available for local level accounting. Drop out of trained staff is very high. One alternative is automation which is not looked at as yet.

Conclusion

Financial Inclusion of poor has gathered momentum and holds prime importance in the agenda of planners and policy makers; recognizing importance of inclusive growth of the economy. Notwithstanding that financial system of the country, encompassing institutional and non-institutional players, being one of the strongest among the emerging economies; is unable to provide financial services to majority of the population. The institutional suppliers of credit avoid the poor due to policies of risk aversion and asset based lending programmes. While it has been established beyond doubt that there is solid relation between

finance and poverty, a new paradigm is required for financial inclusion to achieve poverty alleviation. Microfinance has been increasingly recognized as an alternative to provide financial services to masses mobilizing thrift and supplying credit gradually linking with the mainstream financial institutions. Unlike the Government sponsored subsidized developmental programmes, the poor are not supplied grants but are provided empowerment to come out of the low income trap and vicious circle of poverty by mobilizing small savings. This has resulted in real empowerment of the poor improving credit worthiness, reducing delinquencies and achieving better socio economic status. Hence it is imperative to extend the outreach by scaling up of microfinance programmes into the distant and unbanked centres identified by the RBI. The weaknesses identified in this regard under the four pillars of the financial system; namely supply, demand, intermediation and regulation should be confronted with suitable corrective strategies.

References

Basu, P and Srivastava, P. (2005), *Scaling Up Microfinance for India's Poor*, World Bank Policy Research Working paper, 3646. Accessed from *http://econ.worldbank.org*, dated 15th February 2008.

Rao, Satish (2004), Foreword to *Low Income Households Access to Financial Services, International Experience, Measures for Improvement and the Future.*, Au. Fernanado, N.A., EARD Special Studies, Asian Development Bank, Philippines.

Barth, J.R. (2006), *Rethinking Bank Regulation: Till Angels Govern*, New York: Cambridge University Press.

Karmakar, K.G. (1999), *Rural Credit and Self Help Groups*, Sage Publications, New Delhi.

Chavan, Pallavi (2004), *Banking Sector Liberalization and the Growth and Regional Distribution of Rural Banking*, in Ramachandran and Swaminathan (forthcoming 2004).

Government of India, Labour Bureau (2004), *Rural Labour Enquiry Report on General Characteristics of Rural Labour Households*, 55th Round of NSSO, 1999-2000 (www. ADD).

Hossain, M. (1993), Credit for Alleviation of Rural Poverty: The Grameen Bank in Bangladesh, *Tropicultura*, 11, 3, pp. 115-121.

Kim Kyung-Hwan (1995), *Access to Credit, Term of Housing Finance and Affordability of Housing*, Housing Finance International 9(4), June 22-27.

Micro Credit Summit (2007), Declaration and *Plan of Action*, available at *www.microcreditsummit.org/ decalaration.htm*

Mosely, P. (1999), Micro-Macro Linkages in Financial Markets: The Impact of Financial Liberalization on Access to Rural Credit in Four African Countries, *Journal of International Development*, 11:367-384.

Ramachandran, V. K. and Swaminathan, Madhura (2002), Rural Banking and Landless Labour Households, Institutional Reform and Rural Credit Markets in India," *Journal of Agrarian Change*, 2, 4, Oct., pp. 502-544.

Rao, Smriti (2004), *Women's Self-Help Groups and Credit for the Poor: A Case Study from Andhra Pradesh* in Ramachandran and Swaminathan (forthcoming 2004).

Ramakumar, R. (2004), *Formal Credit and Rural Workers' Households in Kerala: A Case Study of a Malabar Village*, in Ramachandran and Swaminathan (forthcoming 2004).

Official website of the Reserve Bank of India, *www.rbi.org.in*

Official website of NABARD, *www.nabard.org.in*

6

FINANCIAL INCLUSION: CHALLENGES AND OPPORTUNITIES IN THE LIBERALISED ERA

M. Anilkumar & S. Resia Beegam

The banking industry has shown tremendous growth in volume and complexity during the last few decades. Despite making significant improvements in all the areas relating to financial viability, profitability and competitiveness, there are concerns that banks have not been able to include vast segment of the population, especially the under privileged sections of the society into the fold of basic banking services. Financial inclusion is a means to achieve inclusive economic growth. Financial inclusion involves bringing into banking fold all those who presently stand excluded from the purview of banking. The 11th plan draft approach paper has correctly identified that to achieve higher sustainable and equitable growth for the country it would be imperative.

Meaning of Inclusion

Inclusion is a process of covering or bringing in. Inclusive growth implies that all individuals and groups of individuals and all sections of society including the poorest of the poor should be made active participants in the growth process. They actively involved in the efforts at development at the micro level. On account of such participation they will become beneficiaries of economic growth. All should be enabled to come to the main stream of productive and economic life.

Financial Inclusion

Financial inclusion is delivery of banking services at an affordable cost of the vast sections of disadvantaged and low income groups. Unrestrained access to public goods and services is the sine qua non of an open and efficient society. As banking services are in the nature of public good, it is essential that availability of banking and payment services to the entire population without discrimination is the prime objective of the public policy. Financial inclusion involves bringing into banking fold all those who presently stand excluded from the purview of banking.

RBI's Policy on Financial Inclusion

1. When bankers do not give the desired attention to certain areas, the regulators have to step in to remedy the situation. This is the reason why the RBI places a lot of emphasis on financial inclusion.
2. With a view to enhancing the financial inclusion as a proactive measure the RBI in its annual policy statement of the year 2005-206, while recognizing the concerns in regard to the banking practices that tend to exclude rather than attract vast sections of population, urged banks to review their existing practices to align them with the objective of financial inclusion.

Areas of Concern by Banks

1. The banking industry has shown tremendous growth in volume and complexity during the last few decades.
2. Despite making significant improvements in all the areas relating to financial viability, profitability and competitiveness,

there are concerns that banks have not been able to reach and bring vast segment of the population, especially the under privileged sections of the society, into the fold of basic banking services.

3. Efforts are being made to study the causes of financial exclusion and design strategies to ensure financial inclusion of the poor and disadvantaged.
4. The reasons may vary from country to country and so also the strategy but all out efforts are needed as financial exclusion can truly lift the standard of life of the poor and the disadvantaged.

Consequences of Financial Exclusion

The consequences of financial exclusion will vary depending on the nature and extent of services denied. It may lead to increased travel requirements, higher incidence of crime, general decline in investment, difficulties in gaining access to credit or getting credit from informal sources at exorbitant rates and increased unemployment etc. The small business may suffer due to loss of access to middle class and higher income consumers, higher cash handling costs, decline in remittances of money. According to certain researches, financial exclusion can lead to social exclusion.

Scope of Financial Inclusion

The financial exclusion has been viewed in a much wider perspective internationally. The Financial Inclusion Task Force in U.K has identified three priority areas for the purpose of financial inclusion.

1. Access to banking
2. Access to affordable credit
3. Access to free face-to-face money advice.

The scope of financial inclusion can be expanded in two ways:

- Through state-driven intervention by way of statutory enactments.
- Through voluntary effort by the banking community itself for evolving various strategies to bring within the ambit of the banking sector the large strata of society.

Indian Scenario

Bank nationalization in India marked a paradigm shift in the focus of banking as it was intended to shift the focus from class banking to mass banking. The rationale for creating RRBs was also to take the banking services to poor people. The branches of commercial banks and the RRBs have increased from 8321 in the year 1969 to 68282 branches as at the end of March, 2005. The average population per branch office has decreased from 6, 40,000 to 16,000 during the same period. However, there are certain under banked states such as Bihar, Orissa, Rajasthan, Uttar Pradesh, Chattisgarh, Jharkhand, West Bengal and a large number of North Eastern states, where the average population per branch office continues to be quite high compared to the national average. The new branch authorization policy of Reserve Bank of India encourages banks to open branches in these under banked states and the under banked areas in other states. The new policy also places a lot of emphasis on the efforts made by the bank to achieve inter alia, financial inclusion and other policy objectives.

Steps Towards Financial Inclusion

In the context of initiatives taken for extending banking services to the small man, the mode of financial sector development until 1980's characterized by:

1. A hugely expanded bank branch and co-operative network and new organizational forms like RRBs
2. A greater focus on credit rather than other financial services like savings and insurance, although the banks and co-operatives did provide deposit facilities.

3. Lending targets directed at a range of "priority sectors" such as agriculture, weaker sections of the population etc.
4. Interest rate ceilings.
5. Significant Government subsidies channeled through the banks and co-operatives, as well as through related Government programmes.
6. A dominant perspective that finance for rural and poor people was a social obligation and not a potential business opportunity.

Challenges

1. Achievement of total financial inclusion is not easy. It will be a national challenge. Commercial banks alone cannot face the challenge single handed. According to Finance Minister Sri.P.Chidambaram, co-operative credit system is one of the critical instruments for reaching out banking services to rural households. He has also opined that unless co-operative credit system reforms are completed, it is not possible to achieve total financial inclusion.
2. Without active involvement and support of State Government, reform of co-operative credit system can not be undertaken. Therefore, State Governments must comer forward and involve themselves actively in the restructuring of co-operative system.

Opportunities

The new opportunities that may crop-up for banks, will be both in the area of deposit mobilization and lending- Financial Inclusion will afford opportunities for banks to increase the number of their savings bank accounts. The outstanding balance in these accounts will be sizeable. In the opinion of Dr.Y.V.Reddy, Governor of RBI, "Banks should move to the masses as a natural process of financial inclusion". Bank should try to collect small deposits of the farmers, rural artisans, people engaged in rural non-farm sector and rural service sector, Self Help Groups and also the Urban poor.

These small deposits will bring about stability on the liability side. Banks will also get new opportunities for lending as a result of financial inclusion. Lending to small farmers, rural artisans, rural non-farm sector, Self Help Groups, small and medium enterprises etc. will be the new opportunities for lending as a result of financial inclusion. The opportunities for lending that can be had in the bottom of the pyramid, particularly in such areas are agriculture, cottage and small scale industries, rural non farm sector, Self Help Groups etc will be enormous.

Advantages

1. People belonging to all sections of society, including the weakest of the weak will get opportunity to come into banking fold.
2. Banking habit will grow by and by and people belonging to all sections of population will get access banking services and various types of banking products. They will be able to acquire and enjoy certain financial aspects also.
3. As a result of growth of banking habit, payments through banking channels will increase and grow. This will enable people to avoid risks associated with holding of cash and cash transactions.
4. Lending programmes of banks and micro credit will empower people at the bottom and this will enable them to escape their poverty themselves. Access to credit, certain financial assets and deposit products will empower people considerably. Creation of wealth by individuals through utilization of bank credit for productive purposes, will lay a firm foundation for inclusive growth.
5. Financial inclusion will help banks to augment their business volumes. The new business from the freshly included category

of customers will be a substitute for the business lost on account of the process of disintermediation.

Steps Towards Financial Inclusion

In the context of initiatives taken for extending banking services to the small man, the mode of financial sector development until 1980's was characterized by:

1. A hugely expanded bank branch and co-operative network and new organizational forms like RRBs.
2. A greater focus on credit rather than other financial services like savings and insurance, although the bank and co-operatives did provide deposit facilities.
3. Lending targets directed at a range of "priority sectors" such as agriculture, weaker sections of the population etc.
4. Interest rate ceilings.
5. Significant Government subsidies channeled through the banks and co-operatives, as well as through related Government programmes.
6. A dominant perspective that finance for rural and poor people was a social obligation and not a potential business opportunity.

The Way Forward

The banks should come out of inhibited feeling that very aggressive competition policy and social inclusion are mutually elsewhere, the mass banking with no-frills etc can become a win-win situation for both. Basically banking services need to be "marketed" to connect with large population segments and these may be justifiable promotional cost. The opportunities are plenty:

1. In the context of India becoming are of the largest micro-finance markets in the world especially in the growth of women's savings and credit groups (SHGs) and the sustaining success of such institution.

2. The IBA may explore the possibility of a survey about the coverage in respect of financial inclusion keeping in view the geographical spread of the banks and extent of financial services available to the population so as to assess the constraints in extension of financial services to hither to unbanked sections and for initiating appropriate policy measures.
3. It may be useful for banks to consider franchising with other segments of financial sector such as co-operatives, RRBs etc so as to extent the scope of financial inclusion with minimal intermediation cost.
4. Since large sections of low income groups transactions are related to deposits and withdrawals with a view to containing transaction costs, 'simple to use' cash dispensing and collecting machines akin to ATMs, with operating instructions and commends in vernaculas would greatly facilitate financial inclusion of the semi-urban and rural populace.

Conclusion

It is becoming increasingly apparent that addressing financial inclusion will require a holistic approach on the part of the banks in creating awareness about financial products, education and advice on money management, debt counseling, savings and affordable credit. Banks should adopt "banking for all" as a goal on the lines of national goals like "health for all", "education for all' etc. Further, efforts must be made to move from the concept of 'anytime, anywhere banking' to 'anytime, anywhere and to everyone banking'.

References

Hindu Business Line, December 22, 2005.

Dr. K.K. Ammannaya (2007), Financial inclusion–Tasks and Strategies, *Southern Economist*, January 1, .

Shri V. Leeladhar (2005), Deputy Governor, RBI Reports.

Shri V. Leeladhar, (2006), Financial Inclusion:Taking Banking Services to the Common Man, *RBI Bulletin*, January, 2006.

Lecture on "Taking Banking Services to the Common Man-Financial Inclusion", Shri V. Leeladhar, Deputy Governor, at the FED bank, Hormis Memorial Foundation at Ernakulam on December 2, 2005.

Das Gupta, Rajaram (2002), "Priority Sector Lending: Yesterday, Today and Tomorrow", *Economic and Political Weekly*, October 12.

7

ICT AND FINANCIAL INCLUSION: AN INDIAN PERSPECTIVE

V. Arockia Jerold

Part-I

Financial Inclusion and Indian Economy: The Concept, Significance and Challenges

A well functioning financial system empowers individuals, facilitates better integration with the economy, actively contributes to development and affords protection against economic shocks. Inclusive finance - through secure savings, appropriately priced credit and insurance products, and payment services – helps vulnerable groups such as low income groups, weaker sections, etc., to increase incomes, acquire capital, manage risk and work their way out of poverty. In India, the focus of the financial inclusion at present is confined to ensuring a bare minimum access to a savings bank account without frills, to all. Internationally, the financial inclusion has been viewed in a much wider perspective. Having a current account/savings account on its own, is not regarded as an accurate indicator of financial inclusion. 'Financial

Inclusion' efforts should offer at a minimum, access to a range of financial services including savings, long and short term credit, insurance, pensions, mortgages, money transfers, etc. and all this at a reasonable cost.

The Indian economy is growing at a steady rate of 8.5% to 9% in the last five years or so. Most of the growth is from industry and services sector. Agriculture is growing at a little over 2%. The potential for growth in the primary and SME sector is enormous. Limited access to affordable financial services such as savings, loan, remittance and insurance services by the vast majority of the population in the rural areas and unorganised sector is believed to be acting as a constraint to the growth impetus in these sectors. Access to affordable financial services-especially credit and insurance-enlarges livelihood opportunities and empowers the poor to take charge of their lives. Such empowerment aids social and political stability. Apart from these benefits, FI imparts formal identity, provides access to the payments system and to savings safety net like deposit insurance. Hence FI is considered to be critical for achieving inclusive growth; which itself is required for ensuring overall sustainable overall growth in the country.

The financially excluded sections largely comprise marginal farmers, landless labourers, oral lessees, self employed and unorganised sector enterprises, urban slum dwellers, migrants, ethnic minorities and socially excluded groups, senior citizens and women. While there are pockets of large excluded population in all parts of the country, the North East, Eastern and Central regions contain most of the financially excluded population.There are a variety of reasons for FI. In remote, hilly and sparsely populated areas with poor infrastructure, physical access itself acts as a deterrent. From the demand side, lack of awareness, low incomes/assets, social exclusion, illiteracy act as barriers. From the supply side, distance from branch, branch timings, cumbersome documentation and procedures, unsuitable products, language, staff attitudes are common reasons for exclusion. All these result in higher transaction cost apart from procedural hassles. On the other hand, the ease of availability of informal credit sources makes these popular even if costlier. The requirements of independent documentary proof of identity and address can be a very important barrier in having a bank account especially for migrants and slum dwellers.

State Governments can play a pro-active role in facilitating FI. Issuing official identity documents for opening accounts, creating awareness and involving district and block level functionaries in the entire process, meeting cost of cards nd other devices for pilots, undertaking financial literacy drives are some of the ways in which the State and district administration have involved themselves. India Post is also looking to diversify its activities and leverage on its huge network of post offices, the postman's intimate knowledge of the local population and the enormous trust reposed in him. Banks are entering into agreements with India Post for using post offices as agents for branchless banking. The Finance Minister in his budget for 2007-08 has announced the setting up of two funds for FI; the first called Financial Inclusion Fund for developmental and promotional interventions and the other called Financial Inclusion Technology Fund to meet cost of technology adoption of about $ 125 million each. The scope of these funds is being worked out. Setting up of financial literacy centres and credit counseling on a pilot basis, launching a national financial literacy campaign, forging linkages with informal sources with suitable safeguards through appropriate legislation, evolving industry wide standards for IT solutions, facilitating low cost remittance products are some of the initiatives currently under way for furthering FI.

The recent developments in banking technology have transformed banking from the traditional brick-and-mortar infrastructure like staffed branches to a system supplemented by other channels like automated teller machines (ATM), credit/ debit cards, internet banking, online money transfers, etc. The moot point, however, is that access to such technology is restricted only to certain segments of the society. Indeed, some trends, such as increasingly sophisticated customer segmentation technology have led to restricted access to financial services for some groups. There is a growing divide, with an increased range of personal finance options for a segment of high and upper middle income population and a significantly large section of the population who lack access to even the most basic banking services. This is termed "financial exclusion". These people, particularly, those living on low incomes, cannot access mainstream financial products such as bank accounts, credit, remittances and payment services, financial advisory services, insurance facilities, etc.

Deliberations on the subject of Financial Inclusion contributed to a consensus that merely having a bank account may not be a good indicator of financial inclusion. Further, indebtedness as quantified in the NSSO 59th round (2003) may not also be a reflective indicator. The ideal definition should look at people who want to access financial services but are denied the same. If genuine claimants for credit and financial services are denied the same, then that is a case of exclusion. As this aspect would raise the issue of credit worthiness or bankability, it is also necessary to dwell upon what could be done to make the claimants of institutional credit bankable or creditworthy. This would require re-engineering of existing financial products or delivery systems and making them more in tune with the expectations and absorptive capacity of the intended clientele. Based on the above consideration, a broad working definition of financial inclusion could be as under:

> "Financial inclusion may be defined as the process of ensuring access to financial services and timely and adequate credit where needed by vulnerable groups such as weaker sections and low income groups at an affordable cost."

By financial inclusion, we mean delivery of banking services and credit at an affordable cost to the vast sections of disadvantaged and low income groups. The various financial services include savings, loans, insurance, payments, remittance facilities and financial counseling/advisory services by the formal financial system. An open and efficient society is always characterized by the unrestrained access to public goods and services. As banking services are in the nature of public goods, financial inclusion should therefore be viewed as availability of banking and payment services to the entire population without discrimination of any type.

Barriers to Financial Inclusion

There are several barriers to financial inclusion, some are characteristics of service providers and some are of customers. The following are the characteristics of financial service providers which add to financial exclusion:

- *Banking network:* There are no bank branches in remote areas/tribal areas and difficulties in closure/mergers/ shifting of bank branches which were hither to operated in tribal areas/remote rural areas
- *Hours of operation of bank branches in rural areas:* Timings are inconvenient for the poor people as they have to go for farm operations (or) go to wage earning. In that case visiting branch during daytime would mean loss of wages for a day.
- Lack of information about the financial services.
- *Restrictions at bank*: Personal identification, minimum balance, price of the product, technologies adopted at branches some times restrict the people.

Problems Encountered in the Initial Stages

- *Social & Economic position:* Low-income people normally do not feel the need to bank as the transaction carried out by them is mostly in cash that too with low amount.
- *Information:* Many times people do not want to disclose the information which would be required for accessing any financial service.

- *Identification/Introduction:* Poor people, mostly, do not have any identification/introduction, which is accepted by banks to open an account (or) access other financial services.
- Financial literacy: Lack of understanding of financial services and the operations to be carried out is also a hindrance.
- Absorptive capacity : Poor people do not have much absorptive capacity for all the financial services.
- Need for different financial services.
- Large geographical spread of customers: The spread of customers is very thin which makes the operation of reaching out to them a costly affair.

Regional Rural Banks

Post-merger, RRBs, with 14494 branches, represent a powerful instrument for financial inclusion. Their role and relevance in financial inclusion is crucial as:

- In rural areas, they account for 37% of total offices of all Scheduled Commercial Banks.
- 91% of the total workforce in RRBs is posted in rural and semi-urban areas as compared to 38% for other Scheduled Commercial Banks.
- In rural areas, RRBs account for 31% of deposit accounts and 19% of deposit amount of all Scheduled Commercial Banks. Lower average deposit amount per account in RRBs as compared with commercial banks implies their better reach to small depositors.
- Share of RRBs in loan accounts is an impressive 37% in rural areas.
- Of all the scheduled commercial banks, RRBs account for 34% of branches in NE, 30% in Eastern and 32% in Central regions. Incidentally, these regions manifest financial exclusion of a high order.
- Of the total 29.25 lakh SHGs credit linked by the banking system (as on 31 March 2007), 31% linkage is done by

RRBs. More significantly, the more backward a region, greater is the share of RRBs. In North Eastern Region, it is 56%, Central region 48% and Eastern region 40%.

- RRBs have also played a significant role as Self Help Promoting Institutions (SHPIs). As many as 104 RRBs (31 March 2006) are functioning as SHPIs with grant assistance from NABARD.

Part-II

Models Available for Financial Inclusion

With the objective of ensuring greater financial inclusion and increasing the outreach of the banking sector, the RBI has permitted banks to use the services of NGOs /SHGs, MFIs and other civil society organisations as intermediaries in providing financial and banking services through the use of Business Facilitator and Business Correspondent Models.

Business Facilitator Model

Under the BF Model, banks may use intermediaries such as NGOs, farmers clubs, cooperatives, community based organisations, IT-enabled rural outlets of corporate entities, post offices, insurance agents, well functioning Panchayats, village knowledge centres, agri-clinics/agri-business centres, Krishi Vigyan Kendras and KVIC/ KVIB units for providing facilitation services. It has been clarified that BF model adopts the following services:

- Identification of borrowers and fitment of activities,
- Collection and preliminary processing of loan applications,
- Creation of awareness about savings and other products, education and advise on

  managing money and debt counseling,
- Processing and submission of application to banks,
- Promotion and nurturing of SHGs

- Monitoring and hand holding of SHGs/credit groups/ others, and
- Follow-up for recovery.

Business Correspondent Model

Under the BC Model, NGOs/MFIs set up under the Societies/ Trust Act, Societies registered under Mutually Aided Cooperative Societies Acts or the Cooperative Societies Acts of States, Section 25 Companies, Registered NBFCs not accepting public deposits and post offices may act as BCs. Banks have been advised to conduct due diligence on such entities and ensure that they are well established,enjoy good reputation and have the confidence of local people. In addition to the activities listed under the BF Model, the scope and activities to be undertaken by BCs will include:

- Disbursal of small value credit,
- Recovery of principal/collection of interest,
- ollection of small value deposits,
- Sale of micro-insurance/mutual fund products/pension products/other third
  party products, and
- Receipt and delivery of small value remittances/other payment instruments.

ICT–The Driving Force for Low-cost Inclusion Initiatives

The use of IT solutions for providing banking facilities at doorstep holds the potential for scalability of the FI initiatives. Pilot projects have been initiated using smart cards for opening bank accounts with bio metric identification. Link to mobile or hand held connectivity devices ensure that the transactions are recorded in the bank's books on real time basis. Some State Governments are routing social security payments as also payments under the National Rural Employment Guarantee Scheme through such smart cards (see pictures below). The same delivery channel can be used to provide other financial services like low cost remittances and insurance. The use of IT also enables banks to handle the enormous rise in the volume of transactions of millions of households for processing, credit scoring, credit record and follow up.

The use of IT is inevitable to improve the usage of existing branch infrastructure. Increasing outreach and up scaling number of accounts at each branch will require bankers to move out of their branches and source clients and then look at low cost delivery alternatives once the account relationship is established. Opening a no frills account with a small overdraft or GCC is only the first step in building the relationship which would require sustained efforts to ensure that the banking relationship with the customer is fashioned to meet his needs. IT can reduce cost and time in processing of applications, maintaining and reconciliation of accounts and enable banks to use their staff at branches for making that critical minimum effort in sustaining relationship especially with new accountholders. In rural areas customers cannot be expected to come to branches in view of opportunity cost and time and hence banks will have to reach out through a variety of devices such as weekly banking, mobile banking, satellite offices, rural ATMs and use of Post offices. In urban and even in rural areas where mobile phones have penetrated, banks could use mobile technology for facilitating banking transactions. Mobile phones can be used to transfer funds real time from and to bank accounts and could make remittances and payments at very low cost. Once the data base and track record is established, a multitude of financial services can be offered including savings, remittance, transaction banking such as receipt of salaries, pensions and payments for utilities, loan including home loans, insurance and MF products. Here the branches can render more business and variety of products to existing clientele as also source new customers within the area of operation. Financial inclusion offers a huge potential for business in terms of resources and assets and banks therefore need to take aggressive steps to use technology, business processes and personnel to be able to exploit this potential in innovative and creative ways.

The recent developments in banking technology and expansion of telecommunication network in the hinterlands of the country have provided the perfect launch pad for extending banking outposts to remote locations without having to open bank branches in the area. The Committee feels that this could be achieved by leveraging technology to open up channels beyond branch network and create the required banking footprints to reach the unbanked so as to extend banking services similar to those dispensed from branches. In short, technology has to enable the branch to go where the customer is present, instead of the other way around.

Further, RBI's Annual Policy for 2007-08 also urged the banks to scale up efforts for IT-based financial inclusion and develop technologies that are highly secure, amenable to audit and follow widely accepted open standards to allow inter operability among the different systems adopted by different banks. The enabling provisions and support of RBI has facilitated successful pilot projects in use of IT for extending the banking outreach for the "excluded". These projects are premised on technology which uses hand-held devices and connectivity with host computers through General Packet Radio Service (GPRS)/Global System for Mobile Communications (GSM)/Code Division Multiple Access (CDMA)/landline networks. The devices also come in several forms like Simputers (Simple Inexpensive Multi-lingual Computers)/personal digital assistants, programmed mobiles, etc. There are also rural bio-metric ATMs which have been introduced by banks and found to be very popular among rural masses. Some major banks are introducing low cost rural ATMs for cash dispensing and other services in rural areas.

Remittance Needs of the Poor

The credit needs and avenues for safe custody of savings for the poor have been recognized as areas of substantial gaps and have been sought to be addressed by expansion of bank branches, cooperative credit structure and microfinance initiatives. However, the remittance needs have traditionally been thought to be well met by money orders from Post Office, sale of traveler's cheques, demand drafts by banks and through informal sources, including physical carrying of cash by the poor themselves and their relatives and friends.

The poor need a remittance system to send money to their families when they migrate out of their villages or towns. Situations often arise when migrant workers in a city remit money to their families in the village or when parents in the village need to remit money to their children in the city. Other cases of remittance could arise on account of transfer payments by Government or remittances of miscellaneous nature. As such the service they need should meet the following criteria:

(a) *Accessible service:* The product should be available to them without unnecessary hassle. Entry barriers such as existing relationship with banks, possession of checkable accounts or filling up long forms act as deterrents in accessing the services.

(b) *Timeliness and certainty of delivery:* Predictability of delivery at the recipient's place is important for those who depend on remittances for meeting their basic needs.

(c) *Cost effectiveness, affordability and value for money services:* The remittance needs are mostly repetitive and small value. The present system of remitting through post offices is costly. Other sources are risk prone, further adding to the cost of the service.

(d) *Receipt of delivery status:* Timely confirmation of delivery is a requirement for poor people who have limited access to communication facility.

With new technology and computerization of banking operations, new remittance products have been introduced in the market, which have increased the speed, cost effectiveness and efficiency of the payments and settlement system. These include the National Electronic Funds Transfer (NEFT), Electronic Clearing System (ECS), Real Time Gross Settlement (RTGS) and ongoing endeavour at cheque truncation system leading to a national payment and settlement system.

Part-III

ICT Products that Support Effective Financial Inclusion

Automated Teller Machines (ATMS)

Automated Teller Machines (ATMs) conduct many transactions that would otherwise require staff attention: they furnish account information, accept deposits, draw down on pre-approved loans and transfer funds. The use of ATMs frees loan officers to focus on personalized services and the machines can potentially deliver a broader range of services. ATMs are most effective for banks and financial institutions that accept savings and want to serve customers in multiple locations and/or during non-business hours. A single machine can cost as much as Rs. 8 to 10 lakh and requires reliable electric and communications connections. Banks generally consider ATMs when high transaction volumes put pressure on staff, traditional operating hours do not suit client needs and when decided to offer a range of financial services.

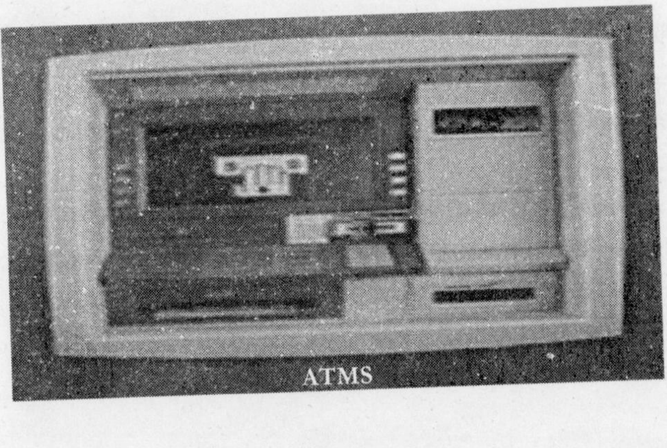

ATMS

Typical ATMs have two input devices (a card reader and keypad) and four output devices (display screen, cash dispenser, receipt printer, and speaker). Not visible to the client is a communications mechanism that links the ATM directly to an ATM host network. The ATM functions much like a PC; it comes with an operating system (usually OS/2) and specific application software for the user interface and communications. Whereas most ATMs use magnetic strip cards and personal identification numbers (PINs) to identify account holders, other systems may use smart cards with fingerprint validation. The ATM forwards information read from the client's card and the client's request to a host processor, which routes the request to the client's financial institution. If the cardholder is requesting cash, the host processor signals for an electronic funds transfer (EFT) from the customer's bank account to the host processor's account. Once the funds have been transferred, the ATM receives an approval code authorizing it to dispense the cash. This communication, verification and authorization can be delivered several ways. Leased line, dial-up, or wireless data links may be used to connect to the host system, depending on the cost and reliability of infrastructure. The host systems can reside at the client's institution or be part of an EFT network. The EFT network may support debit card transactions using PINs or credit card transactions using a signature. Point-of-sale services that use PINs are also possible.

Benefits

- Flexible account access allows clients to access their accounts at their convenience.
- Bank/MFI personnel are not required to be present for transactions and have more time to serve clients.
- Increased hours of operation fit client schedules.
- More clients can be reached beyond the branch network, such as in smaller population centers.
- More low-cost funds are available because ATMs make it easier for clients to deposit savings.

Mobile Biometric ATM

For biometric access, customers have to register their finger prints with the branch in which they maintain their accounts. The mobile ATMs would identify the customer based on his/her finger print. However, personal identification number (PIN) facility would also be available. The customer would also be guided by voice in local languages on how to use the ATM. "Besides, many educated customers are preferring biometric ATMs as it adds to the safety and security of their money. Keeping this in view, public sector banks are planning to take this technology to the masses.

Salient Features of Mobile Bio Metric ATM:

- The bio metric ATMs caters to the need of illiterate and semi-literate people as it works on finger print of the account holder which is scanned at the time of issue of ATM card.
- The ATM will give an audio instruction in Telugu colloquial language to the account holder for easy operations.
- The ATM has dual facility where PIN as well as finger prints operation can be done.
- The ATM will stop at different locations as per the week's schedule approved by RBI.
- The ATM will cover essentially un-banked or under banked regions.

Smart Cards

Smart Cards can be used for financial services, such as managing savings accounts, disbursing loans or making transfers. During enrollment, all relevant client information, account balances and individual credit or other limits are loaded onto the card through a recording device attached to a PC. Some unique form of personal identification, such as the numeric markers of the client.s fingerprint, may also be stored on the card. During visits to a

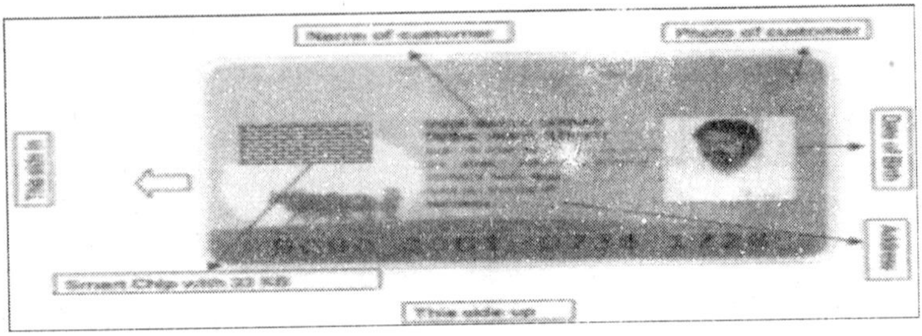

Smart Cards

branch office, the smart card functions as an electronic passbook on which transactions can be recorded once, speeding up the process and improving accuracy. Banks and financial institutions that seek to automate transactions for clients or are attempting to reduce the use of paper in operations may consider smart cards using smart card readers. Smart cards may be part of a fully computerized information system that can transmit data from a central site to the client instantly. As part of an integrated system, however, implementing smart cards generally requires the purchase and implementation of associated technologies, such as automated teller machines (ATMs) or personal digital assistants (PDAs) and may function effectively only with reliable electric and communications networks.

A smart card is a wallet-sized plastic card with an embedded computer chip that can process information (microprocessor chip) or simply store data (memory chip). Smart cards also come in the "contact" and "contactless varieties". A contact smart card is inserted into a smart card reader that connects to the card's conductive micro module (typically a gold plated area on the surface). Through this connection, software on a personal computer (PC) or ATM may transmit commands and data to the reader and the smart card. A contactless card can be held two to three inches away from the reader because the reader and the card are designed with antenna. Despite providing a very fast card interface, the cost of these cards and readers generally restricts their use to high-volume access applications, such as for automatic, no-stop highway toll plazas. Smart card technology is partially standardized. Chip operating systems (COS) are typically proprietary to the card manufacturer, whereas reader interface systems follow standards such as Javacard, Open Platform, and PC/SC to ensure that smart cards are compatible in various readers. The EMV (EuroPay, MasterCard, Visa) standard is becoming the norm in the financial services market and most manufacturers plan to comply with this.

Benefits

- Automated transactions.
- More secure user identity and account information.
- Built-in limits on credit and other accounts.
- With stored data, less or no need for reader to access central server.
- No repetitive form filing.
- Quicker administrative functions.
- Improved transaction accuracy.

Costs

The following are indicative costs for contact cards with microprocessor chips, since these are the most commonly used smart cards for microfinance applications.

- Rs. 250-400 per card.
- Rs. 5000-15000 for each card reader (Card Acceptance Device, or CAD).
- Set-up or installation fee to deploy card readers.
- Monthly or annual service fee for support & Communications charges (modem dial-up, leased lines)

Biometrics

Biometrics technology measures an individual's unique physical or behavioral characteristics, such as fingerprints, facial

Biometrics

characteristics, voice pattern and gait, to recognize and confirm identity. Although the technology is still new, growing awareness of the importance of data security is increasing adoption steadily. For some organizations, low-cost biometric solutions may be more convenient and secure than the passwords and personal identification numbers (PINs) that these institutions currently use to restrict access to financial data. Biometrics technology may be an option for any organization that uses physical cards, documents, passwords, or identification numbers to secure data stored in electronic format on a computer or Automated Teller Machine (ATM). However, biometrics technology to secure individual client transactions generally requires additional implementation. With these biometric applications, some portable client-held device, such as a Smart Card, is also required to store each client's biometric template.

The general purpose of all biometric technologies is to capture and store information at an enrollment stage to compare at a later verification stage. In the capture process, software assigns values to a biometric image and stores these values in a template that requires far less storage than the image itself. During verification, when the client initiates a transaction, the system scans the client's biometric (e.g., voice pattern, retinal image, fingerprint, etc.), matches this scan against the stored template and approves or rejects it. It sends this result to the business software to either proceed with or halt the client's transaction. A secure audit trail is also recorded for each match attempt. The False Rejection Rate measures how often an authorized user's biometric data is rejected by the system; and the False Acceptance Rate measures how frequently an unauthorized person gains access to secure resources. Manufacturers use these measures to monitor and determine the effectiveness (security and ease of use) of their systems.

Benefits

- Greater security-biometrics link a person to an action.
- Convenience-clients have no identification number or password to remember.
- Local verification-clients hold their identity information (e.g., on a Smart Card), so there is no need to verify identity via a central repository or server.
- Verification is swift and does not require staff.
- User identity is stored safely and is tamper free.

Costs

The following are indicative costs of a biometric fingerprint system that verifies identity and passes match/no-match results to other software (e.g,. the transaction application). The costs below assume the use of smart cards, since these systems furnish the greatest potential and flexibility for MFI applications.

- A smart card for each client costs Rs. 250-400 per card.
- Software programming routines to develop the reader-MIS interface cost Rs. 40000-100000.
- A set-up or installation fee to deploy card readers will be charged.
- Basic fingerprint readers cost Rs. 2500-6000, or fingerprint/card readers cost Rs. 4500-10000.

Some smart card readers come with built-in fingerprint capability to authenticate the bearer of the actual card. This raises the price of the reader but increases security and eliminates the need to integrate multiple components.

Part-IV

Corporate Experiences Relating to the Use of ICT for Financial Inclusion

Initiatives taken by banks in the ICT enabled financial inclusion are given below:

Experience of Corporation Bank

A project implemented by Corporation bank at select locations across four Southern States has used modern ICT applications at remote rural locations. The project uses biometric card based authentication devices, which are used by the bank's Business Correspondents at the villages. The Bank is providing basic banking services to the rural people through these low cost devices, without the concomitant costs associated with setting up of an Extension Counter/ATM or a Branch and thus aiming to bring down significantly the transaction costs in rural banking. This model reportedly brings in a win-win situation for both the Bank and its rural customer. The services are made available close to their homes, obviating the need to spend time and money on transport to reach the branch. The roll out and maintenance costs of this model are only a fraction of running a conventional branch. The Bank developed the new operating model to cover a large number of un-banked villages. The Bank developed the new operating model to cover a large number of un-banked villages. The various steps taken by the Bank in this regard were:

- A village survey was conducted to assess the present level of household income generation and the potential of credit requirements in future;
- The household survey report served as an enabling tool to arrive at a total economic view of the families surveyed, potential for savings and the extent of credit that can be delivered;
- While conducting the survey, the Bank observed that many of the villages were reluctant to visit the bank

branches for various reasons like long distance to be travelled, time lost, difficulty in following procedures and reluctance to visit branches for small value transactions.

- The Bank adopted a branchless banking model in select locations in four Southern States using a small Point Of Transaction (POT) device developed by two local vendors using a bouquet of locally available ICT applications.
- The adoption of new technology facilitated basic identification of the customer based on the survey details, eliminated procedural hassles like filling up challans, cheques, etc. for depositing/withdrawing money, provided automated voice guidance to the users in local language, etc. The device adopted was sturdy with a battery back-up to supplement long hours of power outage and could be connected to a car battery. The device was installed at the premises of the Business Correspondent at the village and the customers at village could visit the Business Correspondent at their convenience to carry out cash deposit or cash withdrawal. To facilitate transactions at the Business Correspondent's level, biometric cards containing the photograph and the basic KYC details of the customer were provided to identified villagers.
- The Bank has recently introduced on a pilot basis a loan product which would facilitate loan withdrawals and repayments involving small sums at the Business Correspondent level.
- The Bank is also planning to introduce remittance products for the card holders and factor in Government payouts such as pension, NREGP payments, etc. through the card holder's account.
- The Bank plans to commence a project to disburse group loans through the Business Correspondent to SHGs.
- The Bank intends to provide ancillary services like Utility Payments, Mobile bill payments, etc., through this account.

Experience of Andhra Bank

The State of Andhra Pradesh has been a great success story in micro finance and Andhra Bank plays a significant role in this story. The bank has 1289 branches spread all over the country and 918 branches are located in Andhra Pradesh. The rural and semi-urban branches constitute 59.89 per cent of the total branches giving an ample scope to be a forerunner in helping the poor and play a pivotal role in the mission of financial inclusion. The huge network of branches in rural/semi-urban areas provides a natural edge for the bank besides its robust financials and dedication and committed workforce.

Opening of No Frills Accounts

Possessing a bank account is a minimum requirement for any citizen so that banking channels are kept open to him.The bank has so far opened 1,41,826 no-frills accounts,with average balance of Rs. 430/- per account and Rs. 5/- for opening of account. A pilot scheme for achieving 100% financial inclusion by providing no-frills accounts has been implemented in Srikakulam district in Andhra Pradesh and Ganjam district in Orissa, where we happen to be the lead bank, in collaboration with other banks. This was a gigantic task and required a lot of coordination amongst banks, educating the customers, making due identification, etc.The task, however, was successfully completed by March 2007. It is proposed to extend the scheme to all other districts in the State of Andhra Pradesh.Access to minimum credit is increasingly being seen as a "right" of the customer, rather than a "facility" sanctioned by banks after so much of scrutiny. The bank has initiated steps to cover households to meet the credit needs for economic activities under the existing schemes and also to initiate steps for sanction of "General Purpose Credit cards" to the eligible and needy. This is expected to materialize at the earliest. SHGs are the most important vehicles of financial inclusion. The bank is in the forefront of SHG movement in the country with much emphasis in Andhra Pradesh. The bank also aims at preparing the individuals to avail viable loans by providing them necessary training to secure purpose based finance. Therefore, the SHGs and individual members are being trained in nine Rural Development Institutes of the bank. All the SHGs who have paid their bank loans promptly will be eligible for interest relief from Government of Andhra Pradesh i.e. the ultimate interest paid by the SHG is only 3% per annum. It is aimed to disburse Rs. 1000 crore during this year. The bank has also introduced some innovative systems for the benefit of members of SHGs like SHG Credit Cards, Janashree Bima Yojana Scheme (life cover), Swasthya Bima Yojana scheme (health cover), etc.

Andhra bank has installed several ATMs in rural and semiurban areas. However the constituents coming under financial inclusion are mostly illiterate and would not be in a position to use PIN numbers, etc. To facilitate the operation of ATMs by these people, for the first time, the bank has introduced biometric ATMs and also mobile ATMs carrying biometric facility. This is a modest beginning and will pave the way for more and more people getting benefited by this initiative.

The bank has also participated in a pilot project in Warangal district of Andhra Pradesh along with six other banks in payment of wages under National Rural Employment Guarantee Programme & Pensions under Social Security scheme through "smart cards": Six banks namely Andhra Bank, State Bank of India, State Bank of Hyderabad, Andhra Pradesh Grameena Vikas Bank, Union Bank of India and Axis Bank have taken up six mandals in Warangal district and are implementing the project with the support from Rural Development Department, Government of Andhra Pradesh. Connectivity is an issue while payments are made on line through cards. However, it has been overcome since business correspondents are doing the payments offline and transmitting the data when connectivity is vailable. The bank is enrolling suitable organisations as business correspondents. These business correspondents will in turn appoint Customer Service Points (CSPs) for payment at village level. At present, Village Organisation leaders are being utilized for this purpose. (around 10-15 SHGs federated at village level is called village organization) The correspondents also act as a facilitator for provision of micro finance, savings, and other financial services of the bank and financial Institutions.

The bank is offering micro insurance products like group insurance, life insurance, insurance to farmers to Pattabhi Agri Cards, insurance to SHGs, etc.The bank has selected 21 'Model' villages for overall development and 100% coverage of SHGs The bank, in coordination with the state government, has initiated necessary steps to bring the tenant farmers under one roof (Rythu Mithra Groups- RMGs/Joint Liability Groups-JLGs) to enable them to access institutional credit.The bank has initiated steps in mapping indebtedness of the farmers and implementing m through Prime Minister's relief package to farmers in 16 districts in Andhra Pradesh.

Future Plans of Andhra Bank

1. To extend the smart card scheme to all our lead districts viz. Srikakulam, Guntur, East Godavari, West Godavari, Ganjam and Gajapathi districts in First Phase and to cover the remaining districts in Andhra Pradesh by March 2009.
2. To give loans through smart cards to the farmers and other weaker sections.
3. To install more biometric ATMs in rural and semi urban areas.
4. To open exclusive Micro Finance branches
5. To introduce "Mobile" bio-metric ATMs.
6. To open Financial Literacy centers in all six Lead Districts by March 2008.
7. To finance more number of Urban Self Help Groups.
8. To implement total financial inclusion project in selected slums in urban areas.
9. To cover all SHGs under Micro Insurance by March 2009.

10. To cover all Tenant Farmers in service area of the bank through Joint Liability Groups (JLGs).
11. To develop 'Model' villages in each of 22 districts in Andhra Pradesh.

Experience of the State Bank of India (SBI)

The objective of State Bank of India in the present day context is to ensure financial inclusion of the whole population irrespective of areas and sectors. The 'inclusion' phenomenon cannot be confined to few pockets of area and people. The important question is increasing outreach and deepening penetration. There are two ways of doing it: (i) through the brick and mortar rural branches, (ii) outsourcing all the functions to a business correspondent in a particular area, viz., a state or with the help of business facilitators at a local level. Large scale roll out and rapid scaling up again is not possible without suitable technology intervention which is easy to use, robust, dependable and, at the same time, costefficient. SBI's answer to financial inclusion is the 'SBI Tiny project',which can in simple terms be defined as a "Bank in a Box".The entire set up consists of a cell phone which serves as POS machine, a finger print reader and a tiny printer, all of which can be packed into a 10 inch by 10 inch box. All these work on rechargeable batteries. SBI Tiny accounts (no frills accounts) are opened on the smart cards. The smart card is akin to an e-purse and stores information about the customer, the account number, finger prints as well as the balance in the account. The smart card can handle up to 16 accounts including loan accounts. This card is highly secure as it works on the bio-metric validation of the customer. The card works on the Radio Frequency Identification (RFID) technology. SBI is today using this technology in our smart cards which work in conjunction with a mobile or a hand held connectivity device which works on Near Field Communication Technology (NFC). Transactions are possible both in online and off line mode. It also permits the real time updation of balances in the card. By issuing a smart card to the rural customer, the cost of the transaction is reduced because we are dispensing with paper based transactions and shifting the actual operation of transacting on the account away from the branch to Customer Service Point/Provider (CSP) at the outlet in the location of the rural customer. SBI is running pilots at several places like Aizawl (Mizoram), Medak and Warangal (Andhra Pradesh), Pithoragarh (Uttarakhand) and West Garo Hills (Megalaya). Andhra Pradesh has been identified by our bank for carrying out disbursements Under national Rural Employment Guarantee Programme (NREGP) and other rural development schemes through SBI Tiny Card accounts in Warangal and Medak districts. The scheme is also being extended to areas like Chamoli and Pauri in Uttrakhand and Titabar in North East.

Concluding Observations

It is becoming increasingly apparent that addressing financial exclusion will require a holistic approach on the part of the banks in creating awareness about financial products, education, and advice on money management, debt counseling, savings and affordable credit. The banks would have to evolve specific strategies to expand the outreach of their services in order to promote financial inclusion. One of the ways in which this can be achieved in a cost-effective manner is through forging linkages with microfinance institutions and local communities. Banks should give wide publicity to the facility of no frills account. Technology can be a very valuable tool in providing access to banking products in remote areas. ATMs cash dispensing machines can be modified suitably to make them user friendly for people who are illiterate, less educated or do not know English. To sum up, banks need to redesign their business strategies to incorporate specific plans to promote financial inclusion of low income group treating it both a business opportunity as well as a corporate social responsibility. They have to make use of all available resources including technology and expertise available with them as well as the MFIs and NGOs. It may appear in the first instance that taking banking to the sections constituting "the bottom of the pyramid", may not be profitable but it should always be remembered that even the relatively low margins on high volumes can be a very profitable proposition. Financial inclusion can emerge as commercial profitable business. Only the banks should be prepared to think outside the box. A mechanism has to be developed for regulating and supporting the growth of mobile payments and banking in India. This is the key to the success of "Financial Inclusion". This mechanism presently does not exist and hence, there is confusion between telecom operators and banks as to how the M-Commerce system will work. There are many small initiatives which are presently underway to kick start mobile banking and payments. Their success will tell us how the under banked of India will pay tomorrow. The purpose of this article is to stress that, despite the vast size, heterogeneity and infrastructural constraints, it is very much practical to use ICT-based solutions to extend the financial services in the rural regions of our country as a conscious business strategy. It only requires appropriate vision enabled by suitable business model, appropriate technology choices and collaborative efforts of the different players in the arena.

References

Annual Policy Statement for 2006-07 by Dr. Y.V. Reddy, Governor, RBI

Banking Statistics, RBI, 2003 and Rural Population (India) Census, 2001.

Times of India, December 31, 2007

Recommendations of the Working Group on Micro Finance & Rural Credit.

The Economic Times, December 28, 2007.

Times of India, June 17, 2007.

Official Website of the Reserve Bank of India, www.rbi.org

Official Website of NABARD, *www.nabard.org*

8

NGOs AS INTERMEDIARIES BETWEEN GOVERNMENT, BANKS AND SELF HELP GROUPS IN IMPLEMENTATION OF MICRO CREDIT SCHEMES

M. ANBALAGAN & MS. A. DHANALAKSHMI

Introduction

The New Economic Policy and Livelihood Concern of the Poor

The Government of India initiated the New Economic Policy in 1991 largely due to the persuasion of international institutions such as IMF and World Bank and also to modify the economy through Structural Adjustment Programmes (SAP) to cope with global business. SAPs brought in a number of changes in the economy. With this background the IMF and World Bank combined with WTO in particular enforced a number of controlling mechanisms and also a standard set of menu that has been proposed by them and imposed as conditionalities and suggestions on debtor countries. As a result, our rural are left without any financial assistance for debt relief as subsidy linked loan from government. Therefore, credit squeeze was brought in where even the poor were indirectly asked to reduce their expenditure. But credit is increasingly considered as panacea in fighting poverty, and often considered as vehicle to effect social change. So, the unemployment, underemployment, an poverty rate has increased among rural people. In the absence of money-fetching jobs people some how have to gain access to money.

Part-I

Micro Credit and Role of NGOs in Implementing SHG Scheme

Concept of Micro Credit

Microcredit is the extension of very small loans (microloans) to the unemployed, to poor entrepreneurs and to others living in poverty who are not considered bankable. These individuals lack collateral, steady employment and a verifiable credit history and therefore cannot meet even the most minimal qualifications to gain access to traditional credit. Microcredit is a part of microfinance, which is the provision of a wider range of financial services to the very poor.

Microcredit is a financial innovation which originated in Bangladesh where it has successfully enabled extremely impoverished people to engage in self-employment projects that allow them to generate an income and, in many cases, begin to build wealth and exit poverty. Due to the success of microcredit, many in the traditional banking industry have begun to realize that these microcredit borrowers should more correctly be categorized as pre-bankable; thus, microcredit is increasingly gaining credibility in the mainstream finance industry and many traditional large finance organizations are contemplating microcredit projects as a source of future growth. Although almost everyone in larger development organizations discounted the likelihood of success of microcredit when it was begun in its modern incarnation as pilot projects with ACCION and Muhammad Yunus in the mid-1970s, the United Nations declared 2005 the International Year of Microcredit.

The *World Bank* estimates that there are now more than 7,000 microfinance institutions, serving some 16 million poor people in developing countries. CGAP experts estimate that 500 million households benefit from these small loans. *Cambodia* and *Kenya* were put forward as examples. Asia and the Pacific region represent 83% of the opened accounts in developing countries, which is equivalent to 17 accounts for 100 persons. In November *1997*, more than 2000 delegates from 100 countries gathered at a Microcredit *Summit* in *Washington, DC,* with the goal of reaching 100 million of the world's poorest families, with credit for self-employment and other financial and business services by the year *2005*. Support for these goals has come from prominent world leaders and major financial institutions. Micro Finance may be good instrument for poverty alleviation using cooperative structure as a strategy. World Bank (2001)[1].

The *Economic and Social Council* of the *United Nations* proclaimed the year *2005* as the *International Year of Microcredit* to call for building inclusive financial sectors and strengthening the powerful, but often untapped, entrepreneurial spirit existing in communities around the world. There are five goals associated with "The Year" which are:

1. Assess and promote the contribution of microfinance and microcredit to the SHGs;
2. Increase public awareness and understanding of microfinance and microcredit as vital parts of the development equation;
3. Promote *inclusive* financial sectors;
4. Support sustainable access to financial services, and
5. Encourage innovation and new partnerships by promoting and supporting strategic partnerships to build and expand the outreach and success of microcredit and microfinance for all.

Microcredit Awarded Nobel Peace

Grameen Bank and its founder *Muhammad Yunus* were awarded the *Nobel Peace Prize* for 2006. *The press release* states:

"The Norwegian Nobel Committee has decided to award the Nobel Peace Prize for 2006, divided into two equal parts, to Muhammad Yunus and Grameen Bank for their efforts to create economic and social development from below. Lasting peace can not be achieved unless large population groups find ways in which to break out of poverty.

Micro-credit is one such means. Development from below also serves to advance democracy and human rights. Muhammad Yunus has shown himself to be a leader who has managed to translate visions into practical action for the benefit of millions of people, not only in Bangladesh, but also in many other countries. Loans to poor people without any financial security had appeared to be an impossible idea. From modest beginnings three decades ago, Yunus has, first and foremost through Grameen Bank, developed micro-credit into an ever more important instrument in the struggle against poverty. Grameen Bank has been a source of ideas and models for the many institutions in the field of micro-credit that have sprung up around the world. Every single individual on earth has both the potential and the right to live a decent life. Across cultures and civilizations, Yunus and Grameen Bank have shown that even the poorest of the poor can work to bring about their own development.

Micro-credit has proved to be an important liberating force in societies where women in particular have to struggle against repressive social and economic conditions. Economic growth and political democracy can not achieve their full potential unless the female half of humanity participates on an equal footing with the male. Yunus's long-term vision is to eliminate poverty in the world. That vision can not be realised by means of micro-credit alone. But Muhammad Yunus and Grameen Bank have shown that, in the continuing efforts to achieve it, micro-credit must play a major part."

Microfinance Merger

Kiva was founded in October 2005 by Matt and Jessica Flannery.[2] It is run by a team with experience in *microfinance* and technology.[3] The founders came up with the idea for Kiva, which means "unity" in Swahili, after spending time in East Africa.[4]

Kiva.org,[5] was the first person-to-person micro-lending Website that enabled an individual to lend money to a micro-entrepreneur in the developing world. This came to be known as "the merger between Microfinance and Web 2.0" due to its ability to create atransparent, connective and affordable option for anyone on the Internet to lend directly to the working poor. Inspired by Mohammad Yunus and Grameen Bank, microcredit was taken online. Kiva allows *microfinance*[6] institutions around the world, called "Field Partners", to post profiles of qualified local *entrepreneurs* on its website. Lenders browse and choose an entrepreneur they wish to fund. Kiva aggregates loan capital from individual lenders and transfers it to the appropriate Field Partners to disburse and administer. As the entrepreneurs repay their loans, the Field Partners remit funds back to Kiva. Once a loan is fully repaid, the Kiva lenders can withdraw their principal or re-loan it to another entrepreneur.

MicroPlace.com, a wholly-owned subsidiary of eBay, was launched on October 2007. This website also caters to the micro-borrower with a little difference from Kiva.org. The big difference between MicroPlace and Kiva...is that loans will be securitized (and therefore potentially trade-able), and lenders will earn interest. Unlike Kiva, lenders on MicroPlace invest in microcredit by purchasing securities. Funds generated by these sales are then invested in microcredit institutions around the world. MFIs, in turn, solicit clients, make loans and collect payments-they do their normal day-to-day business. Once client payments are in, the institutional investors receive their loan (plus interest) who can then pay back their investors-people who purchased those original securities. It's not as simple a model as Kiva's, but its differences are very important.

Kiva is a non-profit as it's very difficult to become a SEC-registered broker/dealer. MicroPlace, on the other hand, had the institutional and financial backing of eBay, allowing it to go through the complex regulatory application process and to put up the necessary money for the SEC to sign off. Lenders' funds are transferred to Kiva through *PayPal,* which does not collect its usual fees in this case[7]. Field Partners generally charge interest from their borrowers, although Kiva claims to keep track of how much interest is charged and will not work with those charging unfair interest rates[8]. Kiva lenders do not receive any interest because of US Government regulations[9] Kiva claims that its borrowers have a historical repayment rate of about 99.7%[10].

Part-II

Micro Credit in India: Some Recent Developments

The characteristic of the poor with low incomes, very little savings, frequent credit requirement in small doses for various pressing needs do not corroborate with the banking procedure which resulted in alienating the banks from lending to poor individually. Further the high transaction costs, the perceived risks due to the absence of any security and experience of bad recovery in poverty alleviation programmes compounded the perception. In view of this and with a view to developing a supplementary credit delivery mechanism to reach the poor in a cost-effective, efficient and sustainable manner with built-in advantages to both banks and their rural clients, NABARD launched in February 1992 the pilot project on linking Self Help Groups with banks in consultation with RBI/Banks/NGOs. The Reserve Bank of India gave guidelines of Banks.

The Government of India is mulling some regulation for the Microfinance/Microcredit industry in India and in his budget speech on 28 February 2006, the Finance Minister P. Chidambaram[11] said "I had proposed major initiatives in respect of micro finance in the last Budget. RBI has since issued guidelines to enable banks to appoint banking correspondents and banking agents. A window to access ECB funds has also been opened. A Bill to provide a formal statutory framework for the promotion, development and regulation of the micro finance sector will be introduced in this session".

At a seminar on microfinance organised by the Confederation of Indian Industry (CII) and the Small Industries Development Bank of India (SIDBI) in Delhi, in September 2006, the Chairman & Managing Director of the Indian Bank, K.C. Chakrabarty,[12] said "Micro Finance Institutions are limited in their delivery-most are simply engaged in lending. Micro finance is also about saving, insurance, and investment. Sadly, these products are not being delivered. So far, micro finance initiatives have failed to link the beneficiaries to the capital market, and have met with little success when it comes to developing micro-entrepreneurship. In most of rural India, people still borrow to meet their daily consumption, not to fund an income generating enterprise".

Micro credit serves best those who have identified an economic opportunity and who are in a position to capitalise on that opportunity if they are provided with a small amount of ready cash. Thus, those poor who work in stable or growing economies, who have demonstrated an ability to undertake the proposed activities in an entrepreneurial manner, and who have demonstrated a commitment to repay their debts (instead of feeling that the credit represents some form of social re-vindication), are the best candidates for micro credit." (Satyamurti & S. Haokip 2002)[13].

NGOs as Intermediaties

The New Economic Policy brought a number of changes in our economic structure. Slowly and steady the people faced unemployment and unemployment rather seriously and, as a result, flow of money in the hands of lower middle class and poor have been reduced. Lack of money posed a serious threat to the livelihood issues of the rural mass in particular. There is no instrument by which money could be supplied to them. But people need to gain access to money for their survival. Through NGOs intervention and enablement they started realize that unless they have money in their hands, invest it properly and produce something that will sell in the market, their survival will still be a question mark.

NGOs play an important role in the society. Due to the changing needs of the society the NGOs not only need to continue to play their role but also expand into newer areas. They have understood the social reality to an extent that they can no longer continue the model of charity if they have to cope with the present situation as intermediaries. NGOs play multi-dimensional roles as the only direct link between several actors in the economy both as Community Based Organisations and as Civil Society Organisations. The emergence of SHGs among the poor as CBOs is the effort of NGOs. The situation warrants the effective intervention of a promotional agency with altruistic outlook for the formation of Self Help Groups (Srinivasan Girija, 2002)[14].

The NGOs are involved either as facilitators playing a catalytic role in formation of Self Help Groups and nurturing them in the initial period or as financial intermediaries i.e. providing loan assistance (micro-credit) to SHGs/individuals till they are formally linked with Banks, NABARD, RMK and TNCDW, as a strategy, are encouraging small NGOs to take SHG promotion and linkage as an add-on activity (World Bank Report, 2000) [15]. Technical support is extended in the form of quality training and capacity building to these NGOs. NABARD, RMK and TNCDW also provide small financial assistance to NGOs for taking up promotion of SHGs in order to obtain both NGOs as well as SHGs (Prasad, R.R. 2003)[16]. The more attractive scheme with less effort is "Self Help Group". It is a tool to remove poverty and improve the rural development. The intermediary role of promoting, facilitating and strengthening of groups have to be taken up by reputed NGOs and their services are indispensable for the development of people living below poverty line, between rural or urban.

Origin and Concept of SHGs

The origin of SHGs is from the brainchild of Grameen Bank of Bangladesh, which was founded by Mohammed Yunus. SHGs were started and formed in 1975. In India NABARD is initiated in 1986-87. But the real effort was taken after 1991-92 from the linkage of SHGs with the banks. A SHG is a small economically homogeneous affinity group of the rural poor voluntarily coming together to save small amount regularly, which are deposited in a common fund to meet members emergency needs and to provide collateral free loans decided by the group. (Abhaskumar Jha 2000).[17] They have been recognized as useful tool to help the poor and as an alternative mechanism to meet the urgent credit needs of poor through thrift (V. M. Rao 2002)[18] SHG is a media for the development of saving habit among the women (S. Rajamohan 2003).[19] SHGs enhance the equality of status of women as participants, decision-makers and beneficiaries in the democratic, economic, social and cultural spheres of life. (Ritu Jain 2003).[20] The basic principles of the SHGs are group approach, mutual trust, organization of small and manageable groups, group cohesiveness, sprit of thrift, demand based lending, collateral free, women friendly loan, peer group pressure in repayment, skill training capacity building and empowerment (N. Lalitha, 2002).[21] As women's SHGs or sangha have been promoted by a wide range of government and non-governmental agencies, they now make up 90% of all SHGs *(http://www.jammuandkashmirbank.com/trust/jul_sep_2002/leadstory.html).*[22]

Formation of SHGs

Self Help Groups are voluntary associations of people with homogenous background and interest, perceived of genuine need to help each other and work together for securing greater economic and financial strength for their development. The groups can both be informal as well as formal having regular thrift and create common fund so that members can avail micro credit (ranging from Rs. 300/- to 1000) to meet their immediate domestic needs and as a temporary relief. SHGs are working in democratic style. The number of members in a group is restricted to 20. Among them a member is selected as an 'animator' and two members are selected as the representatives. The animator is selected for the period of two years. The group members meet every week. They discuss about the group savings, rotation of sangha funds, bank loan, repayment of loan, repayment of loan, social and community action programmes. Further, NGOs facilitated SHGs to avail Microfinance (beyond micro credit) to invest in any Income Generating Activity.

How Self-help Groups Work

As women's SHGs or sangha have been promoted by a wide range of government and non- governmental agencies, they now make up 90% of all SHGs. Therefore, the majority of the issues discussed in this paper are particularly relevant for women. As Indian women do not generally have the same opportunities to migrate for wage work as men due to social obligations and taboos, it is particularly important for women to improve employment and income earning opportunities in situ, and in a way that is compatible with their role in child care. The rules and regulations of SHGs vary according to the preferences of the members and those facilitating their formation. A common characteristic of the groups is that they meet regularly (typically once per week or once per fortnight) to collect the savings from members, decide to which member to give a loan, discuss joint activities (such as training, running of a communal business, etc.), and to mitigate any conflicts that might arise. Most SHGs have an elected chairperson, a deputy, a treasurer, and sometimes other office holders. It appears as though the vast majority of rural SHGs invest the loan amounts in a mix of consumption and productive purposes. As credit needs of the poor are determined in a complex socio-economic milieu, where the dividing line between credit for 'consumption' and 'productive' purposes is rather blurred, it is difficult to adopt the traditional banking approach to lending and to insist that loans are not used for consumption. Most SHGs therefore start without any external financial capital by saving regular contributions by the members. These contributions can be very small (e.g. 10 Rs. per week). After a period of consistent savings (e.g. 6 months to one year) the SHGs start to give loans from savings in the form of small internal loans for micro enterprise activities and consumption. Only those SHGs that have utilised their own funds well are assisted with external funds through linkages with banks and other financial intermediaries.

Most development initiatives working through SHGs are specifically targeting the poorest people. For example, the World Bank funded Andhra Pradesh District Poverty Initiatives Project aims, amongst others, at supporting investment in sub-projects proposed by grass-root institutions of the poor to accelerate their entry and expand their involvement in social and economic activities. In order to reach the poor, this project used a three- fold system of targeting: geographic targeting (selection of the poorest districts, and within these the poorest mandals), group targeting (through formation of group-based activities for the poor) and self targeting (through a focus on small, technologically manageable investments that are attractive primarily to the poor organising themselves into common interest groups) (World Bank 2000).[23] But, it is generally accepted that SHGs often do not include the poorest of the poor, for reasons such as:

(a) Social factors (the poorest are often those who are socially marginalised because of caste affiliation and those who are most skeptical of the potential benefits of collective action).

(b) Economic factors (the poorest often do not have the financial resources to contribute to the savings and pay membership fees; they are often the ones who migrate during the lean season, thus making group membership difficult).

(c) Intrinsic biases of the implementing organisations (as the poorest of the poor are the most difficult to reach and motivate, implementing agencies tend to leave them out, preferring to focus on the next wealth category). Efforts are made to overcome this bias, e.g. through participatory wealth ranking at the community level, or by using indices to identify the poorest. Simanowitz *et al.* 1999[24] argue that active poverty-targeting is required to make sure that the poorest are included in microfinance programs. But including them in SHGs is not enough-programs need to be designed such that realistic investment opportunities for these poorest households exist.

Thus, from a social empowerment point of view, the SHG mechanism seems to be very effective for the very poor and disadvantaged. But from an IGA development point of view, it is necessary to bring in the element of selectivity and eligibility, bearing in mind that not everybody has entrepreneurial potential and capabilities. The question then arises how the SHG mechanism could at the same time be an appropriate mechanism for IGA development. Once SHGs are established and start saving, they generally attempt after some time to gain access to larger amounts of capital in order to broaden the range of micro-enterprises available to them. The linkages between SHGs and banks are discussed here under.

Sources of Capital and Links Between SHGs and Banks

SHGs can only fulfill a role in the rural economy if group members have access to financial capital and markets for their products and services. While the groups initially generate their own savings through thrift (whereby thrift implies savings created by postponing almost necessary consumption, while savings imply the existence of surplus wealth), their aim is often to link up with financial institutions in order to obtain further loans for investments in rural enterprises. NGOs and banks are giving loans to SHGs either as "matching loans" (whereas the loan amount is proportionate to the group's savings) or as fixed amounts, depending on the group's record of repayment, recommendations by group facilitators, collaterals provided, etc.

SHGs are increasingly linking up with financial institutions to obtain formal credit. It is estimated that there are now 500,000 SHGs in India, with a membership of 8 million people, who are linked to about 20,000 rural outlets of more than 440 banks, with an advance portfolio of more than 240 million $ (Wilson 2002) [25]. This has been a tremendous achievement, considering that during the first four years after NABARD first introduced its SHG linkage programme (i.e. between 1992 and 1996), less than 3,000 groups were borrowing from banks. In India, micro-finance has been defined by the task-force on Micro-finance constituted by the National Bank for Agriculture and Rural Development (NABARD) as "provision of thrift, credit and other financial services and products of very small amounts to the poor to enable them to raise their income and improve their living standards". The upper limit of amount is fixed at Rs.25000 to be categorised as micro-finance. (Satyamurti & S. Haokip 2002) [26].

How SHGs Save?

Self-help groups mobilise savings from their members, and may then on-lend these funds to one another, usually at apparently high rates of interest which reflect the members' understanding of the high returns they can earn on the small sums invested in their micro-enterprises, and the even higher cost of funds from money lenders. If they do not wish to use the money, they may deposit it in a bank. If the members' need for funds exceeds the group's accumulated savings, they may borrow from a bank or other organisation, such as a micro-finance non-government or animation, to augment their own fund. The system is very flexible. The group aggregates the small individual saving and borrowing requirements of its members, and the bank needs only to maintain one account for the group as a single entity. The banker must assess the competence and integrity of the group as a micro-bank, but once he has done this he need not concern himself with the individual loans made by the group to its members, or the uses to which these loans are put. He can treat the group as a single customer, whose total business and transactions are probably similar in amount to the average for his normal customers, because they represent the combined banking business of some twenty 'micro-customers'.

Any bank branch can have a small or a large number of such accounts, without having to change its methods of operation. Unlike many customers, demand from SHGs is not price-sensitive. Illiterate village women are sometimes better bankers than some with more professional qualifications. They know that rapid access to funds is more important than their cost, and they also know, even though they might not be able to calculate the figures, that the typical micro-enterprise earns well over 500% return on the small sum invested in it (Harper, M, 1998, p. 15)[27]. The groups thus charge themselves high rates of interest; they are happy to take advantage of the generous spread that the NABARD subsidised bank lending rate of 12% allows them, but they are also willing to borrow from NGO/ MFIs which on-lend funds from SIDBI at 15%, or from 'new generation' institutions such as Basics Finance at 18.5% or 21%.. NABARD is presently operating three models of linkage of banks with SHGs and NGOs *(http://www.nabard.org/roles/mcid/shgbanklink.htm)*[28].

Model-1

In this model, the bank itself acts as a Self Help Group Promoting Institution (SHPI). It takes initiatives in forming the groups, nurtures them over a period of time and then provides credit to them after satisfying itself about their maturity to absorb credit. About 16% of SHGs and 13% of loan amounts are using this model (as of March 2002).

Model-2

In this model, groups are formed by NGOs (in most of the cases) or by government agencies. The groups are nurtured and trained by these agencies. The bank then provides credit directly to the SHGs, after observing their operations and maturity to absorb credit. While the bank provides loans to the groups directly, the facilitating agencies continue their interactions with the SHGs. Most linkage experiences begin with this model with NGOs playing a major role. This model has also been popular and more acceptable to banks, as some of the difficult functions of social dynamics are externalised. About 75% of SHGs and 78% of loan amounts are using this model.

Model-3

Due to various reasons, banks in irst, they promote the groups, nurture and train them and then approach banks for bulk loans for on-lending to the SHGs. About 9% of SHGs and 13% of loan amounts are using this model.

Once SHGs are established and start saving, they some areas are not in a position to even finance SHGs promoted and nurtured by other agencies. In such cases, the NGOs act as both facilitators and micro- finance intermediaries. F generally attempt after some time to gain access to larger amounts of capital in order to broaden the range of micro-enterprises available to them.

Part–III

CRHSE: A Study

In view of the foregoing analysis, it is felt important to understand how Centre for Rural Health and Social Education (CRHSE) has changed the face of the Self Help Group Product, the strategies adopted by CRHSE with respect to the SHGs–the formation, training and guidance in marketing. To study how women Self Help Groups products are branded and marketed in the rural markets. Finally the achievements of CHRSE has been presented in this paper.

CRHSE: An Overview

Centre for Rural Health and Social Education, located at Yelagiri hills has been stablished in 1978 and it efficiently, effectively and excellently headed by the founder director Karmayogi Dr. Bennet Benjamine. The main objectives of the project are to promote self supporting health systems among the rural and tribal people through education and training; to develop a community-based health system which is inexpensive; to evolve programmes promoting the welfare of the women, landless, the unemployed and the socially oppressed in the rural and tribal areas. It organises field-based skills and training in community health and development, provides technical support through programme evaluation and consultancy services, promotes environmental awareness through programmes like formation of eco-cells and community forest action group. Apart from the above, CRHSE is now came forward to house 50 children who are orphaned by the Tsunami strike in its Human Resource Development Centre (HRDC) on Yelagiri Hills beyond the barriers of Caste, Creed or Community. This programme has been implemented at present 50 children are benefited, which includes the provision of Food, Accommodation, Clothing, Health Care, Education and Placement in life.

CRHSE has Got the Following Main and Ancillary Objectives

The main objectives are "to evolve programmes promoting the welfare of working women, the unemployed, the landless and poor peasants, the down-trodden and of the economically and socially depressed people in the rural and tribal areas". The ancillary objectives are: enable SHGs to achieve autonomy and sustainability through Cluster Level Federations, build capacity of CLF for independent and democratic decision-making, hand over responsibilities of support of SHGs so that NGO can concentrate on training, linkages and quality control, to reduce NGOs burden of managing large number of SHGs with increasing outreach. Apart from the above the CRHSE has taken additional responsibility to facilitate linkage between SHGs and Govt. Banks, Agencies etc., enhance bargaining power over the rights, privileges of SHGs, access development information and marketing linkages, access policy-making bodies, building solidarity, mutually share experiences and expertise, assist weaker SHGs, achieving sustainability through branding their products and assisting them in marketing their products in the rural markets through "SEM" Brand.

"SEM" Mahalir Federation (CRHSE Model)

The CRHSE has developed a model called "SEM" Mahalir Federation. It is a Network of several SHGs in a given area (20 SHGs) for economic and social empowerment of women members and their capacity-building. It step up development of women through collective effort. And it is a democratic body, uniting SHGs for common cause (of SHGs, by SHG for SHGs). CRHSE's implement the above objectives through the following functions, namely the main and ancillary functions, presented here:

1. Platform for sharing information, experience and expertise.
2. Strengthening member SHGs.
3. New Group formation.
4. Training & Facilitation of new SHGs.
5. Monitoring and improving performance of SHGs on a monthly basis.
6. Participatory Grading of SHGs.
7. Ensuring Internal Audit once in six months.
8. Motivating SHGs for Community Action Programme.
9. Linking SHGs with Government, Banks, Agencies, Markets, Insurance companies, etc.
10. Identification ad Utilisation of Local Resources.
11. Facilitating Banding and Marketing f SHG products and purchase of stocks.

12. Organising Skill/Training programmes.
13. Facilitating proper Books of Accounts, Registers etc.
14. Ensuring adequate representation of women in Panchayats and attendance in Grama Sabha meetings.
15. Lobbying to get infra-structural facilities for villages.
16. Creating awareness and advocacy for women's rights.

Achievements of CRHSE

This NGO had already built 1045 SHG falling under the Federation of "SEM" Mahalir Manrams (CRHSE Model). It is the network of several SHGs in a given area for economic and social empowerment of women, their capability building, and it is a democratic body uniting SHGs for common cause. The registered SHGs covering in them about 18700 rural and tribal women all of whom live below poverty line. Their total savings up to 31.03.06 was Rs. 2,16,88,812/=, internal loan amounting to Rs. 4,34,56,154. In all 414518 members have been benefited through micro-credit. The members of SHG engage themselves in different Income Generating Activities (CRHSE Annual Report, 2006).[29]

The Real Issues to be Tackled are

Based on the above analysis, it appears that there exist a number of unsolved issues relating to healthy development of micro credit as a tool of poverty alleviation and rural development. Such real issues include, primarily the following:

1. Whether micro-credit is an appropriate tool for poverty reduction efforts ?
2. What is the impact of micro-credit on rural indebtedness?
3. What is the impact of micro-credit on rural economy?
4. What is the real default rate of micro-credit clients?
5. Cost of group formation and problems of over convergence?

Concluding Observations

Now one could imagine the achievements of SHGs with the guidance of NGOs acting as the levers between SHGs and Banks. There are many advantages of Linkage Programmes enjoyed by both Banks and Self Help Groups. It is evident that the NGOs organized rural people as SHGs and motivated them to save and create common fun, which in turn facilitated members to use money through micro-credit in a small way and it relieved them from the oppressive money lenders. Therefore the role of NGOs in general and CRHSE in particular are indispensable for the socio-economic revolution of our economy, especially in alleviating the poverty of those living below poverty. "SEM" Federation of SHGs enabled "Women centric approach to developrnent and poverty alleviation of SHGs" to "a frame work for sustainability." Micro-credit paved the way to avail micro financial in initiatives from banks to generate income, which led to many micro enterprises. In the long run micro enterprises will emerge as macro enterprises to face the global competitions.

Notes

1. World Bank Report (2001), The Mirco-Finance Revolution: Sustainable Finance for the Poor, pp. 121.
2. "Kiva Facts At A Glance" on *kiva.org*
3. Los Angeles *Times* Article on Kiva"
4. "Official Kiva.org Facts & Statistics Alexa.com-Kiva.org traffic details Extra Helping by Rob Walker, January 27, 2008, New York, *Times Magazine.*
5. "What We Do" on Kiva.org
6. "Supporters" on Kiva.org
7. Kiva FAQ: When I pay through PayPal, is PayPal Taking a fee?: "Kiva.org is the first organization PayPal is supporting by providing free payment processing."
8. Kiva FAQ: Do Kiva.org's Field Partners charge interest to the entrepreneurs?: "Our Field Partners are free to charge interest, but Kiva.org will not partner with an organization that charges exorbitant interest rates."

9. Kiva FAQ: Do I get interest on my loan?: "Providing interest to our lenders is legally complex and we hope to provide this option soon as the regulations of the US Government allow."

10. Kiva FAQ Will I get my money back?: "To date, Kiva.org's repayment rate is 99.74%."

11. P. Chidambaram, 28th February. 2006. In the Budget Speech.

12. C.K. Chakrabarty (2006), Seminar Proceedings on Micro-finance.

13. Satyamurti, V. and Haokip S. (2002), Micro-finance: Concepts and Delivery Channels in India. New Delhi: AIAMED. *http://www.alternative-finance.org.uk/cgibin/* summary.pl?id=151&language=E.

14. Srinivasan Girija (2002), Linking Self Help Groups with Banks in India. Small Enterprise Development, December Vol. 13, No. 4, pp. 47-57.

15. The World Bank, South Asia Regional Office. Project appraisal document on a proposed credit in the amount of SDR 82.9 million (US$111.0 million equivalent) to India for the Andhra Pradesh District Poverty Initiatives Project. Report No: 20089-IN. Mar 20, 2000.

16. Prasad R.R. (2003), Women's Empowerment through NGO Interventions: Approach, *Kurukshetra*, June 2003, pp.4-11.

17. Abhaskumar Jha (2004), "Lending to the Poor: Designs for Credit", *EPW*, Vol. XXXV, No.8 and 9.

18. Rao, V.M. (2003), Women Self Help Groups, Profiles from Andhra Pradesh and Karnataka", *Kurukshetra*, Vol. 50, N0. 6, pp. 26-32.

19. Rajamohan, S. (2003) , "Activities of Self Help Groups in Virudhunagar District-A Study, TNJC, pp. 25-29.

20. Ritu Jain, (2003), "Socio-Economics Impact Through Self Help Groups", *Yojana*, Vol. 47, No. 7, pp. 11-12.

21. Lalitha, N. (2002). "Women Thrift and Credit Groups-Breaking the Barriers at the Gross Roots", *Peninsular Economist*, Vol. XII, No. 2, pp. 188-195.

22. *(http://www.jammuandkashmirbank.com/trust/jul_sep_2002/leadstory.html).*

24. Simanowitz, A., Nkuna, B. and Kasim, S. (1999, updated June 2000), Overcoming the Obstacles of Identifying the Poorest Families: Using Participatory Wealth Ranking (PWR), the CASHPOR House Index (CHI), and Other Measurements to Identify and Encourage the Participation of the Poorest Families, Especially the Women of Those Families. Meeting of Councils Plenary Papers. *http://www.alternativefinance.* org.uk/cgi-bin/ summary.pl?id=282&language=E.

25. Wilson, K. (2002), The Role of Self Help Group Bank Linkage Programme in Preventing Rural Emergencies in India. Paper presented at the Seminar

on SHG-bank Linkage Programme at New Delhi on 25th and 26th November 2002. Delhi: Micro Credit Innovations Department, National Bank of Agriculture and Rural Development.

26. Satyamurti, V. and Haokip S. (2002), Micro-finance: Concepts and Delivery Channels in India. New Delhi: AIAMED. *http://www.alternative-finance.org.uk/cgibin/* summary.pl?id=151&language=E.

27. Harper, M. (1998), Why are commercial banks not entering the micro-finance market? Paper produced as consultant to SDC, October 1998. *http://www.alternativefinance. org.uk/cgi-bin summary.pl?id=32&language=E*

28. *(http://www.nabard.org/roles/mcid/shgbanklink.htm)*

29. Annual Report, CRHSE (2006).

9

FINANCIAL INCLUSION FOR INCLUSIVE GROWTH

James Manalel

The economic growth that India has attained in recent years is truly remarkable so much so that it is now customary to discuss the growth story of China and in the same fashion that of India. For a country that has long been accustomed to a humble (Hindu rate) growth rate of 3 to 4 per cent to attain a three-fold increase of around 9 per cent is no mean achievement! Yet can we say that India is really shining? Is there something mission in this wonderful growth story? These doubts arise because despite the overall growth in the GDP, the benefits of economic growth have not equitably reached different parts of the society. The rural and agricultural sector, in particular, has not gained the desired momentum of growth and development (Shetty, 2006). Agriculture which is still India's most important sector is growing only at a little over 2 per cent. Vast segment of the population, especially the underprivileged sections of the society have not been touched by this growth story. One out of every five Indian is still below poverty line! Clearly, a trillion-dollar economy that boasts of the highest number of billionaires in Asia must include the two-thirds of India that remains 'unbanked' before staking a claim to wider progress. In other words, India's economic prosperity has been severely marred by the fact that it has not been inclusive. In a democracy, economic growth, if it is to be sustainable, has to be inclusive of all categories and sections of the people.

The objective of this paper, however, is to examine the question of inclusiveness of growth only from the angle of financial inclusion. The basic assumption here is that financial inclusion is critical for achieving inclusive growth and only such a growth is sustainable. The paper after explaining the concept of financial inclusion and the dimension of the problem of financial exclusion proceeds to analyse the reasons for financial exclusion and the impact it has on especially the marginalized sections of the society. This is followed by a review of the policies and strategies adopted in our country in order to tackle this challenge. The paper concludes with a note on possible course of action for the future.

What is Financial Inclusion?

Financial inclusion (FI) according to the Committee on Financial Inclusion is delivery of financial services at an affordable cost to the vast sections of disadvantaged and low-income groups (Ministry of Finance, 2008). The various financial services include credit, savings, insurance, payments and remittance facilities. The objective of Financial Inclusion is to extend the scope of activities of the organised financial system (viz., the banking system) to include within its ambit all categories of population without any discrimination. Financial Inclusion rests on three pillars viz. access to financial services, affordability of such services and actual utilization of such services (Shetty, 2006). Financial Inclusion can be achieved only if all the three pillars show affirmative results. Thus, the ABC of Financial Inclusion is Advice, Banking and Credit. It must also be noted that while for developing countries like India, generally the process of Financial Inclusion starts with opening of savings bank accounts the process, at a later stage, must also incorporate credit facilities and other financial services such as insurance. Hence internationally financial inclusion has been viewed in a much wider perspective.

What is Financial Exclusion?

Another way of understanding financial inclusion is by analyzing what is financial exclusion. Financial exclusion signifies the lack of access by certain segments of the society to appropriate, low-cost, fair and safe financial products and services from mainstream providers. Financial exclusion is thus a key policy concern, because the options for operating a household budget, or a micro/small enterprise, without mainstream financial services can often be expensive (Mohan, 2006). This process becomes self-reinforcing and can often be an important factor in social exclusion, especially for communities with limited access to financial products, particularly in rural areas. It is now well documented that countries with high levels of inequality record higher levels of financial exclusion (Kempson, 2006). Financial exclusion can be thought of in two ways. One is exclusion from the payments system –i.e. not having access to a bank account. The second type of exclusion is from formal credit markets, requiring the excluded to approach informal and exploitative markets.

The scope of financial inclusion can be expanded in two ways (Leeladhar, 2005):

(a) through state-driven intervention by way of statutory enactments (like the Community Reinvestment Act in USA, or making it a statutory right to have bank account as in France).

(b) through voluntary effort by the banking community itself for evolving various strategies to bring within the ambit of the banking sector the large strata of society.

After nationalisation of major banks in India in 1969, there was a significant expansion of branch network to unbanked and under banked areas and stepping up of lending to agriculture, small industry and business. Hence, in recent years, the focus is on establishing the basic right of every person to have access to affordable basic banking services.

International Experience in Promoting Financial Inclusion

It must be pointed out that Financial Inclusion is a concern not only of developing economies. An interesting feature which emerges from the international practice is that the more developed the society is, the greater the thrust on empowerment of the common person and low income groups. Thus, there is a Financial Inclusion Task Force in the UK and they have set up a Financial Inclusion Fund. Further they have created Post Office Current Account for those unable or unwilling to access a basic bank account. In the USA, between 9.5 per cent and 20 per cent of households lack a bank account. To correct this situation, a civil rights legislation known as the Community Reinvestment Act, has been enacted which ensures affirmative action by banks for financial inclusion (Shetty, 2006).

In Canada the Access to Basic banking Services Regulations was introduced to ensure that all Canadians obtain personal bank accounts without difficulty. In 1984 the Banking Act made access to a bank account a legal right in France and in Sweden, banks cannot refuse to open a saving or deposit account under Section 2 of the Banking Business Act of 1987. Thus two major kinds of policy responses have been implemented by central banks in response to financial exclusion: codes of practice and specific legislation. Countries such as France and Belgium have undertaken initiatives to require banks to open an affordable account with bare minimum facilities. Several other countries have introduced specific legislation that gives both, a universal right to a bank account and, spells out the precise nature of banking services to be provided as in France, Sweden etc.

Magnitude of the Problem in India

Extent of Exclusion

1. One common measure of financial inclusion is the percentage of adult population having bank accounts. Going by the available data on the number of savings bank accounts and assuming that one person has only one account, (which assumption may not be correct as many persons could have more than one bank account) we find that on an all India basis only 59 per cent of adult population in the country have bank accounts–in other words 41 per cent of the population is unbanked. In rural areas the coverage is 39 per cent as against 60 per cent in urban areas (Thorat, 2007). Further, within the country, there is wide variation across states. For instance, the ratio for the state of Kerala is as high as 89 per cent while for Bihar it is only 33 per cent. In the North Eastern States like Nagaland and Manipur, the coverage was a meagre 21 per cent and 27 per cent, respectively. The Northern Region, comprising the states of Haryana, Chandigarh and Delhi, has a high coverage ratio of 84 per cent. The unbanked population is higher in the North Eastern and Eastern regions. Another point is that compared to the developed world, the coverage of our financial services is quite low. For instance, as per a recent survey commissioned by British Bankers' Association, 92 to 94 per cent of the population of UK has either current or savings bank account (Leeladhar, 2005).
2. The extent of exclusion from credit markets is much more, as the number of loan accounts constituted only 14 per cent of adult population. In rural areas, the coverage is just 9.5 per cent against 14 per cent in urban areas. Here also the credit coverage was significantly low in North Eastern, Eastern and Central Regions (Thorat, 2007).
3. The survey of indebtedness carried out by the NSSO reported that in 2002, three out of four rural households and four out

of five urban households do not have bank loan. In the eleven years from 1991 to 2002 the banking system added only 4 per cent of rural households as its customers (Srinivasavan, 2007).

4. 51.4 per cent of farm households have no access to formal or informal sources of credit while 73 per cent have no access to formal sources of credit. Further, despite the vast network of bank branches, only 27 per cent of total farm households are indebted to formal sources (of which one-third also borrow from informal sources). Farm households not accessing credit from formal sources as a proportion to total farm households is especially high at 95.91 per cent, 81.26 per cent and 77.59 per cent in the North Eastern, Eastern and Central Regions respectively. Thus, apart from the fact that exclusion in general is large, it also varies widely across regions, social groups and asset holdings. The poorer the group, the greater is the exclusion. (Ministry of Finance, 2008).

5. An even more disquieting trend was revealed by the recent All-India Debt and Investment Survey (AIDIS, 2002). It showed that while over a period of 40 years, the share of non-institutional sources of credit for cultivator households had declined sharply from about 93 per cent in 1951 to about 30 per cent in 1991, with the share of money lenders having declined from 69.7 per cent to 17.5 per cent, in more recent years (2002), the share of money lenders had again increased to 27 per cent, while that of non-institutional sources overall rose to 39 per cent (See, Tables 1 and 1a). In other words, notwithstanding the outreach of banking, the formal credit system has not been able to adequately penetrate the informal financial markets. Some of our past achievements like reduction in the stranglehold of moneylenders it appears is likely to be lost and our poor farmers left to the clutches of moneylenders (Mitra,2007; Chavan, 2007).

6. The share of deposits and credit in rural and semi urban areas have been showing a declining trend while it is increasing in

metropolitan areas. The total number of savings accounts as percentage of number of households was 137 in rural areas and 244 in urban areas in 1991. Despite reforms, by 2005, the position was no better at 131.5 in rural areas and 213 in urban areas. With respect to advances (credit accounts), it was even worse for rural households during the same period. The percentage of households with credit accounts fell from 44.3 per cent to 32.2 per cent during the same period (Mohan, 2006).

Table 1

Relative Share of Borrowing of Cultivator Households #

(per cent)

Sources of Credit	*1951*	*1961*	*1971*	*1981*	*1991*	*2002 $*
Non-institutional	92.7	81.3	68.3	36.8	30.6	38.9
of which:						
Money lenders	69.7	49.2	36.1	16.1	17.5	26.8
Institutional	7.3	18.7	31.7	63.2	66.3	61.1
of which:						
Co-operative societies, *etc.*	3.3	2.6	22.0	29.8	30.0	30.2
Commercial banks	0.9	0.6	2.4	28.8	35.2	26.3
Unspecified	-	-	-	-	3.1	-
Total	100.0	100.0	100.0	100.0	100.0	100.0

: Borrowing refers to outstanding cash dues.

$: AIDIS, NSSO, 59th Round, 2003.

Source: All India Debt and Investment Surveys, *Quoted in* Mohan, 2006.

7. There were 10 states in India which had more than half the adult population not having a deposit account and as many as 15 states in which less than one in ten adults had a loan account (Srinivasan, 2007).

8. Between rural and urban households, the share of institutional sources was lower in rural areas as compared to urban areas between 1991 to 2002. In other words, urban households relied less on non-institutional sources, particularly the moneylenders. But this did affect the cost of borrowed funds. The interest rate differntial between urban and rural housholds was more pronounced in the case of non-institutional sources at 4.2 per cent (Subba Rao, 2007).

Table 1a
Distribution of Credit by Credit Agencies

	1971	*1981*	*1991*	*2002*	*1981*	*1991*	*2002*
Credit Agencies	*Rural*				*Urban*		
	Cultivator Households				*Self- Employed*		
Institutional Agencies	31.7	63.2	66.3	61.1	57.7	67.1	67.2
Government	7.1	3.9	5.7	1.7	8.9	3.1	1.7
Co-op Society/Bank	22.0	29.8	23.6	30.2	15.6	14.5	22.4
Commercial Bank	2.4	28.8	35.2	26.3	31.2	24.7	33.6
Insurance	0.1	0.4	0.2	0.3	1.9	1.3	2.1
Provident Fund	0.1	0.3	0.5	0.2	0.1	0.3	0.2
Other Institutions	0.0	0.0	1.1	2.4	0.0	23.2	7.3
Non-Institutional Agencies	68.3	36.8	30.6	38.9	42.3	30.1	32.8
Landlord	8.1	3.7	3.7	0.9	0.8	0.6	0.4
Agricultural Money Lender	23.0	8.3	6.8	9.9	6.5	1.4	2.2
Professional Money Lender	13.1	7.8	10.7	16.9	9.1	9.9	17.4
Traders	8.4	3.1	2.2	2.6	5.9	3.7	1.8
Relatives and Friends	13.1	8.7	4.6	6.2	14.2	9.8	8.7
Others incl. doctors etc	2.6	5.2	2.6	2.4	5.8	4.6	2.4
	Non-Cultivator Households				*Others*		
Institutional Agencies	10.8	36.7	55.3	45.9	61.8	72.2	79.8
Government	3.4	4.5	7.6	3.8	19.7	16.8	11.1
Co-op Society/Bank	6.0	13.9	14.2	19.5	19.1	19.2	19.3
Commercial Bank	0.8	17.3	27.9	19.5	14.8	19.3	27.4
Insurance	0.2	0.0	0.6	0.2	2.3	1.4	4.4
Provident Fund	0.4	1.0	1.5	0.5	5.9	5.4	3.0
Other Institutions	0.0	0.0	3.4	2.4	0.0	10.1	14.6
Non-Institutional Agencies	89.2	63.3	40.6	54.1	38.2	24.4	20.2
Landlord	12.6	8.4	4.9	1.1	1.1	0.5	0.0
Agricultural Money Lender	23.8	11.4	8.2	10.2	1.2	0.7	0.2
Professional Money Lender	18.7	13.4	9.8	27.0	8.8	8.7	10.7
Traders	10.9	5.8	3.6	2.7	3.8	1.2	0.6
Relatives and Friends	19.0	14.4	8.8	9.8	16.2	9.5	6.9
Others incl. doctors etc	4.2	9.6	5.4	3.3	7.1	3.8	1.7
	All Households				*All Households*		
Institutional Agencies	29.2	61.2	64.0	57.1	59.9	70.0	75.1
Government	6.7	4.0	6.1	2.3	14.6	11.1	7.6
Co-op Society/Bank	20.1	28.6	21.6	27.3	17.5	17.2	20.5
Commercial Bank	2.2	28.0	33.7	24.5	22.5	21.6	29.7
Insurance	0.1	0.3	0.3	0.3	2.1	1.4	3.5

Contd...

	1971	1981	1991	2002	1981	1991	2002
Credit Agencies	*Rural*				*Urban*		
	All Households				*All Households*		
Provident Fund	0.1	0.3	0.7	0.3	3.2	3.3	2.0
Other Institutions	0.0	0.0	1.6	2.4	0.0	15.5	11.9
Non-Institutional Agencies	70.8	38.8	32.7	42.9	40.1	26.8	24.9
Landlord	8.6	4.0	4.0	1.0	1.0	0.6	0.2
Agricultural Money Lender	23.1	8.6	7.1	10.0	3.6	1.0	0.9
Professional Money Lender	13.8	8.3	10.5	19.6	8.9	9.2	13.2
Traders	8.7	3.4	2.5	2.6	4.8	2.2	1.0
Relatives and Friends	13.8	9.0	5.5	7.1	15.2	9.6	7.6
Others incl. doctors etc	2.8	5.5	3.2	2.6	6.6	4.2	1.9

Source: NSSO(2005), Household incidence of indebtedness in India as on 30.6.2002, 59th Survey (January-December 2003), Report No 501 (59/18.2/2.

9. The World Bank-NCAER RFAS *Rural Finance Access Survey* showed that only 41 per cent of rural households have a deposit account from a formal source. The survey further indicated that rural banks served primarily the needs of the richer rural borrowers–66 per cent of large farmers were having a deposit account, and 44 per cent had access to credit. At the same time the rural poor were facing severe difficulties in accessing savings and credit from the formal sector–70 per cent of marginal/landless farmers were not having a bank account and 87 per cent had no access to credit from a formal sector. (Shetty, 2006).
10. With regard to the distribution of bank branches, though the share of rural and semi urban offices had gone up substantially, it is seen that after the reforms, in recent years (1996-2005) the share of rural sector has come down significantly. (See, Table 2).
11. Another trend noticed is the worsening of the number of people served per branch in the rural areas. The population served per branch has increased in rural areas and it was worst in North East, Eastern and Central Regions; and it is seen

that the problem has actually worsened during the period after the reforms (1991-2005). This explains the lower than average number of savings account per 100 persons in these three regions. (Mohan, 2006).

Table 2
Distribution of Bank Branches

(Per cent)

	Offices		
	1969	*1996*	*2005*
Rural	22.2	51.2	45.7
Semi-urban	40.4	21.3	22.3
Urban	19.2	15.2	17.6
Metropolitan	18.2	12.3	14.4
Total	100.0	100.0	100.0

Source: Reserve Bank of India.

12. At the same time there is evidence (NCAER,2003) that there has been a surge in financial savings in rural areas, but these are not reflected in the growth in the number of households with bank accounts. This is reflective of the problem of financial exclusion.

Who are the Excluded?

Having seen the immensity of the problem of financial exclusion, it would be instructive to examine who are the excluded categories. The financially excluded sections largely comprise marginal farmers, landless labourers, oral lessees, self employed and unorganised sector enterprises, urban slum dwellers, migrants, ethnic minorities and socially excluded groups, senior citizens and women. While there are pockets of large excluded population in all parts of the country, the North East, Eastern and Central regions contain most of the financially excluded population. This clearly brings out the grievousness of the problem.

Consequences of Financial Exclusion

Consequences of financial exclusion will vary depending on the nature and extent of services denied. It may lead to increased travel requirements, higher incidence of crime, general decline in investment, difficulties in gaining access to credit or getting credit from informal sources at exorbitant rates, lack of financial planning, limited options for providing for old age and increased unemployment, etc. The households and micro and small enterprises are forced to deal entirely in cash and are susceptible to irregular cash flows. The small business may suffer due to loss of access to middle class and higher-income consumers, higher cash handling costs and delays in remittances of money. From the macroeconomic standpoint, being without formal savings can be problematic in two respects. First, people who save by informal means rarely benefit from the interest rate and tax advantages that people using formal methods of savings enjoy. Second, informal saving channels are much less secure than formal saving facilities (Mohan, 2006). Both poverty and financial exclusion result in a reduction of choices which affects social interaction and leads to reduced participation in society. In fact, there are researches which have shown that financial exclusion can lead to social exclusion also (Kempson *et al*, 2000).

Benefits of Inclusion

Access to financial institutions will bring several benefits to the consumer, regulator and the economy alike. Access to affordable financial services-especially credit and insurance-enlarges livelihood opportunities and empowers the poor to take charge of their lives. Such empowerment aids social and political stability. Apart from these benefits, financial inclusion imparts formal identity, provides access to the payments system and to savings safety net like deposit insurance. Establishment of an account relationship can pave the way for the customer to avail the benefits of a variety of financial products, which are not only standardised, but are also provided by institutions that are regulated and supervised by credible regulators, and are hence safer. The bank accounts can also be used for multiple purposes, such as, making small value remittances at low cost and making purchases on credit. Furthermore, the regulator benefits, as the audit trail is available and transactions are conducted transparently in a medium that can be monitored. The economy benefits, as greater financial resources become transparently available for efficient intermediation and allocation, for uses that have the highest returns. In other words, the single gateway of a banking account can be used for several purposes and represents a beneficial situation for all the economic units in the country (Mohan, 2006).

Difficulties in Promoting Financial Inclusion

There are a variety of reasons for financial exclusion. These include:

- Small-sized transactions;
- Customers scattered over wide areas;
- Lack of clearly-defined property rights;
- The risks faced by small producers need to be assessed and factored into product pricing.

In remote, hilly and sparsely populated areas with poor infrastructure, physical access itself acts as a deterrent. From the demand side, lack of awareness, low incomes/assets, social exclusion, illiteracy etc., act as barriers. From the supply side, distance from branch, branch timings, cumbersome documentation and procedures, unsuitable products, language, staff attitudes are common reasons for exclusion. All these result in higher transaction cost apart from procedural hassles. On the other hand, the ease of availability of informal credit sources makes these popular even if costlier.

Government/RBI policy towards Financial Inclusion

Historically, the Government of India and the Reserve Bank have been making efforts to increase banking penetration in the country. Some of these measures include the creation of State Bank of

India in 1955; introduction of social control in 1967 and nationalisation of commercial banks in 1969 and 1980; initiating the Lead Bank Scheme in 1970; establishing regional rural banks (RRBs) in 1975; introducing a Self-help Group (SHG)-Bank Linkage Programme in 1992 and formulating the Kisan Credit Card scheme (KCC) in 1998 are some of the major milestones in this regard. Notwithstanding these improvements, financial inclusion found a place in policy documents only very recently.

Bank nationalization in India marked a paradigm shift in the focus of banking as it was intended to shift the focus from class banking to mass banking. There has been an unprecedented expansion in branch expansion and deposit mobilisation especially in favour of the rural and semi urban areas. Other measures like credit planning, requiring a minimum credit-deposit ratio of 60 per cent for rural and semi urban branches, lead bank scheme and service area approach, interest rate ceilings, poverty alleviation/ employment gurantee schemes such as IRDP, lending targets directed at a range of 'priority sectors' such as agriculture, weaker sections of the population, Small scale industry, etc., have been extremely relevant in this respect. Yet as we saw in our analysis of the dimensions of the problem of financial exclusion the picture is far from satisfactory. There is a tremendous scope for financial coverage if we have to improve the standards of life of those deprived people.

The Reserve Bank has, therefore, taken a number of measures in recent years to tackle financial exclusion by enhancing access to banking services to promote greater financial access. The following are the important ones among them:

- Banks have been urged to make available a basic banking 'no frills' account either with 'nil' or very low minimum balances as well as charges that would make such accounts accessible to vast sections of the population. Regional Rural Banks have also been advised to allow limited overdraft facilities in 'no frills' accounts, without any collateral.

- Banks are required to make available all printed material used by retail customers in the concerned regional language.
- All State Level Bankers' Committee (SLBC) convener banks have been advised to initiate action for identifying at least one district in their State/Union Territory for, 100 per cent financial inclusion. So far 104 districts have been identified and 100 per cent financial inclusion has been achieved in the Union Territory of Puducherry and in 24 districts in Andhra Pradesh, Gujarat, Haryana, Himachal Pradesh, Karnataka, Kerala and Punjab.
- The 'know your customer' (KYC) procedure for opening 'no frills' accounts has been simplified so that people from low-income groups do not face problems in opening new accounts. As a result of the measures taken for financial inclusion, there was an increase of 6 million new 'no frills' bank accounts between March 2006 and March 2007.
- The Kisan Credit Card (KCC) scheme was introduced in 1998-99 to provide adequate and timely credit support to the farmers from the banking system in a flexible, hassle-free and cost-effective manner. Since the inception of the scheme, 26.6 million KCCs have been issued by the public sector banks, with limits amounting to Rs. 94,712 crore. Recently banks have been asked to consider introducing a General Purpose Credit Card (GCC) facility in the nature of revolving credit up to Rs.25,000 without insisting on security or purpose at deregulated interest rates at their rural and semi-urban branches. Fifty per cent of the GCC loans are treated as part of the banks' priority sector lending (indirect finance to agriculture).
- A simplified mechanism for one-time settlement of overdue loans up to Rs. 25,000/- has been suggested for adoption. Banks have been specifically advised that

borrowers with loans settled under the one time settlement scheme will be eligible to re-access the formal financial system for fresh credit.

- Guidelines have been issued to banks to enhance their outreach by utilising the 'business facilitators' and 'business correspondents' models. The business correspondents (BC) model allows banks to do 'cash in-cash out' transactions at the location of the BC and allows branchless banking. Banks are also entering into agreements with Indian postal authority for using the wide network of post offices as business correspondents.
- Banks are encouraged to make use of information and communication technology (ICT) using bio-metric smart cards and mobile hand held electronic devices for receipts and disbursement of cash by their agents such as business facilitators/correspondents.
- The recommendations of the Working Groups constituted by the Reserve Bank to suggest measures for enhancing provision of banking services, strengthening financial institutions and improving currency and payments systems in under-banked regions of the country such as the North-Eastern Region, Chattisgarh, Uttarakhand and Bihar are also under implementation.
- Special Drive for Financial Inclusion in Scheduled Caste/ Scheduled Tribe and Minorities Concentrated Districts.
- Other measures include setting up pilot projects for credit counselling and financial education. A multilingual website in 13 Indian languages on all matters concerning banking and the common man has been launched by the Reserve Bank on 18th June 2007.

Financial Education

In the context of financial inclusion, financial education is a very important factor in the access of such excluded groups to finance.

Financial education is the process by which financial consumers/ investors improve their understanding of financial products and concepts, and develop the skills and confidence to make informed choices to improve their financial well-being (RBI, 2007). In countries with diverse social and economic profile like India, financial education is particularly relevant for people who are resource poor and who operate at the margin and are vulnerable to persistent downward financial pressures. One of the major hindrances in the way of delivery of financial services is the lack of basic knowledge and lack of awareness of the products and services available from the banks. It is important to note that the Financial Inclusion Task Force of the United Kingdom, one of the pioneers to talk of financial inclusion, has identified access to free face-to-face money advice as an important component of financial inclusion, apart from access to banking and access to affordable credit (Shyamala, 2006). People need information and advice when they either save their money or get into debt. Such information and guidance can best be delivered by appropriate mechanisms and if such effective mechanisms are put in place through the banks, they in turn would reinforce the demand for financial services. In India, the need for financial education is even greater considering the low levels of literacy and a large section of the population being still out of the formal financial set up. As per an OECD study (OECD,2005), the provision of education programmes for the un/underbanked groups can play an important role in encouraging un/underbanked consumers to enter into or make better use of the financial mainstream and contribute to keeping them as savers for the long-term.

Credit Counselling Centres

Another project that has been drawn up under the leadership of RBI is the literacy-cum-counselling centres. The absence of proper credit counselling coupled with inadequate financial literacy levels have often resulted in the consumers being forced towards costlier options and eventual debt traps. It will, therefore, be in the interest of banks themselves to help individual borrowers through appropriate credit counselling (Reddy, 2006). A few banks have, therefore, taken initiatives to set up some centres in rural/semi-urban areas to offer financial education and credit counselling services. The objective of these centres is to advise people on gaining access to the financial system including banks, creating awareness among the public about financial management, counselling people struggling to meet the repayment obligations and helping in rehabilitation of borrowers in distress.

Role of Technology in Financial Inclusion

The use of IT solutions for providing banking facilities at doorstep holds the potential for scalability of the financial inclusion initiatives (Thorat, 2007). Pilot projects have been initiated using smart cards for opening bank accounts with bio metric identification. A mention must be made of projects like 'e-Choupal' and 'Param' which have been brought forth through private sector initiative. Some State Governments are routing social security payments as also payments under the National Rural Employment Guarantee Scheme through such smart cards. The use of IT also enables banks to handle the enormous increase in the volume of transactions for millions of households for processing, credit scoring, credit record and follow up.

Use of Intermediaries

One of the ways in which access to formal banking services has been provided very successfully since the early 90s is through the linkage of Self Help Groups (SHGs) with banks. SHGs are groups of usually women who get together and pool their savings and give loans to members. Usually there is a NGO that promotes and nurture these groups. National Bank for Agriculture and Rural Development has played a very significant role in supporting group formation, linking them with banks as also promoting best practices. The SHG is given loan against guarantee of group members. The recovery experience has been very good and there were 29.25 lakh SHGs linked to banks touching around 40 million households through its members. Banks provide credit to such groups at reasonable rates of interest. However the size of loans is quite small and are used mostly for consumption smoothening or for very small businesses. Agriculture is largely untouched by most of them. But in recent years in some SHGs, credit is provided for agricultural activities and other livelihoods and could be several times the deposits made by the SHG (Thorat, 2007). So also there is the problem of uneven spread of these SHGs with the major concentration being in the South. Most of the SHGs have been linked to public sector banks in view of the latter's dominant presence in the rural areas. According to the Committee on Financial Inclusion (headed by Dr. C. Rangarajan) the SHG-Bank Linkage Programme can be regarded as the most potent initiative since Independence for delivering financial services to the poor in a sustainable manner.

Micro Finance Institutions (MFIs)

MFIs have drawn attention to an entire sector of borrowers who had been previously poorly served by the formal financial sector- and MFIs have demonstrated how to make lending to this sector a viable proposition. However, the rates of interest charged are quite high, typically 24 to 30 per cent, mainly on account of the high transaction cost for the average loan size that can be quite small. For commercial banks, the lower cost of funding, advantages of size and scale gives scope for cross subsidization and their interest rates are more competitive compared to the MFIs, but they have not been as successful in dealing with the last mile issue. The partnering with SHGs and MFIs with reasonable cost of funding by the banks is therefore seen as a more optimal approach (Reddy, 2005). Interestingly, the CEO of a nationalised bank had described the role of the banks for a rural household as: Agriculture for the head of the household, Education for the son, Enabling the daughter to take up an alternative activity and Women SHGs fior the mother (Nair, 2006). In other words, banks have to adopt a holistic approach and should try to forge linkages with the various MFIs and the local communities. The Committee on Financial Inclusion has even suggested for a separate category of Micro finance–Non Banking Finance Companies (MF–NBFCs), which could provide thrift, credit, micro-insurance, remittances and other financial services up to a specified amount to the poor in rural, semi-urban and urban areas.

Thus, we can see that RBI and the Government have been adopting a two-pronged strategy to generate greater awareness and expand the reach of banking services viz., empowerment and protection. Financial inclusion should be seen as the first stage of the process of empowerment. This is strengthened by inculcating awareness among the masses through financial education. Concurrently, an advisory mechanism in the form of credit counseling is being encouraged to help distressed borrowers and bring them within the fold of formal finance. As regards protection, a Banking Codes and Standards Board of India has been established recently to ensure a comprehensive code of conduct for minimum standards of banking services to be offered by banks (Mohan, 2006).

Agenda for the Future

That the Government and RBI (including also NABARD) are fully seized of the need for financial inclusion is clear from the diverse measures that they have introduced ever since independence. Recent years have witnessed more concerted and comprehensive measures in this direction. Much more action is likely now that the recommendations of the Rangarajan Committee on Financial Inclusion is being implemented. Already, the Government has announced in the budget for 2007-08 the setting up of two funds for financial inclusion, viz., Financial Inclusion Fund for Development and Promotional Interventions, and the Financial Inclusion Technology Fund to meet the cost of technology adoption, each with an initial corpus of Rs.500 crores. The Rangarajan Committee has also recommended to set up a

National Mission on Financial Inclusion (NaMFI) to bring about financial inclusion within a specific time frame. It has also suggested the launching of a National Rural Financial Inclusion Plan (NRFIP) with a target to achieve finanancial inclusion of at least 50 per cent of the households by 2012 and the rest by 2015. The need for revitalising the RRBs and Co-operative sector has been highlighted in the report.

In this context it has to be pointed out that if one makes a close observation it can be seen that most of the measures introduced by the Government/RBI have been from the supply side such as building up a network of financial institutions including commercial banks, regional rural banks, co-operatives societies, and more recently the encouragement given to MFIs and SHG-Banks linakage. So also the emphasis on directed credit programmes such as targets for priority sector lending. Clearly, demand side efforts, such as financial education, and credit counselling etc., which will empower the people to demand the disired services, have not received the same level of attention. Hence, the recommendations of the Rangarajan Committee calling for demand side measures needs to be given more serious appreciation and action. Above all, banks and other financial institutions have to realise that financial inclusion is good business and not charity. Increasingly, banks and other financial intermediaries have to see the extension of rural credit and micro finance as business opportunities and not as an obligation to do forced directed lending. As C.K. Prahalad (Prahalad, 2005)has stated "the future lies with those companies who see the poor as their customers". It may appear in the first instance that taking banking to the sections constituting "the bottom of the pyramid", may not be profitable but it should always be remembered that even the relatively low margins on high volumes can be a very profitable proposition. The experience of telecom and organised retail business attests to the efficacy of an expanded customer base as a viable business model of growth. If the corporate world has taken to rural areas and urban slums like never before, why then do banks have such a different view on such a large numbers of economically active people? There is no reason why banks should be an exception. They have to be imaginative enough to unlock the enormous market potential of this huge untapped market out there. Financial inclusion will then emerge as an eminently profitable business. In this way by doing commercially profitable business financial inclusion will lead to inclusive growth as well.

References

Chavan, Pallavi (2007), "Access to Bank Credit", *Economic and Political Weekly*, Vol. 42, No. 31, August 04-10, pp. 3219-3224.

Kempson, E., J. Caskey, C. Whyley and S. Collard (2000), *In or out?*, Financial Services Authority, London.

Kempson, E. (2006), "Policy Level Response to Financial Exclusion in Developed Economies: Lessons for Developing Countries", Paper Presented at the Conference, Access to Finance: Building Inclusive Financial Systems, World Bank, Washington, D.C.

Leeladhar, V. (2005), "Taking Banking Services to the Common Man–Financial Inclusion", Commemorative Lecture at the Fedbank Hormis Memorial Foundation at Ernakulam, December, 2. *http://www.rbi.org.*

Ministry of Finance (2008), "Recommendations of the Committee on Financial Inclusion", Press Releases, February, 5.

Mitra, Rana (2007), "Financial Inclusion: Meeting the Challenge", *People's Democracy*, Vol. XXXI, No. 16, April, 22.

Mohan, R. (2006), "Economic Growth, Financial Deepening and Financial Inclusion", Address made at the Annual Bankers' Conference 2006 at Hyderabad, November, 3. *http://www.rbi.org.*

Nair, M.V. (2006),"Indian Banking: Shaping an Economic Powerhouse—Financial Inclusion", Presentation to FICCI on 17th *July. http://ficci.com/*

NCAER (2003), *India Market Demographics Report 2002*, NCAER, New Delhi.

NSSO(2005), *Household Incidence of Indebtedness in India as on 30.6.2002*, 59th Survey (January-December 2003), Report No. 501 (59/18.2/2).

OECD (2005), *Improving Financial Literacy: Analysis of Issues and Policies,* OECD, Paris.

Prahalad, C.K. (2005), *The Fortune at the Bottom of the Pyramid: Eradicating Poverty Through Profits*, Wharton School Publishing, Pearson Education, Inc.

Reddy, Y.V. (2006), "Micro Finance: Reserve Bank's Approach", *Reserve Bank of India Bulletin*, Vol. LIX, No. 9, September, pp. 841-846.

Reddy, Y.V. (2006), "Credit Counselling: An Indian Perspective", *Reserve Bank of India Bulletin,* Vol. LX, No. 10, October, pp. 1117-1120.

RBI (2007), *Annual Report 2006-07,* Reserve Bank of India, September.

Shetty,V.P. (2006), "Challenges of Inclusive Banking", Speech given at the Institute for Development and Research in Banking Technology (IDRBT), Hyderabad, September 2.

Srinivasan, N. (2007), " Policy Issues and Role of Banking System in Financial Inclusion", *Economic and Political Weekly,* Vol. XLII, No. 30, July 28-August 3, pp. 3091-3095.

Shyamala, Gopinath (2006), "Inclusive Growth: Role of Financial Education", Special Address at BANCON-2006, Hyderabad, November, 4. *http://www.rbi.org.*

Subba Rao, K.G.K. (2007), Financial Inclusion: An Introspection", *Economic and Political Weekly*, Vol. 42, No. 5, February 03, February 09, pp. 355-360.

Thorat, Usha (2007), "Financial Inclusion—The Indian Experience", Speech made at the HMT-DFID Financial Inclusion Conference 2007 at Whitehall Place, London, June,19. *http://www.iibf.org.in.*

10

HOUSING FINANCE BY COMMERCIAL BANKS IN INDIA IN THE EMERGING SCENARIO: SOME STRATEGIC IMPERATIVES

P. K. MANOJ

Introduction

Many of the nations of the developing world had initiated economic deregulation measures during the eighties and nineties of the twentieth century. These reform measures have had significant impact on the financial systems of the respective nations. India has been no exception to the above general trend. As a result of the ongoing financial sector reforms initiated in India in the early nineties, the banking industry of the nation has been undergoing many radical changes, which in turn have got many far reaching implications which include, inter alia, cut-throat competition, dwindling profit margins, tighter supervision by both the national and international regulatory authorities and above all increasingly discerning customers. To cope up with these changes, it has become imperative for commercial banks to re-engineer their business models, re-position their products and after all to project themselves differently before their customers. Besides, for survival and growth in such an increasingly competitive market characterized by quite diverse and highly discerning customers, banks need to change their business strategies on a regular basis. Accordingly, banks have to offer their customers a range of 'tailor-made' and 'as you like it' products, often having very short life cycles. This may necessitate identification of un-served and under-served market segments, offering suitable products to such segments. Such a policy can help improve the business growth and profitability of the individual banks, and at the same time ensure a more balanced and equitable development of the nation as a whole. In the above context, this paper seeks to have a closer look into the housing finance portfolio of commercial banks in India and to analyse as to why there is an imminent need for repositioning their credit strategies in favour of the low income and marginalized sections of the society. Unlike in the past when rural lending as well as other priority sector advances were undertaken primarily as a part of compliance with the Governmental policy of directive lending, currently there is an increasing revelation by many of the players that such "dirty" lending could be profitable as well. The emergence of innovative and replicable models, already time-tested in other countries, most importantly the micro finance model, supports the above argument. In the above context, this paper seeks to suggest pragmatic strategies for sustainable and inclusive housing finance in India. The paper gives an overview of significance of housing to the Indian economy, the changing landscape of Indian housing finance industry, the increasing prominence of commercial banks and after all the utmost significance of inclusiveness in housing finance. Thus, after considering the relevant international experiences and national realities, strategies for more effective and inclusive housing finance for banks in India have been suggested.

Objectives of the Paper

(1) To study in brief the housing situation in India, the problem of housing shortage, and also the significance of housing to the nation as a whole, from an international perspective;

(2) To analyse the changing landscape of institutional finance for housing in India in the post reforms period focusing on the ongoing second phase of the reforms process (viz FY 1997 to FY 2007), and also the pattern of the relative performance of the agency groups;

(3) To study the enhanced significance of inclusiveness in housing finance in India, from the perspective of balanced and sustainable economic development.

(4) To study as to the role of Indian commercial banks in providing housing finance in the emerging scenario, and also to suggest suitable strategies for business growth by catering to the housing finance needs of the poor in India, using emerging but time-tested models.

Analytical Significance

During the late nineties, the reduced credit off-take to the industrial sector because of the general slump in the industry coupled with gradually falling interest rates had fuelled the growth of retail credit in India. Retail banking (particularly, housing finance) used to contribute considerably towards profitability during that recession-hit period. Though this trend continued till 2005, since then there has been somewhat a moderation in the trend. This has been because of various reasons which include, inter alia, (i) indications of industrial revival resulting in enhanced credit needs from the industrial sector, thus reducing the relative prominence of retail credit, and (ii) not-so-encouraging attitude from the regulatory authorities who have issued warning signals against excessive lending and also imposed stricter norms for discouraging over exposure like, higher risk weight, higher provisioning etc. (This is particularly relevant in the case of housing finance.) In the current scenario, retail credit is no more as attractive to the banks as in the past because of growing pressures on interest margins as well as growing delinquency rates; nor is it the only alternative before them because credit to industrial and corporate sectors is gradually picking up. In this scenario, banks have to identify hither to un-served or under-served markets, and also devise appropriate business strategies and feasible business models for tapping the business potential from such markets.

In the Indian scenario, (i) housing shortage is still on the rise year after year in spite of the commendable growth rate in institutional housing finance over the last one decade, (ii) large majority of the housing shortage relates to the low income and other marginalized sections of the society, (iii) traditional credit appraisal norms of banks and other financial intermediaries exclude vast majority of the poor from availing housing finance from the formal institutional system, (iv) the share of co-operative housing sector which traditionally meet the credit needs of the common man and the poor is fast diminishing and this sector has virtually vanished from the scene, and (v) the specialized housing finance schemes of the Government are grossly insufficient to meet the housing finance needs of the poor, and further recent statistics (2007) show that these schemes have failed to meet even one-fourth of their respective targets set. It is in the above context that a study as contemplated above assumes high level of research significance.

Methodology and Data Sources

The study is descriptive-analytical and exploratory in nature. It is descriptive-analyitical to the extent that it provides an overview of the current scenario in respect of housing situation in India, problems of growing housing shortage and exclusiveness, significance of inclusive housing development for the national economy etc. The study is exploratory also to the extent that it considers international best examples in respect of inclusive housing (social housing) and seeks to replicate the same in the

Indian scenario and accordingly to formulate appropriate macro level strategies and models, with due respect to the peculiar features characteristic of Indian economy. The data sources for the study are mainly the authentic secondary data from such sources as the publications of Reserve Bank of India, Indian Banks' Association, Indian Institute of Banking & Finance, reputed business dailies and other periodicals, and so on. The data so collected are thoroughly analysed using commonly used statistical tools to arrive at meaningful conclusions.

Organization of the Paper

Broadly falling in line with the objectives set for the paper as noted above, the remainder of the paper is organized into the following four main parts. Part–I deals with the housing situation in India, the problem of housing shortage, and also the significance of housing to the nation as a whole. Part–II discusses the changing landscape of housing finance in India with special reference to the second phase of the ongoing era of financial deregulation (FY 1997–FY 2007) and also the pattern of the relative prominence of the major institutional groups. Part–III points out the enhanced need for inclusiveness in institutional housing finance in India, and lastly Part–IV discusses as to what should be the role of commercial banks in providing housing finance (particularly rural housing) in the emerging scenario, suggests sustainable strategies, and also appropriate models for the same. Part–IV is followed by the concluding remarks of the author.

PART-I

Housing Situation in India, Pattern of Housing Shortage and the Significance of Housing

Housing has been one of the top priorities for the various governments in India since the seventies. The need for housing has been increasing at a phenomenal pace in India and so also the need for housing finance. Since the growth in supply of housing could not keep pace with the growth in its demand, housing shortage has been on the rise over the years. Housing finance industry which was relatively dormant till the early nineties underwent sweeping changes ever since the initiation of financial sector deregulation measures. Financial deregulation measures brought about several changes in this industry, the first and foremost being the fast growth rate in the industry coupled with cutthroat competition among the industry players. This trend has been quite prominent since the entry of commercial banks into this arena in the late 1990s, consequent to the decision of the Reserve Bank of India (in 1995) to permit banks to freely lend for housing purpose. Accordingly, there has been a surge in the growth of retail (personal) loans segment of banks, comprising predominantly of housing loans. This is evident from the fact that housing loans disbursed by banks as a percentage of their total loans has increased from just 2.79% as of end-March 1997 to as high as 12.52% as of end-March 2007. Thus, there has been an unprecedented growth rate in the disbursement of housing loans by banks, and as of 31 March 2007 the outstanding balance of housing loans by all banks in India stands at Rs.230689 Crore, as against just Rs.7946 Crore as of 31 March 1997, the growth rate being 35.82 %CAGR (for the eleven years' period, FY 1997-'2007).

However, in spite of the impressive growth in housing finance over the years, there are growing apprehensions regarding its inclusiveness, i.e. accessibility to the common man, the underprivileged sections of the society to housing finance etc. It is widely recognized that formal housing finance system, particularly the commercial banks (CBs)–most dominant among the players – is fast becoming exclusive in operations, with nearly 90% of the total housing credit going to the rich and upper middle income group, primarily the salaried class. The case of housing finance companies (HFCs)–the second largest intermediary group –is quite similar in this regard. The poor and other marginalized sections are often deprived of adequate credit facilities for housing. Whether the above weakness of Indian banking system be converted into its own strength through appropriate marketing strategies and models? The paper dwells into the above issue in a systematically in the following paragraphs.

Overview of Housing Situation in India: an International Perspective

Housing, as a financial service is comparatively new in India, the earliest mortgages being provided in 1978. There was no well established and effective housing finance system even afterwards, though some housing finance companies (HFCs)–mostly those promoted by a few major CBs–and a number of co-operative housing societies functioning under a few apex co-operative housing federations (ACHFs) could meet the ever growing housing finance needs to a limited extent. The major source of housing finance was the house building advance (HBA) provided by the employers, which in turn was available only to salaried people of certain organized sectors. In fact the real impetus for the emergence of a dynamic housing finance system has been the financial sector deregulation measures in the early nineties, more prominently in the second phase of such reforms in the late nineties. As a result the CBs have entered into this market aggressively, greatly increasing the number of players thus resulting in fierce competition in the market. Since then the organized housing finance sector in India comprises of three major institutional groups viz. CBs, HFCs and ACHFs. The aggressive entry of CBs has resulted in their market share growing at very fast rates over the years, eventually overtaking the share of HFCs in 2002-'03. The trend continues thereafter. Though HFCs have also been growing fast, their relative share in the total market has been gradually declining, the same being eaten away by the CBs, since the latter group has been growing much faster. Another noteworthy trend is the gradual disappearance of the ACHFs from the market. (Table 1).

Table 1
Housing Loan Disbursements by Various Institutional Agencies

(Rupees in Crores)

Name of the Agency Group	*FY: 2001*	*FY: 2002*	*FY: 2003*	*FY: 2004*	*FY: 2005*
Commercial Banks (CBs)	5553.11	8566.41	23553.70	32816.39	50398.00
Housing Finance Companies (HFCs)	12637.85	14614.44	17832.01	20862.23	26000.00
Co-operative Housing Federations	867.72	677.58	641.48	623.08	421.10
Total	19058.68	23858.43	42026.86	54301.70	76819.10
Overall Growth Rate (Year to Year)	—	25.18 %	76.15 %	29.21 %	41.47 %

Source: *Report on Trend & Progress of Housing in India* for 2001-2005, NHB, New Delhi.)

As is clear from Table 2 above, the problem of housing shortage is still acute in India, in spite of the significant growth in housing finance disbursements over the last so many years (43% CAGR for the five years ended FY 2006). In fact the housing shortage grew almost 4 times during the period 1991 – 2007. It is noteworthy that the mortgage to GDP ratio in India as of 2005 stood at an abysmal level of 7.25% as against 7% in China, 54% in USA, 57% in UK, 17% in Thailand, 40% in European Union and 40% in Malaysia. Though India's position has significantly improved from 3.4% (2001) to 7.25% (2005), it is observed that it quite low compared with other nations of the world (Table 3, Figure 1).

Table 2
Housing Stock and Shortage, 1991-2007 (Million Nos.)

Year	*Housing Stock (Nos in Million)*				
	Pucca	*Semi-Pucca*	*Kutcha*	*Total*	*Housing Shortage*
1991	29.80	06.20	03.20	40.70	08.23
1997	40.07	06.64	03.35	50.08	07.57
1998	42.13	06.72	03.37	51.85	07.36
1999	44.28	06.80	03.40	53.67	07.18
2000	46.55	06.83	03.42	55.56	06.93
2002	41.17	08.08	02.74	55.80	10.56
2007	47.49	09.16	02.18	66.30	24.71

Source: Compiled from: *Annual Report 2006-'07*, Ministry of Housing & Urban Poverty.
Alleviation, Govt. of India; cited in *The Economic Times dt. 13 Aug. 2007*, Chennai Ed.).

Table 3
Mortgage to GDP Ratio in Various Countries (as of FY 2005)

(in Percentages)

Country	*India*	*China*	*USA*	*UK*	*Thailand*	*EU*	*Malaysia*
Mortgage to GDP Ratio	3.4	7.0	54.0	57.0	17.0	40	34

Source: *Report on Trend & Progress of Housing in India 2005*; NHB, Govt. of India, p. 07.

Note: The ratios, as above, relate to FY 2001. The ratio of India has improved over the years and as of FY 2005, the same is 7.25%. Reference, as in Figure 1.1 above, page 11.

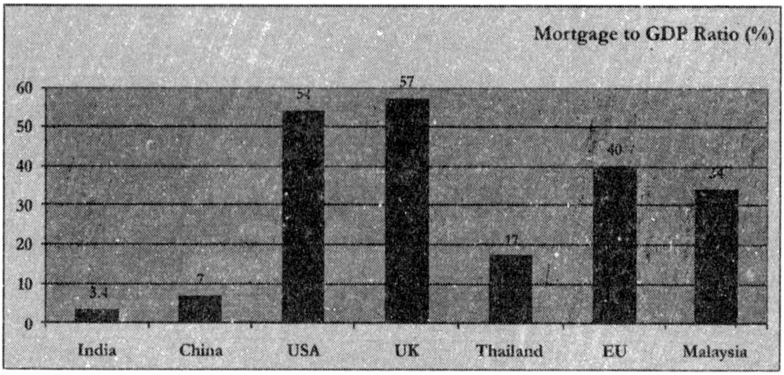

Figure 1: **Mortgage to GDP Ratio in Various Countries**

Source: *Report on Trend & Progress of Housing in India 2005*; NHB, Govt. of India, p. 07.

Another dimension of the housing situation in India is the gradually growing interest rates on housing loans as well as indications of gradual slowing down of the housing finance system resulting in a moderation in the incremental growth rates of housing loan disbursements. This trend is similar to the global trend in this regard which is discussed in the next paragraph.

Global Trends in Housing: Slow Down and Apprehensions Regarding Sustainability

It is observed that trends in Indian housing are broadly following the global trend in this regard. There are apprehensions regarding the formation of housing bubble (real estate bubble, in a broader sense). It is believed that the property values, which have registered huge increase during the period till 2005, may fall by at least 10 to 20 per cent in the near future. In some parts of the country, the property values have skyrocketed and have become more than double during the said period. Since a downward trend is inevitable for any cyclical movement and also since India has almost reached the peak level in respect of property values at least in certain pockets of the country, there is the likelihood for the burst of the housing bubble. The global trend in respect of housing prices is eventually that of downward. As per the statistics of 'The

Economist' (quarterly report on housing), the annual rate of house price inflation has slowed down since the last quarter of 2005 in top 10 out of the 20 countries. (Table 4).

Table 4
House Price Indicators of 'The Economist'–Top Twenty Countries

Country	*Latest*	*2004-'05 on a year earlier*	*% Change (1997-2006)*	*Country*	*Latest*	*2004-'05 on a year earlier*	*% Change (1997-2006)*
Denmark	23.3	22.8	115	New Zealand	08.8	15.8	105
Sth. Africa	14.7	17.8	351	Australia	08.3	02.3	135
Belgium	11.8	20.8	118	Italy	06.2	07.3	92
France	11.1	14.8	137	Netherlands	06.2	05.5	97
Canada	10.8	05.2	69	United States	05.9	13.2	102
Spain	10.8	12.8	173	China	05.6	06.2	NA
Ireland	10.6	08.2	253	Hong Kong	03.0	08.0	-43
Sweden	10.5	10.5	124	Switzerland	01.8	01.3	17
Britain	10.2	02.9	196	Germany	00.7	04.8	NA
Singapore	10.2	03.9	NA	Japan	-02.7	-04.7	-32

Source: "Banking Scene: Global", *Indian Banker,* Vol. II, No. 4, April 2007, pp. 39-40.

In view of the above, it is clear that Indian housing situation is passing through a transition stage, and is largely following the global trend in this regard. Regarding housing finance disbursements, there are clear indications of slowing down in the growth rates thus resulting in a consolidation at the current level or slightly lower level. (This aspect is discussed in greater detail in Part–IV of the paper). In respect of property values also the system has almost reached the peak broadly in line with the developments in majority of the other countries. As already discussed, Indian system has the chronic problem of fast growing housing shortage. It seems that special alternative housing schemes are required to tackle this problem. Similar problem exists in many of the recently deregulated developing economies in more or less similar manner. It is worth pointing out here that some of these transition economies have been able to tackle their housing problem reasonably well with such alternative housing schemes, like, special schemes like 'social housing'. (This aspect is dealt in detail in Part -IV of the paper).

Significance of Housing: Housing as the Growth Engine for the Economy

Housing development has got many strategic advantages particularly for a developing nation like India. Housing investment provides the necessary impetus for the whole economy to grow.

Linkages, Multiplier Effects, and Economic Development

Housing industry has got linkages, both forward and backward, with about 250 ancillary industries. Thus, a small initiative in housing would propel multiplier effects in the economy through the generation of demand. It is estimated that Re.1 investment in housing can increase GDP by Re. 0.78 due to multiplier effects. Because of linkage effects, additional demand is created and spending capacity of the people is enhanced. This drives the entire economy. Besides, housing investment increases the people having lower income and relatively higher marginal propensity to consume (MPC). The higher MPC increases demand for consumption goods thus resulting in higher GDP. Thus housing sector has got a cardinal role to play in ensuring prolific and sustained growth, particularly in recessionary situations. Housing can kick start a recession-hit economy. Once the economy picks up, housing investment needs control.

Housing Sector is a Top Employment Generator in the country, and Rural Housing has Got Vital Role in Economic Development, as an Additional Growth Engine

Housing sector is one of the top employment generators in any economy. This feature is of utmost significance for developing economies like India, and is particularly relevant in respect of rural housing. Initiation of rural housing, for instance, would lead to infusion of housing which in turn will have spillover effects through increase in employment and rural incomes. This would revitalize the rural economy to take up new projects and programmes like rural roads, irrigation works etc. As per the estimates of National Building Organization (NBO), two million housing units per year will lead to creation of additional 10 million man years of direct employment and another 15 million man years of indirect employment. Through income effect rural housing can prove itself to be an additional growth engine for the economy, in the form of rural prosperity.

Part-II

Changing Landscape of Housing Finance in India

The housing finance market in India has undergone radical changes over the last three decades. Accordingly, clear changes are observed in the structure of the market, types of institutional intermediaries and industry growth rates. Broadly, there have been three distinct phases. In the initial phase starting from the late seventies and ending in late nineties the market was characterized by specialized housing finance institutions like HFCs. In the second phase, starting from late nineties (1998) and ending in 2003, commercial banks have entered into this arena aggressively resulting in fast growth rate and fierce competition. The third phase has started from 2003 and is continuing currently. The market has more stabilized with an oligopolistic character and currently the largest four players (viz. ICICI Bank, SBI, HDFC and LICHFL). That is, the largest two banks in India (ICICI in the private sector and SBI in the public sector) along with the largest two HFCs (HDFC in the private sector and LICHFL in the public sector) currently account for more than 80% of the incremental market share. (Exhibit. 1).

***Exhibit 1:* Radical Changes in Indian Housing Finance Market: Three Distinct Phases**

Phase-I (Upto Late 1990s)	*Phase-II (1998-2003)*	*Phase-III (2003 Onwards)*
• Specialized Lenders (HFCs), HFCs sponsored by CBs, Insurance companies, Builders and other companies.	• Aggressive entry of CBs • HFCs lose market share • Irrational competition and rapid disbursements • Credit quality concerns	• Oligipolistic market • Top 3-4 players share over 80% of the market • Sustained growth (25%) • More rational market.

Role of Co-operative Sector in Housing Finance: Constantly Declining Trend

Co-operatives as an institutional mechanism for satisfying various needs of the people emerged from the principles of 'self-help' and 'co-operative effort'. Historically co-operative credit institutions have been playing a vital role in extending credit to the agricultural and rural sectors. In was in the early 20th century that the co-operative housing movement evolved in India with the objective of fulfilling the desire of a 'common man' of owning a home. The role played by housing co-operatives over the years in financing the housing needs of their members has been remarkable. The co-operative sector is expected to play a lead role particularly in land acquisition, allotment of land and housing sites to encourage group housing and development of amenities. As of FY 2005, it is estimated that there are more than 92,000 primary housing co-operatives at the grass-root level with a membership of over 6.5 million represented by 26 Apex Co-operative Housing Federations (ACHFs) at the state/union territory level. The National Co-operative Housing Federation of India (NCHF) has been promoting, guiding and coordinating the activities of housing co-operatives at the national level since its inception in 1969. In addition, NCHF also helps the member Federations in improving their financial, organizational and technical capabilities. Table 5 shows the sanctions and disbursements of housing loans by ACHFs during the period of five financial years, 2000-'01 to 2004-'05. The Table clearly shows a constant declining trend in sanctions and disbursements of housing loans by ACHFs throughout the period. Obviously, as the ACHFs are declining in their outreach and performance over the years, so does the inclusiveness of the housing finance in the whole country.

Changing Profile of the Housing Finance Industry in India: Growing Presence of CBs, Declining Share of HFCs and Gradual Disappearance of ACHFs

Table 6 and Figure 2 show the relative share of the total housing loan advances by the different institutional intermediaries in the

Indian housing finance market, over a period of five years ended FY 2004-'05. Table 7 and Figure 3 show the trend in respect of the growth rates (Y to Y) of these agencies in loan disbursals over the four years' period ended FY 2004-'05.

Table 5
Lending Operations of ACHFs–Constantly Declining Trend

Particulars	*2000-2001*	*2001-2002*	*2002-2003*	*2003-2004*	*2004-2005*
Loan Sanctioned	842.81	730.12	672.99	595.45	432.10
Loan Disbursed	867.72	677.58	641.58	623.08	421.10
Growth Rate (Disbursals)	—	-21.91 %	-05.33 %	-02.87 %	-02.88 %

Source: National Co-operative Housing Federation of India, cited in *Trend & Progress of Housing in India-2005*, National Housing Bank, Govt. of India, New Delhi, p. 26.)

Table 6
Relative Share of Different Players in the Organized Housing Finance Industry

(in Percentages)

Particulars	*2000-2001*	*2001-2002*	*2002-2003*	*2003-2004*	*2004-2005*
Commercial Banks	29.14	35.91	56.04	60.43	65.61
Housing Finance Companies	66.31	61.25	42.43	38.42	33.84
Co-operative Sector	04.55	02.84	01.53	01.15	00.55
Total	100.00	100.00	100.00	100.00	100.00

Source: Computed from *Report on Trend & Progress of Housing in India*; 2001–2005; NHB.

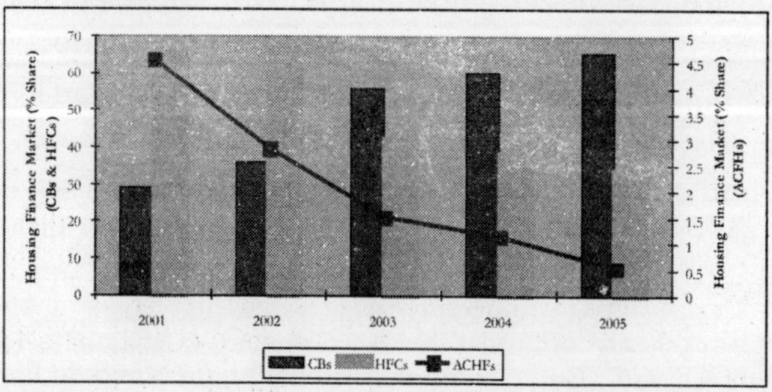

Figure 2: **Changing Landscape of the Housing Finance Industry in India**

Source: Computed from *Report on Trend& Progress of Housing in India*, 2001-2005; NHB.)

Table 7
Growth Rates (Y to Y) of the Major Intermediary Groups in using Finance

(in Percentages)

Particulars	*2001-2002*	*2002-2003*	*2003-2004*	*2004-2005*
Commercial Banks	54.26	174.95	39.33	53.58
Housing Finance Companies	15.64	22.02	16.99	24.63
ACHFs	-21.91	-05.33	-02.87	-02.88
Industry (Overall)	25.18	76.15	29.21	41.47

Source: Computed from *Report on Trend & Progress of Housing in India*, for 2001 to 2005.

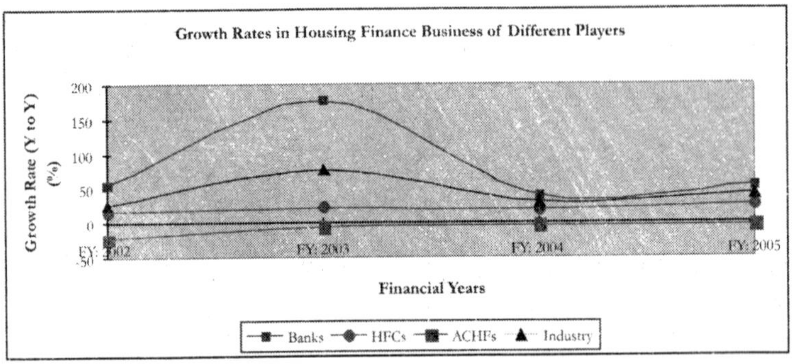

Figure 3: **Growth Rates (Y to Y) of the Major Players in the Housing Finance Industry.**

Source: Computed from Report on Trend & Progress of Housing in India; for 2001 to 2005.)

Exhibit 2

Housing Finance Industry in India: Changing Landscape

- CBs are fast becoming the most dominant players in the housing finance market, as their relative share is goes up every year. Their share is likely to constantly go up in the future.
- Though HFCs have been growing significantly over the years in absolute terms, their relative market share is coming down, as their growth is slower than that of CBs.
- The share of co-operative sector in housing finance (ACHFs) has been drastically coming down every year both in absolute and relative terms and as per the latest position their stake is negligibly small or, rather virtually nil.

Part-III

Appreciable Growth, but Growing Exclusiveness: Need for Alternative Models

On the one hand there is significant growth in housing finance disbursals over the years, thus resulting in a reasonably high mortgage to GDP ratio of about 9% (estimated) as of FY 2007. On the other hand, an equally important and probably more important fact remains viz. the reach of the formal housing finance system is gradually moving away from the majority of the population–the poor and the lower middle income group. This necessitates the need for urgent policy measures for making the system more inclusive and hence more sustainable in the long run. The fact that vast majority of the population is un-served or under-served by the current system has been specifically pointed out by the industry regulator, National Housing Bank (NHB) itself in its recent report viz. Trend & Progress of Housing in India 2005. Besides, the fact of losing inclusiveness of the system is reflected in the pattern of the growth rates of the major players (viz. CBs, HFCs and ACHFs) as discussed in the foregoing section whereby it has been observed that the co-operative sector institutions (ACHFs)–the financial intermediaries which are the most inclusive of all (Exhibit 3)–have almost disappeared. Thus,

***Exhibit 3* : General Profile of the Customers in Housing Finance: Agency-wise Details**

ACHFs		*CBs and HFCs*
Types of Customers	% Share	• Mostly to middle to high income group, and that too salaried class, high level of urban concentration also. (Nearly 90%)
Economically Weaker Section (EWS) and Low Income (LIG)	75	
Middle Income (MIG)	18	• Majority of the population is un-served/under-served [the low income group (LIG), the self-employed, rural populace etc.]
High Income (HIG)	07	
Total	100	

Ref: (1) *Trend & Progress of Housing in India 2004*, NHB, Govt. of India. p. 113,
(2) *Trend & Progress of Housing in India 2005*, NHB, Govt. of India. p. 54.

it appears that unless the major players viz. CBs and HFCs are made more inclusive through appropriate policy initiatives the situation is very likely to become worse in the future. Accordingly, it follows that providing shelter to those in the middle income, low income as well as other marginalized sections of the society is the need of the hour. (Exhibit 3.)

The above state of affairs necessitates modification of the strict income-based credit dispensation as followed by the CBs and HFCs. Being the most dominant player in the market, increasingly so in the future, CBs probably have got the most important role to play in this regard. There has been a pro-rich orientation in respect of housing loans disbursed by both the major types of housing finance intermediaries viz. CBs and HFCs. Table 8 shows this trend in respect of housing finance exposures by the CBs in India (FY 2000-'01 to 2004-'05). Table 9 shows the trend in respect of a typical HFC (viz. LIC Housing Finance Ltd.) for the period (FY 2000-'01to 2006-'07).

Table 8
Average Size of Housing Loan Sanctions (Incremental) (Commercial Banks)

(Rupees in Lacs)

Financial Year	*FY 2001*	*FY 2002*	*FY 2003*	*FY 2004*	*FY 2005*
Av. Loan Amount	01.02	01.81	02.00	02.81	03.45

Ref: *Trend & Progress of Housing in India 2004*, NHB, Govt. of India, New Delhi, p. 113.

Table 9
Average Size of Housing Loan Sanctioned by a Typical HFC (LICHFL)

(Rupees in Lacs)

Financial Year	*FY 2001*	*FY 2002*	*FY 2003*	*FY 2004*	*FY 2005*	*FY 2006*	*FY 2007*
Av. Loan Amount	03.13	03.31	03.83	04.26	05.07	05.92	08.27

Ref: *Annual Report of LICHFL, 2006-'07*, LICHFL. p. 33.

Note: In fact, LICHFL is having 97% of its total housing portfolio under the individual residential housing category. Information in respect of the entire HFC segment or that of other major players is not available.

As is evident from Tables 8 and 9, the housing finance exposures by CBs and HFCs are increasingly becoming pro-rich, pro-salaried class and exclusive of the poor. To a large extent these are pro-urban also. They assess credit-worthiness of the customers based on income criterion wherein the income from salary, business, or profession is taken into account. Because of better stability of income, they always prefer the salaried class. It is estimated that more than 90 per cent of the individual housing finance exposures of CBs and HFCs goes to the salaried class and the balance mainly goes to the business or professional class, the share of agriculturists and other rural populace being quite small. In the case of project financing (i.e. financing housing societies, builders, developers etc.) it is obvious that the ultimate beneficiaries are always the rich. Though the government earmarks specific amounts to be disbursed to the poor through various schemes like Golden Jubilee Rural Housing Finance (GJRHF) scheme, the same is only a meager portion of the total housing finance portfolio of these agencies. Moreover, here also these loans are available only to those who fulfil the income-based eligibility criteria stipulated by these agencies. Often, the assessment criteria are more or less similar to those of general schemes, except for slight changes as stipulated by the regulatory or refinancing agencies. According to the latest estimates (2007) of National Sample Survey Organization (NSSO), there exits a huge disparity between the number of dwelling units targeted and the number of units constructed, in respect of both of the special housing finance schemes for the poor viz. (i) housing for economically weaker section, (ii) housing for low income group. Table 10 is self-explanatory in this regard.

Table 10

Housing for the Poor: Wide Gap between the Targets and Achievements

Name of the Housing Scheme	*Target for 2006-'07 (Units) (Nos)*	*Achievement (Units) (Nos) till Aug. 2007 & Growth %*
Housing for Economically Weaker Section	1,14,000	22,960 (20.14%)
Housing for Low Income Group	24,003	2,251 (09.38%)

Source: NSSO Estimates (2007) cited in *The Economic Times*, Chennai Ed. dt.13 Aug.

In short, in respect of specialized schemes also, the really deserving sections of the society do not have access to the system, rather a handful of rich and affluent among such sections alone are benefited out of such schemes.

Inclusive Housing: the Worst Challenge, and also the Best Opportunity

In view of the foregoing, it appears that making Indian housing finance system inclusive is one of the worst challenges in the days to come. This involves making it pro-poor, pro-rural and hence more equitable. However, the above challenge may also be looked into as an emerging opportunity for the financial intermediaries which are starving for credit-worthy and profitable customers. This is because of the fact that the poor and the marginalized need not be defaulters of credit facilities.

International experiences show the contrary. That is, if the poor are provided with credit facilities, they prove themselves to be quite creditworthy, the repayment track record being as high as 95 per cent or even more. Such a system is self-sustainable and would ensure equitable economic development. The Grameen Bank experience of Bangladesh is a classic example in this regard and many national governments have already replicated the same or are in the process of the same. As already noted, in Indian scenario, the role of commercial banks–the largest agency group and increasingly so in the future–is quite vital in this regard.

Part-IV

Role of Commercial Banks in Housing Finance: Some Strategies for Inclusive and Sustainable Housing Finance and Development in India from a Global Perspective

Housing Loan Exposure by Indian Banks in the Future: How Much is Sustainable?

Commercial banks provide finance for housing purpose as a retail banking product. Retail banking refers to a very large and comprehensive range of financial products like, residential mortgage loans (home loans, as is commonly called), loans for consumer durables, auto finance, deposit products, loans against equity shares, credit cards, debit cards, personal loans, loans for Initial Public Offer (IPO) so on and so forth. However, of these varying products housing loans occupy a very prominent place and in general it accounts for nearly 50% of the total retail banking portfolio of Indian commercial banks.

The relative prominence of housing finance is because of the fact that these loans are comparatively safer; are supported by mortgage of the property financed and the default rate on an average is less than 1%, annualized. Further, housing loan offers many tax benefits for the beneficiaries because of the priority status that it enjoys. Table 11 gives the trend in respect of incremental retail credit exposures by all scheduled commercial banks in India for the last four years' period ended FY 2007. Table 12 gives the position in respect of outstanding amounts of retail

Table 11

Break up of Retail Credit Portfolio (Incremental) of Banks in India

Particulars	*FY: 2004*	*FY: 005*	*FY: 2006*	*FY: 2007*
Housing Loans	89449	134653 (50.54)	179060 (33.4)	224481 (25.4)
Consumer Durables	6256	3810 (-39.10)	4469 (17.3)	7296 (63.3)
Credit Card Receivables	6167	8405 (36.27)	12434 (47.9)	18317 (47.3)
Other Personal Loans	87170	120120 (37.80)	179720 (49.62)	237766 (32.30)
Total Retail Loans	189041	266988 (41.2)	375683 (40.9)	487860 (29.9)
Total of all Loans	864271	1105725 (27.94)	1473723 (31.0)	1893775 (28.5)
Retail Credit as a % of the Total Credit	21.9 %	24.10 %	25.50 %	25.80 %
Housing Credit as a % of the Total Credit	10.35 %	12.18 %	12.15 %	11.85 %

Source: Compiled from, *Report on Trend and Progress of Banking in India* for 2004 to 2007.

Note: Figures in brackets show the percentage variation over the previous year.

Table 12

Break up of Outstanding Retail Credit (Personal Loans) Exposure by Banks in India (FY: 1997 to 2007)

Particulars	*FY 1997*	*FY 1998*	*FY 1999*	*FY 2000*	*FY 2000*	*FY 2000*	*FY 2003*	*FY 2004*	*FY 2005*	*FY 2006*	*FY 2007*
Housing Loans (Rs in Crores)	946	9632	12377	18525	25412	32825	49066	51981	75173	185181	230689
Consumer Durables (Rs in Crores)	974	1322	1906	2781	3463	3214	3222	8274	8655	7101	9151
Other Personal Loans (Rs in Crores)	19282	23799	25306	30332	37065	46480	61654	132256	178011	167799	215663
Total Personal Loans (Rs in Crores)	28201	34753	39589	51639	65940	82519	113942	192511	261839	360081	455503
Total Bank Credit (Rs in Crores)	284373	329944	382425	460081	538434	655995	755968	764383	972587	1443920	1841878
Personal Loans as a % of Bank Credit	09.92%	10.53%	10.35%	11.22%	12.25%	12.58	15.07%	24.19%	26.92%	24.94%	24.73%
Housing Loans as a % of Bank Credit	02.79%	02.92%	03.24%	04.03%	04.72%	05.00%	06.49%	06.80%	07.73%	12.82%	12.52%

Source: Compiled from, *Statistical Tables relating to Banks in India*, RBI for FY 1997 to 2007.

credits by all commercial banks for the eleven-years' period (viz. FY 1997 to FY 2007) representing the second phase of the ongoing financial sector deregulation measures. From Tables 11 and 12, it may be noted that there is a gradual slow down in the retail credit growth rate *vis-à-vis* the total credit since the last two years (ie, FY 2006 and FY 2007). This slow down is quite prominent in respect of housing loans.

As is obvious from the trend revealed by Tables 11 and 12 there is going to be a consolidation in the retail portfolio of banks in the days to come. Accordingly, the outstanding balance of housing loan advances of banks is likely to be stagnant at the current level of about one-fourth (25%) of the total outstanding balance of all loans. Besides, in respect of incremental exposures also, the share is likely to be the same, ie. roughly one-fourth (25%) towards retail credit.

Another notable feature is about half of the retail credit outstanding (and also, incremental credit), or one-eighth (12.5%) of the total bank credit outstanding (and also, incremental credit) goes to housing sector. Now, it is quite logical to project the housing advances of CBs for the next 5 years at the current rate (25%) and also double the rate (50%) to test the sustainability. Table 13 shows the projections as above for the next 5 years' period (FY 2008 – FY 1012).

From Table 13 above, it may be noted that even double the growth rates in housing finance disbursements by commercial banks in India is quite sustainable for the next five years. This is because, even in such a case the mortgage to GDP ratio is likely to be just 28 %. On the other hand, if the present growth rates continue, the same may be just about 12%. The huge and growing housing shortage in the country (24.71 million units as of FY2007) (Table 2) and fast pace of financial exclusion, thus points to urgent measures to double the housing finance growth rate with thrust on reaching the hitherto un-reached viz. the poor and the low-income populace. This in turn necessitates the need for adoption of alternate models of service delivery, norms for appraisal of

Table 13
How much the Housing System (CBs) can Grow? Projections till FY 2012

(Rupees in Crores)

Particulars	*FY 2007 (Actual)*	*FY 2008 (Projected)*	*FY 2009 (Projected)*	*FY 2010 (Projected)*	*FY 2011 (Projected)*	*FY 2012 (Projected)*
GDP@ (Factor Cost)	4130500	4502245	4907447	5349117	5830538	6355286
Housing Loans (CBs)*	224481	280601	350752	438440	548049	685062
Housing Loans (HFCs)#	33488 (Estimate)	36837	40520	44573	49030	53933
Total Housing Loans	257969	36837	40520.7	44572.77	49030.05	53933.05
Mortgage to GDP*#	6.25 %	7.05 %	7.97 %	9.03 %	10.24 %	11.63 %
Housing Loans (CBs)**	224481	336721.5	505082.3	757623.4	1136435	1704653
Housing Loans (HFCs)##	33488 (Estimate)	40185.6	48222.7	57867.3	69440.7	83328.9
Mortgage to GDP**##	6.25 %	8.37 %	11.27 %	15.25 %	20.68 %	28.13 %

Source: Computed from the Data given in Table 4.1) .

Notes:

@ GDP (at factor cost) for the next five years are projected at the an assumed rate of 9%.

* Projections are made at the current growth rate of 25% over the next 05 year' period.

\# Projections at an assumed rate of 10% over the next 5 years period

** Projections are made at an optimistic growth rate of 50%, (ie. double the current rate)

\## Projections at an optimistic rate of double the expected rate of 10%

*# Mortgage to GDP ratio projected (with assumed growth rates of 25% and 10% for CBs and HFCs respectively, considering two major intermediary groups, CBs and HFCs.

**## Mortgage to GDP ratio projected (with assumed growth rates of 50% and 20% for CBs and HFCs respectively, considering two major intermediary groups, CBs and HFCs.

credit worthiness of customers, and after all a conducive regulatory and legal framework that can facilitate the intermediaries to proceed accordingly. To design such a model, the special features of the housing finance system in India need to be considered, along with study of international success stories in respect of housing for the poor and the marginalized.

Housing Development in India: Private Participation is an Imminent Need

The investment in housing in India, during the pre-reforms and post-reforms era are shown separately in Table 14. The investments during the various Plans by the Public and Private sector are shown separately in Table 15.

Table 14
Housing Investment in India during Pre-reform and Reforms Periods

(Amount Rupees in Crores)

Particulars	*Pre-reforms period 1950–51 to 1990–91*		*Reforms period 1991–92 to 2001–02*	*Changes in %*
Total plan outlays in the economy	585282		1657200	283.15
Total plan outlays in housing	62185 (10.62)		247530 (14.94)	398.05
Public sector outlay in housing	6345 (10.20)	62185 (100)	57370 (23.18)	904.18
Private sector outlay in housing	55840 (89.80)		190160 (76.82)	240.54
Investment in rural housing	1067 (1.72)	62185 (100)	14190 (5.73)	1229.90
Investment in urban housing	61118 (98.28)		233340 (94.27)	281.79

Source: Compiled from *Five Years Plan documents* (I–IX), planning commission, GOI.)

Note: Figures in parenthesis represent percentage to total.

From Tables 14 and 15, it may very well be observed that there has been quite significant increase in the housing investments in India since the 1980s. This is much more prominent in the post-reforms era (that is, since the 1990s). Further, it may be noted that public sector investment in housing which was just one-tenth of the total during the pre-reforms era has become almost three-fourth in the post-reforms era. Another noteworthy feature is the increased thrust on rural housing during the post-reforms period. This is evidenced from the increase in the absolute figures; the

Table 15
Investment for Housing during the Various Plan Periods

(Amount in Rupees Crores)

Five Year Plan	*Public Investment*	*Private Investment*	*TotalInvestment*	*%Increase (Total)*
First Plan (1951-56)	250	900	1,150	—
Second Plan (1956-61)	300 (20)	1,000 (11.11)	1,300	13.04
Third Plan (1961-66)	425 (41.67)	1,125 (12.50)	1,550	19.23
Fourth Plan (1969-74)	625 (47.06)	2,175 (93.33)	2,800	80.65
Fifth Plan (1974-78)	796 (27.36)	3,640 (67.36)	4,436	58.43
Sixth Plan (1980-85)	1491 (87.31)	18,000 (394.50)	19,491	339.38
Seventh Plan (1992-97)	2,458 (64.86)	29,000 (61.11)	31,458	61.40
Eighth Plan (1992-97)	31,500 (1181.53)	66,000 (127.59)	97,500	209.94
Ninth Plan (1997-2002)	52,000 (65.08)	99,000 (50.00)	1,51,000	54.87
Tenth Plan (2002-07)*	4,15,000 (698.08)	3,11,300 (214.44)	7,26,300	380.99

* The figures pertaining to 2002-2007 are estimated figures as per the Plan Documents.

Source: *Report on Trend and Progress of Housing in India 2003*, NHB, New Delhi., p. 79.

Note: Figures in Brackets show percentage increase over the previous Plan period.

total amount of which during short span (1992 to 2002) in the post-reforms period has reached 12.3 times the corresponding figure during the pre-reforms period of four decades (1951 to 1991). In relative terms also it has improved from the meager 1.72 percent to 5.73 per cent i.e. an increase of more than 4 per cent. In spite of such huge incremental investments and also significant increase in the mortgage to GDP ratio (about 9% as of 2007), the housing problem is very acute. Moreover, the most critical problem is that of meeting the housing needs of the low-income and middle-income groups. In short, private participation is essential for fast housing development in India.

Models for Affordable Housing Finance Development: Cross Country Experiences

Some classic examples of affordable housing finance and development worth consideration. These success stories mostly relate to the recent past, often during the post-deregulation era. It may be noted that these are replicable in India, if the legal and regulatory set up is changed.

In China, the housing market was liberalized only during the late nineties. For people living in sub-standard living conditions, a 'one-time' equity grants based on the market value of their existing housing are given to enable them to access mortgage instruments. Land leases are auctioned to developers to supply housing on a home ownership basis. Developers are provided incentives in the form of tax reductions or tax exemptions. Accordingly, China could develop more than 20 million housing units during the last five years.

Chile has pioneered in the up-front capital subsidy programme in 1977. This programme has eliminated all slums from Chilean cities. Here, on the supply side, social housing is built by the private sector. On the demand side, subsidies are given to poor families to increase effective demand for the private 'social' housing. Chile has set aside 05.8 % of its national budget for providing such subsidies.

South Africa (along with Singapore, Cuba and Sweden) has got one good success story in providing housing for the poor called social housing. Here minimum standards for housing and services are fixed by the Government. A viable market for low-cost housing is established through subsidy programme. This has been made possible through establishing partnership with housing institutions, communities, the private sector and NGOs. Thus, 1.4 million houses with secure tenure have been constructed in the last ten years for the poorest of the poor.

In Thailand, "The Baan Mankong" (meaning "Secure housing" in Thai) Program has channeled government funds through the Community Organizations Development Institute. Thai Government has earmarked a budget of about US$ 470 million for the infrastructure subsidy and housing loan interest subsidy. This works out to US$ 1650 per family. Accordingly, Thailand puts its existing slum communities (and their community networks) at the center of a process of developing long-term, comprehensive solutions to problems of land and housing.

Apart from the four global success stories (viz. China, Chile, Thailand and South Africa) in respect of urban housing poverty alleviation as discussed above, other glaring examples (that followed more or less similar pattern of participatory or partnership form of development) include Brazil, Egypt, Mexico, and Tunisia. In all these countries, the respective central government has been in the 'driving seat' in the implementation of inclusive policies for housing, land reforms and regularization. Some low-income or middle-income countries like Colombia, El Salvador, Philippines, Indonesia, Myanmar and Sri Lanka, have managed to prevent slum formation by anticipating and planning for growing urban populations by investing in low-cost and affordable housing.

In view of the above success stories, it appears that non-availability of proper housing is by and large a reflection not of market failure but of societal failure. The poor must have access to housing in homes they can afford. Since market forces will never provide housing that the poor can afford, and further market forces will never have the ability to do so until these masses cease being poor, it is up to government to take the initiative. The government can stimulate the creation of sustainable and affordable housing for the poor through the involvement of private sector. Reform measures in (i) the land (grant of land security to poor, reduced government interventions in land market), (ii) finance (down marketing housing finance, fiscal incentives to the private sector developers, micro-finance institutions), (iii) capital subsidies targeted subsidies in various forms (like, up-front subsidies to the poor, or through savings institutions, or to the developers).

In Indian scenario also, private participation is very much essential for rapid housing development in the country. Research shows that there has been significant increase in public investment in housing over the years. spending One of the key requisites for such initiatives to be successful is that of ensuring a governance system that is open, transparent and is able to implement the 'rule of the law' in its true letter and spirit.

Inclusive Housing in India: a Micro finance Approach through PPP Route

In view of the foregoing analyses it appears that: (i) micro finance in housing appears to be the most pragmatic model for affordable housing development, (ii) private investment is essential for fast housing development for which the most appropriate model appears to be that of PPP (Public-Private Partnership) model. Thus, a housing micro finance model under PPP route seems the most appropriate in the Indian context in the ongoing scenario. The success stories of other nations as well as current developments in a few developing nations also support the above approach. Accordingly, the marketing approach suggested in the Indian context is as follows:

(1) SHG-Bank Linkage Model for Housing Micro finance for the time being (Adhoc Model);

(2) Comprehensive Public-Private Partnership (PPP) Model (Ultimate Model).

The adhoc model is suggested because it serves as a model that is relatively easy to adopt at present, while the comprehensive PPP model as suggested would require appropriate policy initiatives from the government which .require considerable time and political will power.

SHG-Bank Linkage Model for Housing Micro finance (Adhoc Model)

Micro finance as a means of financial inclusion is fast picking up in India, though micro finance in housing is yet to pick up momentum. The reasons that deter the growth of housing micro finance are mainly (i) fragile structure of MFIs, (ii) lack of adequate collateral security for the lenders. (Manoj) (2004) [15]. A few favourable developments in this reagrd in India include.

(i) The Draft Micro finance Sector (Development and Regulation) Bill, 2007 has been tabled in the Parliament in March 2007. It aims at regulation of micro finance institutions. The Central Government is seriously considering passing this Act at the earliest.

(ii) Two micro finance funds of Rs. 500 crores each, viz. (i) Financial Inclusion Fund, and (ii) Financial Inclusion Technology Fund, have been announced by the Government. (Oct. 2007).

As India is fast becoming one of the largest micro finance markets in the world (Table 16), the vast network of SHGs would propel the growth of hitherto dormant housing micro finance market in India. Table 16 shows that there has been impressive growth in SHG-Bank linakge programme of NABARD over the last 09 years. With this much strong network, it appears that housing micro finance through SHG linkage can pick up fast in India.

In terms of outreach, the SHG-bank linkage programme of NABARD as mentioned above is the largest of its kind and the fastest growing in the whole world. This linkage could take three different forms, (i) Bank–SHG Members, (ii) Bank-Facilitating Agency-SHG Members, (iii) Bank-NGO-MFI-SHG Members.

These three models have relative shares of 16%, 75% and 09% respectively. Obviously, the second model with three agencies viz. banks, facilitating agencies (like NGOs, Community organizations etc.) and SHGs is the most popular one currently. Regarding housing micro finance also this model appears to be the most suitable.

Table 16
SHG–Bank Linkage Programme: Imprssive Growth over the Years

Financial Year	*Total SHGs financed by banks (in '000s)*		*(Amount in Rupees Crores)*			
			Bank Loans		*Refinances*	
	During the Year	*Cumulative*	*During the Year*	*Cumulative*	*During the Year*	*Cumulative*
1992-99	33	33	57	57	52	52
1999-00	82	115	136	193	98	1507
	(147.9)	(247.9)	(138.1)	(238.1)	(88.6)	(188.6)
2000-01	149	264	288	481	251	401
	(82.3)	(129.9)	(112)	(149.2)	(155.5)	(167.0)
2001-02	198	461	545	1026	396	796
	(32.6)	(74.9)	(89)	(113.4)	(57.9)	(98.8)
2002-03	256	717	1022	2049	622	1419
	(29.5)	(55.4)	(87)	(99.6)	(57.2)	(78.1)
2003-04	362	1079	1856	3904	706	2125
	(41.4)	(50.49)	(81)	(90.6)	(13.4)	(49.7)
2004-05	539	1618	2994	6898	968	3092
	(49.1)	(50.0)	(61)	(76.7)	(37.1)	(45.5)
2005-06	620	2239	4499	11398	1068	4160
	(15.0)	(38.3)	(50.3)	(65.2)	(10.3)	(34.5)
2006-07*	686	2924	6643	18041	1299	5459
	(11.0)	(30.6)	(47.6)	(58.3)	(21.6)	(31.2)

(The figures in brackets indicate annual percentage growth.)
(* - Provisional)

Source: NABARD, cited in *Report on Trend and Progress of Housing in India 2007*, RBI.

Comprehensive Public-Private Partnership (PPP) Model of Housing Micro Finance

As already noted, the ultimate aim should be that of a comprehensive PPP model for housing micro finance. As per this model, the central government has to take the lead role – the role of the main enabler or facilitator.

The government provides fiscal concessions (tax rebates, exemptions, tax holidays etc.) for builders and developers for constructing low cost houses in notified rural areas with clear specifications regarding the minimum quality, size etc. as well as the maximum cost of constructions. Apart from fiscal concessions as above, faster clearance of all necessary conditions, grant of requisite permissions and sanctions (like, transfer of title, building permits etc.) may also be offered to them so that it is practically possible to construct such houses with relative ease. Besides, intermediaries (like NGOs, community organizations etc.) having Self Help Groups (SHGs) involved in housing development, as well as micro finance institutions (MFIs) floated by such organizations be supported by the government both (i) through financial assistance, and (ii) by providing guarantee for the housing loans that members such MFIs take from financial intermediaries. Further, commercial banks be given refinance at concessional rates for financing such housing projects. Also, financial intermediaries be provided refinance at concessional rates for onward lending (as individual housing loans) to poor people belonging to some government-recognized MFI.

Firstly, the builders are getting incentives from both the government and financing agencies so that they will find it feasible to undertake such projects.

Secondly, the financing agencies are getting finance at concessional rates for lending both (i) to individuals (belonging to recognized SHGs), and (ii) to projects taken up by builders and developers that is recognized by the government or satisfy the requisite norms stipulated by the government.

Thirdly, the poor people belonging to recognized SHGs are getting affordable housing through easier finance, and also guarantee support from the government through the respective MFI. The government may encourage financing income generating activities of MFIs also, so that repayment of loans become easier for the members.

Figure 5 shows a comprehensive model for affordable and sustainable housing in India, as proposed in the foregoing paragraphs.

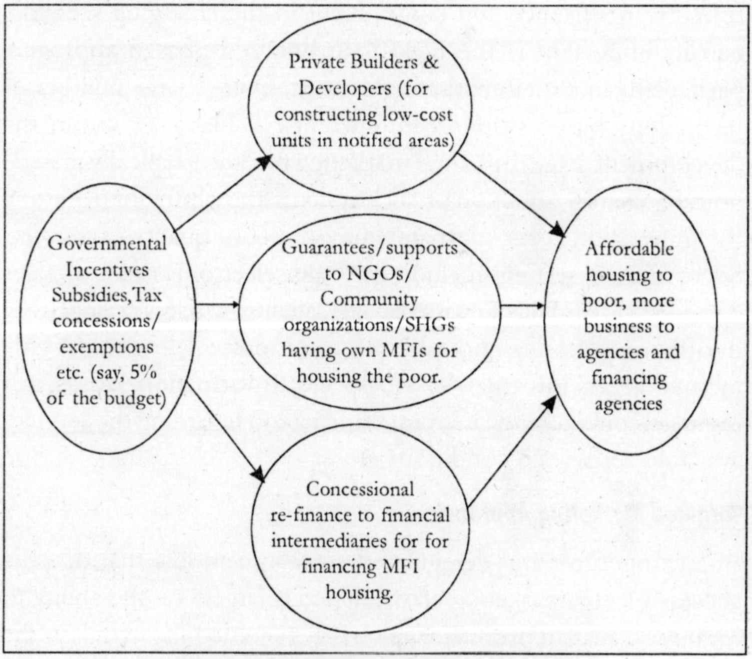

Figure 4: **A Model for Affordable Housing based on Micro finance (PPP) Approach**

Generic Strategies for Marketing of Housing Loan Products to Rural Customers

A few generic considerations that might be followed by banks while going for marketing their housing loan products to rural customers are given in the following paragraphs.

Balanced and Phased Approach towards Technology-based Systems

Technology has to be considered as an enabler for cost-cutting and higher order customer service and not as an end in itself.

Factors that deserve special attention include, inter alia, include facts such as: (i) considerable percentage of the customer population (percentage varies between various customer segments) still prefers manual service delivery through bank branches, and (ii) Technology Readiness (TR) of customers vary between different customer segments. While technology adoption is of primary significance and is imminent in the emerging scenario, equally important is the need to maintain a phased approach, particularly in a rural marketing context. Quite a large number of technology based systems are currently available or are in the development stage. In a rural marketing parlance, typically in rural housing finance, adoption of such systems are helpful for (i) cutting the transaction costs, (ii) maintaining superior quality of service. Some of such systems include, inter alia, electronic point of sales devices (like, card reader with dial up/satellite/wireless connectivity or offline processing), portable electronic devices, low cost ATMs in rural areas, information kiosks etc. Information kiosks, for instance, could provide relevant information regarding the services available, terms and conditions etc.

Targeted Marketing Approach

In a competitive and deregulated environment like that of ours success of any marketing effort depends largely on the ability to create and sustain products which offer "something extra" to the customers. Whatever is really important here is to understand as accurately as possible what is important to customers; with the intention of delivering superior quality service consistently. That is, service expectations of customers and variations in these expectations across different customer segments have to be analyzed and understood well. This in turn requires that these changes are sensed on an ongoing basis through systematic and rigorous consumer research and such other studies. As already noted, the levels of TR as well as other tastes and preferences of customers vary widely in a highly heterogeneous society like that of India, the need for proper segmentation of customers assumes added significance. Further, tailor-made methods of advertisement, market research studies, customer feedback surveys etc. have to be used for each segment for better effectiveness. Modern data mining softwares can provide valuable inputs regarding profile of the existing customers in respect of their credit worthiness (quality of servicing loans) and can even predict future probability of default in these accounts. In a rural marketing context, initiation of sophisticated systems as above may involve considerable time. But, it appears that the orientation needs to be that of targeted marketing always.

Emphasis on Product & Process Innovation

The role of a bank marketer today is no more limited to his functional area. Rather, it is quite strategic in nature. He has to play a vital role in product and process innovation with a view to ensure superior quality service (ie. service with "something extra") consistently. This should be based on information gathered through systematically designed customer feedback surveys, market studies etc. Excellence in customer service has become the most important factor influencing business growth in today's competitive business scenario. Product and process innovation on an ongoing basis is more like an imperative than a choice in any marketing setting.

Customer Feedback Systems

For improving the service standards and hence to ensure customer satisfaction, bank marketers worldwide adopt innovative techniques for capturing valuable feedback from customers and design their service strategy in the light of their feedback. The pursuit of more accurate data regarding the customers' expectations for improving the customer feedback mechanism, has resulted in a wide variety of information-gathering techniques. Further, traditional methods of data collection by way of direct mails and telephone surveys have often proved themselves to be quite unsuccessful since these are considered an annoyance by many a modern customer. Experts in this field advise a comprehensive and balanced approach to customer feedback surveys. Thus, specific survey techniques have to be carefully matched to specific customer groups. This is more relevant in India because of wide heterogeneity of the market, especially in a rural context.

Scientific Assessment of the Cost of Delivery of Services

The cost of delivery of services has to be computed scientifically for meaningful decision-making regarding pricing our product. While separate cost accounting departments are already in place in prominent manufacturing organizations, the same is yet to get adequate significance in many of the banks. But the fact is that, in service organizations like banks also, by the application of the latest techniques of cost accounting like Activity Based Costing (ABC), the cost of delivery of a service can be found out with reasonable accuracy. This in turn facilitates better profit planning and rational pricing of the bank products. In an era when bank products have to be modified overnight because of severe competitive pressures, existence of a well established cost accounting department and proper co-ordination of its activities with those of marketing department can bring about very meaningful business decisions..

Balancing of Social Responsibility and Profits: Focus on Profits for Sustainability

As financial inclusion in general and rural housing in particular involves a delicate balancing between social and economic (profit) considerations, it is imperative that banks have to follow a conscious policy of profit for sustainability, as they need not extend housing loans at the cost of their profitability and operational efficiency. Of late, it is widely recognized that profit for sustainability is something which any financial inclusion endeavor can strive for. (*Adams and Von Pischke, 1992*, pp. 1463-70; *Yaron, 1992*) [1] It is in this context that scientific assessment of cost of delivery of services, as suggested in the last paragraph, assumes vital significance.

Creation of Long Term Relationships

The bank marketer should focus on long term relationships rather than short-term business gains. Only such kind of relationships can ensure sustained growth and profitability in an industry like banking. This is particularly relevant in respect of housing finance because the advances are typically for long periods ranging from ten to twenty years. Further, long-term relationships, if properly built-up can bring in additional business to the bank through word of mouth; and banks can also benefit through cross-selling of products (universal banking). It is the human factor in the service delivery that creates and develops such relationships most.

Need for Micro Insurance and Securitization for Micro finance Assets

To give a further boost to micro finance initiatives, particularly housing micro finance, it is essential that micro insurance–that is, provision of insurance services to low income households–needs to be developed. Similarly, mortgage securitization in general and the one relating to housing microfinance in particular, needs to be developed as the same is in its infancy in India. In the current Indian scenario, commercial banks can take the lead role in promotion of both these schemes, provided the necessary regulatory measures are initiated by the Government.

Concluding Observations

In view of the foregoing, it may be stated that in the ongoing era of financial deregulation the need for balanced and equitable economic growth is of vital significance. As such, financial inclusion in general and low-income (affordable) housing finance in particular, need to be promoted. Many studies have pointed out that inclusive lending need not at all be at a loss to the lenders. Rather these are may a time a profitable business proposition. Micro finance is a classic example in this regard and is fast emerging in India. However, housing micro finance is yet to pick up momentum in India. Bank marketers have the responsibility to cash in on this huge and growing market in India. Apart from promising reasonable returns it ensures a number of advantages to the nation as a whole and ensures fast and equitable economic development.

Further, it appears that customer centricity, cost management, long-term relationships and technology–four interrelated factors –are going to be the hallmarks of success in rural housing finance in India in the future. In view of the foregoing discussions, it is meaningful to frame a typical model for development of rural housing in India. (Figure 5) As shown, it comprises of three main parts. 'Foundations', the most basic component, is the requisite macro level infrastructure which includes, (i) conducive legal and regulatory environment (uniform stamp duty/central registry for

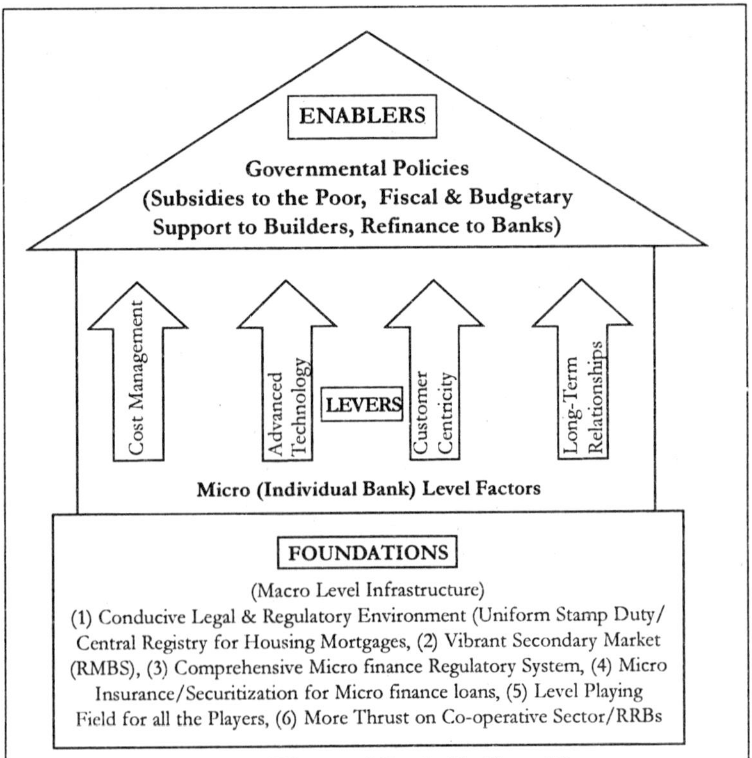

Figure 5: **"House of Equitable Growth": A Model for Housing Finance in India**

housing mortgages, (ii) vibrant secondary market (RMBS), (3) comprehensive micro finance regulatory system, (4) micro insurance/securitization for micro finance loans etc. The second part called 'Levers' represent the factors that promote housing at the micro (individual bank) level viz. (i) cost management, (ii) technology, (iii) customer focus, and (iv) and long term relationships. Lastly, 'Enablers' as the term connotes, represents the Governmental responsibilities towards bringing about an financial administration that is conducive for equitable housing development. That is, adequate budgetary and fiscal support to the poor beneficiaries, financial intermediaries and agencies involved in development of affordable housing.

References

Adams, D., Von Pischke, J.D. (1992), "Micro Enterprise credit Programs: déjà vu", *World Development*, Vol. 20, No.10, pp.1463-70.

Bhattacharya, C. (2006), Services Marketing: Concepts, Planning and Implementation, Excel Books, New Delhi., First Edition.

Buckley, Robert M. (1996), Housing Finance in Developing Countries, Macmillan, London.

Baron, Steve. and Harris, Kim. (2004), Services Marketing: Text and Cases, Palgrave, Houndmills, Basingstoke, New York, N.Y. 10010 (Reprint).

Cherunilam, Francis and Heggade, Odeyar D. (1987), Housing in India, Himalaya Publishing House, New Delhi.

Coles, Adrian (2004), 'Housing Microfinance: A Guide to Practice', Kumarian Press Inc, 1294, Bluehills Avenue, Bloomfield, CT06002, USA, Jan.

Ferguson, Bruce (1999), "Micro-finance of housing: a key to housing the low or moderate-income majority?", *Environment and Urbanization*, Vol. 11, No.1, April, pp. 185-199.

Gupta, R. G. (1995), Shelter for the Poor in the Fourth World, Shipra Publications, Delhi.

Harman, W.C. (1975), Housing and Social Policy, Prentice Hall, U.S.A.

'Housing: Who Benefits ?', *Economic and Political Weekly*, Editorial, May 15, 2004.

"Enterprise CRM in Banks" (*www.hp.com*), in Rao, K Nageswara.(Ed.), Retail Banking, ICFAI Books, Hyderabad, 2003, pp.143-166.

Knapschaefer, Johanna (2002), "Banking on Customer Focus", in Kaushesh, Anshul (Ed.), Marketing of Financial Services, ICFAI Books, Hyderabad, pp. 41-47.

Kotler, Philip (2004), Marketing Management, Pearson Education (Singapore) Pte. Ltd., Indian Branch, Delhi.

Manoj, P. K (2003). 'Retail Banking: Strategies for Success in the Emerging Scenario', *IBA Bulletin*, Vol. XXV, No.11, November, pp.18-21.

Manoj P. K. (2004), "Dynamics of Housing Finance in India", Bank Quest, Vol.75, No. 3, Sept.

Mathur, G.C. (1980), "Housing the Poor", *Yojana*, Vol. XXIII, No. 24, January 01.

Nair, Tara S. (1999), "Housing: The Missing Concerns", Commentary, *Economic and Political Weekly*, Vol. XXXIV, No. 28, July 10, p. 1871.

Report on Trend and Progress of Banking in India 1996 - 2007, RBI, New Delhi.

Report on Trend & Progress of Housing in India 1999-2005, NHB, New Delhi.

Sharma, K.S. R. N. (1989), Housing Finance in India: Some Issues, Indian Institute of Public Administration, New Delhi.

Statistical Tables relating to Banks in India, 1996-2007, RBI, New Delhi.

Skinner, Steven, J., Marketing: Text & Cases, All India Publishers & Distributors, Poonamallee High Road, Chennai., Second Edition.

Wadhva, Kiran (2003), 'Housing Friendly Budgets', *Economic and Political Weekly*, Commentary, January 11.

11

BANKING SECTOR REFORMS IN INDIA AND THEIR IMPACT

K. Aiyadurai

Background

The Indian economy has been undergoing rapid changes in its attempt to integrate with global economy. The programme of stabilisation and structural reforms initiated by the Government since 1991, have already started yielding positive results. Along with the changes taking place in the real sectors of the economy, the financial sector too has been undergoing significant transformation. These changes have far reaching impact on the banking sector and capital market, which are important constituents of the financial sector.

The Indian financial system in the pre-reform period (i.e., prior to 1991), catered to the needs of planned development in a mixed economy, where the public sector had a dominant role in the economic activity. This required huge development expenditure, which was met through Government's dominanance of ownership of banks, automatic monetisation of fiscal deficit and subjecting the banking sector to large pre-emptions-both in terms of the statuary holding of statutory liquidity ratio and cash reserve ratio and the complex structure of administered interest rates, guided by social concerns, resulting in subsidation. These were the major factors which distorted the interest rate mechanism and adversely affected the viability and profitability of the banks, by the end of 1980s.

Impact of Financial Sector Reforms on Credit Management

The initiation of financial sector reforms has put tremendous pressures on the Banking System. It has now to function under more competitive conditions. Banks have to adjust their programmes and policies to changing environment with a sharp focus on profitability under more transparent conditions.

Prudential Norms

The developments in the Capital market and Money Market and emergence of new financial instruments like GDR Commercial Paper have resulted in diminished role for Banks as financial intermediaries.

The Banks have to concentrate on maintaining Asset quality and reducing NPA level. They have to look closely at the "Balance Sheet Risks". Any expansion of "Risk Assets" has to necessarily go with Capital Adequacy Planning.

With liberalisation in foreign exchange segment, Banks have to learn to operate with thin margins on Foreign Currency lending and at the same time manage the exchange risk on the funds raised.

Scientific Risk Management

With increasing complexities of business and proliferation of new business, risk assessment has assumed large importance. Scientific risk management has to be built into Credit Management.

Default risk is now more pronounced due to (i) Severe competition in the business from within the country and outside,

(ii) Risk of technological obsolescence with rapid advancement in science and technology.

Credit Monitoring & Recovery

Management of Non-performing assets (NPA) poses a real challenge to banks. High levels of NPA threaten the very survival of Banks. A clear cut strategy in this regard is called for. Perhaps each Bank has to lay down a tolerable percentage level of NPA for (a) each segment of the market (viz. large corporate, small corporate, SSI, Trade, Overseas lending, personnel segment. Agriculture, other priority) depending upon its portfolio size in each segment, and (b) for major Industry/Trade group in which it has taken large exposure. This may help the Banks to build a default risk costing in pricing the product for each segment/Trade and Industry and closely monitor the lending.

Credit follow up and supervision playa crucial role in NPA management. Banks have to develop and build appropriate information system which can throw up warning signals so that banks may reduce. Exposures to any particular segment/Trade in time or altogether come out of any Trade/Account where warranted.

Having initiated fundamental changes, the financial sector, particularly the banking sector, is now under an obligation to demonstrate the efficacy of the reforms undertaken so far.

Therefore, there is a three fold agenda:

1. To take stock of various changes that have taken place in the banking sector so far.
2. To make an assessment of how the banks in general have been able to cope with these changes and
3. To foresee the issues emerging out of this transition and chalk out strategies as to how best to prepare themselves to manage these changes successfully.

There are three focus areas, which represent the current banking reforms adequately.

Focus Area One is Managing Rural Banking. Combining public good with private enterprise is the essence of the liberalization philosophy. The implication of this to the banking sector is unambiguous. Banks have to make rural banking, an integral part of their commercial character. Over the last 25 years since nationalization, a very sound foundation has been laid for rural finance in terms of a wide network branches, a substantial deposit base and an enormous range of bankable activities. The next stage, obviously is to provide a commercial orientation to rural finance. We have reached a stage in evolution on rural banking, where we can confidently replace a system based on doles, subsidies and direct patronage with a system based on commercial co-operation and partnership. Such a transition would of course throw up many basic questions such as how far the element of concession is to be removed from rural lending? How far can new banking innovations be introduced purposefully and profitably into rural operations? What institutional innovations are required to bring rural credit on commercial lines?

The Second Focus Area is Managing financial Risks. Indian banks traditionally have been exposed mainly to one type of risk, namely, credit risk. This is by and large, true of the post nationalization period also when the decision making in the banks was largely dictated by directives and ground rules. But the current banking reforms have exposed the banks to a wide range of risks. Capital management, asset-liability management, interest rate management, exchange rate management, manpower management, profit management-practically all areas of day to day banking have to contend with degrees of risk now. Deregulation is meant to bring about the integration, through the marke: mechanism, of the various related markets like the forex market, call money market. the capital market and the stock market. As this process of integration proceed5. developments in different markets are bound to affect each other. Life for banks under deregulation can hardly be smooth. Hiccups are bound to occur more often than not!, 21 times, the hiccups can end up in virtual choking, as has happened recently, when the forex and call money markets were subject to wild gyrations. Banks will require great deal of expertise to foresee such risks to protect themselves or to exploit it as the case may be. The survival of the individual banks, therefore, we' largely depend on how far they will be successful in managing these multiple risks.

The Third Focus Area is Managing New Challenges: Liberalization without competition will be, indeed, like enacting Hamlet without Prince of Denmark. Enhancing efficiency by fostering competition is the underlying principle of liberalization. The banking sector has already had a liberal dose of reforms under this head. The doors of Indian banking have been opened for private banks as ,well as foreign banks. In the South especially, the banks have also to contend with the mounting competition from the growing number of Non Banking Financial Institutions and unincorporated agencies. And, as the various financial markets continue to be widened and deepened, the disintermediation of banking both at the wholesale and at the retail level will get accelerated adding to competition.

Banks therefore have to necessarily to learn to live with competition. There is no choice. Harping on a level playing field, will remain a wishful thinking. Banks can at best hope for equal opportunities, which they have been given now. The ultimate test of success of the financial sector reforms is how far banks have been able to improve their service to customers, both as depositors and borrowers. In the financial sector reform, the institutions immediately affected are the banks, since banks typically dominate the financial systems in the early stages of financial development. Banks are eager to provide short-term financing to the various economic entities. Banks are also distinguishable from other financial institutions by a unique characteristic which gives them power to provide means of payment in non-cash transactions. As reform of the financial system takes root, it is the banking system which comes to :(ace increasing competition from non-banks and the capital market. A recent study has drawn. the following lessons from the experience of several developing countries which introduced financial liberalization programmes. First, a system or prudential regulation is the first step in financial .sector reforms. Second, the speed and nature of interest rate liberalization has to take into account the pace with which problem, banks and their debtors can be restructured. Recapitalising the weak banks and restructuring their portfolios must receive attention in this context. Third, the success of the financial liberalization programmes critically depends upon maintaining macro economic control during the reform period. Fourth, introduction of convertibility should move from trade to current to capital account.

Reforming the Financial Sector in India

The Indian financial system comprises an impressive network of banks and financial institutions and a wide range of financial instruments. There is no doubt that there has been a considerable widening and deepening of the Indian financial system, particularly in the last two decades. The extension of banking and other financial facilities to a large cross-section of the people stands out as a significant achievement. As a ratio GDP at current prices, bank deposits increased from 18 per cent in 1969-70 to around 42.0 per cent in 1994-95. All the indicators of financial development, such as, the 'finance ratio', 'financial inter-relations ratio' and 'importance of financial institutions in the economy and growth of financial flows in relation to economic activity.

Major Elements of Reform

Pre-emption and Interest Rate Structure

In terms of administered structure of interest rates, we have come a long way in terms of lending rates for different slabs of borrowing were rationalised into six. A minimum lending rate prescription for large borrowers was introduced in 1988. After the recent changes, there are only two rates of interest prescribed on the lending side and on the deposit side, there is only the prescription of a maximum rate on deposits up to two year maturity. A continuous and a careful step by step approach has thus adopted in terms of deregulation of the interest rate structure.

Prudential Norms

Prudential reforms introduced in India relate to income recognition, provisioning fur bad and doubtful debts and capital adequacy. A proper definition of income was essential in order to ensure that banks take into account income which is actually realized. Banks are now required to make provisions on advances depending on the nature of assets. The provisioning requirement ranges from 10 per cent to 100 per cent depending on the category of the asset. A capital risk weighted asset ratio system has also been introduced more or less ir: conformity with international standards. Indian banks which have branches abroad an': foreign banks operating in India have already achieved this norm. As at the end of Ivfarch 1995, 13 public sector banks had attained the minimum CRAR of eight per cem. 11 banks at least four per cent and the remaining three banks less than four per cent.

The process of re-capitalisation has been facilitated primarily by a large equity-capital injection, made by the Government of India to the nationalised banks. In addition, several banks have also been allowed to access the capital market to raise equity on their own. The State Bank of India was able to enter the capital market in December 1993 and raise Rs. 2,532 crore with an equity-cum-bond issue. It must be mentioned that through this operation the share holding of the RBI in the State Bank of India has come down from 98.2 per cent to 66.3 per cent.

Similarly, for the nationalised banks, The Banking Companies (Acquisition and Transfer of Undertakings) Act, 1970/1980 was amended in June 1994 so as to enable nationalized banks to raise capital by public issue of shares with the Government of India at all time holding not less than 51 per cent of the shares in each bank. Taking advantage of this, the Oriental Bank of Commerce accessed the capital market to strengthen its capital base. This

Act, was further amended in January 1995 allowing .reduction in the paid up capital of a nationalized bank before making any public issue, by canceling any other paid up capital which is lost or is unrepresented by available assets.

Competition

A more competitive environment is also being created. Banks are already facing competition from non-bank finance companies on the lending and deposit sides and ~m mutual funds and other similar institutions on the deposit side. They therefore need to gear themselves up to meet this challenge. But significantly, banks are also tying competition from within their industry. While existing banks have been allowed greater flexibility to expand operations, new banks are now being set up in the private sector. So far nine new banks have commenced banking business. While these new banks with their concentration on select areas and select segments may offer stiff competition in these markets, the improvement in the overall efficiency of public sector banks will have to come from within and from the need to improve their profitability.

Efficiency

With financial liberalization, integration of domestic markets with the external markets and computerisation of financial information, the risk associated with the financial transactions are assuming complex forms. Banks, even in the normal course, are exposed to credit and market risks, which can be decomposed into interest rate risk, price risk, foreign exchange risk and liquidity risk. These risks get heightened with changes in the financial sector environment following liberalization and globalization. Banks therefore need to be fully seized of the importance of controlling various types of risks. Apart from upgrading their risk management methodology, banks must adopt more comprehensive asset-liability management practices. Assets-liability management is a continuous process of planning, organizing and controlling asset and liability volumes, maturity rates and yields. It involves an assessment of the various types of risks and actively alerting the banking system when such an active management of financial risk has become necessary. Comprehensive measurement and management of risk should receive adequate attention. Improving the profitability and viability is only one aspect of enhancing the performance of banks. The other is how adequately and satisfactorily banks are able to meet the demands of customers. The ultimate test of success of the financial sector reform is truly customer satisfaction; customer-as a borrower and a depositor. Through the various reform measures we are laying the foundation for an efficient and a well-functioning banking system. A renewed and a reinvigorated banking system can play an important role in accelerating economic growth. Significant changes have already taken place. It has however miles to go. But the steps that are being taken are in the right direction. The first phase of the banking sector reform concentrated on such factors as pre-emptions, interest rate structure, prudential norms and supervisory oversight.

Second Phase of Reforms

Financial Sector Reforms were initiated as part of the overallstructnral reforms airrl'ed at improving the productivity and efficiency of the economy. The Financial Sector Reforms recognize the fact that the Indian Banking System had over the years grown and that the geographical and functional coverage of the banking system have been truly impressive. However, questions have been raised from time to time on the viability of the banking institutions. Concerns have also been expressed about the deterioration in the quality of services provided by banks. It is with a view to finding solutions to these problems that Financial Sector reforms were initiated. The broad objective of the reform bas thus. been to create a banking system that is both viable and efficient There are four building blocks which have formed part of the Banking Sector Reforms. They are:

(a) Modifying the policy framework;
(b) Improving the financial soundness and credibility of banks;
(c) Creating a competitive environment; and
(d) Strengthening of the institutional framework.

Policy Framework

The improvements in the policy framework are aimed at removing and reducing the external constraints bearing on the profitability and functioning of commercial banks. In effect, an attempt has been made to bring down very substantially, the pre- emptions in the form of reserve requirements and to give greater freedom to banks in the determination of interest rates. The reductions in the reserve requirements have indeed been very substantial. This has had the effect of both expanding the lendable resources of banks as well as to improve the profitability. Between November 1995 and January 1997 the Cash Reserve Ratio had been reduced by five percentage points. Such a reduction has not happened in the past. The de-regulation of the interest rate structure has given a high degree of freedom to banks in determining the deposit rate and the lending rates. Obviously this has put greater responsibility on the banks and banks have to manage this freedom judiciously.

Financial Soundness and Health

In trying to improve the financial health and credibility of banks, a major step has been to introduce internationally accepted prudential norms relating to income recognition, asset classification, provisioning and capital adequacy. The framework suggested a minimum of eight per cent capital to risk-weighted assets ratio which includes both on and off balance-sheet items. The aim of this system is to relate capital to the risk of the portfolio of assets held by a bank. Further, at least four per cent risk weighted assets was to be in the form of pure capital that is equity capital and free reserves. In looking at the pressures and influences on banking, it is difficult to over estimate the importance of the capital ratios now imposed on banks.

Impact of Financial Sector Reforms

One has begun to see the impact of the financial sector reforms, both on the financial results as well as in the services provided. Operating profits have gone up. All banks except two have met the minimum capital adequacy ratio. Sixteen public sector banks have capital adequacy ratios over 10% and five between 9 %and 10%.

Reduction in NPAs has come down from 23 per cent in 1992-93 to 9.2 per cent in 2002-03. The percentage of net NPAs to Net advances was 9.18 per cent. For purpose of international comparisons, it is this figure that should be taken into account. The Priority sector advances accounted for 47 per cent of the total NPAs and non-priority sector for the balance.

The mid term review in November 2003, reviewed the progress of implementation of various developmental as well as regulatory measures in the banking sector, but emphasized facilitating the ease of transactions by the common person and strengthening the credit delivery systems, as a response to the pressing needs of the society.

These reform measures have had major impact on the overall efficiency and stability of the banking system in India. The present capital adequacy of Indian banks is comparable to those at International level. There has been a marked improvement in the asset quality, with the percentage of gross non performing assets to gross advances for the banking system reduced from 14.4% in 1998 to 7.2% in 2004. The reform measures have also resulted in an improvement in the profitability of the banks The Return on Assets of the banks rose from 0.4% in the year 1991-92 to 1.2% in 2003-04 .Considering that, globally the RoA has been in the range 0.9% to 1.5% for 2004, Indian banks are well placed. The banking sector reforms also emphasized the need to review the man power resources and rationalise the requirements, by drawing a realistic plan, to reduce the operating cost and improve the profitability. During the last five years, the business per employee for public sector banks more than doubled to around Rs. 25 million, in 2004. Implementation of Basel II is fast approaching. This rests on three fundamental issues namely minimum capital requirements, supervisory review process and market discipline. The implementation of advanced approaches for credit risk requires much more preparation and poses several challenges for the banks as well as the supervisors. The post Basel II era will belong to the banks with proper risk management systems.

Basel II implementation

Basel II implementation is widely acknowledged as a significant challenge faced by both banks and the regulators internationally. It is true that Basel II implementation may be seen as a compliance challenge. While it may be so for some banks, I would venture to mention that Basel II implementation has another dimension which offers considerable opportunities to banks. I would like to highlight two opportunities that are offered to banks, viz., refinement of risk management systems; and improvement in capital efficiency

Comprehensive Risk management: Under Basel I banks were focused on credit and market risks. Basel II has brought into focus a larger number of risks requiring banks to focus on a larger canvas. Besides the increase in the number of risks, banks are now beginning to focus on their inter-linkages with a view to achieve a more comprehensive risk management framework. Basel II implementation, therefore, is being increasingly seen as a medium through which banks constantly endeavour to upgrade the risk management systems to address the changing environment. Further, in the initial stages, banks were managing each risk in isolation. It is no longer adequate to manage each risk independently. Enterprises worldwide are, therefore, now putting in place an integrated framework for risk management which is proactive, systematic and spans across the entire organisation.

Banks in India are also moving from the individual silo system to an enterprise wide risk management system. While the first milestone would be risk integration across the entity, banks are also aware of the desirability of risk aggregation across the group both in the specific risk areas as also across the risks. Banks would, therefore, be required to allocate significant resources towards this endeavour.

Capital Efficiency: Basel II prescriptions have ushered in a transition from the traditional regulatory measure of capital adequacy to an evaluation of whether a bank has found the most efficient use of its capital to support its business i.e., a transition from capital adequacy to capital efficiency. In this transition, how effectively capital is used will determine return on equity and a consequent enhancement of shareholder value. In effect, banks may adopt a more dynamic approach to use of capital, in which capital will flow quickly to its most efficient use. This revised efficiency approach is expected to guide the return-on-equity strategy and influence banks' business plans. With the extension of capital charge for market risks to the AFS portfolio this year and the coming into force of Basel II norms in March 2007, banks would need to shore up the capital levels not only for complying with these requirements but also for supporting the balance sheet growth. With a view to enhancing the options available to banks for augmenting their capital levels, the Reserve Bank has recently permitted banks to issue new capital instruments, including perpetual instruments. A notable feature of these instruments is that these are designed to help banks in not only managing their capital effectively but also efficiently.

Enhancing corporate governance

The issues related to corporate governance have continued to attract considerable national and international attention in light of a number of high-profile breakdowns in corporate governance. This becomes all the more relevant for banks since they not only accept and deploy large amount of uncollateralized public funds in fiduciary capacity, but also leverage such funds through credit creation. Banks are also important participants in the payment and settlement systems. In view of the above, legal prescriptions for ownership and governance of banks in Banking Regulation Act, 1949 have been supplemented by regulatory prescriptions issued by RBI from time to time.

In view of the importance of the banking system for financial stability, sound corporate governance is not only relevant at the level of the individual bank, but is also a critical ingredient at the system level. Effective risk management systems determine the health of the financial system and its ability to survive economic shocks. To a large extent, many risk management failures reflect a breakdown in corporate governance which arise due to poor management of conflicts of interest, inadequate understanding of key banking risks, and poor Board oversight of the mechanisms for risk management and internal audit. Corporate governance is, therefore, the foundation for effective risk managements in banks and thus the foundation for a sound financial system[1]. Therefore, the choices which banks make when they establish their risk management and corporate governance systems have important ramifications for financial stability. These systems can affect how the institution functions and how others perceive it in the marketplace[2].

A good "governance culture" is crucial for financial stability but since it is an 'intangible', rules may not be able to capture its essence effectively. Therefore, banks may have to cultivate a good governance culture building in appropriate checks and balances in their operations. There are four important forms of oversight that should be included in the organisational structure of any bank in order to ensure appropriate checks and balances: (1) oversight by the board of directors or supervisory board; (2) oversight by individuals not involved in the day-to-day running of the various business areas; (3) direct line supervision of different business areas; and (4) independent risk management, compliance and audit functions. In addition, it is important that key personnel are fit and proper for their jobs. Although some ownership structures might have the potential to alter the strategies and objectives of a bank, these banks will also face many of the same risks associated with weak corporate governance. Consequently, the general principles of sound corporate governance should also be applied to all banks irrespective of their unique ownership structures[3].

Compliance with International Accounting Standards

One of the prime international standards considered relevant for ensuring a safe and sound banking system is the 'Core Principles for Effective Banking Supervision' issued by the Basel Committee on Banking Supervision (BCBS). Accounting standards are now a part of the set of twelve standards that have been identified by the Financial Stability Forum as conducive to a robust financial infrastructure. Financial reporting and prudential supervision have slightly different perspectives. While the former is oriented towards capturing the historical position, the latter has a forward looking element particularly with reference to measurement of impairment and capital. An important challenge, therefore, is to ensure that accounting standards and prudential frameworks are mutually consistent. While working towards achieving this consistency between the two sets of standards, it is essential for the regulators to be in a position to address any implications that the changes in accounting standards may have for the safety and soundness of banks[4].

Derivative activity in banks in India has been increasing at a brisk pace. While the risk management framework for derivative trading, which is a relatively new area for Indian banks (particularly more in respect of structured products), is an essential pre-requisite, the absence of clear accounting guidelines in this area is matter of significant concern. It is widely accepted that as the volume of transactions increases, which is happening in the Indian banking system, the need to upgrade the accounting framework needs no emphasis. The World Bank's ROSC on Accounting and Auditing in India has commented on the absence of an accounting standard which deals with recognition, measurement, presentation and disclosures pertaining to financial instruments. The Accounting Standards Board of the Institute of Chartered Accountants of India (ICAI) is considering issue of Accounting Standards on the above aspects pertaining to financial Instruments. These will be the Indian parallel to International Financial Reporting Standard 7, International Accounting Standards 32 and 39. The proposed Accounting Standards will be of considerable significance for financial entities and could therefore have implications for the financial sector. The formal introduction of these Accounting Standards by the ICAI is likely to take some time in view of the processes involved. In the meanwhile, the Reserve Bank is considering the need for banks and financial entities adopting the broad underlying principles of IAS 39. Since this is likely to give rise to some regulatory/prudential issues all relevant aspects are being comprehensively examined. The proposals in this regard would, as is normal, be discussed with the market participants before introduction. Adoption and implementation of these principles are likely to pose a great challenge to both the banks and the Reserve Bank.

Outsourcing Risks

Banks are increasingly using outsourcing for achieving strategic aims leading to either rationalisation of operational costs or tapping specialist expertise which is not available internally. 'Outsourcing' may be defined as *a bank's use of a third party, including an affiliated entity within a corporate group, to perform activities on a continuing basis that would normally be undertaken by the bank itself.* Typically outsourced financial services include applications processing (loan origination, credit card), document processing, investment management, marketing and research, supervision of loans, data processing and back office related activities etc. Outsourcing might give rise to several risks including, strategic risk, reputation risk, compliance risk, operational risk, exit strategy risk, counterparty risk, country risk, access risk, concentration risk and systemic risk. The failure of a service provider to provide a specified service, ensure security/ confidentiality, comply with legal and regulatory requirements can lead to financial losses/reputational risk for the bank and could also lead to systemic risks for the entire banking system in a country. It would therefore be imperative for the bank outsourcing its activities to ensure effective management of these risks. It is in this background that RBI has issued draft guidelines on outsourcing, which is intended to provide direction and guidance to banks to effectively manage risks arising from such outsourcing activities. The underlying principles for any outsourcing arrangement by a bank are that such arrangements should neither diminish the bank's ability to fulfill its obligations to its customers and the RBI nor impede effective supervision by RBI. Outsourcing banks, therefore, should take steps to ensure that the service provider employs the same high standard of care in performing the services as would be employed by the banks if the activities were conducted within the banks and not outsourced. Accordingly, banks are not expected to outsource any activity that would result in their internal control, business conduct, or reputation being compromised or weakened.

Application of Advanced Technology

Technology is a key driver in the banking industry, which creates new business models and processes, and also revolutionises distribution channels. Banks which have made inadequate investment in technology have consequently faced an erosion of their market shares. The beneficiaries are those banks which have invested in technology. Adoption of technology also enhances the quality of risk management systems in banks. Recognising the benefits of modernising their technology infrastructure banks are taking the right initiatives. While doing so, banks have four options to choose from: they can build a new system themselves, or buy best of the modules, or buy a comprehensive solution, or outsource. In this context banks need to clearly define their core competencies to be sure that they are investing in areas that will distinguish them from other market players, and give them a competitive advantage[5]. A further challenge which banks face in this regard is to ensure that they derive maximum advantage from their investments in technology and avoid wasteful expenditure which might arise on account of uncoordinated and piecemeal adoption of technology; adoption of inappropriate/inconsistent technology and adoption of obsolete technology.

Capacity Building

As dictated by the changing environment, banks need to focus on appropriate capacity building measures to equip their staff to handle advanced risk management systems and supervisors also need to equally equip themselves with appropriate skills to have effective supervision of banks adopting those systems. In the likelihood of a high level of attrition in the system, banks need to focus on motivating their skilled staff and retaining them[6]. Skill requirements would be significantly higher for banks planning to migrate to the advanced approaches under Basel II. Capacity building gains greater relevance in these banks, so as to equip themselves to take advantage of the incentives offered under the advanced approaches. A relevant point in this regard is that capacity building should be across the institution and not confined to any particular level or any particular area. The demand for better skills can be met either from within or from outside. It would perhaps be worthwhile to first glean through the existing resources to identify misplaced or hidden or forgotten resources and re-position them to boost the bank's efforts to capitalise on available skills. This does not undermine the benefits that a bank may derive by meeting their requirements from the market, but is only intended to prioritise the process.

Concluding Observations

The global challenges which banks face are not confined only to the global banks. These aspects are also highly relevant for banks which are part of a globalised banking system. Further, overcoming these challenges by the other banks is expected to not only stand them in good stead during difficult times but also augurs well for the banking system to which they belong and will also equip them to launch themselves as a global bank.

Notes

1. Reserve Bank of India, *BULLETIN*, June 2005, Volume LIX , No. 6.
2. Reserve Bank of India, *BULLETIN*, August 2005, Volume LIX, No. 8.
3. S.P. Muthukrishnan and S. Narayanan (1995), Papers Presented at the Eighteenth Bank Economist Conference.
4. Materials from Indian Overseas Bank Staff training Centre, Coimbatore
5. Y.V. Reddy (2005), Talk on Banking Sector Reforms in India- an Overview, at the Institute of Bankers of Pakistan, Karachi, Pakistan, May 18.
6. Inaugural address by Shri V. Leeladhar, Deputy Governor, Reserve Bank of India, at the seminar on "Indian Banks and Global Changes", Organized Jointly, by the Indian Merchants' Chamber and Indian Banks Association, Mumbai on January, 2006.

12

BANCASSURANCE: A MARKETING CHANNEL

ARAVIND J. & GABRIEL SIMON

Introduction

Bancassurance is the new buzzword in the Indian banking industry. The business of banking around the globe is being changed due to integration of global financial markets, development of new technologies, universalisation of banking operations and diversification in non-banking activities. The financial service sector in India is under going transformation with increasing changes noticed in their external and internal environments. The external environment in changing because of the golbalisation of financial sector industry and the growth of borderless markets and stiffer competition. The internal environment is too changing owing to the induction of new technology, new systems and marketing approaches. Banks are turning to be financial super markets with convergence in operations. Cross marketing of financial products is seen as a potential market. This has opened up an emerging concept of Bancassurance.

Bancassurance, which is also known as Allfinanz (Germany), is the arrangement where by the branches of a bank distribute insurance products developed by insurance companies to bank customers. Bancassurance in its simplest form is the distribution of insurance products through a bank's network of branches. It tries to exploit the synergies between both banks and insurance companies.

Objectives of the Study and Methodology

This study seeks to examine the possibilities of Bancassurance as a channel for cross marketing and the marketing of strategies involved. The Kerala context is taken as the background for the study and the operations of HDFC Standard Life in the state of Kerala forms the focus of the study. The data for the study was collected through an interview with the officials of HDFC.

I

Benefits of Bancassurance

Bancassurance is beneficial to banks, insurance companies and customers. Banks get a commission income while distributing insurance policies; insurance companies view Bancassurance as a new channel for distributing their policies and customers are getting both banking and insurance services under one roof. Thus banks view Bancassurance as a new strategy for earning income and insurance companies, a new channel for insurance distribution. Bancassurance primary banks on the relationship the customer has developed over a period of time with the bank. And pushing risk products through banks is a cost-effective affair for an insurance company compared to the agent route, while, for banks, considering the falling interest rates, fee based income coming in at a minimum cost is more welcome. The benefits of Bancassurance are numerous which include benefits to banks, insurance companies and customers.

To Banks

1. Can cross sell insurance products.
2. Can generate greater fee income.
3. Can retain large customer base.
4. Means of product diversification.

To Insurance Companies

1. Can increase their market share.
2. Can improve their premium turnover.

To Customers

1. Ensures quality products.
2. Ensures delivery at door steps.
3. Ensures insurance at reduced competitive price.

Bancassurance in India started picking up after the Insurance Regulatory and Development Authority (IRDA)'s notification on corporate agency regulation in October 2002, which allowed banks to act as an agent of only one life and one non-life insurer. With the opening up of insurance sector and with so many players entering the insurance industry, it is required by the insurance companies to come up with innovative products, create more consumer awareness about their products and offer then at a competitive price. At this juncture, banking sector was thought of as a potential distribution channel useful for insurance companies.

II

Regulatory Framework of Bancassurance

Banks Governed by Reserve Bank of India Insurance Companies Governed by Insurance Regulatory and Development Authority.

Regulations by R.B.I

The R.B.I has prescribed entry guidelines under the following 3 options for banks wanting to diversity into insurance:

I. Joint Ventures (J.V.) for insurances business with risk participation is allowed for banks which have:

- Net worth not less than Rs. 500 crores :
- Credit Risk Adequacy ratio (CRAR) not less than 10 %.
- Reasonable level of non-performing assets;
- Net profit continuously for the last 3 years.
- Satisfactory track record of the subsidiaries, if any.

II. Banks which are not eligible for joint ventures participation as above, can make investments up to 10% of the net worth of the bank or Rs. 50 crores which ever is less, in Insurance Company for providing infrastructure and service support, provided they fulfil the requirements of CRAR, NPA and Net profit as per (ii), (iii) and (iv) above.

III. Any commercial bank may undertake Insurance business on fee basis, as an agent of Insurance companies, with no risk participation.

Regulations by IRDA

The IRDA guidelines for bancassurance are:

- Each Bank that sells Insurance must have a Chief Insurance Executive to handle all the Insurance activities.
- All the People involved in selling should undergo mandatory training at an Institute accredited by IRDA and pass the examination conducted by the authority.

  IMAGE (Indian Bank Management Academy for Growth and Excellence) has been accredited by IRDA as an agent's training institute.
- Banks can become corporate agents for one Insurance company.
- Banks cannot become Insurance brokers

III

Models of Bancassurance

Bancassurance is evolutionary and there are many different models adopted around the world based on regulatory framework in that country. Let us examine the worldwide models under the following heads.

Distribution Alliance

Under this distribution agreement model, the bank agrees to leverage its branch network and strong customer relationships to sell the insurance products for a distribution fee. This model is a sound and conservative and involves low investments.

Joint Ventures

The joint venture model is the most prevalent of the Bancassurance business models, particularly in Asia. In joint ventures, the bank and the insurance work in a more integrated manner than under distribution model. Distribution fees are split between both parties and some degree of customer information may be shared. This model is less expensive and risky.

Merger and Acquisitions

Under merger and acquisitions, either a bank acquires/merges with an insurer or vice versa. This model was scarcely utilized due to various national government laws forbidding mergers between banks and insurers. This model is highly integrated.

Build or Buy Own Insurance Operations

This model seeks to develop in-house expertise in Bancassurance. The advantage of this model is that the institution has complete control over the process and there are fewer cultural differences to address. But a significant investment is required for this model.

The partnerships in India fall mostly into first model, i.e., distribution alliance. Only 5 banks have gone for second model.

There is no instance of third and fourth model in India. The current BANCASSURANCE RELATIONSHIPS IN INDIA is presented in the following Table 1.

Table 1
Existing Bancassurance Relationships In India

Insurance Company (Life)	*Banks Marketing the Insurance Products*
HDFC Standard	HDFC Bank, Union Bank of India, Indian Bank
ICICI Prudential	ICICI Bank, Union Bank of India, Indian Bank
Birla Sunlife	IDBI Bank, City Bank, Development Credit Bank, Bank of Rajasthan, Catholic Syrian Bank, Karur Vysya Bank,
Tata AIG	HSBC Bank, IDBI Bank, Union Bank of India
SBI Life	State Bank of India
ING Vysya	Vysya Bank, Bharat Overseas Bank.
Bajaj Allianz	Standard Charted Bank, Syndicate Bank
Met Life	Dhanalakshmi Bank, Karnataka Bank, J & K Bank
Aviva	Canara Bank, Lakshmi Vilas Bank, ABN Amro., American Express
LIC	Corporation Bank, Oriental Bank of Commerce, Indian Overseas Bank, Bank of Punjab, Vijaya Bank, Centrian Bank, The City Union Bank Ltd.
Bajaj Allianz	J & K Bank, Bank of Rajasthan, Bank of Punjab, Karur Vysya Bank, Lord Krishna Bank, Karnataka Bank
Royal Sun Alliance	City Bank, Standard Charted Bank, American Express
Tata AIG	HSBC, IDBI, Union Bank of India, Development Credit Bank
ICICI Lombard	ICICI Bank
National Insurance Co.	City Union Bank
United India	Punjab National Bank, Andhra Bank, South Indian Bank, Federal Bank, Indian Bank.
New India	Union Bank of India

IV

Analysis and Findings

The analysis revealed that the firm could generate significant progress in premium income since its cross marketing alliance.

The growth rate in premium was 129 per cent, it was as high as 176 per cent for renewal premium and 173 for group business Table 2.

Table 2
Financial Result of HDFC Standard Life

Parameters	*April-March 2004-05*	*April-March 2005-06*	*% Growth*
Total Received Premium	668.40	1532.21	129.23
(i) New Business	486.15	1028.94	111.65
(ii) Renewal	182.25	503.27	176.14
Group Business	49.40	1.5.15	173.58

Source: www.hdfcinsurance.com.

The main Bancassurance products of the firm are given in Table 3. The products included 8 savings plan and 3 pension plans.

Table 3
Insurance Products Offered to Bank Customers

Saving Plans	*Pension Plans*
Unit Linked Young Star	Unit Linked Pension
Unit Linked Young Star Plus	Unit Linked Pension Plus
Endowment Assurance Plan	Personal Pension Plan
Unit Linked Endowment	
Unit Linked Endowment Plus	
Protection Plan	
Money Back Plan	
Children's Plan	

Source: Primary data.

An attempt was made to identify the most preferred products. As details of premium were not disclosed, market preference was identified on the basis on total sales. Accordingly the preferred products were Unit Linked Young Star and Unit Linked Young Star Plus. The features of these products were as given in Table No.4. The common benefits were the primary reason for preference. According to the respondents, the maximum preferences for these products were in THIRUVALA region of Kerala. This region is basically dominated by a huge NRI population and that could be a unique selling proportion for the firm

Table 4
Product Details

Best Moving Products	*Common Benefits*	*Region/Location*
Unit Linked Young Star Unit Linked Young Star Plus	*Insurance Coverage* (i) Death benefit (ii) Critical illness benefit *Tax Benefits* (i) U/S 80 C (ii) U/S 10 (10D)	Thiruvalla region occupies the first place in the marketing of insurance through banks.

Source: Primary data.

The micro survey reveals the potential for Bancassurance in the state and the need to exploit the potential to the fullest extent. Cross marketing and linkage with banking operation make this a preferred channel and proposition an acceptable to Keralities.

References

Dr. P. Viswanadhan (2005), Bancassurance in India-An Alternative Channel of Insurance Distributor, *Indian Journal of Marketing*, November.

Dr. Meena Sharma (2007), Bancassurance: Opportunities and Challenges for the Banks, *The Journal of Indian Institute of Banking of Finance*, April-June.

Reserve Bank of India, Insurance: The Indian Experience, RBI Occasional Paper 2003, June.

www.bimaonline.com

13

SECURITISATION ACT AND FINANCIAL ASSETS RESTRUCTURING OF INDIAN BANKS: AN ANALYSIS

Manoj Pillai

The Indian Banking system, considered to be one of the crucial facets of Indian Economy, has undergone tremendous change over the years. Even though the Banking sector in India has shown spectacular progress since nationalization, there has been significant decline in productivity and efficiency resulting in erosion of profits. The presence of Non Performing Assets (NPAs) has had an adverse impact on the banking system. Their continued amelioration in absolute terms proved survival extremely difficult. Banks which functions as intermediaries have to be financially sound and stable and they should enjoy public confidence to be able to impact an efficient and effective service role1. The Non-performing Assets are the bad debts and non recovered loans of the bank which now stands at over Rs.50, 000 crores. Table 1 shows the volume of non performing assets of the scheduled commercial banks.

Table 1
Non Performing Assets of Scheduled Commercial Banks. (Rs. In Crores)

All Scheduled Commercial Books	*FY 2003*	*FY 2004*	*FY 2005*	*FY 2006*	*Total*
Gross NPAs-year Beginning	21863	68,698	64,439	59,124	70,153
Additions	21863	24122	20396	21408	87,789
Reductions and write off	23,302	28034	25,320	28717	1,05,373
Gross NPAs-Year closing	68,714	64786	59515	51815	52569

Source: Compiled from *Report on Trends and progress of Banking in India 2006*, RBI, GOI.).

Defining Non-Performing Assets (NPAs)

The Non Performing Assets can be divided into the following three broad groups:

(a) Sub-Standard

(b) Doubtful

(c) Loss

The Reserve Bank of India has not prescribed clear and objective definitions for these categories to ensure uniform, consistent and logical basis for classification of assets. Broadly stated, substandard assets would be those which exhibits problems and would include assets classified as non-performing for a period not exceeding eighteen months. Doubtful assets are those which include assets classified as non performing and would also include loans in respect of which instruments are overdue for a period exceeding eighteen months. Loss assets are those accounts where the loss has been identified but the amount of loss has not been written off. Table 2 shows the frequency distribution of Net Non Performing assets to Net Advances of Scheduled Commercial Banks.

Casual Dynamics of Non-Performing Assets

There are numerous reasons for the high level of NPAs ranging from both policy and environmental factors. According to the Reserve Bank of India's statistics 40 percentage of the total banking credit is given to the priority sector viz. Agriculture, Small industry,

Table 2
Net NPAs to Net Advances of Scheduled Commercial Banks

(Frequency Distribution)

Year	*Public Sector Banks*		*Private Sector Banks*		
	SBI Group	*Nationalized Banks*	*Old*	*New*	*Foreign Banks*
I	*II*	*III*	*IV*	*V*	*VI*
2001-02 Up to 2 per cent	0	0	1	1	20
Above 2 per cent and up to 5 per cent	4	4	2	3	4
Above 5 per cent and up to 10 per cent	4	12	13	5	1
Above 10 per cent	0	3	6	0	14
2002-03 Up to 2 per cent	1	3	1	3	21
Above 2 per cent and up to 5 per cent	6	6	4	2	2
Above 5 per cent and up to 10 per cent	1	8	13	4	5
Above 10 per cent	0	2	2	1	8
2003-04 Up to 2 per cent	6	5	2	4	19
Above 2 per cent and up to 5 per cent	2	9	9	5	4
Above 5 per cent and up to 10 per cent	0	4	7	0	3
Above 10 per cent	0	1	2	1	7
2004-05 Up to 2 per cent	7	10	4	5	22
Above 2 per cent and up to 5 per cent	1	8	11	3	2
Above 5 per cent and up to 10 per cent	0	2	5	1	2
Above 10 per cent	0	0	0	0	4
2005-06 (P)					
Upto 2 per cent	7	15	11	6	26
Above 2 per cent and upto5 per cent	1	5	7	2	0
Above 5 per cent and upto 10 per cent	0	0	0	2	0
Above 10 per cent	0	0	0	0	3

P: Provisional.
Note: Date as on March 31, 2006 are un-audited and provisional.
Source: RBI Annual Report 2006.

Transport, Poverty alleviation programmes etc. and as much as 47% of non performing assets originates from this sector. There are other forms of direct credit whether it is through pressure from the Government and institutions such as Board of Industrial and Financial Reconstructions for Banks to continue nursing sick accounts. The populist 'Loan-Melas' and cancellations of debts granted to large proportion of peasants, artisans and rural poor also result in mounting NPAs. Similarly sizable amount of Non Performing assets have also originated as a result of unreturned corporate debts and loans outstanding with the medium and small entrepreneurs. The High level of NPAs can also be attributed to the inherent weakness prevalent in our legal system. The legal procedures in India are tardy and torturous and it takes years to settle a case. No doubt part of the NPAs may have been the result of banker's inaptitude or bonafide decisions going wrong but a substantial chuck can be attributed to political meddling which polluted the repayment ethos.

Table 3 shows the amount of gross non performing assets that has been added during the last four years in all the scheduled commercial banks of India. Table 4 highlights the percentage of net profit provided for NPAs during the last four financial years.

Table 3

Amount of NPAs Added during FY 2003-2006

(Rs. in Crores)

All Scheduled Commercial Banks	*FY 03*	*FY 04*	*FY 05*	*FY 06*	*Total*
Gross NPAs-year Beginning	70,153	68,698	64,439	59,124	70,153
Additions	21,863	24,122	20,396	23,408	87,789
Reduction and write off	23,302	28,034	25,320	28,717	1,05,373
Gross NPAs-Year closing	68,714	64,786	59,515	51,815	52,569

Source: www.arcil.co.in, Newsletter, Nov. 2006.

Table 4

Percentage of Net Profit Provided for NPAs (FY 2003-2006)

(Rs. in Crores)

All Scheduled Commercial Banks	*FY 2003*	*FY 2004*	*FY 2005*	*FY 2006*	*Total*
Provisions for NPAs-Year beginning	30,749	32,254	36,199	34,484	30,749
New Provisions during the year	13,181	18,473	11,630	8,968	52,252
Write off back during the year	12,049	14,031	12,297	12,916	51,293
Provisions for NPAs-year closing	31,881	36,696	35,532	30,536	31,708
Operating Profit	40,682	52,593	51,023	56,560	2,00,858
Net Profit	17,077	22,270	20,959	24,592	84,898

Source: www.arcil.co.in, Newsletter, Nov. 2006.

Thus if one closely analyze all the statistical information it can be easily inferred that the non performing assets have been constantly increasing in all the scheduled commercial banks in India. Similarly the statistics also reveal that the constant rise in the volume of non performing assets has adversely affected the net profitability of the commercials banks of India.

Securitization and Reconstruction of Financial Assets and Enforcement of Security Interest Act (SARFAESI Act), 2002

The Securitization and Reconstruction of Financial Assets and Enforcement of Security Interest Act, 2002 came into effect from June 21, 2002. Under this act the Reserve Bank of India has formulated specific plans to establish assets reconstruction companies and Assets Management Companies to acquire non performing assets of any bank or financial institution The act lays emphasis on the recovery of money, even without the intervention of the court. Section 13(4) of the act empowers the bank to take possession of the secured assets of the borrower including the right to transfer by way of lease, assignment, or sale for realizing the secured assets. The SARFAESI Act is a detailed set of laws relating to the registration and other important policy matters like prudential norms relating to income recognition, classification of assets, provisioning, accounting standards, capital adequacy norms, deployment of funds and acquisition of financial assets which has to be followed by the Assets Reconstruction Companies. Reserve Bank of India believes that since assets reconstruction activity mainly revolves around non performing loan assets, the whole process of assets reconstruction and other related matters have to be evolved with great care and professionalism so that there can be smooth transfer of Non Performing Assets from the scheduled commercial banks to these assets reconstruction companies.

Registration of Assets Reconstruction Companies under the SARFAESI Act

The RBI clearly clarifies that a securitization company or assets reconstruction/management company registered with it can undertake both securitization and reconstruction activities. The guidelines further clarify that an unregistered entity may also conduct the business of securitization or assets reconstruction outside the purview of the act. This specific ruling has enabled all the banks and financial institutions engaged in securitization activities prior to the act to continue the same without registration. However the benefits of enhanced enforcement rights under the act will not be available to them. The Narasimham Committee (II) was appointed to review progress in the banking sector over the past 6 years with particular reference to the recommendation made by the committee on the financial system in 1991.The committee submitted its report to the Government of India on 22nd April 1998. One of the main recommendations was to set up Assets Reconstruction/Management Companies in India to check the Non Performing Assets.

Genesis of Assets Reconstruction Company India limited (ARCIL)

Assets Reconstruction Company India Limited (ARCIL) is a pioneer Assets Reconstruction Company to commence operation in India. It is registered with Reserve Bank of India under sections of the SARFAESI Act, 2002(SARFAESI Act) and registered as a Securitization and a Reconstruction Company. It commenced operations from August 29, 2003.

Sponsors and Shareholding Pattern of ARCIL

ARCIL is sponsored by State Bank of India, Industrial Development Bank of India, ICICI Bank Limited and Punjab National Bank. Table 5 shows the overall shareholding pattern of ARCIL.

Procedure of NPA transfers to ARCIL and Valuation of NPA

ARCIL acquired NPAs by way of "true sale". Once an organization sells NPAs to ARCIL the entire liability of the NPA shifts to ARCIL and the seller has no further interest in that asset. The valuation of NPA and the price offered by ARCIL depends on

Table 5
Shareholding Pattern

(Rs. in crores)

Name of Shareholder	*Amount of Shares Held*	*% to total paid up to equity capital*
Sponsors		
State Bank of India	43.89	19.95%
ICICI Bank Limited	65.08	29.58%
Industrial Development Bank of India	43.89	19.95%
Punjab National Bank	22.00	10.00 %
Sub-Total A	174.86	79.48%
Other Shareholders		
Housing Development Finance Corporation Limited	1.17	0.53%
HDFC Bank Limited	1.17	0.53%
Federal Bank Limited	2.92	1.33%
South Indian Bank Limited	2.92	1.33%
The Karur Vysya Bank Limited	6.38	2.90%
Karnataka Bank Limited	6.03	2.74%
Citicorp Finance (I) Limited	4.40	2.00%
Infrastructure Development Finance Company Limited	19.15	8.71%
Arcil Employees Stock Ownership Trust	1.02	0.46%
Sub-Total B	45.14	20.52%
Total (A+B)	220.00	100.00

Source: *www.arcil.co.in*, *Newsletter*, Nov. 2006.

the nature of the security the lender has over the borrower's assets, the value realizable from the security, and the time to realize that value. There are specific guide lines from the RBI regarding the valuation of NPAs. After acquiring an asset, the ARCIL raises resources through the issue of Security Receipts (S.R) to eligible investors who are called Qualified Institutional Buyers (QIBs). The amount collected from the issue of Security Receipts is utilized towards the payment of the assets purchased from the Banks and financial institutions. Thus ARCIL becomes the legal owner of the assets and Security Receipts holder becomes the beneficial owner. The Security receipts represent the individual rights, title and interest of investors in the financial assets held in the fund floated by ARCIL. These are redeemed out of the realization from financial held by ARCIL.

On detailed analysis of all the cases acquired by ARCIL till March 2005, it is seen that 78 percent of all the units acquired are either fully operating or partly operating, rest 22 per cent of the units acquired are non-operating. If we assess the resolution strategy of the units acquired by ARCIL, it can be seen that 57 per cent of the acquired units have been made operational through restructuring, 30 per cent through merger and acquisition and 13 per cent through the sale of assets and settlement.

Operational Performance of ARCIL

On August 29, 2006 ARCIL had completed three years of its operations. Arcil has acquired total dues of Rs. 22,212 crores belonging to a total of 622 cases upto H1 financial year 2007. Of this Arcil has resolved 204 cases involving Rs. 11,592 crores. The total amount recovered and distributed till H1 financial year 2007 were Rs. 1157 crores. If one analysis the percentage of resolved cases then it can be seen that till financial year 2005 Arcil has resolved 56 percent of the cases it has acquired. Similarly 66 per cent of the total dues involved in cases were resolved out financial year 2005. Table 6 gives all the relevant statistical information relating to the operational performance of Assets Reconstruction Company India Limited.

Table 6
Operational Performance of ARCIL

(In Crores)

Particulars	*During H1 FY07*	*Upto H1 FY 07*
Acquisition No of cases acquired	63	622
Total due	1,286	22,412
No of selling Bank	13	36
Resolution	28	204
Total dues involved in resolved cash	1,741	11,592
% of cases resolved out of cases acquired upto FY05	8%	56%
%of dues involved in cases resolved out of cases acquired upto FY 2005	10%	66%
Exited cases no of exited cases	43	107
Total dues involved in exited cases	759	2,769
Recovery and distribution Amount Recovered and distributed	550	1,157

Source: *www.arcil.co.in*, *Newsletter*, November 2006.

Concluding Observations

It is evident that the Non-Performing Assets in India has adversely affected the profitability and efficient functioning of the banks. The gravity of the situation forced Government of India to introduce drastic and sweeping reforms in the banking sector and the positive results have started to flow. The new RBI guidelines through the securitization act shall definitely provide a healthy platform and concrete directions for regulating securitization activities. During the last four years the aggregate advances of all public sector banks in India have more than doubled (104 per cent) where as gross NPA's was reduced from Rs. 68714 crores in the year 2003 to Rs. 52,569 crores in the year 2006. The present scenario shows that NPA levels have come down despite substantial growth in credit thanks especially to innovative regulations, accounting procedures and above all the establishment of ARCIL.

ARCIL in India is at its infancy stage and the process is yet to gain momentum in India and the banks are yet to utilize the services of ARCIL fully. Assets Reconstruction Companies have been used world wide with varying degree of success. Only time will tell its viability and practicability in the Indian Financial Environment.

References

Chakraborthy, K.C. (2005), Managing NPAs, The Charted and Financial Analyst, October, P.33.

Tannan's Banking Law and Practice in India, India Law House, p. 1275.

Narasimham, M; Banking Sector Reforms: The Rationale and Contents, UBSPD, pp. 364-365.

Majumdar, N.A., Banking Sector Reforms:Second Coming, ed.by Amalesh Banerjee, Kanishka Publication, p. 185.

RBI Annual Report, 2006, p. 136.

Ibid, p. 136.

Anand Chakravarty (2005), ARCIL on Road to Success, Financial Markets, ICFAI Univ. Press.

14

STP AND RISK MANAGEMENT IN E-BANKING

Anil Kumar P. & Jagathy Raj V. P.

Introduction

STP (Straight Through Processing) is the fully automated processing of transaction requests from initiation to settlement. It is the initiation, execution, management and control of a business process from inception to completion, without the need of any human intervention. The needs for STP are many and it indeed is the need of the hour. Speed of technological changes, changing customer expectations, technology advancements, competitive market, need for integration between systems, e-banking, less face-to-face interaction with banks and its customers are some of the major reasons why banks must opt for more and more Straight Through Processing (STP). It eliminates a lot of manual activities and redundant processes in the end-to-end processing and hence reduces human errors, operational costs and operational risks. It provides a higher accuracy for transaction execution and settlement. The fast and efficient transaction processing cycle coupled with the web technology will allow banks to have a greater geographic presence and a competitive position in the market. Increased customer satisfaction and their demand for services will in turn create new revenue options for banks. Adoption of STP will contribute towards improved business efficiencies and streamlined operations. STP will also help to maintain real-time access to account information, improving customer service. It offers a reduced settlement cycle, better transparency and detailed audit for better monitoring of the business cycle and measurement of the performance. By automating the process from initiation, execution through settlement, which reduces manual processes and provide a more timely and accurate processes, will help in better operational risk management. STP thus provides better risk mitigation and compliance to regulatory requirements like Basel II. Careful implementation of STP is very important to achieve the required level of risk management objectives. This paper discusses the concept of STP, its scope and benefits, and also a specific set of techniques for avoidance, reduction, detection, control and monitoring of the operational risks in STP. Falling in line with the objectives as above, Part–I revolves around the concept of STP and Part–II the techniques.

Part-I

STP: The Concept, Scope, Applications and Benefits

What is STP?

STP (Straight Through Processing) is the fully automated processing of transaction requests from initiation to settlement. It is the initiation, execution, management and control of a business process from inception to completion, without the need of any human intervention. Banks are increasingly using STP for various e-banking products offered to their customers like fund transfer (internal and third party), utility bill payments and pay roll processing. STP will streamline back office activities, leading to reduced failures, lower risks, and significantly lower costs per transaction while customers get easy, secure and fast banking services at their home, office or on the move. STP helps in settlement and thus reducing the settlement risk. It also helps in loss data collection and risk reporting, monitoring and control.

STP in banks is all about using a single system to process or control all elements of the work-flow in a financial transaction. STP integrates the front, middle, and back office applications based on standards. A transaction flow or work-flow of any business process can be defined using STP. So the scope of STP expands to the application of processes and activities such as data collection, analysis, processing, monitoring, controlling and reporting which are all vital for any risk analysis.

The Scope of STP

This paper discusses and compares a set of techniques for avoidance, reduction, detection, control and monitoring of the risks in STP through e-banking channels. STP through web is selected for this discussion as, web with proper security is the best suited technology for STP. This paper discuss only EAI (Enterprise Application Integration i.e. STP with in the bank) an its control mechanisms. This paper does not include the STP in B2B (Business to Business or Bank To Bank or Third Party) channels.

STP and Operational Risk Mitigation

Basel II, the the committee on banking supervision, in their final document has already explained the increased importance of Operational Risk Management along with Credit and Market Risk Management guidelines. Today, operational risk has become another critical aspect in risk capital allocation. The proposed new Basel II accord initiated by the Bank of International Settlement is heralding a major effort to radically increase the quantification of operational risk. With the continuous changes in customer requirements, global competition and technology changes banks are opting for more and more STP into their systems. STP in itself is a risk mitigation technique used in operational risk management. STP reduces operational, legal and settlement risks by better identification, control, measurement and management of risks. STP will provide better tracking of loss data of firms in the context of Basel-II.

Relative Merits of Using FTP–A Basel II Perspective

STP will reduce the operational inefficiencies in the operations. It will certainly help in their drive to measure and manage operational losses, better compliance monitoring and reporting, better risk management through comprehensive risk modeling at international standards. The relative merits of using STP is listed in Table 1 below.

The STP System

STP system in its simplest form requires a front end user interface from where customers/users can initiate a transaction and a back end transaction processing system which then evaluates, controls, executes and reports these user requests processing on a real time basis. Users can initiate a transaction from a browser in a PC, mobile device, ATM or any other device which can be connected via LAN or WAN to the bank's back end system. A secure encrypted connectivity to the Bank's back end system and proper user authentication methods are basic requirements to eliminate any risks to the information assets of the Bank. Risk control mechanisms are integrated to the system to limit the exposures of the bank. Other critical parameters of STP that determine the success or failure of the system are speed, accuracy, stability, availability, scalability, integration to other systems and standardization. A true STP system is one that is fully integrated and operates from a single architectural platform with all these features effectively implemented.

Table 1
Merits of Using FTP–A Basel II Perspective

Item	*STP*	*Non-STP*
Operational Risk	Allows better identification, control, measurement and management of risks.	Difficult to manage risks as human roles are involved in modeling.
Loss Data Collection (Required for Basel II operational riskcalculation and reporting)	Automatic tracking from audit trails & reports and history data.	Loss data has to be maintained manually
Settlement Risks	Reduced settlement risks due to the automatic Settlement & Reconciliation provided in time by the system	Delay in processing can cause significant losses
Compliance Monitoring	Compliance rules defined in the system are verified automatically during transaction execution	Users may take subjective or erroneous decisions
Regulatory Reporting	As all details of the transactions are time stamped and logged in system, it can provide all required reports at any future point of time.	Required details for reporting may not be available or may have archived in hard copies.
Risk Modeling	Comprehensive risk modeling at international standards possible	Risk modeling is difficult because of human roles in the processing cycle.

A system that can mitigate operational risk would have a security definition, no needless movement of data, no reconciliation, secure data storage and a stable and secure user interface. A central database system with an integrated and secure web technology would be the right suite for STP.

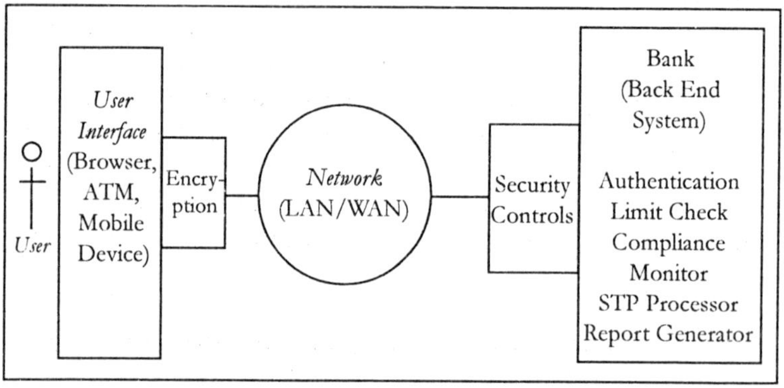

Figure 1: **Overview of an STP System**

Figure 1 depicts an overview of a typical STP system. The figure clearly shows the user along with the five major elements comprising the STP system as discussed above.

Why Use Web Services for STP

Even though different technologies are available for STP, because of the benefits of using web services, for the purpose of discussion, this paper assumes web as the core technology for STP. Some of the central benefits of using web technology for STP are: it is based on open standards, provides better business process management, easier integration, more flexibility and better and cheaper customer service. Web Services offer a platform neutral approach for integrating STP applications, so that it can be used to integrate diverse systems in a way supported by standards rather than proprietary systems. The following Table 2 depicts the components of a typical STP system in various delivery channels like Web, ATM and Mobile Devices.

Table 2
Comparison of STP Using Three Different Channels & Technologies

Item	*Web*	*ATM*	*Mobile Device*
User Interface	Browser: Full Screen, Graphical, Easy to user full key pads, available in PCs and some mobile devices	ATM Screens: Smaller Screen, Graphical, Limited key and limited operation	Mobile Screen:Very small, Graphical, small key pad difficult to use. Limited capabilities.Difficult to enter large amount of data.
	Supports for better data entry	Limited data entry capabilities. Keys needs to be programmed	
Access	PC or Laptop or Mobile Devices	Fixed Locations	Any where, Any time
Cost	Medium	High	Small
Standards	Open (HTTP, HTML)	Proprietary	Proprietary & Open
Integration	Easy	Costly	Difficult if it uses proprietary standards and protocols
Network	Uses public or private network	Normally private network	Public network
Access Control	User Name, Password and and protocols	ATM cards (Plastic or Smart Cards) and PIN Code	User Name & Password
Encryption	Can be Enabled	Can be Enabled	Can be Enabled in some devices
Firewall	Can be Enabled	Not Available	Not Available
Speed & Reliability	Depends on the connectivity	Fast & Reliable	Depends on the connectivity
Functionality	Easy to change or add	Programming Required	Fine turning required for small screens.

Part–II

Risk Management Methods For STP

The following section describes a set of methods to avoid, reduce and detect/control the inherent operational risk during STP.

Risk Avoidance

This section lists a set of techniques which can be used by banks to avoid possible risks in using STP.

Secure Connectivity

As STP transactions get initiated from web pages from an external world and then it get validated and executed in the back-end system of the bank, a secure channel or connectivity is required for user connections. For web based solutions SSL can provide a secure connection by encrypting all the data exchanged between the bank and the user access point. SSL with 64 or 128 bit encryption can be implemented by banks to have higher level of security. Connections or user sessions need to be managed by using session ids generated by cookies or proprietary programs. Table 3 compares the various secure and insecure system connectivities.

Table 3
Comparison of Secure and Insecure Connectivities

Insecure (HTTP)	*Secure Encrypted (HTTPS 64 Bit)*	*Secure Encrypted (HTTP 128 Bit)*
Data is transmitted as clear text over the network. Others can view it	Data is encrypted and transmitted over network using private and public key mechanisms	Improved encryption using 128 bit difficult to crack.

User Authentication

User authentication is the next step in reducing risks associated with the external connections initiated from web pages for transaction processing. A set of mechanisms is suggested below to provide improved security and reduced risk.

Login and Password

Each external or internal user having access rights to the bank system is given a login and password by which the system automatically authenticate them. Generation of login names and passwords, delivery to the customers and management should follow standard procedures. For example, password are encrypted and stored in the database, pin codes are printed in special pin mailers, login names and passwords are forced to have some minimum length and pattern. Customers should be forced to change their password when they first login to the system. A detailed discussion of this topic is beyond the scope of this document.

Challenge Response System

Intruders may try to enter the system by using automated programs which generate logins and passwords at random and then entering it into the web login page. A cleverly designed challenge mechanisms will prevent this. A challenge mechanism is the one which will display a predefined or variable number of digits or alphabets or a combination of both in a specified area in the login page and will force the user to enter this text at the time of logging in. This pattern will change each time this login page is accessed. The challenge code is displayed as a special graphic pattern with characters drawn in a slightly distorted manner. This will avoid the risk of intruders using any character recognition program to identify the pattern and going for an automated login.

Improved Challenge Response Systems

In these mechanisms, the user is provided with an application which can run on a PC, mobile phone or any other device which can encode the challenge pattern displayed in the login page and then generate a new code which the user needs to input for logging in. This will avoid the possibility of some one else logging into the system by using an original user's login and password, which he/she acquired by some means.

Secure Keys/Digital Signatures

Users will be provided with a digital signature in a CD or any other memory device which need to be used for logging in to the STP system. This digital signatures can be set as mandatory for logging in or even it can be configured to be used to initiate certain special transactions like fund transfer, bill payments etc. which are more critical.

Inactivated Logins Even After Production

New logins created are marked as inactive in the system even after login creation and password generation. Access to the system is activated only after confirming the delivery of the password to the customer concerned, by another group of users in the Bank. This eliminates any possibility of the user access being misused by any one in the bank or outside other than the intended customer.

Lock Logins on Invalid Login Attempts

For any invalid login attempts, exceeding a limit(say three times a day), that user login is marked as locked automatically by the system. This will avoid any repeated attempts of invalid logins or automated logins.

Template and Template Approval Mechanisms

This mechanism enforces an approval from the back office for a particular transaction definition, for the first time. Subsequent transactions will go through the system without any approval. This is especially useful when high risk financial transactions like third party fund transfers or bill payments are done through STP. For example, customers generally sent TT or DD to a selected number of their clients or customers or customers pay utility bills for a known set of bills which they receive every month. So, for sending a TT to a client ABC, customer X makes a template through the STP system with all the common details filled in(this is the constant part). This template is then submitted for approval from the back office. Once approved, the templates becomes ready for execution.

Customer can use this template any number of times later to sent TTs to his client ABC by changing only the variable part(like amount, etc). Similarly for utility bill payments also the customer can register his bills with the bank or make templates one time and then pay his/her bills as and when required. This will avoid sending funds from the customer account to unknown parties by any chance.

Additional Passwords/Digital Certificates For Special Transactions

For the initiation of certain financial transactions, which are of higher risks, the user is forced to input an additional transaction password or a digital signature. This provides additional security for such transactions and avoids any misuse.

On Request Assignment of Special Options

Banks are having personal customers and corporate customers. The banking and transaction requirements of these two type of customers are different. For example a personal customer may not open letter of credit or send TTs frequently. So all users by default will get only a predefined set of options. Other options/ services are assigned to the user profile on request by the customer or on bank's discretion.

Multiple Logins

This is another method of avoiding misuse of the system when multiple signatories are involved for a particular customer account or a customer account with single signatory wants to delegate some of his day to day banking requirements to his/her subordinates. A customer is given multiple logins which are grouped together. Profiles and access rights of these logins can be set by the bank on request by the customer of a designated login is given the power to set the profiles of other logins. In the second case there will be one login set as the parent login and a group of attached sub-logins. The parent login is given the authority to manage other logins and their profiles and access rights to accounts and options.

For example, in a company the owner created a login for himself and then created two sub logins, one for his manager and he other for his accountant. Now the owner sets the profile of the other two logins. For example, any transaction initiated by the accountant should be authorized either by the manager or by the owner himself. That is, a transaction initiated by the accountant will not get executed by the STP, rather it will stay in a queue and generate a mail/message to the other two logins saying that a transaction is pending for their authorization. Either the manager or the owner himself can then view this transaction in his own login and they either approves it or deletes this request. This will provide an entry/authorize facility for the customers where one login cannot do specified transactions by themselves. It avoids the necessity of password sharing with in the organization in case of single logins and also avoids the risk of a clerk or accountant initiates financial transactions by using the shared password without the owners or managers approval. Since each user login has got separate profile and access rights, sub logins can be prevented from even viewing the full account information. Risk avoidance techniques are summarized in Table 4.

Risk Reduction

These are methods which will reduce the risk or the exposures of the bank while using STP.

Limits

Limits can be set on the number or value of transactions done through STP. These limits can be set for a customer, for a service, for a transaction or for the bank itself for a specified period of time. Limits set for the customer are called customer level limits and that set for the bank are called bank level limits. An automated transaction processing system for will evaluate these limits at real time and restrict the transactions to stay within this limit. Limit override may be done at special cases as per rules set by the bank.

Table 4
Comparison of Techniques for Risk Avoidance

Access Control Method	*Merits*	*Demerits*
User name & Password	Access is controlled	Risk when used unencrypted Risk of stealing it and using others Crackers using automated tools to crack the password
Challenge Mechanisms		
*Display a challenge code as text	Automated logins can be prevented	Can use OCR readers to read and input challenge code automatically
*Display challenge code as distorted graphical image	Automated logins completely prevented	User has to enter the same code showed on screen. If some one get hold of your password he can login.
*User has to enter an encrypted response to the challenge code displayed on screen	As the challenge code encryption application is run on the users mobile phone or any other device, those who got the password by chance, still cannot login.	User need to download and install a challenge response generator application in his or her mobile device
Secure Keys and Digital Signatures	Can be used as additional security mechanisms for normal logins or for performing special transaction options	User has to carry this key in a separate storage device for enhanced security.
Lock logins automatically after as few number of unsuccessful attempts	Continued unauthorized attempts to login to the system is prevented	User has to contact the Bank and follow a procedure for reactivating it.

Contd...

Access Control Method	*Merits*	*Demerits*
Additional passwords or keys for using financial transaction options	Even if some one hacks into the login, he cannot do any financial transaction	User need to maintain two sets of passwords/keys
Login are maintained inactivated in the system even after password generation	Prevents the use of login by bank users or others who acquired on transit to delivery to the customer	Another set of bank users(different from who produced it) has to be designated for activating the passwords.
On request assignment of certain options	Reduces the risk of having options on the customer's login which he normally does not want to use	User may not know which options are not assigned to his by default
Multiple logins (grouped) Any transaction request entered by one user has to be authorized by one or more user(s) in the same group	Useful for corporate customers where joint signatories exist or for owners who assign the data entry part of web banking to his or her subordinates.	Possible delay in transaction execution.
Same set of users in the bank are not allowed to create and activate the logins.	Any misuse of the login access with in the bank is reduced.	Possible delay in access code generation, delivery and activation

Period Wise (Daily/Monthly/Yearly) Limits

Banks can set daily, monthly, yearly or any other period wise limit for a customers, customer service or for a customer transaction. For example, a customer X may be allowed to have a daily limit of $ 100,000.00 for his web transactions, but he may have a smaller limit of $ 40,000/- for his Letter of Credit transactions. Banks can also set a bank level daily limit for all the STP transactions for a day. This will limit the daily exposure of the bank to the set value.

Transaction Limits

Bank can set transaction limits for individual transactions performed by each customer or for a particular transaction type(say TT). For example each TT transaction of customer X should be less than $ 100,000.00. Bank may also set a limit for total transactions by STP.

Customer Limits

Bank can set a customer level limit for a specific period. For example, the daily transaction limit (total) of customer X is $ 100,000.00

Bank Limits

Bank can set a bank level limit for a specific period. For example, the daily transaction limit (total) of all customers together for fund transfer is X is $ 100,000.00. Risk control methods using limits are summarized in Table 5.

Risk Detection and Control

These are methods which will help the bank as well as the customer to detect any irregularity, if at all it happens.

SMS Notification/E-Mail Notification

Mandatory Email notification or SMS notification is set to a customer profile for pre-defined STP events. This will help

Table 5
Comparison of Limit for Risk Reduction

Control Method	*Merits*	*Demerits*
Customer Limits	Restrict the magnitude of losses in a short duration	Customer may have to contact the bank for any transaction above the limits. User intervention may be introduced to override any such limit.
Bank Limits	Provides treasury control Provides product level control	Service to customers may be affected if these limits are not set properly
Transaction Limits	Restrict any possible loss in a single transaction	User intervention may be introduced to override any such limit.

detect any unauthorized login and transaction as soon as possible. Eg.

- Send an SMS/Email every time the customer logs in.
- Send an SMS/Email when any financial transaction is done.
- Send an SMS/Email when a service is accessed, as requested by the Customer.

Last Login Time & IP Address Logging

Last login time displayed on the customer screen shown just after logging in will help the customer to detect any unauthorized logins. The IP address information logged can be used to trace the intruder access source.

Fraud Monitoring & Intruder Detection System

These are special systems installed in the bank for monitoring the STP access and STP transactions to detect any unusual patterns. For example: Transactions which exceeds limit, number of invalid attempts to the system, number of transactions in a day, etc can be analyzed and reported to the management or the technical department for any further action.

Logging and Reporting

Each and every user accesses and transactions with all the details should be logged and time stamped in the system. This will provide all necessary audit trails and transaction details for the generation of any regulatory or other reports. These reports are to be generated and analyzed on a daily basis. Risk detection and reduction techniques are summarized in Table 6.

Table 6
Comparison of Risk Detection & Reduction Techniques

Control Method	*Merits*	*Demerits*
Notification SMS E-mail	Instant No cost	Cost of messaging Delayed
Login time indication & machine address	Monitor any intruder access and then initiate an investigation	Delayed, losses may have already incurred.
Reporting & Analysis	Detects any abnormal activity	Possible delay in detection
Fault Monitoring and Detection System	Quick and system controlled. Reduces the impact to greater extend.	System cost increases Need for customer wise and bank wise effective detection rules.

Concluding Observations

STP coupled with adequate security and risk control methods, with the advancing technologies, will definitely provide banks the capability to manage operational risk the way compliance and regulatory authorities required. With the kind of customer service requirements, availability, efficiency and globalization, banks would need to go with more and more STP to have a competitive position in the market.

References

International Convergence of Capital Measurement and Capital Standards-A revised framework: Comprehensive version, Basel Committee on Banking Supervision, June, 2006.

Operational Risk–Regulation, Analysis & Management, Carol Alexander, FT-Prentice Hall.

Case Study of BiLogic Systems' STP implementation @Habib Bank AG Zurich worldwide.

Operational risk: the STP mantra, Sabyasachi Bardoloi , manager, Pinnacle Research Group, Pinnacle Systems, Inc., http://www.continuity central.com/feature051.htm, Date: 19th December 2003.

Financial services need straight-through processing, say analysts, *OUT-LAW* News, 08/08/2003, http://www.out-law.com/page-3794.

Straight Through Processing By Sajit Dayanandan, Financial Technologies India Wednesday, July 02, 2003, http://dqindia.ciol.com/content/bank/103070204.asp.

Straight Through Processing, Increase your business agility by gaining full control of your processes (www.softwareag.com/Corporate/Solutions/banking/stp/default.asp).

Straight Through Processing for Financial Services Firms (Paperback), by Hal McIntyre (Author), Paperback, 264 pages, publication dt. Nov. 2007.

15

THE CREDIT CARD AS A CREDIT SCHEME: A SUCCESS WITH SOME ISSUES

N. Brindha

Introduction

A credit card is a system of payment named after the small plastic card issued to users of the system. A credit card is different from a debit card in that it does not remove money from the user's account after every transaction. In the case of credit cards, the issuer lends money to the consumer (or the user) to be paid to the merchant. It is also different from a charge card (though this name is sometimes used by the public to describe credit cards), which requires the balance to be paid in full each month. In contrast, a credit card allows the consumer to 'revolve' their balance, at the cost of having interest charged. Most credit cards are the same shape and size, as specified by the ISO 7810 standard.

Working Mechanism of Credit Cards

A user is issued credit after an account has been approved by the credit provider, and is given a credit card, with which the user will be able to make purchases from merchants accepting that credit card up to a pre-established credit limit. When a purchase is made, the credit card user agrees to pay the card issuer. The cardholder indicates their consent to pay, by signing a receipt with a record of the card details and indicating the amount to be paid or by entering a Personal Identification Number (PIN). Also, many merchants now accept verbal authorizations via telephone and electronic authorization using the Internet, known as a Card Not Present (CNP) transaction.

Electronic verification systems allow merchants to verify that the card is valid and the credit card customer has sufficient credit to cover the purchase in a few seconds, allowing the verification to happen at time of purchase. The verification is performed using a credit card payment terminal or Point of Sale (POS) system with a communications link to the merchant's acquiring bank. Data from the card is obtained from a magnetic stripe or chip on the card. Other variations of verification systems are used by eCommerce merchants to determine if the user's account is valid and able to accept the charge. These will typically involve the cardholder providing additional information, such as the security code printed on the back of the card, or the address of the cardholder.

Each month, the credit card user is sent a statement indicating the purchases undertaken with the card, any outstanding fees, and the total amount owed. After receiving the statement, the cardholder may dispute any charges that he or she thinks are incorrect (Fair Credit Billing Act for details of the US regulations). Otherwise, the cardholder must pay a defined minimum proportion of the bill by a due date, or may choose to pay a higher amount up to the entire amount owed. The credit provider charges interest on the amount owed (typically at a much higher rate than most other forms of debt). Some financial institutions can arrange for automatic payments to be deducted from the user's bank accounts, thus avoiding late payment altogether as long as the cardholder has sufficient funds. Credit card issuers usually waive interest charges if the balance is paid in full each month, but typically will charge full interest on the entire outstanding balance from the date of each purchase if the total balance is not paid.

The credit card may simply serve as a form of revolving credit, or it may become a complicated financial instrument with multiple balance segments each at a different interest rate, possibly with a single umbrella credit limit, or with separate credit limits applicable to the various balance segments. Usually this compartmentalization is the result of special incentive offers from the issuing bank, either to encourage balance transfers from cards of other issuers, or to encourage more spending on the part of the customer. In the event that several interest rates apply to various balance segments, payment allocation is generally at the discretion of the issuing bank, and payments will therefore usually be allocated towards the lowest rate balances until paid in full before any money is paid towards higher rate balances. Interest rates can vary considerably from card to card, and the interest rate on a particular card may jump dramatically if the card user is late with a payment on that card or any other credit instrument, or even if the issuing bank decides to raise its revenue. As the rates and terms vary, services have been set up allowing users to calculate savings available by switching cards, which can be considerable if there is a large outstanding balance.

Because of intense competition in the credit card industry, credit providers often offer incentives such as frequent flyer points, gift certificates, or cash back (typically up to 1 per cent based on total purchases) to try to attract customers to their program. Low interest credit cards or even 0% interest credit cards are available. The only downside to consumers is that the period of low interest credit cards is limited to a fixed term, usually between 6 and 12 months after which a higher rate is charged. However, services are available which alert credit card holders when their low interest period is due to expire. Most such services charge a monthly or annual fee.

Grace Period

A credit card's grace period is the time the customer has to pay the balance before interest is charged to the balance. Grace periods vary, but usually range from 20 to 30 days depending on the type of credit card and the issuing bank. Some policies allow for reinstatement after certain conditions are met. Usually, if a customer is late paying the balance, finance charges will be calculated and the grace period does not apply. Finance charge(s) incurred depends on the grace period and balance, with most credit cards there is no grace period if there's any outstanding balance from the previous billing cycle or statement (ie. interest is applied on both the previous balance and new transactions). However, there are some credit cards that will only apply finance charge on the previous or old balance, excluding new transactions.

The Merchant's Side

For merchants, a credit card transaction is often more secure than other forms of payment, such as checks, because the issuing bank commits to pay the merchant the moment the transaction is authorized, regardless of whether the consumer defaults on their credit card payment (except for legitimate disputes, can result in charge backs to the merchant). In most cases, cards are even more secure than cash, because they discourage theft by the merchant's employees. For each purchase, the bank charges a commission (discount fee), to the merchant for this service and there may be a certain delay before the agreed payment is received by the merchant. The commission is often a percentage of the transaction amount, plus a fixed fee. In addition, a merchant may be penalized or have their ability to receive payment using that credit card restricted if there are too many cancellations or reversals of charges as a result of disputes. Some small merchants require credit purchases to have a minimum amount (usually between $5 and $10) to compensate for the transaction costs, though this is not always allowed by the credit card consortium.

Parties involved

- *Cardholder:* The owner of the card used to make a purchase; the consumer.
- *Card-issuing Bank:* The financial institution or other organization that issued the credit card to the cardholder. This bank bills the consumer for repayment and bears the risk that the card is used fraudulently. American Express and Discover were previously the only card-issuing banks for their respective brands, but as of 2007, this is no longer the case.
- *Merchant:* The individual or business accepting credit card payments for products or services sold to the cardholder.
- *Acquiring bank:* The financial institution accepting payment for the products or services on behalf of the merchant.
- *Independent Sales Organization:* Resellers (to merchants) of the services of the acquiring bank.
- *Merchant Account:* This could refer to the acquiring bank or the independent sales organization, but in general is the organization that the merchant deals with.
- *Credit Card Association:* An association of card-issuing banks such as Visa, MasterCard, Discover, American Express, etc. that set transaction terms for merchants, card-issuing banks, and acquiring banks.

Transaction Network

The system that implements the mechanics of the electronic transactions. May be operated by an independent company, and one company may operate multiple networks. Transaction processing networks include: Cardnet, Nabanco, Omaha, Paymentech, NDC Atlanta, Nova, Vital, Concord EFSnet, and VisaNet.

Affinity partner: Some institutions lend their name to an issuer to attract customers that have a strong relationship with that institution, and get paid a fee or a percentage of the balance for each card issued using their name. Examples of typical affinity partners are sports teams, universities and charities. The flow of information and money between these parties—always through the card associations—is known as the interchange, and it consists of a few steps.

Secured Credit Cards

A secured credit card is a type of credit card secured by a deposit account owned by the cardholder. Typically, the cardholder must deposit between 100% and 200% of the total amount of credit desired. Thus if the cardholder puts down $ 1000, he or she will be given credit in the range of $ 500–$ 1000. In some cases, credit card issuers will offer incentives even on their secured card portfolios. In these cases, the deposit required may be significantly less than the required credit limit, and can be as low as 10% of the desired credit limit. This deposit is held in a special savings account. Credit card issuers offer this as they have noticed that delinquencies were notably reduced when the customer perceives he has something to lose if he doesn't repay his balance. The cardholder of a secured credit card is still expected to make regular payments, as he or she would with a regular credit card, but should he or she default on a payment, the card issuer has the option of recovering the cost of the purchases paid to the merchants out of the deposit. The advantage of the secured card for an individual with negative or no credit history is that most companies report regularly to the major credit bureaus. This allows for building of positive credit history.

Although the deposit is in the hands of the credit card issuer as security in the event of default by the consumer, the deposit will not be debited simply for missing one or two payments. Usually the deposit is only used as an offset when the account is closed, either at the request of the customer or due to severe delinquency (150 to 180 days). This means that an account which is less than 150 days delinquent will continue to accrue interest and fees, and could result in a balance which is much higher than the actual credit limit on the card. In these cases the total debt may far exceed the original deposit and the cardholder not only forfeits their deposit but is left with an additional debt. Most of these conditions are usually described in a cardholder agreement which the cardholder signs when their account is opened.

Secured credit cards are an option to allow a person with a poor credit history or no credit history to have a credit card which might not otherwise be available. They are often offered as a means of rebuilding one's credit. Secured credit cards are available with both Visa and MasterCard logos on them. Fees and service charges for secured credit cards often exceed those charged for ordinary non-secured credit cards, however, for people in certain situations, (for example, after charging off on other credit cards, or people with a long history of delinquency on various forms of debt), secured cards can often be less expensive in total cost than unsecured credit cards, even including the security deposit. Sometimes a credit card will be secured by the equity in the borrower's home. This is called a home equity line of credit (HELOC).

Prepaid Credit Cards

A prepaid credit card is not really a credit card, as no credit is offered by the card issuer: the card-holder spends money which has been "stored" via a prior deposit by the card-holder or someone else, such as a parent or employer. However, it carries a credit-card brand (Visa, MasterCard, American Express or Discover) and can be used in similar ways. After purchasing the card, the cardholder loads it with any amount of money and then uses the card to spend the money. Prepaid cards can be issued to minors (above 13years) since there is no credit line involved. The main advantage over secured credit cards is that you are not required to come up with $ 500 or more to open an account. Also most secured credit cards still charge you interest even though you are not actually "borrowing" any money. With prepaid credit cards you are not charged any interest but you are often charged a purchasing fee plus monthly fees after an arbitrary time period. Many other fees also usually apply to a prepaid card. Prepaid credit cards are often marketed to teenagers for shopping online without having their parents complete the transaction. Because of the many fees that apply to obtaining and using credit-card-branded prepaid cards, the Financial Consumer Agency of Canada describes them as "an expensive way to spend your own money". The agency publishes a booklet, "Pre-paid cards", which explains the advantages and disadvantages of this type of prepaid card.

Salient Features

As well as convenient, accessible credit, credit cards offer consumers an easy way to track expenses, which is necessary for both monitoring personal expenditures and the tracking of work-related expenses for taxation and reimbursement purposes. Credit cards are accepted worldwide, and are available with a large variety of credit limits, repayment arrangement, and other perks (such as rewards schemes in which points earned by purchasing goods with the card can be redeemed for further goods and services or credit card cashback).

Security Overview

Credit card security is based on privacy of the actual credit card number. This means that whenever a person other than the card owner reads the number, security is potentially compromised. Since this happens most of the time when a transaction is made, security is low. However, a user with access to just the number can only make certain types of transactions. Merchants will often accept credit card numbers without extra verification for mail order, but then the delivery address will be recorded, so the thief must make sure he can have the goods delivered to an anonymous address (ie. not his own) and collect them without being detected. Some merchants will accept a credit card number for in-store purchases, whereupon access to the number allows easy fraud, but many require the card itself to be present, and require a signature. Thus, a stolen card can be cancelled, and if this is done quickly, no fraud can take place in this way. For internet purchases, there is sometimes the same level of security as for mail order (number only) hence requiring only that the fraudster take care about collecting the goods, but often there are additional measures. The main one is to require a security pin with the card, which requires that the thief have access to the card.

Security Problems

A smart card, combining credit card and debit card properties. The 3 by 5 mm security chip embedded in the card is shown enlarged in the inset. The gold contact pads on the card enable electronic access to the chip. The low security of the credit card system presents countless opportunities for fraud. This opportunity has created a huge black market in stolen credit card numbers, which are generally used quickly before the cards are reported stolen. The goal of the credit card companies is not to eliminate fraud, but to "reduce it to manageable levels", such that the total cost of both fraud and fraud prevention is minimized. This implies that high-cost low-return fraud prevention measures will not be used if their cost exceeds the potential gains from fraud reduction.

Most internet fraud is done through the use of stolen credit card information which is obtained in many ways, the simplest being copying information from retailers, either online or offline. Despite efforts to improve security for remote purchases using credit cards, systems with security holes are usually the result of poor implementations of card acquisition by merchants. For example, a website that uses SSL to encrypt card numbers from a client may simply email the number from the webserver to someone who manually processes the card details at a card terminal. Naturally, anywhere card details become human-readable before being processed at the acquiring bank, a security risk is created. However, many banks offer systems where encrypted card details captured on a merchant's webserver can be sent directly to the payment processor. Controlled Payment Numbers are another option for protecting one's credit card number: they are "alias" numbers linked to one's actual card number, generated as needed, valid for a relatively short time, with a very low limit, and typically only valid with a single merchant.

Profits and Losses

In recent times, credit card portfolios have been very profitable for banks, largely due to the booming economy of the late nineties. However, in the case of credit cards, such high returns go hand in hand with risk, since the business is essentially one of making unsecured (uncollateralized) loans, and thus dependent on borrowers not to default in large numbers.

Costs

Credit card issuers (banks) have several types of costs:

Interest Expenses

Banks generally borrow the money they then lend to their customers. As they receive very low-interest loans from other firms, they may borrow as much as their customers require, while lending their capital to other borrowers at higher rates. If the card issuer charges 15% on money lent to users, and it costs 5% to borrow the money to lend, and the balance sits with the cardholder for a year, the issuer earns 10% on the loan. This 5% difference is the "interest expense" and the 10% is the "net interest spread".

Operating Costs

This is the cost of running the credit card portfolio, including everything from paying the executives who run the company to printing the plastics, to mailing the statements, to running the computers that keep track of every cardholder's balance, to taking the many phone calls which cardholders place to their issuer, to protecting the customers from fraud rings. Depending on the issuer, marketing programs are also a significant portion of expenses.

Charge Offs

When a consumer becomes severely delinquent on a debt (often at the point of six months without payment), the creditor may declare the debt to be a charge-off. It will then be listed as such on the debtor's credit bureau reports (Equifax, for instance, lists "R9" in the "status" column to denote a charge-off.) It is one of the worst possible items to have on your file. The item will include relevant dates, and the amount of the bad debt. A charge-off is considered to be "written off as uncollectable." To banks, bad debts and even fraud are simply part of the cost of doing business. However, the debt is still legally valid, and the creditor can attempt to collect the full amount for the time periods permitted under state law, which is usually 3 to 7 years. This includes contacts from internal collections staff, or more likely, an outside collection agency. If the amount is large (generally over $1500-$2000), there is the possibility of a lawsuit or arbitration.

Rewards

Many credit card customers receive rewards, such as frequent flier points, gift certificates, or cash back as an incentive to use the card. Rewards are generally tied to purchasing an item or service on the card, which may or may not include balance transfers, cash advances, or other special uses. Depending on the type of card, rewards will generally cost the issuer between 0.25% and 2.0% of the spend.

Networks like Visa or MasterCard have increased their fees to allow issuers to fund their rewards system. However, most rewards points are accrued as a liability on a company's balance sheet and expensed at the time of reward redemption. As a result, some issuers discourage redemption by forcing the cardholder to call customer service for rewards. On their servicing website, redeeming awards is usually a feature that is very well hidden by the issuers. Others encourage redemption for lower cost merchandise; instead of an airline ticket, which is very expensive to an issuer, the cardholder may be encouraged to redeem for a gift certificate instead. With a fractured and competitive environment, rewards points cut dramatically into an issuer's bottom line, and rewards points and related incentives must be carefully managed to ensure a profitable portfolio. There is a case to be made that rewards not redeemed should follow the same path as gift cards that are not used: in certain states the gift card breakage goes to the state's treasury. The same could happen to the value of points or cash not redeemed.

Concluding Observations

While discussing with the credit card holders, we came to know some practical issues with the banks what they are facing, can be listed.

1. Unknown bills added with their card bills, then the queries will prove it as fack ones.
2. Repeated intimations to the paid month dues, which always disturbs the privasy of the people.
3. Without the card holder's concern some insurance policy added, so far.

This culture spoils the youths mindset to spend more and affect the savings habits. Apart from all these issues this credit card culture makes the people to spent more and mobilisation of money gets versatile facets. Credit cards are effective credit schemes through banks world wide is an acceptable truth.

References

Suryachandra Rao (2007), 'Reforms in Indian Banking Sector', *Finance India*, Vol. XXI, No 2, June.

IIB Vision,Volume 2, Issue No. 11

Lawrence. J. Gitman, Principles of Managerial Finance, Pearson Education, India, p. 666–682.

Khan M.Y., Jain. P.K, Financial Management, Tata Mc Graw Hill Publishing Company Limited, New Delhi.

Official Website of the Reserve Bank of India, *www.rbi.org.in*

Official Website of HSBC Bank, SBI Cards, Citi Bank etc.

16

CORPORATE GOVERNANCE IN BANKING AND FINANCIAL INSTITUTIONS IN INDIA

R. VARADARAJAN

Introduction

Corporate Governance structures are essential for shaping enterprise behaviour, including the response by enterprises to these pressures and the associated new investment and growth opportunities. Improving the understanding of corporate governance is therefore of utmost importance. Enhanced understanding will permit the identification of policy priorities and trade-offs as regards the regulatory and institutional environment which conditions corporate governance structures. Corporate Governance is of direct relevance to policy makers because laws, institutions and regulations, on which policy makers exert influence, have a direct bearing for corporate governance structures. Such policy levels include:

- company law
- taxation

- banking and securities regulation
- prudential regulation of pension and insurance sectors.
- stock market regulation and
- bankruptcy legislation

Structural changes in financial markets have led to the emergence of new financial instruments, increased integration of markets, stronger competition and new or radically changed financial institutions. These developments are having an important impact on the functioning of financial governance channels, although not all consequences are well understood. In the context of its regular review of structural changes in financial markets, the OECD, in its analysis of financial systems, will continue its work on structural changes in financial markets and the implications for corporate governance.

Importance of Corporate Governance

Corporate governance is only part of the larger economic context in which firms operate, which includes, for example, macroeconomic policies and the degree of competition in product and factor markets. The corporate governance framework also depends on the legal, regulatory, and institutional environment. In addition, factors such as business ethics and corporate awareness of the environmental and societal interests of the communities in which it operates can also have an impact on the reputation and the long-term success of a company.

While a multiplicity of factors affect the governance and decision-making processes of firms, and are important to their long-term success, the Principles focus on governance problems that result from the separation of ownership and control. Some of the other issues relevant to a company's decision making processes, such as environmental or ethical concerns, are taken into account but are treated more explicitly in a number of other OECD instruments (including the Guidelines for Multinational Enterprises and the Convention and

Recommendation on Bribery) and the instruments of other international organizations.

The degree to which corporations observe basic principles of good corporate governance is an increasingly important factor for investment decisions. Of particular relevance is the relation between corporate governance practices and the increasingly international character of investment. International flows of capital enable companies to access financing from a much larger pool of investors.

Scope of the Study

Corporate governance is affected by the relationships among participants in the governance system. Controlling shareholders, which may be individuals, family holdings, bloc alliances, or other corporations acting through a holding company or cross shareholdings, can significantly influence corporate behaviour. As owners of equity, institutional investors are increasingly demanding a voice in corporate governance in some markets. Individual shareholders usually do not seek to exercise governance rights but may be highly concerned about obtaining fair treatment from controlling shareholders and management. Creditors play an important role in some governance systems and have the potential to serve as external monitors over corporate performance. Employees and other stakeholders play an important role in contributing to the long-term success and performance of the corporation, while governments establish the overall institutional and legal framework for corporate governance. The scope of each of these participants and their interactions vary widely among OECD countries and among non-Members as well. These relationships are subject, in part, to law and regulation and, in part, to voluntary adaptation and market forces.

There is no single model of good corporate governance. At the same time, work carried out in Member countries and within the OECD has identified some common elements that underlie good corporate governance. The Principles build on these common elements and are formulated to embrace the different models that exist. The Principles are non-binding and do not aim at detailed prescriptions for national legislation. Their purpose is to serve as a reference point. They can be used by policy makers, as they examine and develop their legal and regulatory frameworks for corporate governance that reflect their own economic, social, legal and cultural circumstances, and by market participants as they develop their own practices.

The Principles are evolutionary in nature and should be reviewed in light of significant changes in circumstances. To remain competitive in a changing world, corporations must innovate and adapt their corporate governance practices so that they can meet new demands and grasp new opportunities. Similarly, governments have an important responsibility for shaping an effective regulatory framework that provides for sufficient flexibility to allow markets to function effectively and to respond to expectations of shareholders and other stakeholders. It is up to governments and market participants to decide how to apply these Principles in developing their own frameworks for corporate governance, taking into account the costs and benefits of regulation.

Conceptual Framework

The banking and financial institutions sector is not necessarily totally corporate. Some part of it is, of course, but a segment of banks is mostly government-held as statutory corporations or run as cooperatives. In this sense, corporate governance when applied to banking and finance organizations must be understood contextually rather than what the work "corporate" tends to connote. Banking, as a sector, has been unique and the interests of other stakeholders appear more important to it than in the case of non-banking and non-finance organizations. In the case of traditional manufacturing corporation, the issue has been that of ensuring the security and value of the property owners, to the extent of the property contracted, i.e. the equity invested. In the case of banking, the risk involved for the depositors and the possibilities of the contagion effect assume greater importance than of consumers of manufactured products. Further, the involvement of the government is discernibly higher in banks due to the importance of the stability of the financial system and the larger interests of the public. The government does see reason in regulating and controlling the nature of activities, the structure of the boards, the ownership patterns, capital adequacy norms, liquidity ratios, etc. Thus, the market for control is not sufficient enough to ensure proper governance in banks.

Objectives of the Study

A separate and distinct study on corporate governance and shareholder enrichment are scanty, there is a need for a comprehensive study on corporate governance, corporate growth and its impact on shareholder enrichment. The present study is thus an attempt to analyse the concept of corporate governance in banking and financial companies. The objectives are to examine and analyse the recent trends in corporate governance practices in India, to evaluate the integrity and behaviour of selected performance, to measure the impact on banking growth and relationship after globalisation.

Methodology

The present study is both descriptive and analytical in nature. A sample of banking companies whose are actively participating in National Building was considered for the study. The data collected for the present study is mainly secondary data were collected from Annual Report of RBI, Stock Exchanges, Department of Company Affairs and the respective Banking Companies.

Structure of the Financial System in India and Recent Moves for Good Governance

The financial system in India can be broadly categorized as involving the following segments:

- Scheduled Commercial Banks
- Cooperative Banks
- The Rural Banks
- Financial Institutions
- Insurance Companies and
- Non-banking financial companies.

It is evident that over 81% of the assets of all scheduled commercial banks are concentrated in 27 of the public sector banks, of which 19 are the nationalized ones and eight are in the State Bank Group. The State Bank group comprises of the SBI and seven of its associates. Amongst the private sector banks, which account for nearly 11% of the assets, the new private sector banks account for about 37% of these assets. Though numerically small, the size and reach of the public sector banks is significantly high and obviously have far more issues of diversity in stakeholders interests.

Corporate governance is indeed an art of balancing the autonomy and flexibility of the management with checks on strategic decisions, while ensuring that the interests of the shareholders are not sacrificed. It is in this context, that many observe that the government has been insensitive to the issues of governance and has shown preference for undue political mileage arising out of the ownership. Thus, the members of the Board of Directors and the top management continue to be appointed on the basis of a laborious bureaucratic process often steered by political interests. An anachronous situation has been the practice of having RBI nominees on the boards of banks, by which the conflict of interest between a regulator and an independent member often undermines good corporate governance.

Banks and Corporate Governance

Establishing strategic objectives and a set of corporate values that are communicated throughout the banking organization. Setting and enforcing clear lines of responsibility and accountability throughout the organization. Ensuring that board members and qualified for their position, have a clear understanding of their role in corporate governance and are not subject to undue influence from management or outside concerns. Ensuring that there is appropriate oversight by senior management.Effectively utilizing the work conducted by internal and external auditors, in recognition of the important control function they provide. Ensuring that compensation approaches are consistent with the banks' ethical values, objectives, strategy and control environment involves:

- Conducting corporate governance in a transparent manner.
- Ensuring an environment supportive of sound corporate governance.

Banks play a vital role in the economy and the continued strength and stability of the banking system is a matter of general public interest and concern, both in regard to its linkages with the real sector and for providing a payment and settlement system. Banks, as corporate entities, possess certain unique characteristics. As financial intermediaries, they are highly leveraged organizations and until capital standards were introduced, banks could expand business without any linkage with capital. Even with the capital ratios now prescribed, the gearing compared to other entities is significant. Another characteristic is that banks can continue to fund their operations only so long as they enjoy the confidence of the financial markets. Credit institutions are linked to each other through a complex chain of inter-bank relationships which, in the event of difficulty become mechanisms for the acceleration of contagion. The failure of a major institution or a group of institutions, regardless of the reason, is liable to set off through contagion the failure of other institutions and open serious risks in both the banking and financial systems.

The increasing interest in corporate governance is also due to certain other developments such as increasing participation of the public shareholders in public sector banks, the entry of new private banks and the need to access capital markets by all banks. These developments require banks to establish credible and widely accepted corporate governance arrangements, if they have to attract capital, particularly global capital. While the generally accepted principles of corporate governance would also apply to banks, in view of their unique status and safety nets provided to them, certain principles require a reorientation.

Rights of Shareholders

While shareholders of banks enjoy the same rights as other shareholders, I view of the importance of having 'fit and proper' management, transfers of shares beyond a threshold require acknowledgement of the RBI in addition to compliance with other laws. Similarly, in the case of the new private sector banks, the promoters are required to retain their share of 40 per cent for five years in order to ensure that they have a long-term interest in the financial viability of the bank. To limit the control, which any one group can have over the operations of the banks, no person can exercise voting rights in excess of 10 per cent in private sector banks.

Role of Stakeholders

Different laws covers the rights of the stakeholders in banking companies-depositors, creditors and employees and these laws are respected and enforced. Banks also owe a duty to the communities and their activities should be in public interest. The disclosure and transparency measures ensure that all stakeholders have the necessary information that they require.

Disclosure and Transparency

Disclosure and transparency are key pillars of a corporate governance framework because they provide all the stakeholders with the information necessary to judge whether their interests are being taken care of. The banks have how to disclose all significant data such as capital (tier I and tier II), capital adequacy ratio, percentage of net non-performing advances (NPAs) to net advances, provisions toward NPAs and investments, critical cooperating ratios like interest, non-interest income and operating profit to working funds and return on assets. From March 2000, banks will have to disclose, among others, maturity pattern of assets/liabilities, foreign currency assets and liabilities, movements in NPAs and associated provisions and lending exposure to sensitive sectors as may be announced from time to time. With these the disclosure standards in India would generally be on par with international standards.

Responsibilities of the Board

The governance of banks rests with the board of directors. For this reason, much of the debate has been focused on the structure and composition of the board, the board procedures and the responsibility of the board. In the light of deregulation in interest rates and the greater autonomy given to banks in almost all operational matters, the role of boards of directors of even the public sector banks have become more significant. The board should ensure that the bank is run with integrity, complies with all legal requirements and regulatory standards and conducts its business in accordance with high ethical standards. Boards have been required to lay down policies in critical areas such as investments, loans, asset-liability management, and management and recovery of NPAs.

The RBI has also directed the banks to set up audit committees of the board. The audit committee is charged with the responsibility of ensuring the efficacy of the entire internal control and audit functions in the bank, besides compliance with the inspection reports of the RBI, internal and concurrent auditors. To ensure both professionalism and independence of these committees, chartered accountant directors on the board of banks are mandatory members and the chairman is not to be a part of the audit committee. The RBI through various measures has emphasized the primacy of the board of directors and its essential role as the instrument of corporate governance in the affairs of the bank.

The Narasimham Committee has recommended that the RBI nominees from the boards of banks should be withdrawn, as the practice is perceived to be in conflict with the RBI's regulatory and supervisory role. In fact, the RBI has been withdrawing its nominees from the boards of well-managed old private banks.

Corporate Governance : The Role of Banks and DFIs

Banks and development financial institutions (DFIs) in India, particularly DFIs have an important role in the governance of companies where they have their nominee directors. The role of these nominee directors is to protect the interests of the institution and also as members of the board be as responsible as any other director. However, in certain instances where irregularities have been detected, the role of nominee directors has attracted attention. It is generally felt that these nominee directors of term-lending institutions and mutual funds have become a contentious issue.

Issues Relating to Corporate Governance

It is recognized that independence is the corner stone of accountability and that independent boards are essential to a sound governance structure. In India, in most banks, the positions of the Chief Executive Officer (CEO) and the chairman are combined. There has been much debate concerning the wisdom and feasibility of an independent chairman. The Cadbury Committee had stated that there should be a clearly accepted division of responsibilities at the head of a company which will ensure a balance of power and authority such that no one individual has unfettered powers of decision-making. Where the chairman is also the chief executive, it is essential that there be a strong and independent element on the board with a recognized senior member.

One of the principles of sound banking regulation is that 'connected lending' should not be permitted, i.e. lending by banks to directors or companies in which directors are interested. The Banking Regulation Act does not permit such lending. A similar provision/regulation does not apply to financial institutions (FIs) and it is possible for directors on the board of FIs to continue to enjoy borrowing facilities from the FIs. This needs to be reviewed.The other issue relates to the number of non-executive directors. In public sector banks we have currently two whole-time directors, including the CEO. The rest are non-executive directors and nominee directors. Employee directors are also on the board. A suggestion has been made that the number of executive directors should be increased. The Cadbury Committee has suggested that the board should include non-executive directors of sufficient caliber and number for their views to carry significant weight in the board's decisions. Recently, the Monetary Authority of Singapore (MAS) issued a statement on measures to strengthen the banking system. One of the measures relating to corporate governance is to require all local banks to form nominating committees within the boards. The nominating committee will comprise five members of the board where appointments will be made by the board subject to MAS approval.

The Impirical Evidence

The empirical findings of studies by Prowse (1997) of US banks and by Sinha (1998) of UK banks, provide evidence on the effects of board structure, ownership and firm performance on board changes. Prowse (1997) finds that the most important corporate control mechanism in banks is regulatory intervention. In overall terms, the boards of banks are much less assertive than their counterparts in non-financial firms. Sinha (1998) compares the effects of board structures, ownership and performance on top management turnover in UK banks. The results with respect to board monitoring, are consistent with Prowse's findings for US banks. Stockmarket-based performance measures are significant in top management turnover in manufacturing firms, but financial performance measures are significant in two of the three measures of top management turnover in banks. The estimates show that there are differences in the role of the stockmarket and financial performance measures in the two sectors.

Current Scenario

Bleak US economic reports showed the mood of American consumers deteriorating to a point that has signalled recession. Complicating worries aboutan economic downturn,data suggesting bubbling price pressures,raised the possibility of a scenario of simultaneously slowing growth and rising inflation—stagflation. Financial marketstook their cue from the record drop in factory activity in New York, which fellto nearly a five year low. Investment banks in recent months have absorbed $150 billion in mortgage and corporate loan losses and face new pressures to slash spending.Wall Street investment banks, stung debt losses, have cut tens of thousands of jobs, but even more significant cuts are coming in the months ahead amid a bleaker earnings outlook. The estimates also show that, notwithstanding the greater concern of the regulators in the appointment of the board members and ownership changes, non-executive directors are, in fact, less significant in the turnover of top management in banks than in manufacturing firms. However, in high-risk firms, the institutional investors significantly increase the turnover of top management in banks and their influence on the top management turnover is significantly greater in banks than in manufacturing firms.

Concluding Observations

From the analysis, it is clear that effective corporate governance in banks is contingent upon greater, market-based surveillance of banks. Given that the radical option of complete market-based surveillance cannot be implemented because in some instances, the social costs of bank failure may exceed the private costs, the relative effectiveness of market and supervisory surveillance and the specific emphasis in a particular country's regulatory regime is an empirical question. An assessment of relative effectiveness of market versus supervisory discipline is difficult as various studies show that the effectiveness of market surveillance can be compromised by the presence of official surveillance.

In the final analysis, all aspects of the management of banking and financial firms (including compliance) are corporate governance issues. This means that if a banks financial firm behaves hazardously, i.e. to some extent, a symptom of weak internal corporate governance. This may include, for instance, a hazardous corporate structure for the financial firm, lack of internal control systems, weak surveillance by (especially non-executive) directors, and ineffective internal audit arrangements. Corporate governance arrangements were evidently weak and under-developed in banks in many of the countries that has recently experienced bank distress.

References

Anderson, Arthur (1996), *Findings and Recommendations of the Review of Supervision and Surveillance*, July.

Bank of England, (1996), *The Bank's Review of Supervision*, July.

Benston, G. (1998), "Regulating Financial Markets: A Critique and Some Proposals", *Institute of Economic Affairs*, Horbart Paper No. 125, London.

Billet, M.T., J.A. Garfinkel and E.S.O.'Neal (1998), "The Cost of Market versus Regulatory Discipline in Banking", *Journal of Financial Economics*, 48:333-358.

Davies, K. (1995), "Bank Deregulation, Supervision, and Agency Problems", *The Australian Economic Review*, 3rd Quarter, 43-54.

Hall, M.J.B. (1993), "Handbook of Banking Regulation and Supervision", New York: Woodhead-Faulker.

Llewellyn, D.T. (1999c), "The New Economics of Banking", *Societie Universitaire Europeenne de Recherecbes Financieres Special Stud Special Study*, Amsterdam.

Shleifer, A. and R.W. Vishny, (1997), "A Survey of Corporate Governance", *Journal of Finance*, 52:737-783.

Annual Reports of the Reserve Bank of India (RBI) and State Bank of India (SBI).

The Economic Times.

Business Line.

17

ONLINE BANKING IN INDIA: PROS AND CONS

PRASHANT KUMAR & PRASHANT KUMAR

Introduction

'Internet banking' refers to systems that enable bank customers to access accounts and general information on bank products and services through a personal computer (PC) or other intelligent device. In the past, customers rarely noticed the computer systems that made the information systems operate. Today, websites, electronic mail, and electronic bill presentment and payment systems are an important way for banks to reach their customers. National banks have experimented with various forms of online banking for many years. Some of the early experiments involved closed systems where the customers accessed banks through a dial-in or cable TV connection. These systems limited a bank's potential customer base because they required out of area customers to either incur long-distance charges on their phone bills or subscribe to a particular cable TV service to access the bank.

Internet banking involves use of Internet for delivery of banking products & services. Today, with the widespread growth of the internet, customers may use this technology anywhere in the world to access a bank's network. Moreover, with cyber cafes and kiosks springing up in different cities, access to the net is becoming easy. The internet, as an enabling technology, has made banking products and services available to more customers by eliminating geographic and proprietary systems barriers. With an expanded market, banks also may have opportunities to expand or change their product and service offerings. Internet banking is the latest in this series of technological wonders in the recent past involving use of internet for delivery of banking products and services.

Internet banking is changing the banking industry and is having major effects on banking relationships. Banking is now no longer confined to the branches were one has to approach the branch in person, to withdraw cash or deposit a cheque or request a statement of accounts. In true internet banking, any inquiry or transaction is processed online without any reference to the branch at any time. Providing internet banking is increasingly becoming a 'need to have' than a 'nice to have' service. Net banking, thus, now is more of a norm rather than an exception in many developed countries due to the fact that it is the cheapest way of providing banking services. It falls into four main categories, from Level 1- minimum functionality sites that offer only access to deposit account data-to Level 4 sites-highly sophisticated offerings enabling integrated sales of additional products and access to other financial services- such as investment and insurance. In other words a successful Internet banking solution offers:

- Exceptional rates on Savings, CDs, and IRA.
- Checking with no monthly fee, free bill payment and rebates on ATM surcharge.
- Credit cards with low rates.

- Easy online applications for all accounts, including personal loans and mortgage.
- 24 hour accountacces
- Quality customer service with personal attention

The following developments in the Indian banking system have made it possible to use Electronic Technology to each banking transaction like cash receipts, cash payments, transfer of funds, payment of utility bills and payment of dividends and interests etc.:

1. Automated Teller Machines (ATM)
2. Electronic Funds Transfer (EFT)
3. Electronic Data Interchange (EDI)
4. Electronic Clearing System (ECS)
5. Shared Payment Network System (SPNS)
6. Debit Cards/Credit Cards
7. Telephone Banking
8. PC Banking
9. Internet Banking
10. Mobile Banking

Internet banking is the use of Internet as a delivery channel for the banking services, including traditional services, such as opening an account or transferring funds among different accounts, as well as new banking services, such as electronic bill presentment and payment, which allow the customers to pay and receive the bills on a bank's web site.

There are two ways to offer Internet banking. First, an existing bank with physical offices can establish a web site and otter Internet banking in addition to its traditional delivery channels. Second, a bank may be established as a"branchless," "Internet only," or "virtual" bank. Further Internet banking sites offer financial services products to customers in three basic formats:

- Informational only (entry level *Websites):* Presents online information about the different bank services and products to the customer as well as the general public and may include unsecured email contact with no customer identification or verification required. The risk involved here is relatively low, as informational systems typically have no path between the server and the bank's internal network. This level of internet banking may be provided by the bank or be outsourced. While the risk to a bank is relatively low, the server or website may be vulnerable to alteration. Appropriate controls therefore must be in place to prevent unauthorised alterations to the bank's server or website.

- Information exchange (Simple Transactional Websites) or Communicative: customer information such as name, address and account information may be collected or displayed, with possible secure email and/or data transfer. With verification of customer identification (authentication) required. No financial transactions are to be made.
- Transactional (Fully Transactional Websites) : customer account information enquiry, financial transactions such as transfer of funds, payment of bills, application for loans and a variety of other financial transactions with strong customer authentication required.

Such emergence of Internet banking in India is a result of unprecedented competition from non-traditional banking institutions, which now offer banking and financial services over the Internet. The deregulation of the banking industry coupled with the emergence of new technologies, are also responsible for its emergence which enables new competitors to enter the financial services market quickly and efficiently.

Evolution of Online Banking in India

Internet banking, both as a medium of delivery of banking services and as a strategic tool for business development, has gained wide acceptance internationally and is fast catching up in India, with more and more banks entering the fray. India may be said to be on the threshold of a major banking revolution with net banking having already been unveiled. Banking in India has passed through several phases since the times when formal banking activity had commenced. Indian banking industry, today, is in the midst of an IT revolution. The technology changes have put forth the competition among the banks which has led to increasing total banking automation in the Indian banking industry. Out of the over 50,000 branches of public sector banks, only 9,777 branches have been completely computerized while further 13,218 branches gave been partially computerized as on September 30,2001. (IBA, Sept. 2001).

Now private sector banks and foreign banks have an edge over public sector banks as far as implementation of technological solutions is concerned. However, the later are in the process of making huge investment in technology.

The financial reforms that were initiated in the early 90s and the globalization and liberalization measures brought in a completely new operating environment to the banks. Services and products like "Anywhere Banking," "Tele-Banking," "Internet Banking," "Web Banking," "E-Banking" etc. have become the buzzwords of the day and the banks are trying to cope with the competition by offering innovative and attractively packaged technology based services to their customers.

Like most of other activities in banking RBI involved into the act for IT also and set up two committees in quick succession to accelerate thepace of automation of operations in the banking sector. In the early 80s, a high level committee was formed under the chairmanship of Dr. C. Rangarajan, then Governor of RBI, to draw up a phased plan for computerization and mechanization in thebanking industry over a five year time frame of 1985-89. The focus by this time was on customer service and two models of branch automation were developed and implemented. Having gained experience in the earlier mode of computerization, the second Rangarajan committee constituted in 1988 drew up a detailed perspective plan for computerization of banks and for extension of automation to other areas like funds transfer, e-mail, BANKNET, SWIFT, ATMs, Internet banking etc.

The Government of India enacted the Information Technology Act, 2000, generally known as IT Act, 2000, with effect from the 17th October 2000 to provide legal recognition to electronic transactions and other means of Electronic Commerce. Reserve Bank of India set up a 'Working Group on Internet Banking' to examine different aspects of Internet banking (I-banking). The Group agreed that Internet banking is a part of the electronic banking (e banking); the main difference being that in i-banking the delivery channel was Internet, a public domain. Although the concerns of e-banking and i-banking have many things in common, the fact that Internet is a public domain called for additional security measures. It was agreed that the Group would primarily focus its attention on I-banking and to the extent there were commonality between i-banking and e-banking, its recommendation would also apply to e-banking. The Group had focused on three major areas of I-banking i.e., (i) technology and security issues, (ii) legal issues and (iii) regulatory and supervisory issues, RBI had accepted the recommendation of the Working Group and accordingly issued guidelines on Internet banking in India for implementation by banks. The Working Group has also issued a report on Internet banking available on the website of Reserve Bank of India (www.rbi.org.in) covering different aspects of I-banking.

Private and foreign banks have been the early adopters of e-banking while the Public sector banks are also beginning to hold on to the competition. ICICI Bank and HDFC Bank have taken a lead in introducing e-banking in India. ICICI Bank is the first one to have introduced Internet banking for a limited range of services such as access to account information; correspondence for the first time in 1996 and recently, funds transfer between its branches (Rajneesh and Padmanabhan, 2002). ICICI is alsogetting into e trading, thus offering a broader range of integrated services to the customer. Other banks also followed the suit. However, 1996-98 was the period of Internet banking adoption while the Internet banking usage gained importance only in 1999. After ICICI, Citibank, Induslnd Bank and HDFC Bank were the early ones to adopt the technology in 1999. However, Public sector banks initially lagged behind in adoption of the Internet banking technology. Presently almost all the public sector banks are either providing online banking or on the verge of providing such services.

The proposed setting up of a credit information bureau for collecting and sharing credit information on borrowers of lending institutions online would give a fillip to electronic banking. The recommendations of the Vasudevan Committee on technological upgradation of banks in India have also been circulated to banks for implementation 51. In this background, banks are moving in for technological upgradation on a large scale. Internet banking is expected to get a boost from such developments.

Advantages of Online Banking

The Internet has leveled the playing field and afforded open access to customers in the global marketplace. Internet banking is a cost-effective delivery channel for financial institutions. Consumers are embracing the many benefits of Internet banking. Access to one's accounts at anytime and from any location via the World Wide Web is a convenience unknown a short time ago. Thus, a bank's Internet presence transforms from 'brouchreware' status to 'Internet banking' status once the bank goes through a technology integration effort to enable the customer to access information about his or her specific account relationship. The six primary drivers of Internet banking includes, in order of primacy are:

- Improve customer access
- Facilitate the offering of more services
- Increase customer loyalty
- Attract new customers

- Provide services offered by competitors
- Reduce customer attrition

Online Banking Features and its benefits

Online banking facilitates baking from the desk at the click of the mouse. The benefits of such a baking system can be summarized as:

- *Account Information:* Real time balance information and summary of day's transactions.
- *Fund Transfer:* Managing the supply chain network, effectively by using its online fund transfer mechanism. This effects the fund transfer on a real time basis across any bank locations.
- *Request:* This felicitates making any banking request online instantaneously.
- *Account Information:* This is an important component of online banking, making complete database that the bank have available at the terminal. This provides the current balance in the account, day's transaction in the account and details of cash credit limit, drawing power, amount utilized, etc.
- It also provides the benefit of downloading the statement of account as an excel or text/file document file. This statement can be integrated with customer's Enterprise Resource planning system (ERPs) for auto- reconciliation. Such ERP facilitates one to one fund transfer between two linked account and bulk fund transfer.

Information Technology Act, 2000 and Electronic Transactions

During the past decade, the communication system and the digital technology have made dramatic changes in the way business is transacted. A lot of business transactions are carried out now electronically with little regard to geographical dispersion of the trading partners. The law governing commercial transactions has to be consistent irrespective of the jurisdiction in which the trading partners reside.

At present, many legal provisions recognize the paper-based records and documents that should bear signatures. Since electronic commerce eliminates the need for paper based transactions to facilitate e-banking, e-commerce, m-commerce, etc" the IT Act came into existence.

With the increased use of electronic means, it is imperative that evidence of these activities should be available to demonstrate legal rights and obligations that flow from them. Taking cognition of these, the United Nations Commission on International Trade Law (UNCITRAL) adopted Model law on electronic commerce in 1996. The model law provides among other things, that where the law required a signature, that requirement could be met electronically if the electronic signature provided a link between the signer and the record (called the 'data message' in the model law) and evidence of intent to be associated with the record, both to sufficiently reliable for the purposes of the record in the circumstances. This UNCITRAL law is preferred for its universality and harmonious approach. Art 3 of the Draft UNCITRAL Model law says that, in the interpretation of this law, regard is to be had to its international origin and the need to promote uniformity in its application and observance of good faith and questions concerning matters governed by this law which are not expressly settled in it are to be settled in conformity with the general principles on which the law is based.

India is a signatory to the Model Law. In its endeavor to give thrust to Government of India's IT Policy, the Indian Parliament enacted a comprehensive Information Technology Bill, which received president's assent on 9th June 2000. This IT Act, 2000 drawn on the lines of the model law, provides legal recognition for transactions carried out by means of electronic communications. This also encompasses online banking within its purview by providing certain guiding and decisive factors. The aim of Information Technology Act, 2000 is to harmonise consumer protection especially in the use of new technologies and thus facilitate the online banking in the country.

Legal Framework for Electronic Transactions

The act provides legal framework so that the information is not denied legal effect, validity or enforceability solely on the ground that it is in electronic form. This is done by validating and authorising the use of Electronic Data Interchange (EDI), Electronic Records, and Electronic Signatures. It further provides that once a message leaves information system of the originator of the message, it is attributed to him. Thus, repudiation of a secured electronic message is checked and thus the integrity of the data is maintained, in order to have safe and secure online banking transactions. Consequent upon the recognition given to the electronic records, electronic documents and electronic signatures, incidental amendments have also been made in the following Acts:

- The Indian Penal Code, 1860
- The Indian Evidence Act, 1872
- The Banker's Books Evidence Act, 1891 and
- The Reserve Bank of India Act, 1934

The Act purports to include the word 'electronic record' along with the 'record'/'document' appearing in various sections of these Acts. The amendments also purport to include electronic records for the purpose of evidence and impart credence to digital signatures and digital certificates. The amendment to the Indian Penal Code, 1860 also states that for the purpose of Section 446, which deals with forgery of records, a 'register' shall include any list, data or record of any entries maintained in the electronic form as defined in the IT Act.

Similarly, the Banker's Book Evidence Act, 1891 re-defines banker's book as ledgers, daybooks, cash books and account books, and all other books used in the ordinary business of the bank, whether kept in written form or as print outs of data stored in a floppy, disk, tape or in any other form of electro-magnetic data-storage device.

The RBI Act, 1934 has also been amended by the IT Act, 2000 empowering the Central Board to make regulations for fund transfer through electronic means between the banks or between the banks and other financial institutions. Reserve Bank of India has taken the initiative for facilitating real time funds transfer through the real time gross settlement (RTGS) system. With the process of dematerialisation of shares having gained considerable ground in recent years, banks have assumed the role of depository participants. In addition to customers' deposit accounts, they also maintain demat accounts of their clients. Online trading in equities is being allowed by Securities and Exchange Board of India (SEBI). The focus on capital market operations through the web is based on the bank's strategy on tapping customers interested in trading in equities through the internet.

Main Concerns Associated with Online Banking in India

In a survey conducted by the Online Banking Association, member institutions rated security as the most important issue of online banking. There is a dual requirement to protect customers' privacy and protect against fraud. The potential benefits for banks for conducting their business online are manifest, with decreased transaction costs and access to new customers providing seemingly irresistible advantages to conducting business on-line. However, the uptake of Internet baking within India has been slow with only a handful of players providing a true 'Internet banking, service. The two main areas of risk that are inherent in conducting baking transactions over the internet are:

- Preventing unauthorized transactions; and
- Maintaining integrity of customers' transactions;

Preventing Unauthorized Transactions

It will generally be implied into the contract between a bank and its customers that, in the absence of any negligence on behalf of the customer, the bank will be liable for any transactions occurring on the account that have been perpetrated by fraud. It can be said that the relation between a banker and customer is that of a creditor and a debtor with the superadded obligation of honouring customer's orders on the funds n his hands. The extent to which banks in the India can exclude their liability for any losses incurred is governed by the application of the law of contract:

The Indian Contract Act, 1872, prevents contractual terms being enforced against a consumer that are inherently unfair or do not satisfy the test of good faith. Similar to the English Unfair Contract Terms Act, 1977, the Indian Act provides that a party dealing with a consumer can not exclude or restrict its liability in respect of a breach of contract and can not claim to be entitled to render a contractual performance subsequently different from that which was reasonably expected or render no performance at all, except insofar as the contract terms satisfy the requirements of 'reasonableness'.

A shorter reference can be made to the norms under the UK and EU laws. A word on the Banking Code of the British Bankers Association; this code limits the losses for which customers can be liable relating to fraudulent transactions by third parties affecting their accounts. Moreover, the recommendation of the EC relating to 'transactions by electronic payment instrument and in particular the relationship between the issuer and holder' suggests that a limit of ECU 150 be placed on a customer's liability for fraudulent transactions in the absence of extreme negligence on behalf of the customers.

Maintaining Integrity of Customer's Transactions

The risk posed to online banking is related to the confidentiality of customer's transaction history or account details. The ability of hackers to crack encryption products has been widely published and a bank is likely to be liable under these heads:

(i) *Contractual Liability:* In relation to the confidentiality of the customer's transactions, the banks have an implied contractual obligation to keep their customer's affairs secret. The bank will be also liable to its customers and other third parties who are contractually authorized to access its network, and to read information held on it, for loss or damage to those customers and other third parties that arise from inaccurate or faulty information held on the network.

(ii) *Negligent Misstatements:* This pertains to the point of liability of an information service provider for information, which is inaccurate or incomplete, and there is no legislation regarding liability arising from information services. In this regard much will depend on the contractual relationship between a bank and customer. However, similar considerations in relation to the ability of banks to limit their liability to cover the risk of unauthorised transactions apply equally in this context.

Drawbacks and Challenges

For online banking to reach a critical mass, there has to be sufficient number of users and the sufficient infrastructure in place. Though various security options like line encryption, branch connection encryption, firewalls, digital certificates, automatic signoffs, random pop-ups and disaster recovery sites are in place or are being looked at, there is as yet no certification authority in India offering public key infrastructure which is absolutely necessary for online banking. The customer may only be assured of a secured conduit for its online activities if an authority certifying digital signatures is in place.

The communication bandwidth available today in India is also not enough to meet the needs of high priority services like online banking and trading. Banks offering online facilities need to have an effective disaster recovery plan along with comprehensive risk management measures. Banks offering online facilities also need to calculate their downtime losses, because even a few minutes of downtime in a week might mean substantial losses. Proper encryption of data and effective use of passwords are also matters that leave a lot to be desired. Systems and processes have to be put in place to ensure that errors do not take place.

Moreover, users of internet banking services are required to fill up the application forms online and send a copy of the same by mail or fax to the bank. The customer enters into a contractual agreement with the bank for using the internet banking services. In this way, personal data in the applications forms is being held by the bank providing the service. The contract details are often one-sided, with the bank having the absolute discretion to amend or supplement any of the terms at any time. For these reasons, domestic customers are often hesitant to use the internet banking services offered by Indian banks.

The internet is in the public domain whereby geographical boundaries are eliminated. Cyber crimes are therefore difficult to be identified and controlled. In order to promote internet banking services, it is necessary that the proper legal infrastructure is in place. Information Technology Act, 2000, s. 72 casts an obligation of confidentiality against disclosure of any electronic record, register, correspondence and information, except for certain purposes and violation of this provision is a criminal offence.

Suggestions for Making the Online Banking more Effective in India

As the above discussions suggest online banking in the need of the hour and need for the future. Therefore it becomes imperative to make certain changes in the existing online banking scenario to fulfill the emergent needs. This can be summarized as:

- Strengthening the legal regime for crimes committed in relation to online banking and e-commerce. There should be amendment made in the IT Act, 2000 and the Indian Penal Code for increasing the penalty or imprisonment for such crimes. This can work as a deterrent and thus maintain the integrity of online transactions.

- Data security laws should be strengthened to deals with data theft and other similar crimes. This would check the data piracy which has been a cause of concerns these days.
- The communication bandwidth should be increased to meet the high priority services like online banking and trades. Moreover attempts should be made to increase the bandwidth in the semi- rural and semi- urban areas, so that they can also be benefited with such a technological revolution.
- There should be proper encryption of data and effective use of password by the users. Therefore the users should be made aware of proper use of such facilities by awareness campaigns at all levels.
- Public sector banks should take the lead by adoption of such form of banking in all the branches. Since they have presence even in the remotest areas of the country.
- A proper monitoring mechanism should be developed to check the implementation of online banking, especially in the light of 2001 guidelines by RBI for Internet banking.

Concluding Observations

A sound and effective banking system is the backbone of an economy. The economy of a country may function smoothly and without many hassles if the banking system backing it is not only flexible but also capable of meeting the new challenges posed by the technology and other external as well as internal factors. The importance and role of IT for achieving this benign objective may not be undermined. Internet or online banking has ushered a new era of banking in India and rest of the world. This has not only led to the advancement of banking industry per se but has also led to the increase in the banking business over a period of time. Also now it is possible to have a quick access to one's account in a bank which earlier was a tiresome job. This has been possible because of technological advancement, globalization, liberalization and the increase in competition in the market.

But the above development comes with a cost attached to it, i.e, safety and security of ones account and personal information. But over a period of time this lacunas in the banking industry has been taken care by the industry itself. Today we have protection like firewall, data encryption, digital certification etc. This has also been taken care by the Information Technology Act, 2000 which is drawn on the lines of UNCITRAL Model law on electronic commerce.

Such a system of banking is advantageous considering the fact that liquid money flow in the country and in the world in on a rise, thanks to globalization. In short in a fast moving world such a system of online banking is advantageous for the country and the world as a whole.

Inspite of all the advantages and features embedded in such a system of online banking there are many challenges which has to be taken into consideration while advancing further. This includes data protection and data integrity of the customers. Also recent cases suggest that cyber crime is on the rise. This includes cases of online fraud and credit card fraud etc. This suggests that still the environment of online banking in not conducive in India. Moreover, the penetration of online or internet banking has not been successfully done in semi urban and semi-rural areas. This is because of the problem of Internet facility and electricity.

Therefore in order to have a better and efficient banking system in place there is an urgent need for the technological upgradation in all the branches of a bank. There is also a need on the part public sector banks to go for introducing such a system in all the branches, since they have a maximum presence in the country and have a large chunk of banking market in India. Moreover there is urgent requirement to strengthen the laws dealing with online frauds and cyber crimes. This can be done by increasing the penalty or imprisonment. Also since these crimes involve the use of internet and computers, a separate cell for cyber and related crimes should be made in each district.

Thus, internet Banking is the need of the hour, which may not be lost sight of except at the cost of elimination from the competition. The existence of internet banking also becomes inevitable due to the standards required to be matched at the international level. Thus, the domestic as well as the international standards mandates the adoption of internet banking at the earliest possible moment.

References

Internet Banking, Comptroller's Handbook, October 1999, accessed from *www.occ.treas.gov/handbook/intbank.pdf.*

Measuring the quality of e-banking portals, Hans H. Bauer, Maik Hammerschmidt and Tomas Falk, Department of Marketing, School of Business Administration, University of Mannheim, Germany accessed from *www.emeraldinsight.com/researchregister.*

Internet Banking Explodes in Europe says Bluesky, 09 November 1998, Newsbytes News Network, 9 Nov 1998, accessed from *http://www.findarticles.com/p/articles/mi_m0NEW/is_1998_Nov_9/ai_53200203.*

Ahmad Azzouni (2003), 'Internet Banking and the Law: A Critical Examination of the Legal Controls Over Internet Banking in the UK and their Ability to Frame, Regulate and Secure Banking on the Net', J.I.B.L.R., 18(9), 351-362.

Report on internet banking, accessed from *http://rbidocs.rbi.org.in/rdocs/PublicationReport/Pdfs/21595.pdf.*

Virus controls also become much more critical in this environment. See, enterprise under attack, network magazine, issue of November 2003, accessed from: *www.networkmagazineindia.com/200311/cover01.html.*

Towards online banking, network magazine, issue of February 2003, accessed from *http://www.networkmagazineindia.com/200302/feature.shtml*

India opens new vistas for Indian Banks, Network Magazine, Issue of September 2002, accessed from, *http://www.expresscomputeronline.com/20020916/indtrend1.shtml.*

Indian banks cash in on delivery channels, Express Computer, 02 December 2002, accessed from, *http://www.expresscomputeronline.com/20021202/banks1.shtml.*

Central Bank of India partners with TCS for its core banking solution, 16 June 2005, accessed from, *http://www.tata.com/tcs/releases/20050616.htm.*

Legal issues for data protection myths and realities, accessed from *www.certin.org.in/training/21-22april05/legal%20issues%20data%20protection.pdf.*

Pamela Samuelson & Hal R. Varian, The New Economy & Information Technology Policy, 2001, accessed from, *http://www.ischool.berkeley.e du/~hal/Papers/infopolicy.pdf.*

Internet Banking in India–Guidelines, 14 June 2001, DBOD.COMP.BC.No.130/07.03.23/2000-01. The guidelines issued are three in number comprising of: (1) technology and security standards; (2) legal issues; and (3) regulatory and supervisory issues.

Malhotra Pooja and Singh Balwinder (2004), "Status of Internet Banking in India", *Journal of the Management Accountant*, Vol. 39, No. 11, Nov., p. 890.

"Findings of NASSCOM's Internet Survey India"(2002), Accessed from *www.expressindia.com*

18

CORE BANKING SYSTEM: THE TECHNOLOGICAL INNOVATION IN BANKING

ROSHNA VARGHESE

A sound banking system is a *sin qua non* for accelerating the process of economic development. Banks and economic development are intertwined and inseparable to each other. Banking organisations occupy a key position in the economic development of a country. They constitute the core of the country's financial structure and money supply. The banks encourage investments and help capital formation by mobilising savings and lending those funds to prospective entrepreneurs and industrial ventures.

The advancement in technology especially internet and information technology has led to new way of doing business in banking. The technologies have cut down time, working simultaneously on different issues and increased efficiency. Fueled by the evolving business landscape, and the growing competition, financial institutions today are realising the need to adopt core banking technology that can empower them. Banks are looking to transform strategically, and simultaneously leverage day-to-day operations. Of prime significance is a core banking system comprising self-contained services, over which systems can be easily constructed, and then orchestrated into a complete solution. The platform where communication technology and information technology are merged to suit core needs of banking is known as Core Banking Solutions. Here computer software is developed to perform core operations of banking like recording of transactions, passbook maintenance, interest calculations on loans and deposits, customer records, balance of payments and withdrawal are done. This software is installed at different branches of bank and then interconnected by means of communication lines like telephones, satellite, internet etc. It allows the user (customers) to operate accounts from any branch if it has installed core banking solutions. This new platform has changed the way banks are working. Now many advanced features like regulatory requirements and other specialised services like share (stock) trading are being provided. Core banking solutions is very helpful to small industries.

The Context

The reason why the changes could be so substantial is that there is a powerful combination of pressures operating on the industry, and some of these pressures challenge the very core of banking business: information and delivery. A dominant pressure derives from new technology with respect to information, trading and delivery of financial services. Industrial history shows that the development of new technology can have a major impact on any industry and has often done so. This is most especially the case when technology affects the very core of the business–in the case of banking: information, processing and delivery. In this respect, banking is no different from other industries. It is largely technology, and what follows from it, that will transform the banking and financial services industries.

In many countries, financial systems in general, and the banking sector in particular, are passing through a period of substantial structural change under the combined and inter-related pressures of: internal competition; declining entry barriers; changes in regulation; new information, trading and delivery technology; global competitive pressures; and fast-evolving strategic objectives of banks themselves and their existing and potential competitors. A series of universal trends have become evident all of which have major implications for the competitiveness of banks. The impact of these forces has varied in timing and degree between countries though many of the secular pressures on the industry are universal. Banks around the world face formidable challenges: they are losing some of their past monopolies and comparative advantages which have underpinned their dominant position in the financial system. In particular, as entry barriers into banking services are eroded, banks are increasingly facing competition from a wider range of actual and potential suppliers of banking services: the capital markets, money markets, non-banking financial institutions, and also 'non-financial banking institutions'. In addition, the development of electronic banking has in some countries enabled foreign banks to enter hitherto relatively closed domestic retail banking markets. In some cases large corporate customers have been internalising some of their banking operations through 'in-house banks'. In many countries banks are shedding staff and closing branches with the introduction of new technology and alternative delivery systems. At the same time, squeezed by inroads into their traditional businesses and sharper competition, banks are expanding into new areas: insurance, life assurance, unit trusts and other services. These trends are emerging in the context of major structural changes in financial systems: the relative growth of financial markets; the increasing institutionalisation of saving and investment business; the growing role of institutions in other functions of the financial system; the rise in the role of institutional funds managers in the financial system; diversification of financial firms and the steady erosion of traditional distinctions between different types of financial institution; the entry of new types of supplier of financial services; a substantial growth in the variety of new and complex financial instruments; and the globalisation of financial markets.

Core Banking

Core banking is a general term used to describe the services provided by a group of networked bank branches. Bank customers may access their funds and other simple transactions from any of the member branch offices. Core banking is normally defined as the business conducted by a banking institution with its retail and small business customers. Many banks treat the retail customers as their core banking customers, and have a separate line of business to manage small businesses. Larger businesses are managed via the Corporate Banking division of the institution.

Today, more products are being released by banks; these include relief bonds and mutual funds. Corporate clients would like to handle this through a Web interface which may not always be possible. Sometimes for a product that is available at the branch, vendors need to create separate packages to deliver them through different channels such as ATMs (Automated Teller Machine) or mobile phones. For example, in the home loans category, there are different modes of payment such as balloon payment and varying levels of interest. While banks always try and design products to suit customer requirements, at the technology end it is still an ordeal to provide customised products through all channels.

The realm of banking is now moving to non-traditional functions. Though IT for banks and financial services in India matches global standards, we need to make the transition quickly since the definition of banking is changing. Currently vendors only include traditional services, and they are still reactive rather than proactive. While vendors cannot be blamed totally, the need of the hour is to move into the third-generation of core banking solutions, adhere to standards such as RTGS, and make processes seamless across banks. But before this happens, it is imperative that technology should pay attention to the details.

As banks offer more products and services online, security challenges are increasing. Also, regulators around the world are introducing new frameworks and standards across countries to take care of operational risk. Frameworks for operational risk activities such as anti-money-laundering should be built in the core banking solution. For example, to differentiate between a genuine customer and a fraud, the bank will not only need to know the complete customer behaviour but also the transaction details. These features need to be integrated into the core banking solution. They will help the banks identify exceptions (fraudsters) to the manager or person in charge. Currently, this is done offline and is a separate function in banks.

Core Banking in India

In countries such as India and Hong Kong that were a part of the erstwhile British empire, it is only recently that core banking has caught on. This is mainly due to the restrictions by the UK government on free movement of money throughout the region. Also, the IT infrastructure necessary for such services did not exist in these countries until recently. After liberation from the UK, the economies of these countries went through a drastic change - thus the demand for such services increased and the need to meet such demand were met with today's technologies. Most of the nationalized banks in India for example: State Bank of India, Punjab National Bank, Allahabad Bank, HDFC and ICICI Bank today supports core banking. As of 2007, many Cooperative banks in India such as Jain Urban Cooperative Bank, Kangra Central Cooperative Bank, Udaipur Urban Cooperative Bank, Kollam District Cooperative Bank, Kerala State Cooperative Bank and Panchsheel Mercantile Cooperative Bank have started to use and offer centralized Core Banking too. The three standard software used are Flexcube from iFlex Solutions, Finacle from Infosys and B@ncs from TATA Consultancy Services. In countrie such as Japan, core banking is still in its early stages. Although having autonomous reign over their currency for over half a century, the consumers themselves do not see much use for such services - low demand, thus less services. It is only within the last decade that banks started placing ATMs outside the bank premises. Many of the bank services must be done in person at the account holder's registered branch. Japanese banks rely heavily on paperwork and physical evidence, such as the personal chop or Inkan-thus rendering core banking impractical.

Driving Forces in Core Banking

Adopting a next generation core banking solution can help banks innovate and cater to your customers' changing requirements, increase efficiencies, and reduce operational costs across your bank, while improving customer retention. This core system would ideally improve productivity, enable higher processing speeds, and closely align with your bank's overall business strategy.

Increased levels of competition as new entrants in the market come out with innovative products to challenge existing players. The right core banking solution can help your bank to not only innovate, but also achieve economies-of-scale, ensuring that they are able to compete in dynamic and diverse markets.

An Evolving Regulatory Regime

Adopting the use of the right regulatory platform to ensure compliance with numerous regulations such as Basel II and SOX, can help your bank alleviate costs and improve reusability, turnaround times and accuracy.

Streamlined Flow of Information

The right technology will go a long way in ensuring the smooth flow of information at your bank, and eventually lead to efficient decision-making processes.

Customer Experience Management

Like most banks, your bank also wishes to target specific information at customers, and leverage a unified, actionable view of customer experience. Most product innovation today is strongly driven by this parameter.

The Move Towards Service-Oriented Architecture (SOA)

It is becoming increasingly important to have a flexible, robust, future-oriented IT architecture, based on SOA to support integration and consolidation activities. With SOA, your bank can increase operational efficiency, enhance service quality, and improve risk management and regulatory compliance. These core solutions form the backbone of a bank's technical infrastructure, and they constitute a mission-critical element in the financial services industry. The changing face of the regulatory framework of the global banking industry-be it Basel II, AML, KYC or corporate governance - is bringing about a paradigm shift in the way banks approach risk management, capital adequacy, customer-centricity and financial reporting. Customers are increasingly demanding speed, convenience, differentiation and superior service. The move from product-centric banking to customer-centric banking is no longer a matter of debate, but the reality of the day. At the same time, the dynamically changing competitive landscape requires banks to constantly innovate and differentiate.

In all of this, what really enables banks to build a lasting competitive advantage is their ability for continuous process innovation coupled with an optimised speed and cost of response, to the dynamic business requirements. The core banking platform plays a very critical role in determining a bank's technology capability in these areas.

Core banking–Features and Benefits

Now a days all banks are upgrading to provide the facility of core banking to their customers to be in the race. it is one step closer to mix technology with baking for providing convenience of banking to the customers. The customer-centric architecture coupled with the integrated CRM capability, ensures a unified view of the customer, across channels and products. The solution enables banks to effectively manage customer relationship by defining & monitoring service levels, enhancing sales force productivity & creating a differentiating customer experience.

With workflows to automate processes and Straight Through Processing (STP) infrastructure to reduce turnaround times, the core banking solution can help the banks to eliminate nonproductive processes and reduce manual intervention. Additionally, by virtue of being a true web-enabled application, the solution screens are richer, with integrated web applications like chat, information ticker and e-mail, for quick and seamless knowledge dissemination.

Various facilities associated with core banking:

- All branches of the bank are interconnected
- details of the accounts can be viewed online just as login to view email account
- main thing is that one can transfer money online from his account to any account with any bank in ones country
- one can do majority of the transactions cnline that he needed to go personally to the bank to perform it.
- one can perform transactions of his account from the bank counter at any part of the country.

Ingredient's Core Banking System

There are 5 ingredients that form part of the Core Banking system. These are the essential building blocks for the entire bank/ institution.

General Ledger

The absolute Core is the General Ledger of the bank accordingly, the absolute core of the banking system is the General Ledger system, every single financial activity that happens at any location within entire bank has to be reflected in the G.L. system that generates the financial statements for the entire bank which provides any entity to monitor the financial health of the bank.

Throughout the world, almost all banks have all their financial activity reflected in G.L. every night and next morning the G.L. system provides the bank with enterprise wide balance sheet and trial balance report. In short for those who have successfully implemented Core Banking Systems, the concerned entities in the bank know the financial condition of the bank at the beginning of each business day. If one is looking at the financial statements of the whole bank the G.L. System must provide that. If one is in regional office, the G.L. System must provide the financial statements for the region. If one is the branch the G.L. System must provide the financial statements at the branch. Each morning all these entities, at the respective workplaces, see these financial statements reflecting the condition as of close of business yesterday. In a Core Banking System, this is achieved by deploying a centralized G.L. System which provides for thousands of sub legers with. Level's start with individual branch G.L. rolled up to regional G.L. with further rollup of all regional G.L's to bank G.L. financial transactions from various sources throughout the bank update these subsidiary ledgers and the G.L. system then performs rollups to report at branch, region, zone, country wise head office and any other level that is required by the bank / financial institution.

Customer Information System

The next major ingredient of a Core Banking system is the Customer Information System or CIS. Accordingly in the CIS, a customer is identified by uniquely by his/her CIS number and all information related to that customer (name, address, phones, employment, credit history, relatives, family members, and demographic data) is stored along with this unique number. All this is stored in a centralized CIS system allowing the customer to visit any branch to do business with the bank. In addition, CIS stores Customer to account relationships. A single unique customer could have a current account a joint saving account with his wife a time deposit, a car loan and a house loan. The CIS links all these five account to this single unique customer I.D. whenever the customer visits any branch of the bank, all that he does is give his name (and/or address or phone or CIS number) and the CIS system shows the branch staff the information about this customer as well as all the accounts linked to this customer and the latest balance in each of these account.

Deposit System

The third major ingredient is the deposit system. The ability to process various types of deposits is a must. These include current, savings, time deposit and hundreds of variations in each of these. e.g. Simple current accounts, current accounts with overdraft, cash credit accounts, variable rate overdrafts, simple savings, multi-currency savings, time deposits, CDS, variable rate time deposit, recurring deposits, multi-currency, time deposits, and so on. This is required to handle the liability side of the bank/financial institution's business. This all is achieved by having deposits system that are heavily deposit system that are heavily parameterized i.e. by simply setting a parameter "Fixed Rate" or "Variable Rate" the deposit account will be processed by the deposit system using the appropriate rate from the applicable rates. Around the world banks do not open a new deposit account for a customer directly in the deposit system. When the customer wants to open a new deposit account, the branch staff to go the CIS screen verifies the customer details and opens the account. This way, the existing CIS data of the customer remains infect and the CIS information shows that this customer has now increased his relationship with the bank/financial institution. As a result banks who have implemented such systems do not need to have an inter branch reconciliation organization/system.

Loan System

The fourth major ingredient is the loan system. This system handles the asset side of this business. In most banks/financial institutions around the world loans are separated by those to retail customer and those to commercial customers processing requirement of loans to corporate customers is different form retail customers and hence there are loan systems that cater to retail customers and those that cater to commercial or corporate customers. The loan process in a bank involves multiple stems. The loan appraisal and sanction step, the disbursement and monitoring step, the non-performance tracking step the recovery step and the closure. Owing to the fact that a multitude of entities and processes are involved in the appraisal and sanction step, most banks around the world separate the appraisal and sanction step and implement a system called a loan organization system. The other remaining steps of the loan process are handling by the loan system. With authorised access, any staff working in any branch around the country should be able to retrieve the customer loan information on his terminal and help the customer do a financial transaction. These financial transactions are automatically sent to the bank/financial institution's General Ledger and they update the appropriate credits and debits in the subsidiary ledgers in the General Ledger.

Management Information System (MIS)

Once the core deposit and loan business transaction for all customers of the bank are captured and appropriate General Ledger accounts are updated, various users of the Core Banking System throughout the bank need to know what is happening within the entire financial institution. As a result, the fifth major ingredient is the management information system. This enables everybody in the bank to obtain the relevant information from the system in order to carry out their business effectively. MIS is simple terms takes information from the General Ledger, CIS Deposit, Loan Systems and present them to the bank/financial institution. The staff all employees including management. Around the world, typical examples of information that bank staff (each with access rights) retrieves include.

- Branch transaction activity for today (list of all branch transactions).

- Loan activity for a single customer or a group of customer.
- Branch General Ledger report printed at the branch.
- N P A report for the entire bank for all transactions as of yesterday.

New Components

Besides the 5 major ingredients, there are optional components (like a car with options like leather seats, flashing light etc...) that can be added on to the Core Banking Systems to help the bank staff uses them in a more efficient manner, these include:

Delivery Channels

All the 5 major ingredients of a Core Banking system can be operated by a bank staff from any location in the country simple by using their terminal at their workplace. Around the world as banks started focusing on customer relationship management, they realized that customers interact with the entire bank for banking transactions in many ways. Customer can go to the branch, go to an ATM, call on the phone, and log on to the Internet to do their banking transactions. They can use one or more of these delivery channels (Called customer touch paints) to conduct segment and decide on further investment design specific products and services to promote such delivery channels. The Core Banking Systems are production factories creating products and services and tracking them and the delivery channels are distributors and retailers who ensure these products and services are available to the customers whenever they are in the country. Hence, the add-on systems for Core Banking System include;

- Branch Automation system
- ATM Switch and connected ATM
- Call center system
- Internet Banking System

Any transaction done by the customers in any of the above systems goes and updates the Core Banking System like deposit or loan at that in turn updates the Bank's G.L. in the Core.

Concluding Observatios

While banks are beginning to realise the importance of investing to build more sophisticated and complex risk infrastructure, there is also definitely a need for current technology systems to be flexible and scalable as the business grows. Today, most banks want to get a completely integrated solution for retail, corporate, treasury, cash management and third-party distribution-but it is missing in the marketplace. The need of the hour is a solution that offers product- and channel-wise access rules, and policies with the flexibility to make changes in product features on the fly across all channels. This solution should also have the capability to integrate with the external world on standard interfaces, support rule-based workflow engines to define new processes, and provide information on risk management across business lines. At present vendors are not able to keep up with the pace at which products are being introduced by banks. This forces banks to go in for interim solutions. In my view, the big core banking players really need to rework on their product strategies and come out with new products and services much faster than they do now. In the near future, the biggest concern of a bank will be to implement best practices and solutions in the compliance area. With BASEL II and anti-money-laundering norms, banks are required to monitor their operational activities very carefully and quantify the operational risk associated with their business products, services and volumes. This will not be possible without the help of technology. In the coming years, these modules should become an integrated part of core solutions rather than be offered separately. To conclude, banking software solution vendors need to come out from the shell of software development and understand changing business dimensions. They need to develop scalable and flexible solutions on open standards. Finally, they need to react much faster than the changing banking business scenarios and develop more analytical and risk tools within their solutions.

References

Dharmaraj, E. (2005), "Banking Theory Law and Practice", Scitech Publications (India) Pvt. Ltd., Chennai.

Koch, T. W., & Macdonald, S. S. (2005), "Bank Management", (5th Ed), Thomson South-Western, Bangalore.

Llewellyn, D.T. (1995), "Universal Banking and the Public Interest", in A. Saunders and I. Walter (eds), *Universal Banking*, Irwin, New York.

Pithadia, V. (June 6, 2006), "Criticism of Core Banking Concept in India", Retrieved February 14, 2008, from *www.indianmba.com.*

Shekhar, K. C., & Shekhar, L. (2005), *Banking Theory and Practice*, (19th Ed.) Vikas Publishing House Pvt. Ltd., New Delhi.

Van Horne, J.C. (1985), "Of Financial Innovation and Excesses", *Journal of Finance*, 40(3), 621-631.

19

BASEL ACCORD AND INDIAN BANKING INDUSTRY IN THE LIBERALISED ERA

Vijila V . & G. Raju

Introduction

In June 2004, the Basel Accord II on Banking supervision was released by the Basel Committee, (A Committee of banking supervisory authorities that was established by the Governors of the Central banks of the 'Group of Ten' countries in 1975) for adoption by the concerned countries. The deadline for implementing Basel II, originally set for March 31,2007, has now been extended. Foreign banks in India and Indian banks operating abroad are to meet those norms by March 31, 2008, while all other scheduled commercial banks will have to adhere to the guidelines by March 31,2009. But the decision to implement the guidelines remains unchanged.

Evolution of Capital Adequacy Standard

Historically, bank regulates have considered the maintenance of adequate capital by banks as one of the key methods of preservations of bank safety and soundness. Such safety considerations led to the impositions of unlimited liability on bank owners in Scotland which continued up to 1862, In the United states, a double liability system was adopted for national banks when the National banking Act of 1863 created a national banking System. Under double liability system, bank shareholders could lose twice on their bank investment. First: contributed capital was lost if the bank failed. Second: after bank failure, shareholders could be assessed up to the par value of their shares to satisfy creditor claims.In the twentieth century unlimited liability systems came to be replaced by minimum capital requirements and capital to liability the asset standards. The pre-BIS capital adequacy standards had to two distinctive features.

- For computation of capital adequacy rations, all balance sheet assets were given equal weighting regardless of the underlying of risk
- Off Balance sheet items were not considered for capital purposes.

Basel Committee

The eighties witnessed a marked shift in the adoption of capital adequacy standards by bank regulators. The BASEL committee on Banking Supervision(BCBS) comprising of representations and supervisory authorities of the central banks of 12 majar nations developed a set of international capital adequacy guidelines for banks. The objectives for developing the guidelines were three fold.

1. To promote stability to the global banking system.
2. To create a level playing field by removing existing competitive inequalities in the firm of differing national capital adequacy standards.
3. To serve as a reference for the implementation of the proposal in the participating countries by the respective regulatory agencies.

Basel Accord I

The 1988 Basel Accord proposed that capital adequacy of banks is to be measured in respect of their risk weighted asset exposures. Capital adequacy ratio is a measure of the amount of banks capital expressed as a percentage of its risk weighted credit exposures. The Basel I mainly consists of:

1. The constituents of capital
2. The risk weights corresponding to various asset categories.

Constituents of Capital

The Basel Committee prescribes two ties of capital for regulatory purposes.

- Tier I capital
- Tier I capital

The Tier I capital comprises of equity capital and published reserves from post tax retained earnings. The Tier II capital includes undisclosed reserves revaluation reserves, general provisions/general loan loss reserves, hybrid debt capital instruments and subordinated term debt for computation of capital goodwill and investment in subsidiaries (engages in banking and financial activities which are not consolidated national systems)are to be deducted.

The Risk Weights Corresponding to Various Asset Categories

The Basel Accord prescribes that the various balancesheet and off balancesheet exposures of commercial banks are to be multiplied by risk weights proposed by Basel committee on Banking Supervision. The 1988 Accord concentrated only credit risk. The committee used only five risk weights 0%,10%,20%,50% &100%.In respect of off balance sheet items, the exposures are to be multiplied by specified credit conversion factors so that they can be converted in to their credit equivalents and then appropriate risk weights are to be applied. The Accord stipulated that banks will be required. To maintain a minimum of 8% capital in relation to their risk weighted assets(RWA). Tier I capital should be at least 4% of RWA.

The 1988 accord did not cover market risk. In the nineties, the BCBS proposed an amendment to the original Accord to provide capital cushions for market risk inherent set forth two approaches for calculating the capital charge to cover market risks.

1. A standardized measurement frame work development the BCBS itself for calculating market risk for interest rates, equities and currencies.
2. Internally developed models based measurement of market risk.

As per the Market Risk Amendment (1988) eligible capital under both the internal models approach and the standardized approach consists of shareholders equity and retained earnings (Tier I capital). Further the following conditions were also imposed.

- A minimum of 28.5% of market risk should be covered by Tier I capital.
- The Tier III capital is only eligible to cover market risk including foreign exchange and commodities risk. It must have an original maturity of at least 2 years and will be limited to 250% of the banks Tier I capital that is allocated to support market risk.
- The total of tier I and TierII capital should not exceed 50% of the banks total capital.
- In so far as the overall limits in the 1996 Amendment are not breached Tier II elements may be substituted for Tier III up to the same limit of 250%.

Basel Accord II

The Basel I system came to be criticized by concerned parties on three major grounds.

1. It gave an equal risk weigting to all corporate credits irrespective of the differences in their underlying credit risks.

2. It failed to recognize that by undertaking credit portfolio diversification banks can have potential capital savings.
3. It led to extensive regulatory capital arbitrage which adds to the riskiness of bank asset portfolios.

Given the experience with BASEL(1988), the BIS proposed a new capital adequacy framework(1999) also known as Basel II. Base II seeks to rectify most of the defects of Basel I Accord. The objectives of Basel II are the following.

1. To promote adequate capitalization of banks.
2. To ensure better risk management
3. To strengthen the stability of banking system

The aforesaid objectives can not be translated into action in isolation-they are really tied to each other and require an appropriate 'vehicle' of implementation. This , therefore, led to the evolution of the three pillars. They are

1. A minimum capital requirement pillar
2. A supervisory review pillar to ensure that the banks capital is aligned to its actual risk profile.
3. A market discipline pillar to enhance the role of other market participants is ensuring that appropriate capital is held by prescribing greater disclosure.

First Pillar: Minimum Capital Requirement

The first pillar is converned with closer alignment of bank capital with range of perceived risks Basel I categorized risks in respect of credit in broad terms without taking into account individual credit worthiness or lack of it. In other words it does not consider risks involved in individual assets. Under Basel II the above defect is sought be rectified by stipulating higher capital for higher risks and vice versa. This pillar of the Approach seeks to bring about alignment of capital requirement to each bank's actual risk of economic loss. It takes into account all types of risks including market risk, operational risk and credit risk. It prescribes minimum capital requirement having due regard to risk profile of each bank.

Each banking institution must maintain a minimum of 8% capital in relation to its risk-weigted assets/scale of operations. (The RBI however directed that Indian banks must maintain a minimum of 9%). This is also refered to as regulatory capital.

Credit Risk

A bank always faces the risk that some of its borrowers may renege on their promises for timely repayments of loan, Interest on loan or meet the other terms of contract. This risk is called credit risk, which varies from borrower to borrower depending on their credit quality. Basel II requires banks to accurately measure credit risk to hold sufficient capital to cover it.

Market Risk

As part of the stautory requirement in the form of SLR, banks are required to invest in liquid assets such as cash, gold, Govt.and other approved securities. For instance, Indian banks are required to invest 25 per cent of their net demand and term liabilities in cash,gold,Govt.securities and other eligible securities and other eligible securities to comply with SLR requirements. Such investments are risky because of the change in their prices. This volatility in the value of a banks investment portfolio is known as the market risk,as it is driven by the market. The change in the value of the portfolio can be due to changes in the interest rates, foreign exchange rates or the changes in the values of equity or commodities.

Operational Risk

Several events that are neither due to default by third party nor because of the vagaries of the market. These events are called operational risk and can be attributed to internal systems, processes, people and external factors.

Second pillar: supervising review

Pillar II of the new capital framework recognizes the necessity of undertaking effective supervisory review of banks internal assessment of their overall risk. This is to ensure that bank managements exercise sound judgement and set aside adequate capital for these risks. Un using this pillar Bank supervisors namely RBI may evaluate the activities and risk profiles of individual banks in order to determine whether the banks have provided sufficient capital in terms of pillar I and spell-out ways to set right discrepancies if any.

In short it seeks to ensure that a bank:

- Maintains the minimum capital requirement, as stipulated by the first pillar
- Uses appropriate techniques of risk management in measuring and managing risks in relation to the banks risk profile.

Third Pillar: Market Discipline

This pillar is complimentary to the first and second pillar, and aims to:

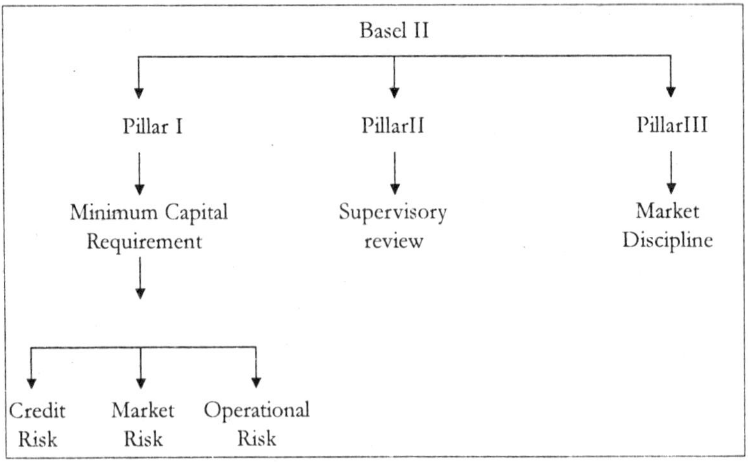

Overview of the Pillars of Basel II

(1) Encourage market discipline through a set of periodical, qualitative and quantitative disclosures to the regulatory authorities an the public in connection with capital, risk exposures and risk assessment processes.

(2) Ensure that the banks disclosures are consistent with "how senior management and the board assess and manage" the risks in the bank, since compliance to minimum capital requirements (as stipulated by the first pillar) is based on the managements internal decision regarding the use of any specified approach/methodology for measuring various risk factors.

Overview of the Key Differences Between Basel I and Basel II

Issue	*Basel I*	*Basel II*
Capital ratio	8% risk weighted assets	No change
Composition of capital	Tier I and Tier II capital	No change
Supervisory review	Not included	New guidance on supervisory review process
Market discipline	Not included	Introduced in new Accord
Operational risk	Implicit within ratio	Specific formula of 15% average gross income in the basic indicator approach
Risk weighing of assets	One-size-fits-all	2 approaches (a) Standardized (b) IRB approach
Residential mortgages (Standardized approach)	50% risk weighting	35% risk weighting
Retail exposures	100%	Treated separately with 75% risk weighting for qualifying exposures

Concluding Observations

The implementation of Basel II promises significant gains for the economy. Risk based capital maintenance by banks will surely enhance financial stability. This will promote risk based pricing, which will ultimately contribute to enhancement of shareholder value. Implementation of Basel II may trigger new developments including merges and acquisitions. In the new scenario there will be increased accent on corporate governance and creation and enhancement of shareholder value in banking institutions.

References

Bagchi, S.K. (2006), "Credit Risk Management", Jaico Publishing House, Delhi.

Bharati. V. Pathak (2003), "Indian Financial System", Pearson Education, Delhi.

Vasant Desai (2005), "The Indian Financial System and Development", Himalaya Publishing House, Delhi.

Leeladhar. V. (2005), "Basel II Accord and its implications", *BIS Review*, March 17.

Ramakrishnan. S. (2006), "Adhering to Basel II Norms is Own the Agenda of all Major Banks", Express Computer, July 3.

Avijit Bakshi (2006), "Basel Opportunities and Challenges Ahead", Banking Finance, March.

20

ROLE OF BANK SUPPORTED INDIAN SEZs IN THE ECONOMIC GROWTH

N. Sreenivasan

Introduction

These are the advanced days of globalization, Liberalisation, with IT and ITES .All types of A to Z corporate units are with their branches in other countries, if not ties with other units internationally. In this Global village, India has gained name and fame for its Export Processing Zones (EPZs), Special Economic Zones (SEZs) and EPZs conversion to SEZs. The set up of first Asia's EPZ was in Kandla port, India, in 1965. To attract larger foreign investments into India, the SEZ policy was announced in April 2000. Now the set up of SEZs is a continuous and highly dynamic global activity. In India, the SEZs are promoted and managed by the Central Government and the individual State Governments. In the State governments to promote SEZs the separate cells are under the Ministries of Finance and Commerce. Thus Indian SEZs are operated as a mix of public sector undertakings that are owned and controlled by the Central or State governments and private enterprises either on their own, as consortiums or in partnership with government owned enterprises. The recent announcement was, by the Andhra Pradesh's Finance Minister, Dr. K Rosaiah during the budget(2008-09) speech, to set up 71 new SEZs that provide 25 lakh employment opportunities.[1]

Indian SEZs operates on a global paradigm of business practices, regulatory framework and the freedom to do business and trade without government restrictions. In India the SEZs have access to all the advantages including the workforce, the supplier base and the ports and logistical infrastructure needed for the global trade.

Indian SEZs are with a large range of incentives from the government. They are a) very low tariffs and barriers, b) exemption from taxation and c) the freedom to operate the business on globally accepted business principles with minimum application of Indian laws and d) least regulatory procedures.

The Indian SEZs attract large foreign investment, (a) to enable the setting up of large manufacturing and service operations in India, (b) to expand on the infrastructure and competitiveness of India, (c) to improve the employment potential in India for its citizens, d) to improve/increase exports and trade revenues and (e) to bring in a global business climate into the country. Thus Indian SEZs are more competitive and global in its outlook and operation.

The RBI enactment was in 1934 and the Nationalisation of 14 Private banks was in 1969, which was a major step in Indian Banking, and this was much earlier to the formation of EPZs/ SEZs. The Banks could not 'Go Hand In Glove' with SEZs until the recent developments and successful Information Technology (IT) Transactions. Analytical Processing of Banking business Developments which were taken place during the last few years all have IT as the pivotal centre-point. The publication of the Financial Sector Technology (FST) Vision in July, 2005[2], led to the new era with significant changes in the current banking sector of the country. Offshore Banking Unit(OBU), Core Banking System(CBS), Internet Banking, Mobile Banking, Mobile Automated Teller Machines (ATMs), multi-functional ATMs, shared ATM services, large scale usage of Real Time Gross Settlement (RTGS) for quick, immediate funds transfer and smart card based cards as part of initiatives etc., all aimed at the Financial Inclusion. These are also some of the landmark developments that influenced the Banking practices every where, not excluding SEZs.

Objectives of the Study

The objective of the study is to compare trends of the Indian Banking to the performance of Indian SEZs that cause the growth of Indian economy.This study reviews the established facts such as (a) the developments in banking due to the considerable growth in Indian IT and IT-enabled services (ITES)[3] (b) the GDP, as software industry has emerged as one of the fastest growing sectors in the Indian economy with a compound annual growth rate (CAGR) exceeding 28 per cent between the financial year (FY) 1999-2000 and FY 2005-2006[4].The industry's contribution to the national GDP has risen from 1.9 per cent in FY 1999-2000 to a projected 4.8 per cent in FY 2005-2006. c) In terms of the segment composition of the Indian IT-ITES industry, as in the previous years, IT services continue to account for a lion's share, contributing over 47 per cent of the total industry revenue in FY 2004-05 (c) The sustained high growth rate of merchandise exports at more than 20 per cent during the last four years(2002-06) is more than twice the current growth of Gross Domestic Product (GDP).[5]

Methodology

This is a review based descriptive study. This article is based on the available secondary data and other research results and reports As the GDP estimates are various organizations, only the absolute figures are given to compare trends.

Organization of the Paper

The paper is organized into four major sections viz. (1) Indian scenario of SEZs, (2) How the Bank policies Supported the SEZs, (3) Growth in Indian GDP and Exports, (4) Conclusion.

Section I

Indian Scenario of SEZs

Indian SEZ Scenario

Earlier Benefits and Incentives to EPZs/ SEZs and Exports

The Government has earlier announced a Special Economic Zones (SEZs) Scheme in April, 2000 to promote exports from the country. The policy provided for setting up of SEZs in the public, private, joint sector or by State Governments. It was also announced that the existing Export Processing Zones could be converted into Special Economic Zones. Accordingly, four Export Processing Zones (EPZs) had been converted in to Special Economic Zones (SEZs) with effect from 1.11.2000. The Government has issued notification for conversion of all the existing Export Processing Zones (EPZs), located at Santa Cruz (Maharashtra), Cochin (Kerala), Kandla and Surat (Gujarat), Chennai (Tamil Nadu), Falta (West Bengal), Visakhapatnam (Andhra Pradesh) and Noida (Uttar Pradesh), into Special Economic Zones. The Government has also granted approval for setting up of SEZs in the private/joint sector/by the State governments at Positra (Gujarat), Dronagiri and Kopta (Maha Mumbai) (Maharashtra), Nanguneri (Tamil Nadu), Kulpi, Salt Lake (Kolkata), (West Bengal), Paradeep and Gopalpur (Orissa), Bhadohi, Kanpur, Moradabad and Greater Noida (Uttar Pradesh), Kakinada and Visakhapatnam (Andhra Pradesh), Indore (Madhya Pradesh), Sitapura (Jaipur) and Jodhpur (Rajasthan), Vallarpadam/Puthvypeen (Kerala) and Hassan (Karnataka).

Salient Features of the Proposed SEZ Legislation are

(a) SEZs are being recognised as deemed foreign territory and supplies from Domestic Tariff Area to SEZ treated as export. This would integrate the zones with the domestic industry.

(b) Existing incentives and facilities such as exemption from Custom/Excise duty for development of SEZ and setting up of units, income tax exemption, exemption from Central Sales Tax, Service Tax etc. are reflected in the proposed legislation to impart stability to the fiscal regime.

(c) Limited domestic market access on the basis of duty forgone proposed.

Agri Export Zones

For the first time, Agricultural Export Zones (AEZs) have been created. The Central Government had sanctioned 48 Agri Export Zones in various States. These AEZs generate substantial direct and indirect employment.The AEZs scheme was introduced to transform select rural regions as regional rural motors of export economy. For the first time, transport assistance was made available for export of fresh and processed fruits, vegetables, floriculture, poultry, dairy products and products of wheat and rice. That lead to diversification of agriculture activity. Policy initiatives taken to promote SEZs are

(a) Duty-free import/domestic procurement of goods for development, operation and maintenance of SEZs and SEZ units;

(b) External commercial borrowing by SEZ units up to US $ 500 million in a year without any maturity restriction through recognized banking channels;

(c) Facility to set up of Overseas Banking units in SEZs;

(d) 100% FDI to SEZ franchisee in providing basic telephone service in SEZs;

(e) Exemption from Central Sales Tax on sales made from Domestic Tariff Area to SEZ units; and Exemption from Service Tax to SEZ units and developers.

The First SEZ BILL 2005[6]

The Special Economic Zones (SEZs) Bill 2005 was passed in Indian Parliament on 9th May, 2005 and accelerated the growth of exports and foreign direct investment (FDI) inflows. The SEZ Bill was aimed at encouraging public-private partnership to develop world-class infrastructure and attract private investment (domestic and foreign), boosting economic growth, exports and employment, and a single window clearance and approval mechanism for establishment of SEZs as well as production units inside the Zones. The SEZ Bill introduced income tax concessions for both SEZ units as well as SEZ developers. SEZ units will be eligible for 100% tax exemption for 5 years, 50% for the next 5 years, and 50% of the ploughed back export profits for the next 5 years. SEZ developers continue to get 100% income tax exemption for 10 years in a block period of 15 years. The salient features of the SEZ Bill relate to the following:

(i) Establishment of SEZ and for setting up of units therein, including requirements, obligations and entitlements;

(ii) Establishment of free trade and warehousing zones to create world class trade-related infrastructure to facilitate import and export of goods aimed at making India a global trading hub;

(iii) Requirements for setting up of offshore banking units and units in International Financial Service Centre in SEZs, including fiscal regime governing the operation of such units;

(iv) Establishment of an Authority for each SEZ set up by the Central Government to impart greater administrative autonomy; and

(v) designation of special courts and single enforcement agency to ensure speedy trial and investigation of notified offences committed in Special Economic Zones.

Post Scenario of SEZ act 2005 and Exports

2006-07

The sustained high growth rate of merchandise exports at more than 20 per cent during the last four years (2002-06) is more than twice the current growth of Gross Domestic Product (GDP).This result is due to stable policy framework provided by the Trade Policy and a continuous, conscious & concerted effort by the Government to reduce trade barriers, that brought down transaction costs and facilitate a favorable international environment[7].

The several benefits are from the Special Economic Zones (SEZs). The SEZ policy aimed at generating greater economic activity and employment by providing a stable, transparent and efficient policy framework for establishment and running of SEZs. The main objectives of the SEZ Act are; generation of additional economic activity, promotion of exports of goods and services, promotion of investment from domestic and foreign sources, creation of employment opportunities and, development of infrastructure facilities[8].

According to Annual report (2006-07) the formal approval was granted to 234 SEZ proposals and in-principle approval to 162 SEZ proposals. Investment in SEZs are upto Rs.1,00,000 crore that included FDI of US $ 5-6 billion by end of December 2007. SEZs created direct employment of 5 lakh jobs. A Special Purpose Tea Fund (SPTF) has been set up under the Tea Board.Under the SPTF, the Government would be providing a subsidy of 25 per cent of the cost. On multilateral trade, throughout the negotiations, India has continued to pursue its national interests across all the areas under the Doha Work Programme. It continued to work constructively with its coalition partners, particularly, the G-

20 and the G-33 in the agriculture, NAMA-11 and other developing country groupings including the African Group, ACP countries, CARICOM, and LDCs in order to secure its development imperatives. The 7th India-EU Summit was held in Helsinki in October 2006. The Summit agreed that both sides move towards negotiations for a broad-based Trade and Investment Agreement. The European Commission is currently seeking a mandate from its Council of Ministers for the launch of negotiations for such an Agreement. The exports from SEZs in the year 2006-07 was Rs. 34,787 crore, which was 52% higher than the previous year's exports[9].

2007

The Empowered Group of Ministers (EGOM) on Special Economic Zones (SEZs) lifted the existing freeze on SEZs, tightened the rules and prescribed a ceiling on the size of SEZs and the fixed upper limit of 5000 hectares. State Governments may prescribe a lower limit.

Jan 2008[10]

The Export Promotion Council for EOUs and SEZ Units (EPCES) organized a function to award the best EPZs and SEZs The total number of awards presented were 47 and are in the fields of gem & jewellery, engineering, plastic products, electronic, computer hardware, services, readymade garments, handicrafts, chemical & allied products, textile products, food products etc.

Minister Kamalnath's 2008-09 years expectation is a growth of 100% and the exports from SEZs are likely to touch Rs.67,000 crore. Exports from SEZs is like to cross Rs.1,00,000 crore in the year 2008-09. EOUs and SEZs encourage manufacturing, exports, and employment generation and accelerate the process of inclusive growth. EOUs and SEZs provide direct employment to over 6.5 lakh people and indirect employment nearly 5 times. EOUs are operating in 27 states and new SEZs have been approved in 22 states. 420 SEZs have already started operations and have already started exporting.

Section II

How the Bank Policies Supported the SEZs

Measures in Banking Sector that influenced SEZs

For the first time, Offshore Banking Units (OBUs), which are exempted from CRR, SLR and give access to SEZ units and SEZ developers to international finances at international rates, have been set up.The Scheme has given leadership role to the State governments in identifying locations and private sector partners for developing SEZ zones[11].

Money Market Instruments[12]

Repos and CBLOs

Money market instruments such as market repo and collateralised lending and borrowing obligations (CBLO) have provided avenues for non-banks to manage their short-term liquidity mismatches and facilitated the transformation of the call money market into a pure inter-bank market.

CPs, CDs and Treasury bills

Issuance norms and maturity profiles of commercial paper (CP) and certificate of deposits (CDs) have been modified over time to encourage wider participation while strengthening the transmission of policy signals across the various market segments.

The abolition of *ad hoc* Treasury Bills and introduction of regular auctions of Treasury Bills paved the way for the emergence of a risk free rate, which has become a benchmark for pricing the other money market instruments.

Set up of Prudential Limits

Set up of prudential notes with the increased market orientation of monetary policy along with greater global integration of domestic markets, the Reserve Bank's emphasis has been on setting prudential limits on borrowing and lending in the call money market, encouraging migration towards the collateralised segments and developing derivative instruments for hedging market risks. This step has been complemented by the institutionalisation of the Clearing Corporation of India Limited (CCIL) as a central counterparty. The upgradation of payment system technologies has also enabled market participants to improve their asset liability management. All these measures have widened and deepened the money market in terms of instruments and participants, enhanced transparency and improved the signalling mechanism of monetary policy while ensuring financial stability.

Enabling Measures that smoothened Flow of Foreign Investments.[13]

(i) Foreign Institutional Investors (FIIs) were allowed to invest in government securities subject to certain limits.

(ii) Introduction of automated screen-based trading in government securities through Negotiated Dealing System (NDS).

(iii) Setting up of risk-free payments and settlement system in government securities through Clearing Corporation of India Limited (CCIL).

(iv) Phased introduction of Real Time Gross Settlement System (RTGS).

(v) Introduction of trading in government securities on stock exchanges for promoting retailing in such securities, permitting non-banks to participate in repo market.

(vi) Recent measures include introduction of NDS-OM and T+1 settlement norms.

Financial inclusion measures

Financial inclusion refers to delivery of banking services at an affordable cost to the vast sections of disadvantaged and low-income groups who tend to be excluded from the formal banking channel. Despite widespread expansion of the banking sector during the last three decades, a substantial proportion of the households, especially in rural areas, is at present outside the coverage of the formal banking system. The Reserve Bank's broad approach to financial inclusion aims at 'connecting people' with the banking system and not just credit dispensation; giving people access to the payments system; and portraying financial inclusion as a viable business model and opportunity. Efforts towards 'financial inclusion' include sensitising the banks to the banking and financial needs of the common person and ensuring access to basic banking facilities. The Annual Policy Statement for 2006-07 urged all banks to give effect to the measures announced by the Reserve Bank from time to time on financial inclusion at all their branches.

'Zero Balance" or 'No Frills'

Introduction of 'zero balance' or 'no frills' accounts has enabled the common person to open bank account. However, providing banking facilities closer to the customer, especially in remote and unbanked areas, while keeping transaction costs low, remains a challenge. This has to be done with affordable infrastructure and low operational costs with the use of appropriate technology. In the Annual Policy Statement for the year 2007-08, banks were urged on May 7, 2007 to scale up their financial inclusion efforts by utilizing appropriate technology, while ensuring that the solutions developed are: (i) highly secure; (ii) amenable to audit; and (iii) follow widely accepted open standards to allow interoperability among the different systems adopted by different banks. Banks have initiated pilot projects utilising smart cards/ mobile technology to increase their outreach. Biometric methods for uniquely identifying customers are also being increasingly adopted.

Pilot Project for 100 per cent Financial Inclusion: Status and Further Action

The convener banks of the State Level/ Union Territory Level Bankers' Committees (SLBC/UTLBC) in all States/Union Territories were advised on April 28, 2006 to identify at least one district in each State/Union Territory for achieving 100 per cent financial inclusion by providing a 'no-frills' account and issue of general purpose credit card (GCC). So far,160 districts have been identified and 100 per cent financial inclusion has been achieved in the whole of Union Territory of Puducherry and in 28 districts in eight States (Andhra Pradesh, Gujarat, Haryana, Himachal Pradesh, Karnataka, Keraia, Punjab and West Bengal). All districts of Himachal Pradesh have achieved financial inclusion. An evaluation of the progress made in achieving financial inclusion in these districts is being undertaken to draw lessons for further action in this regard.

Services to Depositors and Small Borrowers in Rural and Semi-Urban Areas

The Annual Policy Statement for the year 2005-06 proposed a survey for assessing customer satisfaction on credit delivery in rural areas by banks. Accordingly, the National Council of Applied Economic Research (NCAER) was entrusted with the job of carrying out a study on the quality of services rendered by branches of commercial banks to their customers (both depositors and small borrowers) in rural and semi-urban areas. The NCAER study covered 930 bank branches across the country from 30 States/ Union Territories, and included 9,300 depositors and 13,950 borrowers.

Credit Counseling: Setting up of Centres on a Pilot Basis

The Working Group (Chairman: Prof. S. S. Johl) constituted by the Reserve Bank to suggest measures for assisting distressed farmers had recommended that financial and livelihood counselling are important for increasing the viability of credit.

Use of Intermediaries as Agents

In January 2006, the Reserve Bank permitted banks to utilise the services of nongovernmental organisations/self-help groups (NGOs/SHGs), micro-finance institutions (other than NBFCs) and other civil society organizations as intermediaries in providing financial and banking services through the use of business facilitator (BF) and business correspondent (BC) models.

Working Groups on Improvement of Banking Services in Different States/ Union Territories

The Reserve Bank has been initiating measures to improve the outreach of banks and their services, and promote financial inclusion in less developed States/UTs.

Customer Service and Financial Inclusion

The Reserve Bank has taken several measures in recent years aimed at providing customer service at reasonable cost. These measures include enhancing customer protection and disclosures, code of ethics and grievance redressal, among others.

Some Policy measures of BANKs that supported SEZ Units, and SEZ Developers[14]

Sep. 2006, 20: Banks were advised that the exposure of banks to entities for setting up Special Economic Zones (SEZs) or for acquisition of units in SEZs which includes real estate would be treated as exposure to commercial real estate sector with immediate effect and banks would have to make provisions as also assign appropriate risk weights for such exposures as per the existing guidelines.

Oct. 2006 , 18: The banks were advised to ensure that all the loan accounts of the farmers in the specified districts which are overdue as on July 1, 2006 are rescheduled on the lines of package of relief measures for the debt stressed farmers of 25 districts in the states of Andhra Pradesh, Karnataka and Kerala.

Oct. 31, 2006: All SCBs (excluding RRBs) advised that in view of the current macroeconomic and overall monetary conditions, the fixed repo rate under the liquidity adjustment facility (LAF) of the Reserve Bank has been increased by 25 basis points with effect from Second LAF of Oct 31, 2006 to 7.25 per cent from 7.00 per cent. The reverse repo rate under the LAF remains unchanged at 6.00 per cent All other terms and conditions of the current LAF Scheme will remain unchanged.

2006 Nov. 6: In order to facilitate the expansion of Indian corporates' business abroad, the prudential limit on credit and non-credit facilities extended by banks to Indian Joint Ventures (where the holding by the Indian company is more than 51 per cent)/Wholly Owned Subsidiaries abroad was enhanced from 10 per cent to 20 per cent of their unimpaired capital funds (Tier I and Tier II capital).

2006 Dec. 22: It was decided in consultation with the Government of India to allow foreign investment in infrastructure companies in securities market, namely stock exchanges, depositories and clearing corporations, in compliance with SEBI Regulations and subject to the following conditions: (I) foreign investment up to 49 per cent will be allowed in these companies with a separate foreign direct investment (FDI) cap of 26 per cent and Foreign Institutional Investment (FII) cap of 23 per cent; (ii) FDI will be allowed with specific prior approval of FIPB; and (iii) FII will be allowed only through purchases in the secondary market.

2007 Jan. 31: The Reserve Bank decided to increase the fixed repo rate under the liquidity adjustment facility (LAF) by 25 basis points with effect from January 31, 2007 to 7.50 per cent. The reverse repo rate under the LAF remained unchanged at 6.0 per cent. The Reserve Bank advised the SCBs that the Standing Liquidity Facilities provided to banks (export credit finance) would be available at the repo rate, i.e., 7.50 per cent with effect from January 31, 2007.

- The Reserve Bank advised the SCBs that they may undertake short sale of Central Government dated securities, subject to the short position being covered within a maximum period of five trading days, including the day of trade.
- The Reserve Bank advised the SCBs about the increase in the provisioning requirement in respect of standard assets in respect of personal loans (including credit card receivables), loans and advances qualifying as capital market exposure and real estate loans from the present level of one per cent to two per cent with effect from January 31, 2007.
- The Reserve Bank advised the SCBs that the interest rates on fresh Non-Resident (External) Rupee (NRE) Term Deposits for one to three years maturity should not exceed the LIBOR/SWAP rates, as on the last working day of the previous month, for US dollar of corresponding maturities plus 50 basis points (as against LIBOR/ SWAP rates plus 100 basis points effective from close of business on April 18, 2006). The interest rates as determined above for three year deposits will also be applicable in case the maturity period exceeds three years. The changes in interest rates will also apply to NRE deposits renewed after their present maturity period. The Reserve Bank also advised that in respect of FCNR (B) deposits of all maturities contracted effective from the close of business in India as on January 31, 2007, interest shall be paid within the ceiling rate of LIBOR/SWAP rates for the respective currency/corresponding maturities minus 25 basis points (as against LIBOR/ SWAP rates effective from the close of business on March 28, 2006). On floating rate deposits, interest shall be paid within the ceiling of SWAP rates for the respective currency/ maturity minus 25 basis points. For floating rate deposits, the interest reset period shall be six months.

- The Reserve Bank advised that the banks should not grant fresh loans or renew existing loans in excess of Rs. 20 lakh against the NR (E) RA and FCNR (B) deposits, either to depositors or to third parties, with immediate effect. Banks were also advised not to undertake artificial slicing of the loan amount to circumvent the ceiling.

2007 February 12: In pursuance of the Bank's Clean Note Policy, the currency chest holding banks were advised to automate the sorting of notes by installing Note Sorting Machines (NSM) at their currency chests. The tolerance level of reissuable notes in the soiled banknote remittance to the Reserve Bank was changed from the existing 10 per cent to 5 per cent of each remittance, with immediate effect

2007 Jan. 14: Banks were advised that cash reserve ratio (CRR) will be increased by one-half of one percentage point of their net demand and time liabilities (NDTL) in two stages, effective from the specified date.

2007 Feb. 21: Banks were advised to lay down general principles and broad parameters to be followed by them while offering "doorstep" services to their customers and to ensure transparency in respect of the rights and obligations of customers, uniformity in approach and to clearly delineate the risks involved.

- Banks were also advised to take suitable steps to educate their "Agents" to enable them to detect forged and mutilated notes so as to avoid frauds and disputes with the customers.

2007 March 1: All SCBs were advised that they would continue to be exempted from maintaining average CRR with effect from June 22, 2006 on the following liabilities, subject to the maintenance of statutory minimum CRR of 3 per cent on their total demand and time liabilities:(i) liabilities to the banking system in India as computed under clause (d) of the Explanation to Section 42 (1) of the Reserve Bank of India Act, 1934; (ii) credit balances in ACU (US$) Accounts; (iii) transactions in Collateralised Borrowing and Lending Obligation (CBLO) with Clearing Corporation of India. (CCIL); and (iv) demand and time liabilities in respect of their Offshore Banking Units (OBUs).

IT and ITES

The Special Economic Zones (SEZ) Scheme has benefited the IT and ITES industry in many was. It has provided[15]

(a) various incentives to promote exports including duty free import/domestic procurement of goods,

(b) exemption from Central Sales Tax on supplies made from DTA,

(c) exemption from service tax 100 per cent income tax exemption for the first 5 years, 50 per cent for the next 2 years and 50 per cent of ploughed-back profits for the next 3 years.

SEZ Rules, 2006 provided a lower minimum area requirement to support IT industry The Government has approved a number of SEZs in IT/ITES Sector. Approval has been given for setting up of 117 SEZs, out of which 57 pertain to IT Sector i.e. 48.7 per cent of the approved SEZs are in the IT Sector. The hardware, Information Technology Enabled Services- Business Process Outsourcing (ITES-BPO) and engineering and research and development (R&D) services segments accounted for 21 per cent, 18 per cent and 14 per cent respectively.IT-ITES exports from India grew from USD 13.3 billion in FY 2003-04 to USD 18.2 billion in FY 2004-05, with export earnings accounting for 64 per cent of the total IT-ITES aggregate in FY 2004-05. It is estimated that total IT-ITES exports from India will exceed USD 23.9 billion in FY 2005-06. All this cannot be without better performance of SEZsIndia's merchandise exports grew at an accelerated pace during 2005, with exports continuing to record double-digit growth during April-November 2005-06. During 2004-05, India's merchandise exports at US $ 80 billion far exceeded the target. It is anticipated that the export target of US $ 92 billion for 2005-06 will also be exceeded.[16]

Section-III

Growth in Indian Economy

Shri Kamal Nath, Minister for Commerce and Industry, has stated that the EOU/SEZ Sector is playing a very important role in encouraging manufacturing activity, providing substantial employment opportunities, thereby accelerating the pace of economic growth. The units set up under these schemes are already providing direct employment to over 6.5 lakh people[17].

Many of these SEZs are recruiting people from rural areas and providing them training for operations in the SEZs, as we have seen from Gem & Jewellery SEZ in Hyderabad, Textiles units in Mahindra SEZ in Chennai and other new SEZs like Nokia, Flextronics in Chennai, Apache SEZ, Brandix Apparel SEZ, Divy's Laboratories in Andhra Pradesh and Rajiv Gandhi Technology Park in Chandigarh[18].

The average saving rate in India was 10 per cent in the 1950s, which rose to 17.5 per cent in the 1970s and further to 23.4 per cent in the 1990s. The saving rate was 32.4 per cent in 2005-06. The strengthening of economic activity in the recent years has been supported by persistent increase in gross domestic investment rates from 22.9 per cent of GDP in 2001-02 to 33.8 per cent in 2005-06. It may also be noted that over 95 per cent of investment in the country during this period was financed by the domestic savings[19].

There seems to be a general optimism about India's growth prospects in projections made by various agencies such as ABN Amro, Asian Development Bank,Confederation of Indian Industry (cii),Centre for Monitoring the Indian Economy(CMIE), Citigroup, RISIL,Economic Advisory Council to the Prime Minister, CPA, indicus Analytics, International Monetary Fund, JP Morgan, Organisation for Economic Corporation and Development (OECD), National Council for Applied Economic Research (NCAER), Reserve Bank of India (RBI) and Median Projection[20].

Expected Growth of various fields and sectors under SEZs:

(a) Stimulation of foreign and domestic investments into manufacturing sector for production of export.

(b) Sourcing of large requirements of raw material from the domestic area would create backward linkages from the SEZ areas. Similarly the facility of sub-contracting to DTA units would further enhance the capability of DTA units.

(c) Availability of technology and modern management skills in SEZ units would be beneficial for overall economic growth.

(d) Availability of finance at international rates and other international financial and consultancy services.

GDP Growth[21]

Over the last four years during 2003-07, the Indian economy has entered a high-growth phase, with the GDP growth averaging 8.6 per cent per annum. The acceleration of growth during this period has been accompanied by a significant moderation in volatility, especially in industry and services sectors. The structure of domestic output has distinctly shifted in favor of the services sector, while growth in industry is also accelerating. Indian industry appears to have responded well to global competition through restructuring and technological upgradation in recent years. India's growth is mainly driven by domestic consumption, which contributed, on an average, to almost two-thirds of the overall demand. Saving and Investment Balances. A noteworthy feature of the ongoing structural transformation of the Indian economy is the significant increase in domestic saving and investment rates. Domestic investment rate increased from 24.3 per cent in 2000-01 to 33.8 per cent in 2005-06 and domestic saving rate from 23.7 per cent in 2000-01 to 32.4 per cent during 2005-06. The household sector continued to be the major contributor to gross domestic saving with its saving rate placed at 22.3 per cent in 2005-06, while on account of rise in profit, the saving rate of private corporate sector rose to 8.1 per cent in 2005-06. The public sector, which started posting positive saving beginning 2003-04, recorded a saving rate of 2.0 per cent in 2005-06 on account of continuing fiscal improvement as against a negative saving rate of 1.7 per cent in 2000-01. It may be noted that over 95 per cent of investment is financed by domestic savings. Given the fact that Indian per capita income is increasing rapidly and policy efforts towards financial deepening for achieving a more inclusive growth are underway, savings rate in India could even rise further in the medium to long term. The level of saving rates should help continue to finance the investment needs of the economy domestically, without undue dependence on foreign savings. In Indian Economic growth, from an annual average growth rate of 3.5 per cent during 1950 to 1980, the growth rate of the Indian economy accelerated to around 6.0 per cent in the 1980s and 1990s. In the last four years (2003-04 to 2006-07), the Indian economy grew by 8.6 per cent. In 2005-06 and 2006- 07, it had grown at a higher rate of 9.0 and 9.4 per cent, respectively. There is, thus, tangible evidence of self-accelerating growth.[22]

Comparison among Banking, Performance of SEZs, GDP and other Indicators

Since 1991, India has transformed itself from one of the most closed large economies of the world to a relatively more open one, with trade,Exports plus Imports, as a percentage of GDP reaching 40% in 2004 and 45% in 2005 (Table 1)[23].

Table 1
Total Trade as Percentage og GDP

Year	*1990*	*91*	*92*	*93*	*94*	*95*	*96*	*97*	*98*	*99*	*2000*	*01*	*02*	*03*	*04*	*2005*
%	16	17	19	20	20	23	22	23	24	25	27	26	30	31	40	45

Source: World development Indicators.

Table 2

Select Macro Economic Aggregates (Current Prices) (Per Cent) (Base : 1999-2000)

Year	*Annual growth Rate*								
	GDP at factor cost	*NDP at factor cost*	*GNP at factor cost*	*NNP at factor cost*	*Per capita NNP*	*Rate of GDS $*	*Rate of NDS $$*	*Rate of GDCF $*	*Rate of NDCF $$*
1995-96	17.1	17	17.3	17.2	14.9	24.4	16.4	26.2	18.3
1996-97	16.4	16.5	16.6	16.8	14.6	22.7	14.5	24	15.9
1997-98	11.2	11.1	11.3	11.3	9.2	23.8	15.6	25.3	17.3
1998-99	15.3	15.6	15.3	15.6	13.4	22.3	14.1	23.3	15.3
1999-00	10.5	10.4	10.6	10.5	8.5	24.8	16.9	25.9	18.2
2000-01	7.8	7.4	7.4	7	5.1	23.7	15.3	24.3	16
2001-02	9.1	8.6	9.3	8.9	6.9	23.5	14.8	22.9	14.1
2002-03	7.9	7.6	8.1	7.9	6.2	26.4	17.9	25.2	16.6
2003-04	12.5	12.6	12.6	12.7	10.8	29.7	21.6	28	19.8
2004-05 P	12	11.4	11.9	11.3	9.6	31.1	22.9	31.5	23.4
2005-06 QE	13.8	13.8	13.8	13.8	12.1	32.4	24.4	33.8	25.9
2006-07 RE	15.2	15.5	15.4	15.8	14.3	.	.	.	.

P : Provisional; QE : Quick Estimates., RE : Revised Estimates.

$ GDS and GDCF rates are percentages to GDP at current market prices.

$$ NDS and NDCF rates are percentages to NDP at current market prices.

Source: Central Statistical Organization.

There has also been significant improvement in market infrastructure in terms of trading platform and settlement mechanisms. As a result of various reform measures, liquidity in the foreign exchange market increased by more than 5 times between 1997-98 and 2006-07 (Table 3 and 4).

Table 3
Turnover in the Foreign Exchange Market[24]

Year	*Turnover in US $ Billion*			*Share of Spot Turnover in Percentage*		
	Merchant	*Inter bank*	*Total*	*Merchant*	*Inter bank*	*Total*
1997-98	210	1096	1305	57.6	50.3	51.5
1998-99	246	1057	1303	52.9	49.4	50.0
1999-00	244	898	1142	62.3	50.8	53.3
2000-01	269	1118	1387	65.2	45.2	49.1
2001-02	257	1165	1422	64.0	39.8	44.1
2002-03	325	1236	1560	57.9	42.7	45.9
2003-04	491	1628	2118	53.1	48.7	49.7
2004-05	705	2188	2892	48.2	50.5	50.0
2005-06	1220	3192	4413	45.0	52.7	50.6
2006-07 (P)	1787	4727	6514	46.2	54.2	52.0

(P): Provisional.

Table 4
Indian Exports

Year	*Exports Total*	*Growth Rates*	*Year*	*Exports Total*	*Growth Rates*
1970-71	1535.3	—	1987-88	15673.7	25.873
1971-72	1608.2	4.74826	1988-89	20231.5	29.0793
1972-73	1971.5	22.5905	1989-90	27658.4	36.7096
1973-74	2523.4	27.9939	1990-91	32557.6	17.7132
1974-75	3328.8	31.9173	1991-92	44041.8	35.2735
1975-76	4036.3	21.2539	1992-93	53688.3	21.9031
1976-77	5142.7	27.4112	1993-94	69751.4	29.9192
1977-78	5407.9	5.15682	1994-95	82674.1	18.5268
1978-79	5726.1	5.88398	1995-96	106353	28.6416
1979-80	6418.4	12.0903	1996-97	118817	11.7192
1980-81	6710.7	4.55409	1997-98	130101	9.49653
1981-82	7805.9	16.3202	1998-99	139753	7.41926
1982-83	8803.4	12.7788	1999-00	159561	14.1738

Contd...

Year	Exports Total	Growth Rates	Year	Exports Total	Growth Rates
1983-84	9770.7	10.9878	2000-01	203571	27.5816
1984-85	11743.7	20.193	2001-02	209018	2.67572
1985-86	10894.6	-7.23026	1987-88	15673.7	25.873
1986-87	12452	14.2952	1988-89	20231.5	29.0793
2002-03	255137	22.0648	1989-90	27658.4	36.7096
2003-04	293367	14.9839	1990-91	32557.6	17.7132
2004-05	375340	27.9421	1991-92	44041.8	35.2735
2005-06	456418	21.6014	1992-93	53688.3	21.9031
2006-07 P	571642	25.2453	1993-94	69751.4	29.9192

Source: Directorate General of Commercial Intelligence and Statistics.

Section IV

Concluding Observations

All the exim transactions are only through Bank dealings.With out current practice of IT and ITES the speed and volume of transactions could not be that much, more and most Gradual growth in GDP figures, Growth in exports gradually in corresponding years and especially after IT and ITES in Banking are visible with the same trends in raise in absolute values. This confirms the importance and role of e-Bank supported SEZs in increased GDP as well as corresponding Exports and thus in Indian Economic Growth. . However the increase in GDP and EXPORTS absolute figures in the year 2006 and after, and the SEZs are multiplied, this was all due to IT/ITES introduced Banking.

Notes

1. AP Assembly Budget Secession on 16, Feb. 2008, Finance Minister 's Budget Speech, 2008-09.
2. Financial Sector Technology Vision Document, RBI, 2005.
3. 'India's Trade Integration, Realising The Potential' , (An Interim Report was presented to the Working Party of the Trade Committee in January 2007), Organisation for Economic Co-operation and Development, Paris, 26 June 2007.

4. *Ibid*
5. PIB Release, April 03, 2007.
6. PIB Release May 10, 2005.
7. The Annual Report of Ministry of Commerce & Industry (Department of Commerce), 2007.
8. *Ibid.*
9. PIB Release, Statement of Minister Kamalnath
10. PIB Release.
11. PIB Release, Feb. 2004.
12. 'Development of Financial Markets in India' Address by Dr. Rakesh Mohan, Deputy Governor, Reserve Bank of India at the First Indian-French Financial Forum in Mumbai on May 16, 2007. The assistance of Janak Raj, Jai Chander and Partha Ray in preparing this address is gratefully acknowledged.
13. Mohan (2007), as in 'Development of Financial Markets in India' Address by Dr. Rakesh Mohan, Deputy Governor, Reserve Bank of India at the First Indian-French Financial Forum in Mumbai on May 16, 2007.
14. RBI Report on Trend and Progress of Banking in India, 2006-07.
15. PIB Release, 17 MAR 2006.
16. PIB Release, Jan. 01, 2006.
17. IB Release, Jan. 2008.
18. *Ibid*
19. Speech delivered by Dr. Y.V. Reddy, Governor, Reserve Bank of India at the Central Bank of the Russian Federation on July 2, 2007.
20. Valedictory Address by Dr. Rakesh Mohan, Deputy Governor, Reserve Bank of India on August 3, 2007at the Workshop for Top Executives of Banks on Macroeconomic Issues and their Relevance to the Banking System organised by the State Bank of India. Assistance of M.D. Patra and Indranil Bhattacharya in preparing the speech is gratefully acknowledged.
21. India: Development and Reform Experience; and Prospects 1 Address by Dr. Y.V. Reddy, Governor, Reserve Bank of India at the Bank of Mexico, Mexico City on September 12, 2007.

22. Speech delivered by Dr. Y.V. Reddy, Governor, Reserve Bank of India at the Central Bank of the Russian Federation on July 2, 2007.
23. World Development Indicators.
24. 'Development of Financial Markets in India' Address by Dr. Rakesh Mohan, Deputy Governor, Reserve Bank of India at the First Indian-French Financial Forum in Mumbai on May 16, 2007. The assistance of Janak Raj, Jai Chander and Partha Ray in preparing this address is gratefully acknowledged.

References

'India's Trade Integration, Realising The Potential', (*An interim report was presented to the Working Party of the Trade Committee in January 2007)*, Organisation for Economic Co-operation and Development , Paris, 26 June 2007.

AP Assembly Budget Secession on 16, Feb. 2008, Finance Minister's Budget Speech, 2008-09.

Bhattacharya in Preparing the Speech is Gratefully Acknowledged.

Development of Financial Markets in India' Address by Dr. Rakesh Mohan, Deputy Governor, Reserve Bank of India at the First Indian-French Financial Forum in Mumbai on May 16, 2007.

Financial Sector Technology Vision Document, RBI, 2005.

India: Development and Reform Experience; and Prospects 1 Address by Dr. Y.V. Reddy, Governor, Reserve Bank of India at the Bank of Mexico, Mexico City on September 12, 2007.

PIB Release, 17 MAR 2006.

PIB Release May 10, 2005.

PIB Release, April 03, 2007.

PIB Release, Feb. 2004.

PIB Release, Jan. 01, 2006.

PIB Release, Jan. 2008.

PIB Release, Statement of Minister Kamalnath.

RBI Report on Trend and Progress of Banking in India, 2006-07.

Speech delivered by Dr. Y.V. Reddy, Governor, Reserve Bank of India at the Central Bank of the Russian Federation on July 2, 2007.

Speech delivered by Dr. Y.V. Reddy, Governor, Reserve Bank of India at the Central Bank of the Russian Federation on July 2, 2007.

The Annual Report of Ministry of Commerce & Industry (Department of Commerce)-2007.

The Banking System organised by the State Bank of India. Assistance of M.D. Patra and Indranil.

Valedictory Address by Dr. Rakesh Mohan, Deputy Governor, Reserve Bank of India on August 3.

World Development Indicators.

21

GOA MODEL OF SEZ DEVELOPMENT IN INDIA

P. ARUNACHALAM

The Factor-Endowment Model

There is a theory in International Economics known as 'Factor Endowment Theory' which could be used as a 'Model' for 'Special Economic Zones (SEZs)' development in India since Goa, a small state, opposes to have SEZs in Goa in the name of protecting tourism industry and environmental problems. We could make this theory applicable not only to Goa but also to ecologically sensitive states and metro cities. The Factor endowment theory was advocated by two Swedish economists Eli Heckscher and Bertil Ohlin (HO). The HO theory focuses on the difference in relative factor endowments and factor prices between nations as the most important determinants of trade between two countries. The HO theorem postulates that each nation will export the commodity intensive in its relatively abundant and cheap factor and import the commodity intensive in its relatively scarce and expensive factor. The factor price equalization theorem postulates that trade will lead to the elimination of the pre-trade difference in relative and absolute factor prices between nations.

In brief we can simplify the theory as follows. There are two countries. One has lot of capital whereas the second country has abundance of labour. The country which has more capital can concentrate on capital intensive commodities and the second country can concentrate on labour intensive commodities. They can exchange the surplus products between them and share the profit optimally. Though it talks about the international trade between two countries it is very much parallel to Indian states with respect to SEZ. Small states like Goa can concentrate on eco and environmental friendly and responsible tourism related activities. On the other hand the SEZ developers can concentrate on larger states where vast track of land is available for industrialization different purposes.

Development of SEZs in India

The reform process initiated during the late eighties, early nineties have begun to show their impact, and India is taking huge strides in the course of growth and development. However, recognizing that there is no room for complacency, Indian policy makers are moving ahead with due caution and at the same time integrating India with the global economy. Establishing Special Economic Zones (SEZs) is part of Globalization process in India. SEZ is one of the best designed strategic policies of China If implemented properly in India it could resolve some of the fundamental problems like unemployment, regional disparity, removal of poverty, lack of infrastructural facilities, etc. Despite its advantageous there are problems associated with implementation of the scheme. The controversy surrounding SEZs continues to rage and make newspaper headlines across the country. SEZs have occupied centre state in the national consciousness for the last two years due to the events unfolding in Singur and subsequently due to the occurrences in Nandigram. Some call SEZs as potential trigger to the economic growth story of India while some call it the source of mass conflicts. Nandigram as a stark example. The controversy over the SEZs appears to be unending with the latest agitation at Nandigram highlighting the depth of feeling in this country over these new entities. The disturbances have taken place despite West Bengal has dropped the idea of SEZs in Nandigram and started it in Nayachar Island. The doubts of the people who opposed SEZ in Nandigra ultimately proved correct when Nandigram went up in flames as farmers protested against cultivable land being acquired for a chemicals hub in the region proposed by Salim Group of Industries from Indonesia. The TATAs proposal for an automobile project at Singur faced similar opposition from farmers thought it was made clear that this is not an SEZ. The fact is that the entire policy was flawed in many respects from the outset. This included the failure to lay down guidelines in terms of infrastructure development as well as the decision to make government responsible for land acquisition. It is a scheme for which the time has come, but the government will have to rapidly clear the misgivings over the concept both at the political and at the grassroots level.

The controversial SEZs scheme, launched from 10th February 2006 has met with massive protests from those living on land earmarked for such zones in India, where 68 pr cent of the 1.1 billion-plus population live off agriculture. News of dissent in the ruling party over the proposed SEZs in Haryana and Punjab has been making the rounds. Protests are there not only in backward states like Uttar Pradesh, Orissa and Chattisgarh even most advanced states like Maharastra and Gujarat etc. Resistance to these zones has built up rapidly in the country even though most political parties seem to be supporting their creation since they are ruling in some State where they would like them to come up.

SEZs are seen as a strategy for ensuring the continuation of above 9 per cent rate of growth of the economy. If China could succeed, through such a strategic policy, then why not India? There is no much doubt, that the SEZ concept will definitely help India succeed in a tremendous way. The domestic industries will be able to compete in the global market. The SEZs will bring technology and manufacturing skill, employment opportunities, attract FDI, increase exports, etc. The challenge ahead lies in appropriately sequencing to sustain the popular support for reforms and reconciling the conflicting interests of the various reform constituencies. The recent debate about SEZs illustrates the kind of considerations that have to be taken into account in the formulation of policies.

State Governments have a very important role to play in the establishment of SEZs. Representatives of the State Governments, who are members of the Inter-Ministerial Committee on Private SEZ is consulted while considering the proposal. Before recommending any proposals to the Ministry of Commerce and Industry the States must satisfy themselves that they are in a position to supply basic inputs like land, water, electricity, etc.

Though the special economic zone developers are happy with the basic framework of policies and norms formulated by the Centre, the lack of cooperation from the State Governments and some policy-related matters and operational issues have become a matter of concern for them. The SEZ developers have the experience that matter related to land acquisition, tax exemptions and lack of single window clearance mechanism is leading to unnecessary delays in execution of various projects. They are also worried over the non-uniformity of SEZ Act, 2005 and rules framed by various State Governments. When the Centre has allowed the State Governments the flexibility of fixing the area to develop SEZs, some states have sized the opportunity; state like Goa scraped all the proposals due to land problem. Larger states like West Bengal, Andhra Pradesh and Maharashtra have taken the lead in clearing the SEZs proposals, Kerala Government's indecision to approve the 21 proposals pending for developing special economic zones over ideological differences would be setback for industrial development in the state. As many as 21 proposals for the developing SEZs in Kerala are pending at the Chief Ministers office for the last 10 months for want of approval. However, SEZs Nodal Officer and Development Commissioner for South Zone C.J.Mathew has stated that, 'The developers are yet to identify the land to set up SEZs in the state and that is the reason why the proposals are pending with the state.

From the Board of Approvals indications are that the proposals would be scrapped if it fails to obtain the clearance from the concerned State governments. Only after obtaining the state government's approval the proposals can be put up for the Center's assent. According to the SEZs rules, the developer submits the proposal for establishment of SEZ to the concerned state government. The government has to forward the proposal with its recommendation within 45 days to the BOA.

The developers are waiting to invest in Kerala but if the State government fails to respond then they would approach other states like Karnataka and Tamil Nadu, where they are welcome. Despite repeated reminders from the Industries Department the State Government has not forwarded the 21 pending SEZs proposal to the Centre and it speaks of the ideological underpinnings. Revamping the SEZ rules, the inconveniences faced by developers due to control, are being eased out though exemptions on VAT and stamp duties in states like Andhra Pradesh. The other states have announced a rehabilitation price of up to 75 per cent above the registered market rate for the project affected people but Kerala Government rules out any displacement of people. Kerala may not have to pay a high rehabilitation cost considering the extent of people to be shifted. Still, the Stake Government and its bureaucracy have failed to evolve a clear strategy on developing SEZs.

The Export promotion Council for Export Oriented Units and SEZs Panel for SEZ Developers are trying hard to convince the Union Government, particularly the Ministry of Commerce and Industry that is responsible for sanctioning of SEZs, to ask the State Governments to have identical rules and guidelines for development of SEZs, so that SEZ developers can implement their projects faster. The Centre has deputed Development Commissioners in various regions whose job is to coordinate with the State Governments. However, it is not simple as multiplicity of authorities and separate rules and regulations in States make the task difficult. For instance, the Development Commissioners of North region has to deal with seven State Governments. The state should enable single window clearance for all planning requirements. And in case of multi-product SEZs, the States must empower the Development Commissioners with powers to approve the development and building plans.

The SEZs developers also want some changes in policies related to tax exemptions and stamp duty. The Central Act provides for exemption of stamp duty for which the Stamp Act has been duly amended. But the state governments are following different practices for refund. States must provide stamp duty exemption to the developers who have been given in-principal approval, and instead of refund, the State should secure a bank guarantee that is released once the SEZ is notified. Same approach should also be adopted while dealing with issues related to local taxes. This will allow developers to have extra money in his hands that could be utilized in the development of SEZs. The SEZ developers have also demanded abolition of ceiling on land holdings and encourage them to establish infrastructure.

Ever since the government implemented the SEZs Act in 2005, only 1945 kg km land has been earmarked for the projects. Many fresh projects can still be accommodated. Recently, the Center has directed to the State Governments to place a 1 per cent cap on conversion of land for industry. The proactive role of the Government without facilitation by the State Government, it is not possible to buy land for the huge projects. The State Governments should take the onus to ensure that fertile land is not notified for industrialization projects and the projects should now be limited to barren and waste land. This will lead to a win-win situation for the involved parties.

Going by sheer numbers, Southern States and some western states are extracting maximum advantage out of the SEZs policy and the East and North East are losing out. In the North, proactive players like Haryana are turning SEZs into success stories with 32 SEZs approval so far while others are not doing enough. By moving in quickly, Haryana has left behind Punjab where only six SEZs have been notified so far. Apart from market price for land, the state government has specified that families whose land is taken over would get Rs. 10,000 per annum for 33 years. Developers like Reliance are willing to do better since their cordial relations with the local population have neutralized political opposition to SEZ. Vocational training, a job for each family and infrastructure benefits, have also added to the development dimension. Other states have fared no better. Only six SEZ has been notified in Rajasthan. Madhya Pradesh is no better with just ten so far SEZs getting notified so far. The state government seems to be in the process of clearing more but there is a long way to go. Uttar Pradesh has got thirteen projects so far but this is far too less for a state with strong potential due to proximity of the national Capital and availability of land. Jammu and Kashmir, Himachal Pradesh, Uttaranchal fare very poor with one or two proposals.

The success of SEZs in creating economic activity and employment will depend on how state governments treat these projects and initial trends clearly emphases this key aspect. Land is a state subject and no company can snatch real estate away in the name of SEZs without the connivance of the state government concerned. In any case, the Centre has imposed curbs on state acquisition of land and an improved rehabilitation policy.

Goa's Case

Goa is a small State, with an area of just 3,704 square km, and a population of nearly 15 lakh. It has the highest population density of 450 people per square km as against 150 for the all-India average. In this context, giving away 1, 20,770 meters of land from Goa's scarce land resource for 18 SEZs with no benefits to the State was not acceptable to Goa's Movement Against SEZs (GMAS) and the people at large. Many people including former State's Tourism Minister of Goa Matahny Saldanha. Questioning how 18 SEZs can be allowed within the dot-sized Goa? Development has to be totally based on the needs of the State, with a vision for growth and not for the sake of so-called development. They have raised some fundamental questions related to to SEZ in Goa. The numbers of zones quoted by them are 18 but actually the number of zones approved as on 19.10.2007 is 7 only and with this Goa occupies the 11th rank among the SEZ states.

The promoters of the SEZs argue that the main reason for establishing the SEZs in Goa is to generate employment for the locals. The government has been approving projects in the name of the unemployed. Existing industries already employ nearly 80 per cent of the workers who are migrants from the other States. If the unemployment problem in Goa was so serious, there would have been no need for such a migration. The former Chief Minister, Mr Pratap Singh Rane, had approved 15 SEZs and welcomed many more, all in the name of unemployment, growth and development. Anyway, all these SEZs are supposed to generate 9, 27,100 jobs. The question is from where this workforce will come, especially since Goa just does not have the numbers required, nor does it have such a large quantum of skilled or unskilled labour. This obviously means that Goa will witness an influx of 8, 47,100 persons from all over the country, perhaps much more as many workers also bring their families. How can a small State with the highest population density, already facing a serious crunch in water supply and electricity, with no space to dump and dispose of its garbage, sustain such an enormous influx? They question. Now, consider the infrastructure. Existing roads in Goa are narrow, with the number of vehicles rising virtually with every passing day. Imagine the plight of local Goans with lakhs of outside workers settling down in the region. An influx of this kind is bound to change the social fabric and the demography of Goa, with increases in crime rates and other social and economic problems. It will lead to a drastic change in the social and cultural environment of the State. Shri. Kamal Nath Union Minster for Commerce has stated that "The Central Government does not want to thrust upon any state SEZ which is not conducive."

An influx of this kind into Goa will increase the pressure on its scarce land resources, reduce the greenery and disturb the ecological balance, thereby denying Goa its unique environment which is responsible for drawing a large number of tourists to this State, making it the sixth best tourism destination in the world. Besides, there is no revenue for the State as SEZs are exempt from all forms of taxes, and neither the State nor the Centre has any jurisdiction over the SEZs. How can we allow 18 republics within the dot-sized Goa? Development has to be totally based on the needs of the State, with a vision for growth and for the sake of so-called development. This will only destroy the existing development and progress. Interestingly, it must be noted that the demand for cancellation of SEZs in Goa came not from any anti-establishment group or single-minded environmentalists. It came from the grassroots; practically every gram sabha has demanded the abolition of all the SEZs in the State, as well as the SEZ policy. Moreover, the cancellation of SEZs has been the demand of all the political parties, including the ruling Congress coalition and its partners. It is also the demand of practically all the NGOs and the trade unions, as well as Youth for Goa, a forum comprising the students and the youth of Goa. Against this total opposition to the SEZs, the question of a law in force not permitting de-notification of the three notified SEZs appears irrelevant. Under the quasi-federal constitution of India, any State that is in threat of losing its very character and identity has all the rights to seek protection for its existence by demanding the review of the law. Opposing SEZs, IT parks, new townships, special fishing zones, special tourism zones does not mean protest against industrialization. We want industries that are environment-friendly, based on the availability of manpower within the State, and those which are sustainable and not exploitative of labour.

One of the important issues raised by Matahny is quite applicable not only to Goa but also to some small states like Delhi and Pondicherry and Kerala. Kerala occupies 9th rank with 11 approved zones. Kerala also a land scarce state like Goa. Both states have some similarities. One could describe them as green belt states and very much essential for maintaining ecosystem. Although Kerala vigorously pursuing industrialization policy most of these proposals ended up with land problem. Goa's tourism potential has fully been utilized whereas as Kerala's potential not been exploited fully. Therefore small states like Kerala, instead of encouraging SEZ, could concentrate on tourism related and environmental friendly industries. By doing so that greenery of these states would be protected. Another important point raised by the protesters is number of people who registered in employment exchange. Nearly one lakh people registered for employment in the employment exchange. The employment opportunities SEZs are going to generate is not only for the educated people but also the semiskilled, artisans and manual work, etc. when industries are there and definitely employment opportunities would be there. Hence nobody can deny or stop the influx of people from other states into Goa. If all the proposed SEZs (18 as he stated) become operational they can generate 9, 27,100 employment opportunities in 2010 -2012. By that time Maharastra and Karnataka and Andhra Pradesh would be having enough employment opportunities due to a large number of proposed SEZs in these states. Therefore no people or workers from these states migrate to Goa. Another serious issue raised by them is change of demographic imbalance. Being a part of India as a state it has no power or control mechanism to stop people coming to Goa for whatever may be the purpose like searching job opportunities, traveler, doing business, etc. Delhi, Kolkatta and Chennai have a large number of migrant workers from other states.

People should be consulted and farmers should be consulted. An amicable solution should be reached before one finalizes the proposal. Now it is not too late still developers have enough time and opportunities in front of them. From the above argument what we suggest is that to avoid controversies like SEZs in Goa or small states let the developers and the central government concentrate on large states like Madhya Pradesh, Uttar Pradesh, Rajasthan where less number of SEZs were proposed despite a large area of land is available for industrialization.

Goa attracted this much proposals because it is situated on the coastal area like Maharastra and it will be easy for the developers to shift the products through ports. To avoid this type of concentration Government' of India has to increase its budget on infrastructure from 4 per cent at present to 13 per cent. All the state capitals, port cities, and air ports should be well connected with six or eight lane express high way. World class infrastructural facilities will definitely reduce concentration of Industries and also motivate developers to go to a far away place from urban and semi urban areas.

It is the fact that almost all the states except Goa want to have SEZs although most of the SEZs are concentrated on certain states like Maharastra, Andhra Pradesh, Karnataka, Tamil Nadu, Delhi and Gujarat. States like Jammu and Kashmir, Himachal Pradesh, Bihar, and all the North Easter states are completely neglected by SEZs developers even though the concessions and inducements more or less same for all the states in India. Due to a large scale concentration of Industries in certain states people from UP, Bihar and Orissa and West Bengal migrate to other parts of the country in search of jobs and it is creating a lot of problems among the local and the migrant workers. A recent problem in Mahasatra is a clear example for this.

At the same time there are concessions for small states with respect to minimum acres of land needed for different SEZ Zones. Goa is having different kind of experience as far as SEZ is concerned. Goa Government scraped all the proposals submitted to the Board of Approvals, New Delhi for approval. In contrary to Goa's development small states like Kerala pursuing with more

SEZs. In due course Kerala may raise against SEZ due to land problem alone since Kerala also a thickly populated state like Goa. In practical sense they have no surplus land to be distributed for industrialization purpose. One of the major issues Kerala always is facing is distribution of land only. Some of the important industrial schemes Kerala lost due to land problem alone. So government of India can bring some changes in the SEZ Act 2005 so that small states can be spared from developing SEZ. The developers could be encouraged to set up SEZ in larger states. Larger states can accommodate large number of migration people from rural areas and different parts of India. Ecologically and environmentally sensitive states can concentrate on environmental zones, bio-zones and agricultural zones thereby the ecosystem might be maintained. So Factor endowment model is very much suitable for SEZ development in India. It can resolve so many unwanted problems related to SEZ.

Concluding Observations

In India, the major problem the SEZ developers are facing is land only. It is mainly due to over concentration of SEZs near urban and semi urban areas. The important reason for over concentration is infrastructural facilities available in urban areas. To avoid this type of problem what we really needed is establishment of world class infrastructural facilities like six or eight lane express highways connected with all the major ports, airports, state capitals, district and taluk head quarters in India. Similarly the train service also be extended to every nook and corner of the country. Travel time should be reduced to one fourth of present level. Uninterrupted power and drinking water supply should be ensured. If world class infrastructural facilities were available in rural areas automatically developers would move over to the interior India for establishing SEZs. It will reduce pressure on not only small states like Goa, Kerala and Delhi but also metro cities like Kolkatta, Mumbai and Chennai. World class infrastructural facilities are a must at present. Hence government has to increase its expenditure on infrastructural facilities from the current 4 per cent to 14 per cent of GDP. So that pressure on small states would be reduced and states like Goa can concentrate on tourism related industries. SEZs can be established in larger states. What we needed is an 'economic development' which includes each and every person of this country in sharing the benefits of prosperity. Definitely we could say that SEZs would fulfill this objective.

References

http://www.Sez/ in India, Ministry of Commerce and Industry, New Delhi.

http://www.Goa/ website.

Matahny Saldanha (2008), e-paper on "Why Goa does not need SEZs", *Business Line*, January 23.

Dominick Salvatore (1995), "The Hecksher-Ohlin Theory, International Economics", Fourth Edition, Schaum's Outline Series.

22

HR PRACTICES IN INDIAN BANKING SECTOR

Rajashree Vyas

Introduction

Indian banking sector is increasingly becoming one of the challenging sectors and the reasons for this are in plenty. The sector is undergoing a rapid transformation, with more and more global banks setting up offices in India or expanding their existing operations to cash in on India's growth story. The global aspirations of Indian banks are also rising with increasing globalization of Indian corporate. The first and foremost reason is the booming Indian economy. With a persistent challenge of maintaining a double digit growth figure the banking backbone needs to be strong enough and this is making the banking sector an interesting playground even for the private sector too.

A direct consequence of this forks out into a couple of facts:

- Firstly, the increase in the number of player in the market,
- Secondly, the increasing demand from the consumers,

- Thirdly, the maintaining a persistent service quality and there by an increasing market share and
- Fourthly, driving the employees in the banks towards aligning themselves to the changing strategies.

The crux of the matter lies in formulating an effective planning strategy by taking into consideration certain determining parameters like competitor behavior, regulatory laws of the land and customer needs that are going to affect the long-term objectives.

To achieve all these parameters, banks are today facing a tough challenge, the prime challenge being associated with the management of human resources. The fact that the way an organization should manage its manpower should be in tandem with their organization strategy is equally obvious and universal. However the obviousness of this fact is in no way certainly attainable in a dynamic and turbulent industry like banking.

Today banks are becoming increasingly inclined towards their technology upgradation. IT solutions are mushrooming in number in order to support the banking operation, especially the back end. There are ERP solutions, there are web-based and web-enabled solutions, and there are highly efficient dashboard systems in order to monitor the effectiveness of each and every process that is being carried on in the banks. But despite all these there lurks some pertinent questions like:

- What then exactly is the impact of technology on the human resources employed in banking?
- How should an HR Manager in a bank respond to this fast changing scenario?

Changing Competencies

The imperative changes taking place in the banking sector relate to the very basic or the fundamental way of banking. The driving forces behind these changes relate to the forces of competition, productivity and efficiency of operations, reduced operating margins, better asset/liability management, risk management, and increasing the number of touch points-anytime and anywhere banking. The major challenge lies in protecting the down sliding margins due to increase in competition. As a result, in order to protect their share of profit, ever bank in India are engaging them in this rat race of multiplying their volume of operation so as to attain individual economies of scale. In order to achieve this multiplication of operational volume the necessary conditions are:

- Increasing manpower
- Enhancing infrastructural capacity
- Switching to more technology oriented domain of operation.

But the point that is to be noted here is that, mere technology upgradation does not solve the purpose of enhancement of profitability. What lies as a more vital aspect is the lubrication of human intervention in the process. Technology acts as the backend for any successful venture, but what remains in the front end is the human being or the talent pool of the organization.

In a sector like banking which is wholly and solely driven by customer service and customer satisfaction, it is the integration of technology and manpower that gives the banks a competitive edge over others.

One of the best examples in this case is the Bank of China which was once awarded for following "best practice in HR" by China STAFF. BOC was chosen because of the bank's dedication to human resource management and development as acclaimed by the market. What was at the bottomline in case of BOC was the smooth gelling of technological upgradation coupled with human skill enhancement. It is a well-known fact that the technological know how of China was much ahead of India at a particular point of time. But mere implementation was not the key to success. BOC has transformed into a joint-stock enterprise, ahead of its market listing scheduled for early next year. Its human resource management has been the "most profound, complicated and arduous revolution" during its reform process as was stated by Wang Zhaowen, the spokesman of China STAFF.

Having said that the change is challenging, it is very important to lay focus on the changes that are impending in the industry or to be more specific it is vital to note the previous and the existing scenario so as to gauge the magnitude of the change that is essentially to be brought about as a key strategy for the survival of the organization who are playing in the current Indian Banking arena. So far as the employee competency is concerned the following changes are in the primary focus:

Old Competencies	*New Competencies*
Ability to operate in well defined and stable environment	Ability to operative in ill-defined and ever changing environment.
Capacity to deal with repetitive straight-forward and concrete work process	Capacity to deal with routine andabstract work process
Ability to operate in a supervised work environment	Ability to handle decisions and responsibilities
Isolated work	Group work, Interactive work
Ability to operative within narrow geographical and time horizons	System-wide understanding, ability to operative within expanding geographical and time horizons
Broad unspecified knowledge	Specialized knowledge
Procedural competencies	Customer assistance oriented competencies.

Source: Human Resource Management in Banks--Contemporary Issues by Dr. Jacob Mankidy.

The inference that can be drawn from the above mentioned gamut of changes in the industry is that there is a huge task laying ahead in the field of employee reorientation so as to match the changing strategies and a strong enough training module for this strategic alignment. The banking industry, fortunately, is known for a strong training regime though it was more of a ritualistic in nature. Today's situation no longer demands a straight-jacketed training module which takes into consideration the broader spectrum, but what is needed is a specific and focused training which should cater to each and every competency in order to map them with the operational requirement of the organization.

Organizational intervention becomes critical for such a focused and meticulous training module. A framework for a complete human resource development package which will be catering to a all-round employee development taking into consideration the organizational policies and principles, the strategic stance of the organization and on top of all the long term mission and vision of the same. All these will play a determining role because the core function of HR department is not only to facilitate the working of the organization but to take the front-seat in driving the organization towards its objectives. Current HR policies should not only have the operational aspect in focus, but also the financial aspect. The training department should stay focused on the total human capital of the banks and lay emphasis on the integration of human resource strategy with the business strategy.

Strategic Human Resource Management

HR practitioners across the globe have long argued about the fit or the gelling between business strategies and organizational characteristics for being the key determinant ón case of organizational performance. But in today's dynamic work culture coupled with ever increasing competition from every corner has made it a compulsory factor that the strategic entity of the organization be incorporated to the human resource domain.

The framework of strategic human resource management (HRM) provides guidance into both descriptive and prescriptive lines of questioning. Human Resource related activities till the recent past was more of an individualistic in nature taking into consideration the individuals and their performance. This micro approach towards HR policy was effective till there was little or no dynamism in the market and competition was almost negligible as compared to today's situation. It was more of a support system that HR used to serve in those days. But now it is time to look into HR from a macro perspective so as to help the organization emerge into a performance driven organization. If we look into the Indian banking sector, then the past and the present can be classified very strikingly into two categories–the High-Controlled workplace and the High-performance workplace with the following distinctions:

Practice	*High-Controlled workplace*	*High-performance workplace*
Compensation	Low base pay Individual incentive plans High differentials across organization	High base pay Group incentives Low differentials
Training	Low levels, depending on need	High levels, pro-active initiative
Recruitment	Depending on manpower need, less stress on screening.	Highly professional and minutely screened
Workplace management	Little employee involvement	High employee involvement
Job Design	Narrow job roles Steep hierarchy High level of monitoring	Broad job roles Flat Hierarchy Self-motivated work culture

Source: How Will Competition Change Human Resource Management in Retail Banking? A Strategic Perspective by Larry W. Hunter.

The above table reflects some phenomenal distinctions that are observed in case of the two types of organization get-up. The banking sector in India is fast moving towards becoming a high-performance based category and hence demands a change in the policy for all the determining factors like compensation, training, staffing, recruitment, workplace governance and work organization.

Compensation

In case of designing a compensation package, managers should try to find out the key performance indicators and relate the compensation with the employee performance in each of the KPIs. The focus should also be given on the parameters that should play ital role in case of the increments whatsoever made. A specific structure needs to be made if the organization decides to go for a differential pay structure. Employees should not only be given long-term benefits but also short term benefit options be provided to them. All these will lead to the quantification of employee compensation system and this will make human capital budgeting effective policy.

Training and Development

Training and development related planning also needs to be reframed as per the need of the hour. The generic approach of providing a over-view oriented training needs to be replaced by focused and meticulous training regime. Firstly there should be a proper method in order to identify the employees who are in need of training. Post identification of the employees to be trained the training module needs to be befittingly designed so as to fit the requirements of those who are trained, A proper need analysis is very essential. Another aspect of training is the monitoring of the performance of those employees who are trained. This will help the banks to analyze the effectiveness of the training program and also the employee talent factor.

Staffing

The number of employees needed for a particular branch also needs to be properly measured. This may depend on the size of the branch, the number or the volume of transaction happening per day, the total number of customers' catered to by the bank in a particular period of time. Implementation of statistical calculation method will be of great help in this case. All this will help in proper employee allocation so that there is neither over staffing nor under staffing. It is often found in the remote branches of man banks in India that there is a serious lacking of staffs where as in those branches which are in posh areas there is heavy excess of staff. A proper manpower allocation team needs to be developed to study all these factors and to arrive at an effective conclusion.

Recruitment

The role of a efficient recruitment team is in no way negligible in case of any organization. A strong recruitment policy not only provides the organization the right manpower at the right place but also helps an organization in several ways to economized it human capital investments. A proper recruitment policy initially determines the primary roles that they are looking for and then specific skill set requirement should be framed in order to rate the contending candidates. It is very true that if an employee becomes a square peg in a round hole then it is neither beneficial for the employee nor for the organization. Hence hiring the right employee for the right position is very critical.

Work Culture

While determining the work culture in the organization the first thing that needs to be understood is the hierarchy levels in the organization. In Indian Banks, especially in the government banks, it is very prominent that there is a steep hierarchy. This is in no way beneficial in today's organizational needs. A bunch of self motivated work force that is ready to deliver their best is the requirement of the day. And this requires a congenial work culture too. Employees should be given certain level of authority and managerial responsibility so as to develop their sense of belongingness for the organization and to deliver their responsibility in a diligent manner.

Concluding Observations

To conclude, it can be stated that the banking sector in India is floundering with opportunities for becoming a happening industry in itself. This is coupled with the economic reforms and the growth of the country. It is also inevitable that with out a string banking backbone no economy can sustain its growth. However to achieve all this the banking sector needs to undergo a large phase of reform so far as its policies and procedures are concerned. In this paper only the HR related issues are stressed on, but it is very obvious that there are other areas of improvement too. From product planning to technological implementation every where there are specific areas where there needs some stress so as to fight the impending competition from across the globe and emerge as a successful industry.

23

"KANO MODEL APPLIED IN BANKS TO FIND OUT CUSTOMER SATISFACTION"

JEENA KURUVILLA

Introduction

After globalization, the intensified competition and rapid changes in the socio-economic and technological environment had a major impact on the India economic, financial and business environment. With in this environment it is clear that banking institutions face new challenges and increasing risks, as well as increasing business potentials. The recent experience shows that achieving a sustainable development of the banking system is not of interest to the banking institutions themselves, but it is also directly related to the development of the whole business and economic environment, both at regional and national level.

The variety of new banking products that is constantly being developed to accommodate the increased customer needs (firms, organizations, individuals etc) provides a clear indication of the changes that the banking industry has undergone during the last many years. All the banks strive hard to improve upon their operations, effectiveness and performance for the satisfaction of the customers. It can be in terms of accessibility by opening up more and more branches, customer care centers for proper customer relationship management, better ambience and friendly staff for attracting and retaining customers, online banking and ATM facility for convenience etc.

Quality is sought by all organizations, especially in the service sector. This is of main interest, particularly in the banking sector. Empirical evidence has shown that service quality can be seen as one of the main determinants of customer satisfaction, which in turn may influence purchase intentions. Quality has been defined as superiority or excellence, or as the customer's overall impressions of the relative inferiority/superiority of the organization and its services.

Banks can access the customer perception about the varies services and marketing strategy among different customer segment and how much importance needed to be given to each attribute, by using the Kano Model of Customer Satisfaction.

Kano Model of Customer Satisfaction

The Kano Model of Customer (Consumer) Satisfaction classifies product attributes based on how they are perceived by customers and their effect on customer satisfaction. These classifications are useful for guiding design decisions in that they indicate when good is good enough, and when more is better. This model helps to define and prioritize customer needs.

A very astute student of Dr. Ishikawa, Dr. Noriaki Kano, developed this interesting model to address the various ways in which Six Sigma practitioners can prioritize customer needs. This became particularly important when trying to rank the customer's wants and desires in a logical fashion.

Project activities in which the Kano Model is useful:

- Identifying customer needs
- Determining functional requirements

- Concept development
- Analysing competitive products

The Kano Model of Customer satisfaction (Figure 1) divides product/service attributes into three categories: threshold, performance, and excitement. A competitive product meets basic attributes, maximises performances attributes, and includes as many "excitement" attributes as possible at a cost the market can bear.

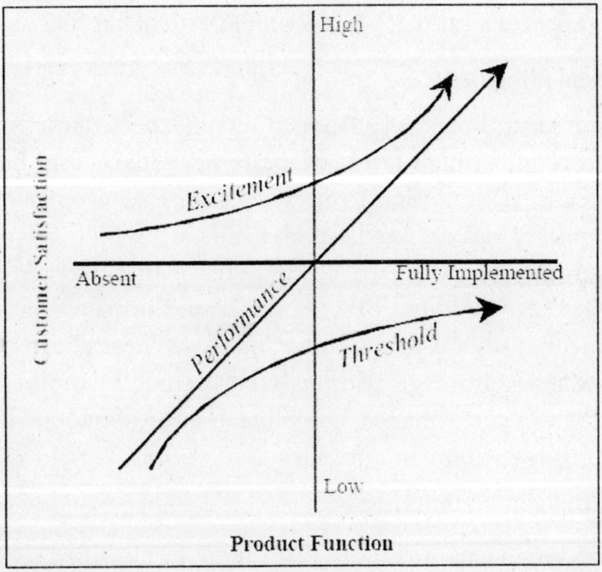

Threshold Attributes

Threshold (or basic) attributes are the expected attributes or "musts" of a product, and do not provide an opportunity for product differentiation. Increasing the performance of these attributes provides diminishing returns in terms of customer satisfaction; however the absence or poor performance of these attributes results in extreme customer dissatisfaction. An example of a threshold attribute in banks is confidentiality.

Performance Attributes

Performance attributes are those for which more is generally better, and will improve customer satisfaction. Conversely, an absent or weak performance attribute reduces customer satisfaction. Of the needs customers verbalise, most will fall into the category of performance attributes. These attributes will form the weighted needs against which product concepts will be evaluated. The price for which customer is willing to pay for a product is closely tied to performance attributes. For example, customers would be willing to pay more for a car that provides them with better fuel economy.

Excitement Attributes

Excitement attributes are unspoken and unexpected by customers but can result in high levels of customer satisfaction, however their absence does not lead to dissatisfaction. Excitement attributes often satisfy latent needs–real needs of which customers are currently unaware. In a competitive marketplace where manufacturers' products provide similar performance, providing excitement attributes that address "unknown needs" can provide a competitive advantage. Although they have followed the typical evolution to a performance then a threshold attribute, cup holders were initially excitement attributes.

Other Attributes

Products often have attributes that cannot be classified according to the Kano Model. These attributes are often of little or no consequence to the customer, and do not factor into consumer decisions. An example of this type of attribute is the cheque number which is of no use to the customer but useful for other banks when the transaction actually takes place.

The first step is to identify the quality characteristics that are typically fuzzy, vague and nebulous. These are referred to as the voice of the customer (VOC). Once the voice of the customer is understood, we can attempt to translate it into quantitative terms known as critical to quality (CTQ) characteristics.

In the case of banks some of the quality characteristics or VOC that have been identified which can lead to customer satisfaction, dissatisfaction, neither satisfied nor dissatisfied (neutral) or delight are Personalized products, Personal Attention, Ambience of the bank, Interest difference, Friendly staff, Banks' reputation, Brand Name, Accessibility and many more.

These are certain attributes identified which are important to the customer in workable terms. After identifying VOC ,the second step is to apply it to the Kano model. Always keeping the customer in mind, and apply the concepts outlined in the Kano Model.

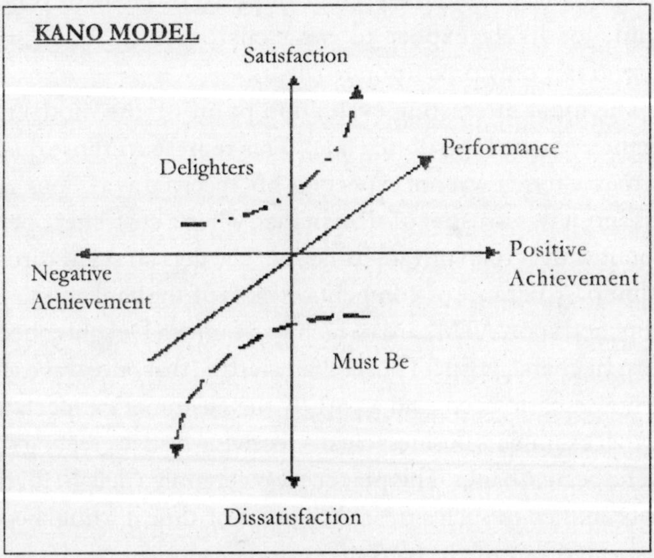

This model is broken down into an (x, y) graph, where the x-axis represents how good the banks are at achieving the customer's outcome(s), or CTQ's. The y-axis records the customer's level of satisfaction the customer should have, as a result of our level of achievement.

The dashed line represents the Must Be's. That is, whatever the quality characteristic is, it must be present, such that if it is not, the customer will go elsewhere! The customer does not care if the product is wrapped in 24-carat gold, only that it is present and is functionally doing what it was designed to do. An example of this would be a client who enters the bank expects immediate service, with adequate staff , adequate seating facility, parking facility etc. These items are not called out for by the customer, but would definitely cause them to go elsewhere if any of these "characteristics" were not present.

The solid line represents the Performance. This line reflects the voice of the customer. The better a bank meeting these needs, the happier the customer is. It is here where the trade-offs take place. Someone wanting vast range of personalized bank products would not likely expect to be a customer of bank which concentrates only on corporate clients.

The most interesting evaluation point of the model is the Delighter (dashed and dotted line). This represents those qualities that the customer was not expecting, but received as a bonus. A few years ago, it was a matter of delight that, when a customer opens an account with certain private banks, he/she gets an ATM card also. As time past, because of competition most of the banks availed this facility, and soon ATM cards which was earlier a Delighter became a Must Be characteristic. Thus, a characteristic that once was exciting was now a basic need, and a part of the customer's expectations. Another example is business clients receiving festive greetings from their respective banks. This practice was certainly a delight for those clients entitled to such a treat. At a point of time it would become an expected part of the banker's customer service.

Once the critical to quality characteristics have been prioritized, the last step involves an analysis of evaluating or assessing just how well a bank can satisfy each of Dr. Noriaki Kano's classifications. By applying this model one can investigate the quality of service, based on the customers' perception.

Application of the Kano Model Analysis

The first thing is to identify a list of qualities the client would be interested in. This list can be formulated by listening to complaints, handing out surveys, holding focus groups and conducting interviews. The information is the voice of the customer. In the case of banks the voice of the customer when related with the Kano customer satisfaction model can be a relatively simple approach to applying the Kano Model Analysis is to ask customers two simple questions for each attribute:

Characteristic	*High Income/Business client*	*Medium Income*
Confidentiality	Must be	Must be
Personal Attention	Must be	Performance
Ambience	Must be	Performance
Rate of interest	Performance	Performance
Friendly staff	Must be	Delighter
Transaction time	Performance	Performance
Range of products	Performance	Delighter
Accessibility	Performance	Performance
Brand Name	Performance	Performance
Personalized Greetings	Delighter	Delighter
Core banking facility	Must be	Performance
Bank's reputation	Must be	Performance
Service cost	Performance	Must be
Investment options	Delighter	Performance
Parking facility	Must be	Performance
Locker Facility	Delighter	Must be

1. Rate your satisfaction if the service has this attribute?; and
2. Rate your satisfaction if the product/service did not have this attribute?

Customers should be asked to answer with one of the following responses:

(A) Satisfied;

(B) Neutral (Its normally that way);

(C) Dissatisfied;

(D) Don't care.

- Basic attributes generally receive the "Neutral" response to Question 1 and the"Dissatisfied" response to Question 2. Exclusion of these attributes in the product has the potential to severely impact the success of the product in the marketplace.
- Eliminate or include performance or excitement attributes that their presence or absence respectively lead to customer dissatisfaction. This often requires a trade-off analysis against cost. As Customers frequently rate most attributes or functionality as important, asking the question "How much extra would you be willing to pay for this attribute or more of this attribute?" will aid in trade-off decisions, especially for performance attributes. Prioritisation matrices can be useful in determining which excitement attributes would provide the greatest returns on Customer satisfaction.
- Consideration should be given to attributes receiving a "Don't care" response as they will not increase customer satisfaction nor motivate the customer to pay an increased price for the product. However, do not immediately dismiss these attributes if they play a critical role to the product functionality or are necessary for other reasons than to satisfy the customer.

The information obtained from the Kano Model Analysis, specifically regarding performance and excitement attributes, provides valuable input for the Quality Function Deployment process. With this attributes listed, the bank can assess how strong or weak are they in trying to satisfy those quality characteristics identified in the above table. The results for a particular bank may be as follows:

The conclusions from this effort can be as summarized by looking at the rows that have a characteristic in the Must Be category. With respect to the business client, the important factors or thresholds are Confidentiality, Personal Attention, Ambience,

Characteristic	*High Income/ Business client*	*Medium Income*	*How good is the bank*
Confidentiality	Must be	Must be	Satisfactory
Personal Attention	Must be	Performance	Weak
Ambience	Must be	Performance	Weak
Rate of interest	Performance	Performance	Satisfactory
Friendly staff	Must be	Delighter	Satisfactory
Transaction time	Performance	Performance	Weak
Range of products	Performance	Delighter	Satisfactory
Accessibility	Performance	Performance	Weak
Brand Name	Performance	Performance	Satisfactory
Personalized Greetings	Delighter	Delighter	Weak
Core banking facility	Must be	Performance	Weak
Bank's reputation	Must be	Performance	Satisfactory
Service cost	Performance	Must be	Satisfactory
Investment options	Delighter	Performance	Weak
Parking facility	Must be	Performance	Satisfactory
Locker Facility	Delighter	Must be	Weak

Friendly staff, Core banking facility, Banks reputation, Parking facility . The Mediocre customer, on the hand, have must be's that included Confidentiality, Service cost, Locker facility.

Of these characteristics, the bank can understand that they are weak in Personal attention, Ambience, Transaction time, Accessibility, Personalized greeting, Core banking facility, Investment options and locker facility.

This exercise allows the bank to better address the needs of the customer, based on their critical to quality characteristics. Now the work begins to minimize the gap of where the bank is with where the bank wants to be.

References

Ullman, David G. (1997), "The Mechanical Design Process", McGraw-Hill, Inc., U.S.A., pp. 105-108, ISBN 0-07-065756-4.

Jacobs, Randy (1999), Evaluating Satisfaction with Media Products and Services: An Attribute Based Approach, European Media Management Review, Winter.

http://www.tukkk.fi/mediagroup/emmr/Previous%20Issues/Satisfaction.htm

Kano, N., N. Seraku, F. Takahashi and S. Tsuji (1984), "Attractive Quality and Must-be Quality", Hinshitsu, *The Journal of the Japanese Society for Quality Control*, April , pp. 39-48.

Randy Jacobs (1999), Evaluating Customer Satisfasction with Media Products and Services, European Media Management Review, Winter.

Vonin and Taylor (1992), vavra *et al.,* 1995, 1997.

Kurt Matzier (2004), Matthias Fuchs and Astrid Schubert, Total Quality Management & Business Excellence, November-December.

24

A STUDY ON THE IMPACT OF ORGANIZATIONAL LEADERSHIP AND CLIMATE ON EFFECTIVENESS

MURALE V.

Theoretical Background

The core objective of the study is to frame a structural equation to prove the relation ship between organizational leadership ,climatic variables and the factors affecting effectiveness such as commitment and satisfaction. Secondly it will facilitate research on the concept of organisational climate by considering behavioral and attitudinal dimensions associated with it Further it will help the practicing managers to identify any weakness if present in the environment and enables them to take corrective action as it has been observed that human performance exceeds the expectation when right changes are incorporated in the work environment.

Organisational climate can be defined as an attribute of the organization ,composed of behaviours ,attitudes and feeling which are characteristic of the organization(Ekvall,1983). The popularity of the term climate has been discussed a lot since the 1960s. It is therefore not surprising that numerous researches and various studies underscores the importance people seen in it ,that led to a now relatively well known and established subject. The term organisational climate refers to the human environment within which employees' do their work. It may refer to the environment within a department, major company unit such as branch, plant or an entire organization Benjamin and Schneider defines "organisational climate as a relatively enduring quality of the internal environment experienced by its members, which can influence their behaviour and can be described in terms of particular set of characteristics of the organization."

A lot number of definitions and concepts about climate have been framed over years " Climate can be defined as an attribute of the organization, composed of behaviors attitudes and feelings which are the characteristics of the organization. According to Ekvall " the climate has originated, evolved and continues to develop in the on going interactions between individuals and organisational settings."(Ekval, 1985). Payne (1971) has described "climate as a molar concept, reflecting the content and strength of the prevalent members of social system, which can be operationally measured through the perception of system members or observational and other objective means". Climate itself is a multidimensional concept (Campbell *et al;* 1970) and incorporates dimensions about interpersonal process and relationships and about how the tasks of the organization are achieved. Glick (1985) defines climate as "a generic term for a broad class of organisational for a broad class of rather psychological variables that describe context for individual's actions. Pitchard and Karos (1973) say that climate is the result of behaviour and policies of members of the organization, especially top management". Payne & Pugh (1976) presented a model of the major influences on organisational climate. The model is based on the idea that the structural variable largely determine the climate, they found two variables that exhibited more consistent correlation with climate, that is decentralization and size of the organization. Purtchard and Karasack (1976) on the other hand seem to regard "values as a determinant of climate." Two organizations having widely diverge value orientation would be expected to have markedly different organisational climate. "Climate can be defined as the organizational phenomena through which leadership works "(Ekvall 11993),This definition underscores the strong influence of leadership upon organizational climate that was confirmed in numerous research strudies carried out in various organizations throughout the world.Research in this area also proved that different leadership styles cause different climate in working groups.leaders can neither male or break organisations by building up a good emotional climate or spoil it by auto cratic style of functioning.

The contemporary researchers in the field of leadership hold the opinion that leaders primary task is to create a positive organizational climate. However it should be kept in mind that climate can also influence leadership style since it is a bi directional relationship The terms organisational climate and organisational culture are often mixed up and it is worth presenting the differences briefly.

Culture can be defined as shared assumptions, beliefs and norms of a group, in the context of an organization and its members. Culture has a powerful influence on the way people live and act; it defines what is 'normal ' and what sanctions follow behavior that is not"normal". It can be said that culture is felt in the implicit rules and expectations of behaviour in an organizations, even though the rules are not formally written knowing what is expected of them. Organisational culture and differentiate the organization from others. Schein (1990) defines culture as follows:

"Culture is

- A pattern of basic assumptions
- Invented, discovered, or developed by given group
- As it learns to cope with its problems of external adaptation and internal integration.

- That has worked well enough to be considered valid and therefore
- Is to be taught to new members as the correct way to perceive, think and feel in relation to those problems" (Schein, 1990).

Culture is the deep structure of an organization, which is rooted in the values, beliefs and assumptions held by organisational members and it has a long term perspective, in contrast climate is often considered as relatively temporary, subject to direct control and largely limited to those aspects of social environment that are knowingly perceived by organisational members (Dension, 1996). Climate is characterized by work requirements, feelings and interpersonal relationships.

As mentioned earlier organisational culture is concerned with the nature of beliefs and expectations about organisational characteristics as being in accordance with their expectations. The stronger the culture is the more it influences the climate. Nevertheless, the borders between cultures are flattening, as both are dependent on each other In this study the researcher has gone for the convenience sampling, as it is more relevant to the study as it was conducted in a highly homogeneous universe.

Organisational effectiveness can be defined as the condition of an organization in which specific derived ends are attained. It has been observed that climate can influence motivation, performance and job satisfaction. The climate does that by creating expectancies, about what consequences will follow from different actions, on the basis of their perception of the organizations climate, as these perceptions tend to lead to motivation. Many behavioural scientists are of the opinion that organisational climate contributes to the overall health and self-renewing capabilities of dyads, team and there by to the entire organization.

The members of the organization and their personalities have a central influence on climate ,each organisationa l members notices it can be describe it in of his or her own experiences and perceptions, Individuals interpret their perceptions and react according to it.

Different climates attract and motivate different kinds of employees by subtly or blatantly defining the "rights and wrongs" and "do's and don'ts" for each organisational member. If people perceive that certainkinds of behaviour will be rewarded, they will be motivated to engage in thosebehaviours. Similarly, if there is a feeling that other behaviours are punished("that's not done around here"), these will be avoided Friedlander and Marguiles (1969) define climate as a dyanamic phenomenon ,which may release, channel, facilitate or constrain the organisation's technical and human resources. It can be viewed as a moderating vaiable between the organisations input like capital ,resources equipment and products and the out comes like profit ,quality, satisfaction and productivity (Ekvall, 1983). Through influencing the in between lying organisational and psychological process.

Ekvall, Arvonen & Wolden (1983) studied the organisational climate in two divisions of a large Swedish Corporation. One division was regarded by management as having been very innovative and successful over the last few years, where the other was thought to have stagnated and to be unable to adapt to changing environment conditions. The climate measures were the average values of the descriptions made by the stagnating ones on the climate dimensions like challenge, support for ideas, freedom and dynamic workforce.

The successful division had significantly higher average values than the stagnating one on the climatic dimensions.

Hellreigal and Slocom (1974) stated that several studies clearly indicated the existence of a relation between climate and job satisfaction. They cited two studies which is based on are analysis at individual level and organisational level respectively. They also claimed to have found many studies demonstrating significant relations between climate and performance, but they also pointed out that these relation are neither as easy to interpret nor as convincing as those referring to job satisfaction.

Payne & Mansfield (1973) studied climate in 14 different organizations, they found climate varied between hierarchical levels in 15 of 20 climate dimensions measured. People at higher level described the climate as less authoritarian, friendlier, more stimulating and more likely to promote innovation than people in lower ranks.

Joyce and Slocum (1984) introduced the concept known as collective climate, by which they meant climatic perception that are common to a group in an organization regardless of whether or not the people concerned form unit in any formal organisational senses. Instead of aggregating the climate descriptions of individuals belonging to same unit or functions they started from the other end, from the climate description themselves. Individuals description where it is similar come to constitute a "collective climate". They claimed that collective climate is related to both work performance and job satisfaction.

Argyres (1958), Forehand and Gilmer (1964) emphasized that to characterize employee perception of the organization, climate has been a central concept in organisational research.

Climate has been studied with quantitative methods like questionnaires. In Ekvalls (1986) opinion members of an organization are reliable reporters of the existing climate since they observe it in their daily processes. According to Anderson& West (1989) climate should be studied in proximal work group, which are defined as the permanent or semi-permanent teams in which individuals interact to perform their tasks. Taken together the climatic dimensions have a special relationship with the level of creativity and innovation inside an organization.

Stern (1970), Pace (1968) and Gorman and Malloy (1972) all identified major climatic factors, each of which concerned fostering people development and encouraging the growth and application of new ideas and methods. Studies by Friedlander Margulies (1969) Kaczka and Kirka (1968), Schneider (1972), Cowsey (1973) and Hall & Lawler (1969) clearly indicate that organisational climate is related to job satisfaction in terms of interpersonal relations, group cohesiveness and task involvement and the like. Sea shore and Yutchman (1967) conclude "the highest level of organisational effectiveness is reached when the organization maximizes its resource procurement.

Optimum is the point beyond which an organization endangers itself because of repletion of its resource producing the environment or the resources or because of this stimulation of countervailing forces within that environment". KhandWalla and Jain (1984) emphasized the job satisfaction as an important indicator of effectiveness. Sutaria and Padaki (1976) examined the job satisfaction of supervisors in bureaucratic, modern and informal organizations .It was found that motivating factors emerged as source of satisfaction and hygiene factors in all three types of organizations. Padaki (1983) found that internally individuals were more satisfied with meaningfulness of work and responsibility. Schein (1970) considered organisational commitment as criterion of effectiveness and it is influenced by personal characteristics, job characteristics and work experience. Balajee (1988) had reported, "Organisational commitment accompanied by satisfaction explains that it is essential for the survival and effectiveness of large work organizations. The fundamental responsibility of management is to create a state of health necessary to carryon its work". Kanungo (1977) defined job involvement as a descriptive belief about the individual's present job. It is a generalized cognitive state of psychological identification with the present job. Involvement is related to three classes of variables, namely personal characteristics like age, sex and education etc, and situational characteristics of the job such as variety of job, autonomy and work outcome like satisfaction and performance on the job.

Child (1974)examined the relationship between organizational structure and organizational performance and found that companies having a high performance less bureaucratic. Stress (1975)reported that adaptability or flexibility was considered asa criterion applied in various models of effectiveness. Fosala and

La Mastro (1990) found that perceived organisational support was positively related to job performance.

The above given review of literature torch light into the nature and extent of relationship existing between organisational climate and organisational effectiveness as a separate variable as total entity of features. This can be explained more on the basis of Model Proposed by Fred Canon (2000) on the basis of his studies.

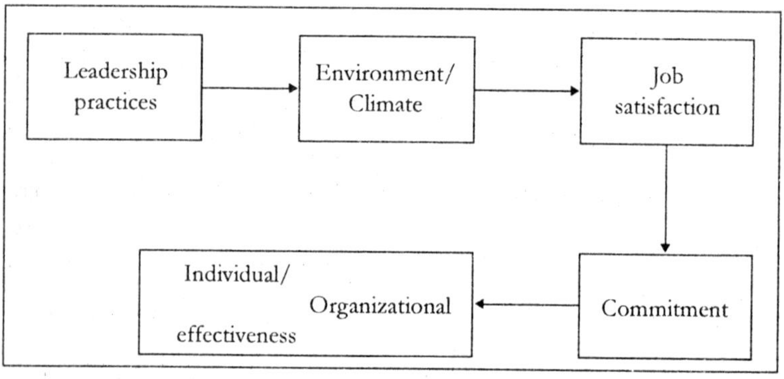

Conceptual Framework for Organizational Framework and Effectiveness

The Model can be explained on the basis of following variables associated with it.

Leadership: This is the Most influencing factor, changes in leadership lead directly to changes in climate ,since it affects the relationship between individuals and enterprise, the attitude of the leaders on followers ,and the style of people who join the organization in senior management position can influence the climate.

The Climate Dimensions: The organisational climate measurement serves as the guidelines for dealing with peoplele ,It gives a clear picture about individuals perception of organisational properties in identifying organisational climate, the six factors considered for measuring climate taken are:

- *Clarity:* The clarity of the individuals about his roles and responsibilities in the organisation.

- *Organisation structure:* The perception about organisational constraints, rules regulations etc.
- *Responsibility:* The degree to which members are able to act independently. The higher the level of autonomy the higher will be the initiative taken by an individual.
- *Standards*: This Indicate the bench mark that the organisation has set for improving its efficiency. The perceptions of degree of challenge and risk in the work situation.
- *Recognition*: The feelings related to being confident of adequate and appropriate recognition.
- *Support*: The emotional security and trust in the organisation, when support for ideas is high employees to each other and encourage others.

The Job satisfaction, job involvement commitment and strategy are considered while measuring the effectiveness elements.

Job Satisfaction: job satisfaction is a set of favourable or unfavourable feelings with which employees views their jobs, more specifically the nature of jobs they do,the quality of supervision they receive ,promotional avenues. Many studies have cited the influence of job satisfaction in employee commitment and performance.

Job involvement: job involvement indicates the extent of people's identification with or ego investment in the job Commitment: The employees' delight in being associated with the present organisation. The involvement that he displays in his job.

Strategy and vision: The strategies are the plans to achieve the goals and the vision are means to images about the future.

The Methodology of the Study

The study was conducted ina major Financial service vertical of a leading firm in India located at Mumbai-the financial hub of India.

Random sampling is applied for data collection. A structured schedule was used for collecting the information from the employees. Likert scale is used in measuring the attitude of the employees. A well-structured questionnaire was deployed for obtaining information about climate. To measure organisational effectiveness a set of questions were designed by the researcher. A sample of 168 employees was selected for the study and data was collected in june 2007 by interviewers for a period of almost a month. In order to reduce biases interviewers used stratifying interviews across the different layer of employees in the organisation.

After collecting data from the field data were coded and analysed by using SPSS software. Factor analysis was carried out to identify factors that are related with the construct . The tools used for the study includes eighted Average, simple percentage. The Technique of Partial Least square Method was used for framing the structural equation.

The study aims at framing a structural equation model which focus on proving relationship impact of climate on effectiveness on the basis of following Hypothesis:

H1: Leadership practices can have a positive influence on organisational climate.

H2: Organisational climate prevailing organisation has a positive influence on job satisfaction.

H3: The sense of job satisfaction has a positive influence on commitment.

Leadership Practices: The leader of a work group has apowerful influence on the expectations of itsmembers.The dimensions related with ledarship practices gives an asseeement of leadership style followed in the organisation and its strength and weakness:The influence of leadership on employees can be measured from the respect which the employees possess towards the top management, The trust I which employees having towards present management style.

Table 1

Leadership Practices	*Score on five pint scale*
Respect for current management team	3.65
Trust in management style	3.45
Respect given for individuals by managers	3.51

The scores indicate that the employees have a considerable amount of respect towards management team. The management teams style of functioning has a positive influence on the employees. Clarity Scores on this dimension reflect employees' sense of being well organised and of having a clear definition of their roles and responsibilities. Score is high when people feel that everyone's role is well defined. It is low when there isconfusion over who has decision-making authority

Table 2

Clarity of role	*Score on five point scale*
Goals of your organisations are clearly communicated	3.58
Clarity of performance criteria and work assignments	3.6

The score Indicates that the employees are informed about their role by the top management team. Organisational Structure, Systems and Procedures. include the formal organisational structure, the design of tasks and jobs, flow of information, and perceptions of control Mechanisms.

Table 3

Organisational structure, system and procedure	*Score on five point scale*
Flexible system of organisational structure	3.68
Authority and responsibility were clearly explained,	3.75
Efficiency of Communication system	3.9
Effectiveness of Monitoring Mechanism	4

The score Indicates that the organisation structure is flexible, conducive of managing situations, and has established standard procedure to monitor performance. Standards Scores on this dimensions measure the feeling of pressure to improve performance and the degree of pride employees take in doing a good job. High scores mean people are always looking for ways to improve performance. Low scores reflect lower performance standards.

Table 4

Standards	*Score on five point scale*
Expertise is required in delivering your responsibilities	3.82
Refresher training is required to perform	3.76
Standards are challenging and require efforts	3.91
Organisation focus on effective training and development of executives	3.83

The scores Indicate the organisations focus on efforts that are aimed continually improving the performance. Responsibility Scores on this dimension reflect the feeling employees have of "being their own boss" and of not having to constantly check decisions with others. High responsibility scores signify that employees are encouraged to solve problems on their own. Low responsibility scores indicate that risk taking and the testing of new approaches tend to be discouraged.

Table 5

Responsibility	*Score on a five point scale*
New Initiatives and good decisions are highly encouraged	3.86
Superiors assigns you with responsibilities	3.82

The score indicates that the employees are assigned with responsibilities to an extent and encouragement is given for employees to make decisions on their own,This implies that organisation is decentralised to a greater degree.This inculcates breeding of new ideaand innovation. Recognition Scores on this dimension indicate the feeling of being rewarded for a job well done. This is a measure of the emphasis placed on reward versus criticism. High-recognition climates are characterised by an appropriate balance of reward and criticism. Lower scores on recognition mean that good work is inconsistently rewarded.

Table 6

Recognition and rewards	*Score*
Management rewards excellent performance	3.8
Increments promotions and other rewards based on performance	3.89
Boss often appreciates your work	3.77

The score indicates that the employees are motivated since theya are rewarded and recognised for their efforts and performance. This will increase the motivation level of individuals and team spirit

Support Scores on this dimension reflect the feeling of trust and mutual support that prevail in the organisation. Support is high when employees feel they are part of a well-functioning team and they sense they can get help when they need it. It is low when employees feel isolated and alone.

Table 7

Support	*Score on a five point scale*
Friendly atmosphere and teamspirit prevails in the organisation	3.84
Fellow workers can respect your feelingsand are quite helpful	3.8
You can trust your friends and team members	3.76
You are encouraged to speak your mind even if it means disagreeing with superiors	3.89

The score indicate an agreeable level of trust and morale among team members in the organisation.A team having high level of morale will be delivering a high quality performance

The Effectiveness Factors

Job satisfaction: Job satisfaction is the amount of pleasure or contentment associated with the job.

Table 8

Job satisfaction	*Score on a five point scale*
Rate the level of satisfaction with regard to following:	
Compensation package	3.84
Career development	4.01
Job profile	3.89
Manager/supervisor	3.9

The score Indicates a moderately agreeable level of satisfaction among the employeesThe satisfied employees will be having high level of job involvement.

Job involvement: Job involved people spend more time on job and turn out better performance, Challenging jobs have skill variety influence employees to get involved with job.

Table 9

Job Involvement	*Score on five point scale*
The level of free time spent on job related activities	3.83
Stay back after office hours to complete the job	3.71
Feels miserable when you have less job	3.93
Job related thoughts dominates me on vacation	3.81

The Job involvement is considered to be a major factor affecting organisational effectiveness.The score indicates an agreeable level of effectiveness. The high level of involvement will result in a strong commitment towards the organisation and job.

Commitment: Scores on this dimension measure employees' sense of pride in belonging to the organisation and their degree of commitment to the organisation's goals. High commitment scores indicate that employees' have a strong sense of personal loyalty to the organisation and commitment to achieving goals. Low commitment scores mean employees feel apathetic towards the organisation and its goals.

Table 10

Commitment	*Score on a five point scale*
Organisation really inspires you to excel	3.88
You are really proud of your organisation	3.84
You are willing to put in a great deal of effort to help you organisation succeed	3.9
The extra amount of time that you spend on accomplishing tasks other than assigned to you	3.77
You are extremely glad that you choose this organisation over others	3.92
You really care about the fate of your organisation	4.06
You feel that you are an integral part of your organisation	3.94

The score indicates a high level of commitment. The organisational commitment is considered as a major factor influencing organisational effectiveness by all the behavioural scientist wh had conducted studies on climate.

Commuication: an organisation's overall commu can have a distinctive impact on the climates of its work units. organisation's strategy can send clear signals to employees about what is expected from them. The study reflects a moderately high commitment scores as result of a clear strategy and the efficiency to clearly communicate the business focus and priorities.

Table 11

	Correlation of Latent Variables			
Construct	*Leadersh*	*Climate*	*Jobsatis*	*commitmt*
Leadersh	1.000			
Climate	0.444	1.000		
Jobsatis	0.341	0.692	1.000	
commitmt	0.301	0.713	0.802	1.000

The impact of climate on effectiveness can be proved using a structural equation.The reliability of the constructs were examined through confirmatory factor analysis and by calculating Cronbach's alpha coefficient. The following Table shows the results of the composite reliability obtained through confirmatory factor analysis and by calculating Crobach alpha (Cronbach 1951) values.

Table 12

Reliability and AVE

Construct	*Composite Reliability*	*AVE*	*Cronbach Alpha*
Leadersh	0.827934	0.546350	0.726489
Climate	0.893417	0.583786	0.855897
Jobsatis	0.849725	0.532786	0.775872
commitmt	0.900700	0.532445	0.873780

The table indicates that alpha value is higher than. 7 and the composite reliability score s are all higher than. 6 the measurement model need not have change the measurement mode. However studies in tids area says that composite reliability is a stronger measure for reliability than alpha value, as the alpha values depends heavily on number of scale items, further composite reliability scores are made after considering measurement errors, taking all this into account the reliability of the scales are fool proof. The structural equation modeling was employed by deploying partial least square method using Visual PLS package, resampling was done using boot strapping mechanism was applied to test the model. The coefficients of the path analysis can be seen in the following table.

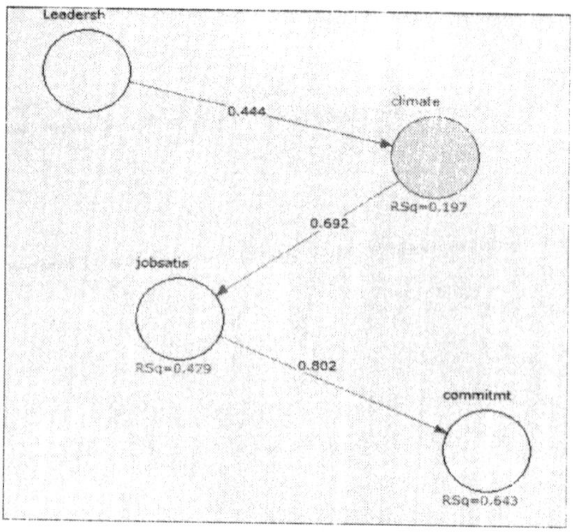

The Path Analysis

Table 13

Structural Models - Bootstrap (n=500)	*Path Co-efficient*
Leadersh - > climate	0.4440
climate - > jobsatis	0.6920
Jobsatis -> commitmt	0.8020

The path coefficients between cognitive- affective loyalty, affective-conative loyalty, and conative- action loyalty are positive in each case and statistically significant at the .01 level. Hence, all the hypothesized relationships in the model were supported by the findings.

Concluding Observations

This study provided empirical evidence for the development of a model which proves relationship between climate and effectiveness. The operational environment of the 21st Century will place tremendous stress upon future units and their leaders. Whether we end up with the current conceptualization of the FCS, a flattened organizational structure, and new operational concepts regarding units of action" or not is, to a large degree, irrelevant. Good leaders and their ability to get the best from their units will remain the key combat multiplier. The study shows impact of influence that leadership has on culture, and climate and the impact of the culture and climate on organizational effectiveness. To have a winning edge the organizations should be focused on determining how best to select and train leaders capable of creating a supportive climate. Now is the time to start seriously addressing these findings... to move beyond survey results and get to the work of solving these issues. Some of these changes can be implemented easily, most will require a concerted effort by leaders at all levels. All center around selecting and then training leaders to develop and sustain supportive command climates within their organization.

References

Anderson, N.R., West, M.A. (1989), "Measuring Climate for Work Group Innovation: Development and Validation of the Team Climate Inventory", *Journal of Organizational Behaviour*, 19, 235-258.

Arnold, J., Cooper, C.L., Robertson, J.T. (1998), "Work Psychology", Harlow: Financia Times, Bass, B.M. (1998), Transformational Leadership: Industrial, Military and Educational Impact. Mahwah, New York: Lawrence Erlbaum Associates.

Block, L. (2003), "The Leadership-culture Connection: An Exploratory Investigation", *Leadership and Organizational Development, Journal*, 24, 318-334.

Buono, A.F., Bowditch, J.L. (1989), "The Human Side of Mergers and Acquisitions", San Francisco: Jossey-Bass Publishers.

Denison, D.R. (1996), "What is the difference between Organizational Culture and Organizational Climate? A Native's Point of View on a Decade of Paradigm Wars", *Academy of Management Review*, 21, 619-654.

Ekvall, G. (1983), "Climate, Structure and Innovativeness of Organizations", The Swedish Council for Management and Organizational Behaviour. Stockholm: FArådet.

Ekvall, G. (1983), "Creative Organizational Climate: Construction and Validation of a measuring instrument", The Swedish Council for Management and Organizational Behaviour.Stockholm: FArådet.

Ekvall, G. (1985), "Organizational Climate: A Review of Theory and Research", The Swedish Council for Management and Organizational Behaviour. Stockholm: FArådet 35.

Ekvall, G., Arvonen, J. (1989), "Change Centred Leadership: An Addition to the Two Dimensional Model", The Swedish Council for Management and Organizational Behaviour.

Stockholm: FArådetFriedlander, F., Margulies, N. (1969), " Multiple Impacts of Organizational Climate and Individual Value System upon Job Satisfaction. *Personnel Psychology*, 22, 171-183.

Maslow, A. (1970), "Motivation and Personality", New York: Harper and Row

Schein, E. (1990), "Organizational Culture", *American Psychologist*, 45, 109-119.

Schneider, B. (1987), "The People Make the Place", *Personnel Psychology*, 40, 437-454.

25

RBI's MONETARY POLICY AND STOCK MARKET PERFORMANCE

K. Sreenivas

Besides, Union Budget, the RBI's monetary and credit policy pursues economic growth with price stability which refers to inflation control. Credit policy aims at credit delivery system to Industry and Agricultural development. The flow of credit to these sectors depends on cost of credit and availability of adequate funds. The factors like interest rate, margin money requirement, resources position, purpose of utilization of credit , general economic conditions etc., affect the credit delivery system. Declared semi-annually, the monetary policy takes stock of the economy's liquidity and inflationary conditions and employs the necessary tools to revive it. Monetary policy can be summarized as the central bank's actions to influence the availability and cost of money and credit in the economy. The primary objective of these actions is to ensure price stability.

The policy directly affects the Banking and Financial System as flow of credit to various activities come from banking system and indirectly affects, trade and industry as the interest rate, credit flow and margin money requirements are dealt with. Agricultural sector is not generally affected as it is always ensured adequate credit through priority sector prescriptions. Monetary policy will seek to answer important questions that impact the well-being of the economy, companies as well as individuals.

Objectives of the Monetary Policy

The monetary police of RBI aim at twin objectives of price stability and growth by ensuring adequate flow of credit to the productive sectors of the economy. While maintaining a judicious balance between price stability and economic growth, the relative emphasis between the two is governed by the prevailing circumstances at a particular time. Apart from these two important goals, there has been a conscious attempt, on the part of RBI in recent years, to maintain orderly conditions in the foreign exchange market and curb destabilizing and self-fulfilling speculative activities. This has assumed strategic importance for the sustainability of the external sector in the face of growing cross border capital flows into the economy.

Instruments of Monetary Policy

The RBI uses different direct and indirect instruments to control credit. Direct instruments include cash reserve (CRR) and/or statutory liquidity ratios (SLR), directed credit and administered interest rates. Indirect instruments generally operate through repurchase (Repos) and purchase and sale of government securities (open market operations). The reforms in the financial sectors have enabled RBI to expand the array of instruments at its command. While the prime target of monetary policy continues to be banks' reserves, the use of the same is sought to be de-emphasized and the liquidity management in the system is being increasingly undertaken through open market operations (OMO), and Repos.

CRR/SLR

Cash reserve ratio (CRR) determines the level of cash banks need to hold against their net demand and time liabilities. Similarly, statutory liquidity ratio (SLR) requires banks to maintain a part of their liabilities in the form of liquid assets (e.g. government securities).

Bank Rate

Bank rate is the rate at which RBI lends to the banking entities to meet their liquidity requirements.

Interest Rates

Credit and interest rate directives take the form of prescribed targets for allocation of credit to preferred sectors or industries and prescription of deposit and lending rates.

OMO & LAF

Liquidity management in the system is carried out through open market operations (OMO) in the form of outright purchases or sales of government securities and daily repo and reverse repo operations under Liquidity Adjustment Facility (LAF).

Market Stabilization Scheme (MSS)

The liquidity impact of large inflows was managed till the year FY04 largely through the day-to-day LAF and OMO. In the process, the stock of government securities available with RBI declined progressively and the burden of sterilization (sucking out excess liquidity) increasingly fell on LAF operations. In order to address these issues, the Reserve Bank in March 2004 signed a memorandum of understanding with the Government of India for issuance of treasury bills and dated government securities under the MSS. The intention of MSS was essentially to ensure liquidity absorption of a more enduring nature by way of sterilization against the day-to-day normal liquidity management operations (*Equitymaster* News Letter, *www.equitymaster.com*).

Recent Measures

With the revival in credit demand and inflation that RBI hiked the CRR to 7%, SLR 25%, Bank Rate 6.0% Reporate 7.75% Reverse Repo Rate 6.00%, PLR 12.75% - 13.25% and Deposit Rate 7.50%-9.60%. (*www.rbi.org.in*). This is in tune with the central bank's reiteration from time to time that it would continue to pursue its objective of economic growth and price stability by controlling inflation.

Stock Market Performance and Monetary Policy

It is always evident that the stocks in the stock market perform well based on the performance of those companies. The interest rate and credit flow in to the market determines the performance of Banking and Auto sectors in particular and other sectors in general. Due to recent monetary policy, the interest rates have increased and credit flow from the commercial banks came down. This mostly affected the stock prices of banking and automobile companies. The Banks' stock prices declined due to lower lending and higher interest rates. Due to higher interest rates, the sales of automobile companies have declined resulted in declining their share prices.

RBI's decision to increase the 'CRR' and 'Repo rate' together to taming inflation, during March 30th to April 7th, BSE and NSE fall 1% and 1.2% respectively. The major losers were Bank and Auto Indices which fell by 2.6% and 5.4% respectively and others also fell slightly.

Table 1

Stock Market Performance during March 30th to April 7th

Index	*As on March 30*	*As on April 7*	*% Change*
BSE SMLCAP	6,471	6,456	-0.2%
BSE PSU	5,922	5,917	-0.1%
BSE OIL AND GAS	6,419	6,370	-0.8%
BSE MIDCAP	5,384	5,320	-1.2%
BSE METAL	8,488	8,624	1.6%
BSE IT	4,899	4,822	-1.6%
BSE HEALTHCARE	3,649	3,647	-0.1%
BSE FMCG	1,739	1,720	-1.1%
BSE BANKEX	6,542	6,372	-2.6%
BSE AUTO	4,869	4,606	-5.4%

Indices	*Price on March 29 (Rs)*	*Price on April 5 (Rs)*	*% Change*	*52-Week H/L (Rs)*
BSE Sensex	12,980	12,856	-1.0%	14,691 / 8,799
S&P CNX NIFTY	3,798	3,752	-1.2%	4,232 / 2,596

Source : *Equity master* News Letter, *www.equitymaster.com*

The gains during April 20th to April 27th 2007 were resulted from the RBI's decision to leave rates unchanged for the time being and this led investors to buy into banking and other interest rate sensitive sectors. Due to this though the BSE and NSE Index increased marginally, the BSE Bank Index And Auto Index have gained substantially by 2.5% and 2.3% and others have small gains and small losses.

Table 2

Stock Market Performance during 20th April to 27th April 2007

Indices	*As on April 20*	*As on April 27*	*% Change*
BSE BANKEX	6,914	7,087	2.5%
BSE AUTO	4,831	4,945	2.3%
BSE PSU	6,353	6,420	1.1%
BSE MIDCAP	5,699	5,734	0.6%
BSE FMCG	1,812	1,821	0.5%
BSE OIL AND GAS	7,052	7,078	0.4%
BSE METAL	9,702	9,726	0.2%
BSE SMLCAP	6,974	6,941	-0.5%
BSE IT	5,055	4,954	-2.0%
BSE HEALTHCARE	3,793	3,696	-2.6%

Indices	*Price on April 20 (Rs)*	*Price on April 27 (Rs)*	*% Change*	*52-Week H/L (Rs)*
BSE SENSEX	13,897	13,909	0.1%	14,724 / 8,799
S&P CNX NIFTY	4,084	4,084	0.0%	4,245 / 2,596

Data Source: *Equitymaster*, News Letter, *www.equitymaster.com*.

The RBI has permitted nine banks, including SBI and PNB, to transfer their investments in non-SLR (statutory liquidity ratio) bonds issued by the development finance institution, IFCI, to available-for-sale (AFS) category from held-to-maturity (HTM) by the end of June 2007. This move will entail a hit of around Rs 7 bn on the bottom line, as the banks will now have to provide for depreciation in the value of these bonds. When the IFCI debt restructuring exercise was undertaken in FY03, the central bank had allowed banks to hold non-SLR bonds issued by IFCI in the HTM category to avoid mark-to-market losses. However, in May 2007, the central bank told the banks to transfer their exposure in the non-SLR bonds and debentures to the AFS category. According to RBI guidelines, only SLR bonds can be held in HTM category. The RBI had given the special concession to the banks when the debt of IFCI was restructured and now wants to withdraw it, since time has lapsed and IFCI's repayment capacity has improved (*Equitymaster* News Letter, *www.equitymaster.com*). Due to these changes, the banks got freedom to some extent and the BSE BANKEX increased by 5.0% and BSE Auto by 2.8% along with other indices except BSE IT Index.

Table 3
Stock Market Performance during 15th June to 22nd June 2007

Indices	*As onJune 15*	*As onJune 22*	*% Change*
BSE BANKEX	7,462	7,835	5.0%
BSE PSU	6,500	6,720	3.4%
BSE MIDCAP	6,181	6,374	3.1%
BSE AUTO	4,675	4,805	2.8%
BSE METAL	10,496	10,745	2.4%
BSE SMLCAP	7,350	7,513	2.2%
BSE OIL AND GAS	7,457	7,594	1.8%
BSE FMCG	1,789	1,818	1.6%
BSE HEALTHCARE	3,795	3,824	0.8%
BSE IT	4,996	4,858	-2.8%

Indices	*Price on June 15 (Rs)*	*Price on June 22 (Rs)*	*% Change*	*52-Week H/L (Rs)*
BSE SENSEX	14,163	14,467	2.1%	14,724 / 9,875
S&P CNX NIFTY	4,171	4,252	1.9%	4,363 / 2,878

Data Source: Equitymaster, News Letter, *www.equitymaster.com.*

It is always evident that the Stock Market reacts when ever there is change in the RBI's policy. This phenomenon is common as RBI is the apex bank which controls the money in the market. Certain external factors which are out side boarders of the country also influence the performance of Stock Market.

Concluding Observations

The monetary policy is not the only policy responsible for the Stock Market performance. In addition to that, the environment of increasing capital inflows through the participation of FII's, cross-border interest rate differentials (eg. Fed rates vis a vis Indian G-Sec rates) and surplus liquidity conditions, exchange rate movement tend to have linkages with interest rate movements in the country. The challenge of the monetary authority (i.e. RBI) is to balance the various choices into a coherent whole and to formulate a policy that can best facilitate the country's economic objectives as well as stock market performance.

References

P. R. Bramhananda (2002), "Elasticites relevant to Monetary Policy", August 31st .

Raghuvir Srinivasan (2007), "FII's Keeping Tabs on the Movers and Shakers", *The Hindu*, September 23rd, .

Inflation Rates as Anchor for Monetary Policy, *Business Line's* Investment World.

S. Balakrishnan (2003), "Monetary Policy with Inflation Bias?, *Business Line*, June 11th .

Report of the Committee on Liberalisation Foreign Institutional Investment, *www.finmin.nic.in*

Websites

www.equitymaster.com

www.moneycontrol.com

www.bse-india.com

www.nse-india.com

INDEX

G

H

M

S

continental

(63)

Rs. 1295

20%

Rs 1036